Yoram Dinstein's seminal textbook is an essential guide to the legal issues of war and peace, armed attack, self-defence and enforcement measures taken under the aegis of the Security Council. This fourth edition incorporates new material on the wars in Afghanistan and Iraq, response to armed attacks by terrorists, recent resolutions adopted by the Security Council and the latest pronouncements of the International Court of Justice. In addition, several new sections consider consent by States to the use of force (as expressed either *ad hoc* or by treaty); an armed attack by non-State actors; the various phases in the Gulf War up to the occupation of Iraq in 2003 and beyond; and immunities from jurisdiction. With many segments rewritten to reflect recent State practice, this book remains a comprehensive and highly readable introduction to the legal issues surrounding war and self-defence. An indispensable tool for students and practitioners.

DR YORAM DINSTEIN is the Yanowicz Professor of Human Rights at Tel Aviv University. Other posts he has held include Stockton Professor of International Law at the US Naval War College (Newport) and Humboldt Fellow at the Max Planck Institute for International Law, Heidelberg. He has written extensively on the law of war, including a companion volume to this book, *The Conduct of Hostilities under the Law of International Armed Conflict* (Cambridge University Press, 2004).

War, Aggression and Self-Defence

Yoram Dinstein

Fourth edition

1004651515 T

CAMBRIDGE UNIVERSITY PRESS
Cambridge, New York, Melbourne, Madrid, Cape Town, Singapore, São Paulo

CAMBRIDGE UNIVERSITY PRESS
The Edinburgh Building, Cambridge CB2 2RU, UK

Published in the United States of America by Cambridge University Press,
New York

www.cambridge.org
Information on this title: www.cambridge.org/9780521616317

Fourth edition © Cambridge University Press 2005

First published by Grotius Publications Limited 1988
Second edition published by Cambridge University Press 1994
Reprinted 1995, 1999
Third edition published by Cambridge University Press 2001
Reprinted 2002, 2003, 2004
Fourth edition published by Cambridge University Press 2005

Printed in the United Kingdom at the University Press, Cambridge

A catalogue record for this book is available from the British Library

ISBN-13 978-0-521-85080-3 hardback
ISBN-10 0-521-85080-0 hardback
ISBN-13 978-0-521-61631-7 paperback
ISBN-10 0-521-61631-X paperback

Contents

Part II   The illegality of war

Introduction to the fourth edition

This is a completely updated edition of a book originally published in 1988 and last revised in the early part of 2001. In the short space of time since then, the international community has gone through the watershed date of 9 September 2001, the ensuing war in Afghanistan and the resumption of the Gulf War. These events have already left their mark on the way in which the *jus ad bellum* is perceived and practised. Moreover, several international legal phrases – like 'material breach' or so-called 'preemptive' self-defence – have percolated from the somewhat rarefied sphere of discourse by scholars and specialists to the public arena of political jousting. The result has been a lot of heat, but not necessarily much light.

The fourth edition examines the new developments in an effort to interpret correctly their proper meaning. As well, the new edition reflects recent judicial pronouncements of the International Court of Justice, relevant decisions adopted by the Security Council, the final Draft Articles on State responsibility as formulated by the International Law Commission and an unprecedented spate of legal literature on the subject of the use of inter-State force.

There are several new supplementary sections in the book. These relate mainly to consent by States to the use of force (as expressed either *ad hoc* or by treaty); an armed attack by non-State actors; the various phases in the Gulf War up to the occupation of Iraq in 2003 and beyond; and immunities from jurisdiction. Additionally, the views expressed in previous editions of the book on interceptive (as distinct from 'preemptive') self-defence and on response to terrorist attacks are further expounded. Other segments of the book have been entirely rewritten with a view to reflecting recent State practice.

From the introduction to the first edition

War has plagued *homo sapiens* since the dawn of recorded history and, at almost any particular moment in the annals of the species, it appears to be raging in at least a portion of the globe (frequently, in many places at one and the same time).

War has consistently been a, perhaps the, most brutal human endeavour. If for no other reason, the subject of war should be examined and reexamined continuously. There is a tendency today to avoid the use of the term 'war', regarding it as arcane and largely superseded by the phrase 'international armed conflict'. However, apart from the fact that the expression 'war' – appearing as it does in many international instruments and constituting an integral part of a host of customary international legal norms – is far from outdated, a general reference to international armed conflicts ignores the important theoretical as well as practical distinctions existing between wars and other uses of inter-State force ('short of war').

This book is divided into three parts. The first part deals with questions like: What is war? When does it commence and terminate? Is there a twilight zone between war and peace? What is the difference between peace treaties, armistice agreements and cease-fires? Where can war be waged and what is the meaning of neutrality? These problems, with their numerous ramifications, seriously impact on the substance of international law.

The focus of the discussion in the second part is the contemporary prohibition of the use of force in international relations. The current state of the law is put in relief against the background of the past. The meaning of aggression, as defined by a consensus Resolution of the United Nations General Assembly in 1974, is explored. The construct of crimes against peace, which is part of the *Nuremberg* legacy, is set out. Some controversial implications of the illegality and criminality of wars of aggression are fathomed, with a view to establishing the true dimensions of the transformation undergone by modern international law in this domain.

The third part wrestles with the complex topics of self-defence and collective security. In the practice of States, most legal disputes concerning the use of force hinge on the alleged exercise of the individual or collective right of self-defence. In fact, more often than not, self-defence is invoked by both antagonists simultaneously. The question when, and under what conditions, self-defence may legitimately take place is crucial. In this context, the scope of an armed attack – giving rise to self-defence – is investigated, and a differentiation is made between armed attacks from and by a State. The functions discharged by the Security Council in the evaluation of self-defence are probed. Other pertinent matters relate to the modality of self-defence, e.g., can armed reprisals or forcible measures for the protection of nationals abroad be harmonized with the law of the UN Charter? Collective self-defence comes under a special scrutiny, and the infrastructure of the various types of treaties in which it is usually embedded is analyzed.

Collective security, as an institutionalized use of force by the international community, is still an elusive concept in reality. The original mechanism devised by the Charter has yet to be activated, although some imperfect substitutes have evolved. An important subject of discourse is the relative powers – actual and potential – of the Security Council, the General Assembly and (in the light of the *Nicaragua* Judgment) even the International Court of Justice.

Table of cases

Table of treaties

Table of Security Council and General Assembly resolutions

TABLE OF GENERAL ASSEMBLY
RESOLUTIONS

Abbreviations

AC	Appeal Cases
AD	Annual Digest and Reports of Public International Law Cases
AFDI	Annuaire Français de Droit International
AIDI	Annuaire de l'Institut de Droit International
AJICL	Arizona Journal of International and Comparative Law
AJIL	American Journal of International Law
ALR	Alberta Law Review
APSR	American Political Science Review
ARIEL	Austrian Review of International and European Law
ASJG	Acta Scandinavica Juris Gentium
AUILR	American University International Law Review
AUJILP	American University Journal of International Law and Policy
AYBIL	Australian Year Book of International Law
All ER	All England Law Reports
Amer.ULR	American University Law Review
Ar.V.	Archiv des Völkerrechts
Auck.ULR	Auckland University Law Review
BFSP	British and Foreign State Papers
BJIL	Brooklyn Journal of International Law
BYBIL	British Year Book of International Law
CJTL	Columbia Journal of Transnational Law
CLP	Current Legal Problems
CTS	Consolidated Treaty Series
CWILJ	California Western International Law Journal
CWRJIL	Case Western Reserve Journal of International Law
CYIL	Canadian Yearbook of International Law
Cam.LJ	Cambridge Law Journal
Col.LR	Columbia Law Review
Cor.LR	Cornell Law Review

DJCIL	Duke Journal of Comparative and International Law
DJILP	Denver Journal of International Law and Policy
DLJ	Denver Law Journal
DSB	Department of State Bulletin
EJIL	European Journal of International Law
EPIL	*Encyclopedia of Public International Law* (R. Bernhardt ed., 1992–2000).
F.	Federal
For.Aff.	Foreign Affairs
GJICL	Georgia Journal of International and Comparative Law
GYIL	German Yearbook of International Law
HICLR	Hastings International and Comparative Law Review
HILJ	Harvard International Law Journal
HJIL	Houston Journal of International Law
Hague Conventions	*The Hague Conventions and Declarations of 1899 and 1907* (J. B. Scott ed., 3rd ed., 1918)
Har.LR	Harvard Law Review
Hof.LR	Hofstra Law Review
HJLPP	Harvard Journal of Law and Public Policy
ICJ Rep.	Reports of the International Court of Justice
ICLQ	International and Comparative Law Quarterly
IJIL	Indian Journal of International Law
ILC Ybk	Yearbook of the International Law Commission
ILM	International Legal Materials
ILQ	International Law Quarterly
ILR	International Law Reports
ILS	International Law Studies
IMT	Trial of Major War Criminals before the International Military Tribunal
IRRC	International Review of the Red Cross
IYHR	Israel Yearbook on Human Rights
IYIL	Italian Yearbook of International Law
Int.Aff.	International Affairs
Int.Con.	International Conciliation
Int.Law.	International Lawyer
Int.Leg.	*International Legislation: A Collection of the Texts of Multipartite International Instruments of General Interest* (M. O. Hudson ed., 1931–50)
Int.Rel.	International Relations
Io.LR	Iowa Law Review
Is.LR	Israel Law Review
JCSL	Journal of Conflict and Security Law

JILE	Journal of International Law and Economics
JPP	Journal of Political Philosophy
JYIL	Jewish Yearbook of International Law
Jur.R.	Juridical Review
Ken.LJ	Kentucky Law Journal
LCP	Law and Contemporary Problems
LJIL	Leiden Journal of International Law
LNTS	League of Nations Treaty Series
LQR	Law Quarterly Review
LRTWC	Law Reports of Trials of War Criminals
MPYUNL	Max Planck Yearbook of United Nations Law
Mar.JILT	Maryland Journal of International Law and Trade
Mer.LR	Mercer Law Review
Mich.JIL	Michigan Journal of International Law
Mich.LR	Michigan Law Review
Mil.LR	Military Law Review
Mod.LR	Modern Law Review
NCLR	North Carolina Law Review
NDLR	Notre Dame Law Review
NILR	Netherlands International Law Review
NJIL	Nordic Journal of International Law
NMT	Trials of War Criminals before the Nuernberg Military Tribunals under Control Council Law No. 10
NWCR.	Naval War College Review
NYIL	Netherlands Yearbook of International Law
NYLSJICL	New York Law School Journal of International and Comparative Law
NYUJILP	New York University Journal of International Law and Politics
PASIL	Proceedings of the American Society of International Law
PSQ	Political Science Quarterly
PYIL	Pace Yearbook of International Law
Peace Treaties	*Major Peace Treaties of Modern History 1648–1967* (F. L. Israel ed., 1967)
RBDI	Revue Belge de Droit International
RCADI	Recueil des Cours de l'Académie de Droit International
RDSC	Resolutions and Decisions of the Security Council
REDI	Revue Egyptienne de Droit International
RGA	Resolutions Adopted by the General Assembly
RGDIP	Revue Générale de Droit International Public

RIAA	Reports of International Arbitral Awards
RIDP	Revue Internationale de Droit Pénal
RSIDMDG	Recueils de la Société Internationale de Droit Militaire et de Droit de la Guerre
SDILJ	San Diego International Law Journal
SDLR	San Diego Law Review
SIULJ	Southern Illinois University Law Journal
SJIL	Stanford Journal of International Law
SJILC	Syracuse Journal of International Law and Commerce
SJLR	St. John's Law Review
Sp.	Special
Supp.	Supplement
TGS	Transactions of the Grotius Society
TICLJ	Temple International and Comparative Law Journal
TILJ	Texas International Law Journal
Tul.LR	Tulane Law Review
UCLR	University of Chicago Law Review
ULR	Utah Law Review
UNJY	United Nations Juridical Yearbook
UNTS	United Nations Treaty Series
UTLR	University of Toledo Law Review
VJIL	Virginia Journal of International Law
VJTL	Vanderbilt Journal of Transnational Law
Vill.LR	Villanova Law Review
Vir.LR	Virginia Law Review
WCR	*World Court Reports* (M. O. Hudson ed., 1934–43)
WILJ	Wisconsin International Law Journal
WLLR	Washington and Lee Law Review
WVLR	West Virginia Law Review
YBWA	Year Book of World Affairs
YJIL	Yale Journal of International Law
YLJ	Yale Law Journal
ZAORV	Zeitschrift für Ausländisches Öffentliches Recht und Völkerrecht

Part I

The legal nature of war

1   What is war?

A.   The definition of war

(a)   The numerous meanings of war

The phrase 'war' lends itself to manifold uses. It is necessary, at the outset, to differentiate between 'war' as a figure of speech heightening the effect of an oral argument or a news story in the media, and 'war' as a legal term of art. In ordinary conversation, political manifestos, press reports or literary publications, 'war' may appear to be a flexible expression suitable for an allusion to any serious strife, struggle or campaign. Thus, references are frequently made to 'war on terrorism',[1] 'war against the traffic in narcotic drugs', 'class war' or 'war of nerves'. As a rule, this is a matter of poetic licence: the metaphor of war merely serves to convey the gravity of the situation. But the metaphor must not be taken literally, lest it create confusion and incongruities derived from the fact that, in legal parlance, the term 'war' is invested with a special meaning.[2] A metaphorical 'war' may admittedly segue into a real war in the legal sense: this is what happened in 2001 when Taliban-led Afghanistan gave a haven to Al-Qaeda terrorists responsible for the outrage of the 11th of September (9/11) (see *infra*, Chapter 7, B, (b), (bb)).

In pursuing the legal meaning of war, a distinction must be drawn between what war signifies in the domestic law of this or that State and what it denotes in international law. War, especially a lengthy one, is likely to have a tremendous impact on the internal legal systems of the belligerents. A decision whether war has commenced at all, is going on, or has ended, produces far-ranging repercussions in many branches of private law, exemplified by frustration of contracts or liability for insurance

---

[1] See National Addresses by President Bush: 'War against Terrorism', [2001] *Digest of United States Practice in International Law* 856, 857, 859.

[2] See H. Tigroudja, 'Quel(s) Droit(s) Applicable(s) à la "Guerre au Terrorisme"?', 48 *AFDI* 81, 87–93 (2002).

coverage.[3] Similarly, there are multiple relevant issues arising in public law, such as constitutional 'war powers' (*i.e.* identification of the branch of government juridically competent to engulf the nation in war);[4] the authority to requisition enemy property; tax exemptions allowed to those engaged in military service in wartime;[5] and criminal prosecutions for violations of wartime regulations (spanning a wide range of topics, from trading with the enemy to rationing of scarce commodities). In consequence, domestic judicial decisions pertaining to war are legion. All the same, one must not rush to adduce them as precedents on the international plane. If a municipal tribunal merely construes the term 'war' in the context of the legal system within which it operates, the outcome may not be germane to international law. Even should a judgment rendered by a national court of last resort purport to set out the gist of war in international law, this need not be regarded as conclusive (except within the ambit of the domestic legal system concerned).

Occasionally, domestic courts – dealing, for instance, with insurance litigations – address the question whether war is in progress not from the perspective of the legal system (national or international) as a whole, but simply in order to ascertain what the parties to a specific transaction had in mind.[6] When insurance policies exclude or reduce the liability of the insurer once death results from war, the parties are free to give the term 'war' whatever definition they desire.[7] The definition may be arbitrary and incompatible with international law. Nevertheless, there is no reason why it ought not to govern the contractual relations between the parties.

At times, the parties to a private transaction mistakenly believe that a wrong definition of war authentically comports with international law. If a domestic court applies that definition, one must be exceedingly careful in the interpretation of the court's judgment. The dilemma is whether the contours of war, as traced by the court, represent its considered (albeit misconceived) opinion of the substance of international law, or merely reflect the intent of the parties.

When we get to international law, we find that there is no binding definition of war stamped with the *imprimatur* of a multilateral treaty in force. What we have is quite a few scholarly attempts to depict the practice of States and to articulate, in a few choice words, an immensely

[3] See Lord McNair and A. D. Watts, *The Legal Effects of War* 156 ff., 259 ff. (4th ed., 1966).
[4] See, e.g., D. L. Westerfield, *War Powers: The President, the Congress, and the Question of War passim* (1996).
[5] See W. L. Roberts, 'Litigation Involving "Termination of War"', 43 *Ken.LJ* 195, 209 (1954–5).
[6] *Cf.* L. Breckenridge, 'War Risks', 16 *HILJ* 440, 455 (1975).
[7] See R. W. Young, 'Note', 42 *Mich.LR* 884, 890 (1953–4).

complex idea. Instead of seeking to compare multitudinous definitions, all abounding with variable pitfalls, it may be useful to take as a point of departure one prominent effort to encapsulate the essence of war. This is the often-quoted definition, which appears in L. Oppenheim's classical treatise on International Law:

War is a contention between two or more States through their armed forces, for the purpose of overpowering each other and imposing such conditions of peace as the victor pleases.[8]

(b) An analysis of Oppenheim's definition of war

There are four major constituent elements in Oppenheim's view of war: (i) there has to be a contention between at least two States; (ii) the use of the armed forces of those States is required; (iii) the purpose must be overpowering the enemy (as well as the imposition of peace on the victor's terms); and it may be implied, particularly from the words 'each other', that (iv) both parties are expected to have symmetrical, although diametrically opposed, goals.

It is proposed to examine in turn each of these characteristic features of war. However, it must be borne in mind that when references are made to the prerequisites of war, no attempt is made – as yet – to come to grips with the central issue of the *jus ad bellum*, viz. the legality of war. Questions of legality will be raised in subsequent chapters of this study. In the meantime, the only question asked is what conditions have to be fulfilled for a particular course of action to be properly designated 'war'.

i. Inter-State and intra-State wars

Of the four ingredients in Oppenheim's definition of war, only the first can be accepted with no demur. 'One element seems common to all definitions of war. In all definitions it is clearly affirmed that war is a contest between states.'[9]

Some qualifying words should nevertheless be appended. International law recognizes two disparate types of wars: inter-State wars (waged between two or more States) and intra-State wars (civil wars conducted between two or more parties within a single State). Traditionally, civil wars have been regulated by international law only to a limited extent.[10] More recently, in view of the frequent incidence and ferocity of internal

---

[8] L. Oppenheim, *International Law*, II, 202 (H. Lauterpacht ed., 7th ed., 1952).

[9] C. Eagleton, 'An Attempt to Define War', 291 *Int.Con.* 237, 281 (1933).

[10] See common Article 3 to the four Geneva Conventions of 1949 for the Protection of War Victims: Geneva Convention (I) for the Amelioration of the Condition of the Wounded and Sick in Armed Forces in the Field, 75 *UNTS* 31, 32–4; Geneva Convention (II) for the Amelioration of the Condition of Wounded, Sick and Shipwrecked Members of Armed Forces at Sea, *ibid.*, 85, 86–8; Geneva Convention (III) Relative to the Treatment

armed conflicts, the volume of international legal norms apposite to them has dramatically increased.[11] Still, a single corpus of law applicable to all armed conflicts (inter-State and intra-State) neither exists nor attracts much support.[12] Hence, Oppenheim was entirely right in excluding civil wars from his definition. In the present study, inter-State armed conflicts will constitute the sole object of our inquiry.

It is immaterial whether each belligerent recognizes the adversary's statehood. War may actually be the device through which one challenges the sovereignty of the other. As long as both belligerents satisfy objective criteria of statehood under international law,[13] any war between them should be characterized as inter-State. Even so, the States involved in an inter-State war must be aligned on opposing sides. If a civil war is raging in Ruritania, and Atlantica assists the legitimate Government of Ruritania (legitimate, that is, in the eyes of the domestic constitutional law) in combating those who rise in revolt against the central authority, the domestic upheaval does not turn into an inter-State war (see *infra*, Chapter 4, G, (a)). In such a case, two States (Ruritania and Atlantica) are entangled in military operations, but since they stand together against the Ruritanian rebels, the internal nature of the conflict is retained intact. By contrast, if Atlantica joins forces with the insurgents, supporting them against the incumbent Government of Ruritania, this is no longer just a civil war. Still, the changing nature of the war does not necessarily affect every single military encounter. The joint war may have separate inter-national and internal strands, inasmuch as specific hostilities may be waged exclusively between two (or more) States, whereas other combat may take place solely between a single State and those who rebel against it.[14] As the International Court of Justice enunciated in the *Nicaragua* case of 1986:

of Prisoners of War, *ibid.*, 135, 136–8; Geneva Convention (IV) Relative to the Protection of Civilian Persons in Time of War, *ibid.*, 287, 288–90. The International Court of Justice held that this common Article expresses general international law. *Case Concerning Military and Paramilitary Activities in and against Nicaragua* (Merits), [1986] *ICJ Rep.* 14, 114. See also Protocol Additional to the Geneva Conventions of 12 August 1949, and Relating to the Protection of Victims of Non-International Armed Conflicts (Protocol II), 1977, [1977] *UNJY* 135.

[11] The growth of this body of law is highlighted in the 1998 Rome Statute of the International Criminal Court, which in Article 8 enumerates a long list of war crimes committed in internal armed conflicts. 37 *ILM* 999, 1006–9 (1998).

[12] See C. Kress, 'War Crimes Committed in Non-International Armed Conflict and the Emerging System of International Criminal Justice', 30 *IYHR* 103, 132–4 (2000).

[13] For these criteria, see J. Crawford, *The Creation of States in International Law* 36 ff. (1979).

[14] See C. Greenwood, 'The Development of International Humanitarian Law by the International Criminal Tribunal for the Former Yugoslavia', 2 *MPYUNL* 97, 118–20 (1998).

The conflict between the *contras'* forces and those of the Government of Nicaragua is an armed conflict which is 'not of an international character'. The acts of the *contras* towards the Nicaraguan Government are therefore governed by the law applicable to conflicts of that character; whereas the actions of the United States in and against Nicaragua fall under the legal rules relating to international conflicts.[15]

Moreover, a country may simultaneously be engaged in both a civil war and an inter-State war, without any built-in linkage between the external and internal foes, although it is only natural for the two disconnected armed conflicts to blend in time into a single war. This is what happened, for instance, in Afghanistan in 2001. The Taliban regime, having fought a long-standing civil war with the Northern Alliance, brought upon itself an inter-State war with an American-led Coalition as a result of providing shelter and support to the Al-Qaeda terrorists who had launched the 9/11 attack against the United States[16] (see *infra*, Chapter 7, B, (b), (bb)). But even as the overall character of the armed conflict was transformed from an intra-State to an inter-State war, some specific hostilities continued to be waged exclusively between the domestic foes (namely, the Taliban forces and the Northern Alliance).

Admittedly, in practice, the dividing line between inter-State and intra-State wars cannot always be delineated with a few easy strokes. Thus, if the internal strife in Ruritania culminates in the emergence of a new State of Numidia on a portion of the territory of Ruritania, and the central Government of Ruritania contests the secession, the conflict may be considered by Ruritania to be internal while Numidia (and perhaps the rest of the international community) would look upon it as an inter-State war. Objectively considered, there may be a transition from a civil war to an inter-State war which is hard to pinpoint in time.

Such a transition may be relatively easy to spot if and when foreign States join the fray. Thus, Israel's War of Independence started on 30 November 1947 as a civil war between the Arab and Jewish populations of the British Mandate in Palestine.[17] But on 15 May 1948, upon the declaration of Israel's independence and its invasion by the armies of five sovereign Arab countries, the war became inter-State in character.[18]

The disintegration of Yugoslavia exposed to light a more complex situation in which a civil war between diverse ethnic, religious and

---

[15] *Nicaragua* case, *supra* note 10, at 114.

[16] See C. Greenwood, 'International Law and the "War against Terrorism"', 78 *Int.Aff.* 301, 309 (2002).

[17] For the facts, see N. Lorch, *The Edge of the Sword: Israel's War of Independence 1947–1949* 46 ff. (2nd ed., 1968).

[18] For the facts, see *ibid.*, 166 ff.

linguistic groups inside the territory of a single country was converted into an inter-State war once a fragmentation into several sovereign States has been effected. The armed conflict in Bosnia may serve as an object lesson. As long as Bosnia constituted an integral part of Yugoslavia, any hostilities raging there among Serbs, Croats and Bosnians clearly amounted to a civil war. However, when Bosnia-Herzegovina emerged from the political ruins of Yugoslavia as an independent country, the conflict transmuted into an inter-State war by dint of the cross-border involvement of Serbian (former Yugoslav) armed forces in military operations conducted by Bosnian Serbs rebelling against the Bosnian Government (in an effort to wrest control over large tracts of Bosnian land and merge them into a Greater Serbia). This was the legal position despite the fact that, from the outlook of the participants in the actual combat, very little seemed to have changed. The juridical distinction is embedded in the realignment of sovereignties in the Balkans and the substitution of old administrative boundaries by new international frontiers.

In 1997, the Trial Chamber of the International Criminal Tribunal for the former Yugoslavia (the ICTY) held in the *Tadic* case that from the beginning of 1992 until May of the same year a state of international armed conflict existed in Bosnia between the forces of the Republic of Bosnia-Herzegovina, on the one hand, and those of the Federal Republic of Yugoslavia (Serbia-Montenegro), on the other.[19] Yet, the majority of the Chamber (Judges Stephen and Vohrah) arrived at the conclusion that, as a result of the withdrawal of Yugoslav troops announced in May 1992, the conflict reverted to being non-international in nature.[20] The Presiding Judge (McDonald) dissented on the ground that the withdrawal was a fiction and that Yugoslavia remained in effective control of the Serb forces in Bosnia.[21] The majority opinion was reversed by the ICTY Appeals Chamber in 1999.[22] The original Trial Chamber's majority opinion had elicited much criticism from scholars;[23] and even before the delivery of the final judgment on appeal, another Trial Chamber of the ICTY took a divergent view in the *Delalic* case of 1998.[24] However, the essence of the disagreement must be viewed as factual in nature.

---

[19] *Prosecutor v. Tadic*, Judgment, ICTY Case No. IT–94–1–T, Trial Chamber, 1997, 36 *ILM* 908, 922 (1997).

[20] *Ibid.*, 933.   [21] *Ibid.*, 972–3.

[22] *Prosecutor v. Tadic*, Judgment, ICTY Case No. IT–94–1–A, Appeals Chamber, 1999, 38 *ILM* 1518, 1549 (1999).

[23] See, e.g., T. Meron, 'Classification of Armed Conflict in the Former Yugoslavia: *Nicaragua's* Fallout', 92 *AJIL* 236–42 (1998).

[24] *Prosecutor v. Delalic et al.*, Judgment, ICTY Case No. IT–96–21–T, Trial Chamber, 1998, 38 *ILM* 56, 58 (1999).

Legally speaking, the fundamental character of an armed conflict as international or internal can indeed metamorphose – more than once – from one stretch of time to another. Whether at any given temporal framework the war is inter-State in character, or merely a civil war, depends on the level of involvement of a foreign State in hostilities waged against the central Government of the local State.

ii.   *War in the technical and in the material sense*   The second element in Oppenheim's definition is fraught with problems. According to Oppenheim, a clash of arms between the parties to the conflict is of the essence of war. He even underlined that war is a *'contention, i.e. a violent struggle through the application of armed force'.*[25] But this is not uniformly in harmony with the practice of States. Experience demonstrates that, in reality, there are two different sorts of war: there is war in the material sense, but there is also war in the technical sense.

War in the technical sense commences with a declaration of war and is terminated with a peace treaty or some other formal step indicating that the war is over (see *infra*, Chapter 2, A–B). The crux of the matter is the taking of formal measures purposed to signify that war is about to break out (or has broken out) and that it has ended. *De facto*, the armed forces of the parties may not engage in fighting even once in the interval. As an illustration, not a single shot was exchanged in anger between a number of Allied States (particularly in Latin America) and Germany in either World War.[26] Nevertheless, *de jure*, by virtue of the issuance of declarations of war, those countries were in a state of war in the technical sense.

Until a formal step is taken to bring it to a close, a state of war may produce certain legal and practical effects as regards, e.g., the internment of nationals of the enemy State and the sequestration of their property, irrespective of the total absence of hostilities.[27] It can scarcely be denied, either in theory or in practice, that '[a] state of war may exist without active hostilities' (just as 'active hostilities may exist without a state of war', a point that will be expounded *infra*, iii).[28] Oppenheim's narrow definition must be broadened to accommodate a state of war that is not combined with any fighting.

War in the material sense unfolds regardless of any formal steps. Its occurrence is contingent only on the eruption of hostilities between the

---

[25] Oppenheim, *supra* note 8, at 202.

[26] See J. Stone, *Legal Controls of International Conflict: A Treatise on the Dynamics of Disputes – and War – Law* 306 (2nd ed., 1959).

[27] See L. Kotzsch, *The Concept of War in Contemporary History and International Law* 248–9 (1956).

[28] See Q. Wright, 'When Does War Exist?', 26 *AJIL* 362, 363 (1932).

parties, even in the absence of a declaration of war. This is where Oppenheim's reference to a violent struggle is completely apposite. The decisive factor here is deeds rather than declarations. What counts is not a *de jure* state of war, but *de facto* combat. Granted, even in the course of war in the material sense, hostilities do not have to go on incessantly and they may be interspersed by periods of cease-fire (see *infra*, Chapter 2, C). But there is no war in the material sense without some acts of warfare.

Warfare means the use of armed force, namely, violence. Breaking off diplomatic relations with a State, or withdrawing recognition from it, does not suffice. An economic boycott or a psychological pressure is not enough. A 'Cold War', threats to use force, or even a declaration of war (unaccompanied by acts of violence), do not warrant the conclusion that war in the material sense exists. It is indispensable that some armed force be employed.

The setting of an intervention in support of rebels in a civil war in another country raises some perplexing questions. What degree of intervention brings about a state of war in the material sense? It appears that the mere supply of arms to the rebels (epitomized by American support of Moslem insurgents against the Soviet-backed Government in Afghanistan in the 1980s) does not qualify as an actual use of armed force (see *infra*, Chapter 7, B, (b), (aa), v). But there comes a point – for instance, when the weapons are accompanied by instructors training the rebels – at which the foreign country is deemed to be waging warfare.[29]

The *jus in bello* – governing the conduct of hostilities in the course of an international armed conflict (see *infra*, B, (a)) – is brought into operation as soon as war in the material sense is embarked upon, despite the absence of a technical state of war. This principle is pronounced in Article 2 common to the 1949 Geneva Conventions for the Protection of War Victims:

> [T]he present Convention shall apply to all cases of declared war or of any other armed conflict which may arise between two or more of the High Contracting Parties, even if the state of war is not recognized by one of them.[30]

Of course, if a state of war exists in the technical sense only – and no hostilities are taking place – the issue of the application of the *jus in bello* rarely emerges in practice.[31]

---

[29] It is noteworthy that a breach of neutrality occurs when military advisers are assigned to the armed forces of one of the belligerents in on-going inter-State war (see *infra*, D, (b), ii).

[30] Geneva Conventions, *supra* note 10, at 32 (Geneva Convention (I)), 86 (Geneva Convention (II)), 136 (Geneva Convention (III)), 288 (Geneva Convention (IV)).

[31] In some extreme instances, even when the state of war exists only in a technical sense, a belligerent may still be in breach of the *jus in bello*. Thus, the mere issuance of a threat to an adversary that hostilities would be conducted on the basis of a 'no quarter' policy

iii. *Total wars, limited wars and incidents 'short of war'* The third component in Oppenheim's definition is that the purpose of war must be the overpowering of the enemy and the imposition of peace terms. His intention, no doubt, was to distinguish between a large-scale use of force (tantamount to war) and a clash of lower intensity (constituting measures 'short of war'). Indeed, when armed units of two countries are locked in combat, the preliminary question is whether the use of force is comprehensive enough for the fighting to qualify as war.

Incidents involving the use of force, without reaching the threshold of war, occur quite often in the relations between States. Border patrols of neighbouring countries may exchange fire; naval units may torpedo vessels flying another flag; interceptor planes may shoot down aircraft belonging to another State; and so forth. The reasons for such incidents vary. They may happen accidentally or be caused by trigger-happy junior officers acting on their own initiative; they may be engendered by simmering tensions between the two countries; they may be the fallout of an open dispute revolving around control over a strategically or economically important area (like oil lands, a major road, a ridge of mountains or a waterway); and other motives may be at play.

In large measure, the classification of a military action as either war or a closed incident ('short of war') depends on the way in which the two antagonists appraise the situation. As long as both parties choose to consider what has transpired as a mere incident, and provided that the incident is rapidly closed, it is hard to gainsay that view. Once, however, one of the parties elects to engage in war, the other side is incapable of preventing that development. The country opting for war may simply issue a declaration of war, thereby initiating war in the technical sense. Additionally, the State desirous of war may escalate the use of force, so that war in the material sense will take shape.

There is a marked difference between war and peace: whereas it requires two States to conclude and to preserve peace (see *infra*, Chapter 2, B, (a), i), it takes a single State to embroil itself as well as its selected enemy in war. When comprehensive force is used by Arcadia against Utopia, war in the material sense ensues and it is irrelevant that Utopia confines itself to responding with non-comprehensive force. Utopia, remaining completely passive, may in fact offer no resistance; nevertheless, war in the material sense can result from the measures taken by the advancing Arcadian

constitutes a violation of Article 40 of the 1977 Protocol Additional to the Geneva Conventions of 12 August 1949, and Relating to the Protection of Victims of International Armed Conflicts (Protocol I), 1977, [1977] *UNJY* 95, 110. *Cf.* Article 23(d) of the Regulations Respecting the Laws and Customs of War on Land (Annexed to Hague Convention (II) of 1899 and (IV) of 1907), *Hague Conventions* 100, 107, 116.

military contingents.[32] If Arcadia proceeds to 'devastate the territory of another with fire and sword', the invasion would be categorized as war in the material sense, discounting what the Utopian armed forces do or fail to do.[33] Hence, the invasion by the Iraqi army and the rapid takeover of Kuwait within a few hours on 2 August 1990 brought about war in the material sense. It would be erroneous to assume that the Gulf War began only when extensive hostilities flared up in January 1991.

Since war in the material sense is derived from deeds rather than words, third parties sometimes feel compelled to investigate the legal position on their own. This may come to pass either because the adversaries keep silent, while their field units are in constant battle, or what they say does not match what they do. 'There is ... room for the view that the opinions entertained by the belligerents need not be given conclusive effect. War may be too important a matter to be left either to the generals or to the contending parties.'[34]

A legal analysis of the true state of affairs, carried out objectively, hinges on a perception of the use of force as comprehensive. Force is comprehensive if it is employed (i) spatially, across sizeable tracts of land or far-flung corners of the ocean; (ii) temporally, over a prolonged period of time; (iii) quantitatively, entailing massive military operations or a high level of firepower; (iv) qualitatively, inflicting extensive destruction. Reliance on any one of the four criteria may prove adequate in certain instances, but generally only a combination of all four will paint a clear picture of the nature of the hostilities.

The use of force need not be unlimited for it to be comprehensive. Oppenheim's definition postulates what is termed nowadays a 'total' war. Many a war is unquestionably 'total' in that it is conducted with total victory in mind. Total victory consists of the capitulation of the enemy, following the overall defeat of its armed forces and/or the conquest of its territory, and if this is accomplished the victor is capable of dictating peace terms to the vanquished. When carried to extremity, a total victory may bring about the complete disintegration of the enemy State (see *infra*, Chapter 2, B, (c), ii). Thus, in unleashing the Gulf War in 1990, the Iraqi aim was to extinguish the political life of Kuwait as a sovereign State. However, when Iraq was completely occupied in 2003, the winning Coalition did not wish to mete out that fate to Iraq whose sovereignty was assiduously respected.

---

[32] See P. Guggenheim, 'Les Principes de Droit International Public', 80 *RCADI* 1, 171 (1952).
[33] T. Baty, 'Abuse of Terms: "Recognition": "War"', 30 *AJIL* 377, 381, 398 (1936).
[34] R. R. Baxter, 'The Definition of War', 16 *REDI* 1, 4 (1960).

Not every war is aimed at total victory. Oppenheim completely overlooked the feasibility of limited wars. Such wars are, in fact, of considerable frequency and import. In a limited war, the goal may be confined to the defeat of only some segments of the opposing military apparatus; the conquest of certain portions of the opponent's territory (and no others); or the coercion of the enemy Government to alter a given policy (e.g., the Kosovo air campaign of 1999; see *infra*, Chapter 10, D, (c)), without striving for total victory. Now and then, it is not easy to tell a limited war (in the material sense) apart from a grave incident 'short of war'. The difference between the two is relative: more force, employed over a longer period of time, within a larger theatre of operations, is required in a war setting as compared to a situation 'short of war'.

A war may be deemed 'total' not only when its goal is the complete subjugation of the enemy. A war is total also when the means, used to attain a limited objective, are total. That is to say, war may be catalogued as total when the totality of the resources (human and material) of a belligerent State is mobilized, so as to secure victory at any cost. Victory at any cost should not be confused with total victory. Surely, more often than not, a State will mobilize its full resources only when the end for which it exerts itself is total victory. But a State may conduct war *à outrance* for a limited reward, like a border rectification, if the issue carries an emotional load of great weight. One must distinguish between the military war aims and the ulterior motives of war. The latter can be strategic, political, economic, and even religious, ideological or cultural. War may have a hidden agenda that transcends the tangible or ostensible gains contemplated.

The counterpart of a limited war fought with unlimited means is a total war waged with less than the totality of the means available. Occasionally, a belligerent – while fighting a war that is total in terms of its objective – refrains from resorting to some destructive (conventional or unconventional) weapon systems, although they are at its disposal and their use is legally permissible. There is a broad array of causes for such self-restraint: lofty moral impulses; a concession to public opinion at home or abroad; a desire to avoid colossal losses; fear of retaliation; or purely military considerations. Either way, hostilities do not lose their legal classification as war only because some weapons remain on the shelf.

For these reasons, it is better to attenuate the rigidity of Oppenheim's definition. War need not be total to be war. At the same time, not every episodic case of use of force by States amounts to war. Only a comprehensive use of force does. The key to the definition of war should lie in the adjective 'comprehensive'.

iv.   War as an asymmetrical phenomenon The last factor in Oppenheim's definition is the implicit symmetry in the positions of the contending parties, as if both necessarily have corresponding objectives. However, the genuine war aims of one adversary are not always a mirror image of the other's. Sometimes, an attacking State may desire solely to gain a limited advantage over a neighbouring country, but the victim is apt to respond fiercely in an effort to crush its adversary once and for all. The opposite scenario is equally conceivable. The attacking State may aim at total victory, whereas the other side sets its sights lower. This is what happened in the first phase of the Gulf War. Although Iraq attempted to annihilate Kuwait, the American-led Coalition which came to the aid of the latter spurned exhortations to march all the way to Baghdad in 1991. Hostilities were therefore suspended upon the liberation of Kuwait (although when the cease-fire terms were continuously disregarded by Iraq, the Coalition resumed hostilities in 2003 and brought about the total collapse of the Saddam Hussein regime; see *infra*, Chapter 10, C, (b)).

This brings us to another core issue. Ordinarily, a state of war is characterized by a specific intention to wage war against the chosen opponent; an *animus belligerendi*. There are those who look upon the manifestation of such an intention on the part of at least one of the belligerents as an essential component in the definition of war.[35] The obvious manifestation of such an intention would be in a declaration of war, if issued.[36] However, the intention to embark upon war may be less self-evident in the absence of a declaration of war. When all is said and done, the intention is usually deduced from the fact of war, and not vice versa.

More significantly, the whole thesis that an *animus belligerendi* is intrinsic to the definition of war – albeit enticing – is insupportable. It is clear that an *animus belligerendi* need not stimulate the attacking State. Just as war can be imposed by Arcadia (the attacking State) on Utopia (the target State) against the latter's will, war can also develop contrary to the original intentions harboured by Arcadia. When it mounts a military incursion into Utopian territory, Arcadia may envisage a brief armed encounter 'short of war'. Yet, inasmuch as it is incapable of controlling the Utopian response, Arcadia may stumble into war. Arcadia acts 'at its peril', since the measures of force to which it resorts can be treated by Utopia as the initiation of war.[37] Thus, the decision whether a seminal use

---

[35] See, e.g., C. Greenwood, 'War, Terrorism, and International Law', 56 *CLP* 505, 513, 515 (2003).
[36] See *ibid.*, 513.
[37] See A. D. McNair, 'The Legal Meaning of War, and the Relation of War to Reprisals', 11 *TGS* 29, 38 (1925).

of force will culminate in a state of war may be taken by the target State (Utopia).[38] Additionally, in some scenarios, the target State (Utopia) – no less than the attacking State (Arcadia) – lacks altogether an *animus belligerendi*. All the same, 'if acts of force are sufficiently serious and long continued', war may unfold between Arcadia and Utopia although 'both sides disclaim any *animus belligerendi* and refuse to admit that a state of war has arisen between them'.[39] Differently phrased, an objective inquiry (conducted, e.g., by Patagonia) may prompt the conclusion that Arcadia and Utopia are in the midst of war although, from the subjective standpoint of its intentions (*animus belligerendi*), neither country desires to wage war.

(c)   A proposed definition of war

As the foregoing discussion should indicate, the term 'war' gives rise to more than a handful of definitional problems. No wonder that the assertion is made that no definition, serviceable for all purposes, can be provided.[40] Still, in the context of the present study, 'war' will have the following meaning:

> War is a hostile interaction between two or more States, either in a technical or in a material sense. War in the technical sense is a formal status produced by a declaration of war. War in the material sense is generated by actual use of armed force, which must be comprehensive on the part of at least one party to the conflict.

B.   *Status mixtus*

In the past, the dominant opinion, as expressed by Grotius[41] following Cicero,[42] was that no intermediate state exists between war and peace (*inter bellum et pacem nihil est medium*). But in the last century, a number of scholars have strongly advocated a reconsideration of the traditional dichotomy in the light of the modern practice of States. In particular, G. Schwarzenberger called for recognition of a '*status mixtus*',[43] and P. C. Jessup urged acceptance of a state of 'intermediacy' between war

---

[38] See E. M. Borchard, '"War" and "Peace"', 27 *AJIL* 114, 114–15 (1933).
[39] See J. L. Brierly, 'International Law and Resort to Armed Force', 4 *Cam.LJ* 308, 313 (1930–2).
[40] See F. Grob, *The Relativity of War and Peace* 189 (1949).
[41] H. Grotius, *De Jure Belli ac Pacis*, Book III, § XXI, I (1 Classics of International Law ed. (text) 592 (1913)).
[42] Cicero, *Philippics*, § VIII, I, 4 (Loeb Classical ed. 366 (1926)).
[43] G. Schwarzenberger, 'Jus Pacis ac Belli?', 37 *AJIL* 460, 470 (1943).

and peace.[44] Other commentators deny that the notion of an intermediate status between war and peace is consonant with contemporary international law.[45]

To the degree that proponents of the *status mixtus* school of thought recognize an independent third rubric, lying outside the bounds of war and peace, and subject to the application of a different set of rules,[46] there is nothing in the current practice of States to provide support for that view. Nor is it justified to speak loosely of a *status mixtus* in the sense of a twilight zone between war and peace. Legally speaking, there are only two states of affairs in international relations – war and peace – with no undistributed middle ground.

Whenever States disagree about the application or interpretation of international law, it is necessary and possible to establish first whether a state of war or of peace is in progress. But this is not to say that the concept of a *status mixtus* is without merit in international law. One must acknowledge, as an observable phenomenon, the applicability of some laws of peace in specific war situations and of some laws of war in certain peace settings. A *status mixtus* is characterized by the simultaneous operation of the laws of war (for some purposes) and the laws of peace (for others).[47]

(a)   Peacetime *status mixtus*

In peacetime, a *status mixtus* exists when States resort to a limited use of force 'short of war'. Because a state of peace continues to prevail, (i) most of the relations between the parties are still governed by the laws of peace, and (ii) the laws of neutrality are not activated between the antagonists and third parties. Nevertheless, the actual fighting will be regulated by the basic rules of warfare. The body of these rules – traditionally called the *jus in bello* – is currently subject to various designations. Increasingly, the name used is 'international humanitarian law'. This appellation – once deemed coterminous with the Geneva Conventions – is nowadays construed as covering also other instruments, such as Hague Convention (IV) of 1907 Respecting the Laws and Customs of War on Land (and the

[44] P. C. Jessup, 'Intermediacy', 23 *ASJG* 16, 17 (1953); P. C. Jessup, 'Should International Law Recognize an Intermediate Status between Peace and War?', 48 *AJIL* 98, 100 (1954).

[45] See G. I. Tunkin, *Theory of International Law* 265–70 (1974).

[46] See, e.g., A. N. Salpeter and J. C. Waller, 'Armed Reprisals during Intermediacy – A New Framework for Analysis in International Law', 17 *Vill.LR* 270, 271–2 (1972).

[47] See G. Schwarzenberger and E. D. Brown, *A Manual of International Law* 151 (6th ed., 1976).

Regulations annexed thereto),[48] as well as customary international law.[49] The present writer prefers the expression 'law of international armed conflict',[50] but it must be perceived that the distinction between the diverse locutions is more semantic than real.

It is generally conceded at the present time that the relevant norms of the *jus in bello* must be implemented in the course of international armed conflicts of whatever type, and not only when a state of war is in effect (*i.e.* even when there is no *bellum*). The broad application of the *jus in bello* is reflected in the very title of Protocol I of 1977, Additional to the four Geneva Conventions, which relates to the Protection of Victims of International Armed Conflicts,[51] viz. not only wars. Common Article 2 of the 1949 Geneva Conventions for the Protection of War Victims (quoted *supra*, A, (b), ii) prescribes that these instruments (wherein the term 'war' figures prominently) shall apply to all cases of armed conflict between contracting States, 'even if the state of war is not recognized by one of them'. It may be inferred from the last words that, if both adversaries jointly refuse to recognize the existence of a state of war, the Conventions are not operational.[52] But the correct legal position appears to be that whenever force is employed in international relations, States are obligated to carry out those norms of the *jus in bello* that are germane to the situation.[53]

Contemporary instruments – dealing, for instance, with prohibited weapons – tend to make it transparently clear that they cover all armed conflicts of whatever scope (not even necessarily inter-State). Thus, under the 1993 United Nations Convention on the Prohibition of the Development, Production, Stockpiling and Use of Chemical Weapons and on Their Destruction, Contracting Parties undertake 'never under any circumstances' to use chemical weapons.[54] The scope of this injunction is so extensive that it transcends any armed conflict. It is true that the Convention expressly permits Contracting Parties to keep certain

---

[48] Hague Convention (IV), *supra* note 31, at 100, 107.

[49] The amalgamation of the two branches of law applicable in armed conflict (the 'Hague Law' and the 'Geneva Law') into 'one single complex system, known today as international humanitarian law' was noted by the International Court of Justice in its Advisory Opinion on the *Legality of the Threat or Use of Nuclear Weapons*, [1996] *ICJ Rep.* 226, 256.

[50] See Y. Dinstein, *The Conduct of Hostilities under the Law of International Armed Conflict* 12–14 (2004).

[51] Protocol I, *supra* note 31, at 95.

[52] See A. P. Rubin, 'The Status of Rebels under the Geneva Conventions of 1949', 21 *ICLQ* 472, 477 (1972).

[53] See *Commentary, I Geneva Convention* 32 (J. S. Pictet ed., 1952).

[54] United Nations Convention on the Prohibition of the Development, Production, Stockpiling and Use of Chemical Weapons and on Their Destruction, 1993, 32 *ILM* 800, 804 (1993) (Article I(1)).

chemicals (such as tear gas) for law enforcement, including domestic riot control.[55] However, it is interdicted to employ these chemicals for military purposes as a method of warfare.[56] The ban covers any international armed conflict (whether characterized as war or 'short of war'), and even internal conflicts rising above the level of riots.[57]

(b)   *Wartime* status mixtus

In some circumstances, widespread hostilities (inflicting a large number of casualties and incalculable damage) are raging between States over a long period of time, yet the parties behave as if nothing out of the ordinary has happened.[58] They continue to maintain full diplomatic relations,[59] go on trading with each other,[60] and otherwise assume a 'business as usual' posture. As pointed out (see *supra*, A, (b), iii), third countries may be driven to probe independently the nature of the hostilities. An impartial examination may lead to the conclusion that in reality war is going on, official protests to the contrary notwithstanding.

This pattern of hostilities is liable to be highly confusing. It seems to be the other side of the coin of a state of war without warfare: here, ostensibly, warfare occurs without a state of war. In actuality, that is not so. If States use comprehensive force against one another, war in the material sense exists.

Once war is going on, the *jus in bello* is supposed to be brought into operation in its amplitude. Can the parties to the conflict, acting in concert, suspend the application of the *jus in bello* (in whole or in part)? To answer the question, a distinction must be drawn between the duties that the *jus in bello* imposes and the rights that it bestows. Belligerents are obligated to discharge in full the duties devolving on them under the *jus in bello*. These duties cannot be evaded even if the parties to the conflict grant a dispensation to one another. But States engaged in war are not compelled by international law to make use of the

---

[55] *Ibid.*, 805–7 (Articles II(7)–(9), III(1)(e)).   [56] *Ibid.*, 806 (Article II(9)(c)).

[57] See W. Krutzsch and R. Trapp, *A Commentary on the Chemical Weapons Convention* 18 (1994).

[58] The Soviet–Japanese armed conflict of 1939 may serve as a good example. See I. Brownlie, *International Law and the Use of Force by States* 389 (1963).

[59] 'Diplomatic relations normally come to an end upon outbreak of war'; yet, '[i]n recent years, there have been many instances where diplomatic relations had been maintained notwithstanding the outbreak of hostilities'. B. Sen, *A Diplomat's Handbook of International Law and Practice* 236 (3rd ed., 1988).

[60] While there is no prohibition of trading with the enemy pursuant to international law, most belligerent States enact domestic legislation to that effect. See McNair and Watts, *supra* note 3, at 343–4.

full gamut of the rights accorded to them. If it so desires, each of the opposing sides is generally empowered not to insist on its rights. Subject to exceptions spelt out by multilateral treaties,[61] a belligerent is entitled to renounce its rights or to leave them in abeyance. Surely, international law does not impede warring States from continuing reciprocal trade, or retaining diplomatic relations, even when their armies are pitted in combat.

In a 1976 International Chamber of Commerce Arbitration, in the *Dalmia Cement* case, P. Lalive pronounced that war must entail 'a *complete rupture* of international relations' between the belligerents, and 'the continued existence of treaties as well as of diplomatic relations between the parties cannot be reconciled with a "state of war"'.[62] As for treaties, this statement is not consonant with the modern trend denying their *ipso facto* termination – and, according to the *Institut de Droit International*, even suspension – upon the commencement of war.[63] While the breaking off of diplomatic relations at the opening of hostilities is still the rule, it can no longer be viewed as an essential aspect of war.[64]

What a wartime *status mixtus* requires is some finesse in appraising the conduct of the belligerents. On the one hand, it ought to be remembered that a state of war exists. Consequently, all wartime obligations must be complied with scrupulously. On the other hand, if the parties wish to preserve a modicum of peace in the middle of war, they are entitled to do so. The only condition is that their behaviour must not run counter to the overriding obligations of the *jus in bello*.

C.   The region of war

War can be waged over large portions of the planet and beyond. The space subject to the potential spread of hostilities is known as the region of war. Actual hostilities may be restricted by the belligerents to a fairly narrow theatre of operations, but the potential is always there. The

---

[61] The four Geneva Conventions expressly rule out the conclusion of special agreements between belligerents, which affect adversely or restrict the rights of protected persons. *Supra* note 10, at 34 (Geneva Convention (I), Article 6), 88 (Geneva Convention (II), Article 6), 142 (Geneva Convention (III), Article 6), 292 (Geneva Convention (IV), Article 7).

[62] *Dalmia Cement Ltd. v. National Bank of Pakistan* (1976), 67 *ILR* 611, 624.

[63] *Institut de Droit International*, Resolution, 'The Effects of Armed Conflicts on Treaties' 61(II) *AIDI* 278, 280 (Helsinki, 1985) (Article 2). *Cf.* comments by the present writer drawing attention to the contrast with the Lalive arbitral award and other sources, *ibid.*, 215.

[64] The Arbitrator himself conceded that the position was not free of doubt. See *Dalmia Cement* case, *supra* note 62, at 623.

combat zone on land is likely to be quite limited in geographic scope, yet naval and air units may attack targets in distant areas.

The region of war consists of the following:

(a)   The territories of the parties to the conflict

In principle, all the territories of the belligerent States, anywhere under their sovereign sway, are inside the region of war. As a corollary, the region of war does not overstep the boundaries of neutral States, and no hostilities are permitted within their respective domains.

Since the region of war comprises the territories subject to the sovereignty of the belligerent States, it includes (i) land areas; (ii) internal waters; (iii) archipelagic waters;[65] (iv) territorial sea; (v) subsoil and submarine areas underneath these expanses of land and water; as well as (vi) the superjacent airspace above them. However, the extension of the region of war to the entire territories of the belligerent States is not immutable. An international (multilateral or bilateral) treaty may exclude from the region of any present or future war a waterway, an island or any other well-defined zone located within the territory of an actual or prospective belligerent. Such a treaty gives rise to the 'neutralization' of the specific zone.[66] Neutralization assimilates the status of an area controlled by a belligerent to that of a neutral territory.

A typical neutralization arrangement is embodied in Article 4 of the 1888 Constantinople Convention on the Suez Canal, where the Contracting Parties agreed that 'no right of war' or 'act of hostility' would be allowed in the Canal and its ports of access, or within a radius of 3 nautical miles from those ports.[67] A parallel provision, explicitly referring to neutralization, appeared in Article 3 of the 1901 Anglo-American Hay–Pauncefote Treaty (in anticipation of the construction of a canal connecting the Atlantic and Pacific oceans).[68]

In 1977, the United States and the Republic of Panama concluded a Treaty Concerning the Permanent Neutrality and Operation of the Panama Canal.[69] In general, the phrase 'permanent neutrality' is to be

---

[65] On the status of archipelagic waters, see E. Rauch, *The Protocol Additional to the Geneva Conventions for the Protection of Victims of International Armed Conflicts and the United Nations Convention on the Law of the Sea: Repercussions on the Law of Naval Warfare* 32 (1984).

[66] See Oppenheim, *supra* note 8, at 244.

[67] Constantinople Convention Respecting the Free Navigation of the Suez Maritime Canal, 1888, 3 *AJIL*, Supp., 123, 124 (1909).

[68] Great Britain–United States, Treaty to Facilitate the Construction of a Ship Canal (Hay–Pauncefote Treaty), 1901, 3 *AJIL*, Supp., 127, 128 (1909).

[69] United States–Panama, Treaty Concerning the Permanent Neutrality and Operation of the Panama Canal, 1977, 72 *AJIL* 238 (1978).

differentiated from the term 'neutralization'.[70] The concept of permanent neutrality applies to the whole territory of a country, with Switzerland as the model. A country placed under a permanent neutrality regime undertakes to remain neutral in all future wars (unless attacked), to conclude no military alliances and to allow no foreign military bases on its soil.[71] No such obligation is imposed on the Republic of Panama in the 1977 Treaty. The permanent neutrality declared therein relates only to the Panama Canal.[72] Respect for the permanent neutrality of the Canal is also a theme of a special Protocol, annexed to the Treaty and open to accession by all the States of the world.[73] In correct legal terminology, the 1977 Treaty and Protocol ensure not the permanent neutrality, but the neutralization, of the Panama Canal.

Neutralization is not restricted to international waterways. Article 6 of the 1921 Geneva Convention on the Non-Fortification and Neutralisation of the Aaland Islands lays down that, in time of war, these islands are to be considered a neutral zone and they are not to be used for any purpose connected with military operations.[74]

Protocol I Additional to the Geneva Conventions incorporates, in Article 60, a detailed stipulation relating to 'demilitarized zones'.[75] Parties to a conflict are forbidden to extend their military operations to zones on which they have conferred by agreement (concluded either in writing or verbally, either in peacetime or after the outbreak of hostilities) the status of a demilitarized zone. Although Article 60 refers to 'demilitarized zones', the exclusion of wartime military operations signifies that the zones have been neutralized.

The two institutions of neutralization and demilitarization 'must be sharply distinguished'.[76] Demilitarization means that a State accepts limitations on (or waives altogether) its right to maintain armed forces and weapon systems, as well as to construct fortifications and military installations, in a certain region.[77] Demilitarization can be a component of neutralization. Conversely, demilitarization may exist without neutralization, just as neutralization may exist without demilitarization. In both instances, a well-defined zone is involved (whereas a permanent

---

[70] See S. Verosta, 'Neutralization', 3 *EPIL* 570, *id.*
[71] See J. L. Kunz, 'Austria's Permanent Neutrality', 50 *AJIL* 418, 418–19 (1956).
[72] Treaty Concerning the Permanent Neutrality and Operation of the Panama Canal, *supra* note 69, at 238–41.
[73] *Ibid.*, 241–2.
[74] Geneva Convention Relating to the Non-Fortification and Neutralisation of the Aaland Islands, 1921, 9 *LNTS* 211, 219.
[75] Protocol I, *supra* note 31, at 118–19.
[76] J. H. W. Verzijl, *International Law in Historical Perspective*, III, 500 (1970).
[77] See J. Delbrück, 'Demilitarization', 1 *EPIL* 999, *id.*

neutrality regime affects an entire State). But demilitarization is designed for periods of peace or at least cease-fire, while neutralization acquires a practical significance only in time of actual warfare. Demilitarization, particularly of a border buffer zone, places the emphasis on the prevention of incidents liable to trigger hostilities. Neutralization is premised on the assumption that hostilities do begin or have begun: the goal is to prevent the neutralized zone from being engulfed in the fighting. In demilitarization, the demilitarized zone serves only as a means to the end of the maintenance of peace, or the observance of a cease-fire, everywhere. In neutralization, the neutralized zone itself is the end: the objective is safeguarding the zone from the spread of warfare raging elsewhere.

The 1959 Antarctic Treaty promulgates, in Article I(1), that 'Antarctica shall be used for peaceful purposes only'.[78] There is no lucid definition of the term 'peaceful purposes'.[79] However, a plain reading of the text would suggest that it eliminates the possibility of warlike activities ('warlike' being the antonym of 'peaceful'). Article 8(4)(b) of the 1988 Convention on the Regulation of Antarctic Mineral Resource Activities – when dealing with non-liability for damage in case of unforeseen disasters – refers to the possibility of an 'armed conflict, should it occur notwithstanding the Antarctic Treaty'.[80] Since an armed conflict can occur only 'notwithstanding' the Antarctic Treaty,[81] it is clear that a regime of neutralization has been imposed on the entire continent. Article I of the Antarctic Treaty also provides for the demilitarization of Antarctica.[82]

(b)   The high seas and the exclusive economic zone

There has never been any doubt that the high seas 'fall within the region of war'.[83] Surprisingly, Article 88 of the 1982 United Nations Convention on the Law of the Sea, echoing the language of the Antarctic Treaty, proclaims:

The high seas shall be reserved for peaceful purposes.[84]

---

[78] Washington Antarctic Treaty, 1959, 402 *UNTS* 71, 72.
[79] See J. Hanessian, 'The Antarctic Treaty 1959', 9 *ICLQ* 436, 468 (1960).
[80] Wellington Convention on the Regulation of Antarctic Mineral Resource Activities, 1988, 27 *ILM* 859, 873 (1988).
[81] Apart from the possibility of a material breach of the Antarctic Convention, an armed conflict may be initiated by a non-Contracting Party. See A. Watts, *International Law and the Antarctic Treaty System* 207 (1992).
[82] Washington Antarctic Treaty, *supra* note 78, at 72.
[83] Oppenheim, *supra* note 8, at 239.
[84] United Nations Convention on the Law of the Sea, 1982, Official Text, 31.

Under Article 58(2), this clause applies also to the exclusive economic zone.[85] A literal construction of the words used in the Convention would connote that the waging of war as such is banned throughout the high seas and the exclusive economic zone.[86]

If taken seriously, the laconic stipulation of Article 88 would bring about a veritable revolution in maritime warfare. 'This is the shortest Article in the Convention, but in spirit it is the most far-reaching: ostensibly it challenges the historic role of the oceans as battlegrounds.'[87] It is hard to believe that 'a one-sentence reference to peaceful purposes', in an inordinately verbose and complex instrument, was intended to produce the momentous results that seem to flow from the text.[88] The provision 'is widely regarded as prohibiting only acts of aggression on the high seas'.[89] Such an interpretation, which allows naval military operations on the high seas only 'if undertaken as an exercise of the right of self-defense',[90] renders Article 88 redundant in the light of Article 301 of the Convention[91] (quoted *infra*, Chapter 4, D). No wonder that some commentators suggest that Article 88 should not be overemphasized.[92] The authoritative San Remo Manual on International Law Applicable to Armed Conflicts at Sea expressly rejects an interpretation of Article 88 which would 'prohibit naval warfare on the high seas'.[93] There is no doubt that the practice of States in maritime hostilities, conducted since the formulation of the Convention, is in stark contrast to the proposition that the text of Article 88 need be taken at face value.

The region of war at sea embraces not only the exclusive economic zone and the continental shelf of belligerent States: hostile actions by

---

[85] *Ibid.*, 19.

[86] See F. Francioni, 'Use of Force, Military Activities, and the New Law of the Sea', *The Current Legal Regulation of the Use of Force* 361, 375–6 (A. Cassese ed., 1986).

[87] K. Booth, *Law, Force and Diplomacy at Sea* 82 (1985).

[88] B. H. Oxman, 'The Regime of Warships under the United Nations Convention on the Law of the Sea', 24 *VJIL* 809, 831 (1983–4).

[89] R. R. Churchill and A. V. Lowe, *The Law of the Sea* 208 (3rd ed., 1999).

[90] R. J. Zedalis, '"Peaceful Purposes" and Other Relevant Provisions of the Revised Composite Negotiating Text: A Comparative Analysis of the Existing and the Proposed Military Regime for the High Seas', 7 *SJILC* 1, 18 n. 72 (1979–80).

[91] United Nations Convention on the Law of the Sea, *supra* note 84, at 104.

[92] See R. Wolfrum, 'Restricting the Use of the Sea to Peaceful Purposes: Demilitarization in Being?', 24 *GYIL* 200, 213 (1981). Interestingly enough, although Wolfrum is of the opinion that military activities on the high seas ought to be restricted on general grounds of freedom of navigation, he does not believe that Article 88 imposes any obligations on States exceeding those of Article 301. R. Wolfrum, 'Military Activities on the High Seas: What Are the Impacts of the U.N. Convention on the Law of the Sea?', 71 *ILS* 502, 505 (M. N. Schmitt and L. C. Green eds., 1998).

[93] *San Remo Manual on International Law Applicable to Armed Conflicts at Sea* 82 (L. Doswald-Beck ed., 1995).

naval and air forces may also be conducted in or over the exclusive economic zone and the continental shelf of neutral countries.[94] All the same, the entitlement of the belligerent States to engage in naval operations in the exclusive economic zone and the continental shelf of neutral countries is 'not unqualified'.[95] Due regard must be given to installations constructed by a neutral coastal State for the exploitation of its economic resources in these areas.[96]

(c)   Outer space

Pursuant to Article IV of the 1967 Treaty on Outer Space, the Moon and other celestial bodies are to be used 'exclusively for peaceful purposes'[97] (once more, in substance, the Antarctic Treaty formula). The precise effect of this phrase in the 1967 Treaty proved controversial.[98] But Article 3 of a further Agreement, concluded in 1979, reiterates the same general principle and elaborates upon it.[99] The 1979 provision specifically prohibits the use of force either (i) on the Moon (and other celestial bodies within the solar system, except Earth); or (ii) from the Moon (and the other bodies) in relation to Earth or man-made spacecraft. It is still not forbidden to fire missiles (from one point on Earth against another) through outer space.[100]

D.   Neutrality

(a)   The basic principles

Neutrality 'presupposes war between some Powers': it is 'the position of a State which does not participate in that war'.[101] The laws of neutrality

---

[94] See *ibid.*, 80.
[95] G. V. Galdorisi, 'Military Activities in the Exclusive Economic Zone: Preventing Uncertainty and Defusing Conflict', 32 *CWILJ* 253, 279 (2001–2).
[96] See *San Remo Manual, supra* note 93, at 108.
[97] Treaty on Principles Governing the Activities of States in the Exploration and Use of Outer Space, Including the Moon and Other Celestial Bodies, 1967, [1966] *UNJY* 166, 167.
[98] See I. A. Vlasic, 'The Legal Aspects of Peaceful and Non-Peaceful Uses of Outer Space', *Peaceful and Non-Peaceful Uses of Space: Problems of Definition for the Prevention of an Arms Race* 37, 44–7 (B. Jasani ed., 1991).
[99] Agreement Governing the Activities of States on the Moon and Other Celestial Bodies, 1979, [1979] *UNJY* 109, 110. See also Article 1(1), *ibid.*, 109. The Treaty is not widely ratified.
[100] See L. Condorelli and Z. Mériboute, 'Some Remarks on the State of International Law Concerning Military Activities in Outer Space', 6 *IYIL* 5, 9 (1985).
[101] E. Castrén, *The Present Law of War and Neutrality* 422–3 (1954).

stem from a realization that, in an interdependent world, neutrals cannot simply ignore a war conducted by other countries. 'The very nature of war causes its effects to extend also to non-participating States and their nationals whether they wish it or not.'[102]

A State may be neutral at the outbreak of hostilities, turning into a belligerent at a later stage; that was the case with the United States in both World Wars. A State starting a multipartite war as a belligerent may also withdraw from the hostilities (provided that the enemy will let it do so) and become a neutral. In fact, a State may be associated with certain other countries in a war against one enemy, staying neutral in another war conducted by the same countries concurrently against another enemy. Accordingly, in the Grand Alliance of World War II, the Soviet Union – while bearing for several years the brunt of the fighting against Germany – remained neutral, until almost the very last moment, insofar as Japan was concerned.

The laws of neutrality are operative only as long as the neutral State retains its neutral status. Once that State becomes immersed in the hostilities, the laws of neutrality cease being applicable, and the laws of warfare take their place. However, if the neutral State is not drawn into the war, the laws of neutrality are activated from the onset of the war until its conclusion.

The laws of neutrality are predicated on two fundamental, closely interlinked, rationales: (i) the desire to guarantee to the neutral State that it will sustain minimal injury by reason of the war; (ii) the desire to guarantee to the belligerents that the neutral State will be neutral not only in name but also in deed (that is to say, it will not assist one of the belligerents against the opposing side). The two pillars of the laws of neutrality are non-participation and non-discrimination.[103]

(b)   Some concrete rules

Without seeking to lay out the broad sweep of the laws of neutrality, it may be advisable to trace several characteristic rules – concretizing the basic principles of non-participation and non-discrimination – which will have some bearing on the discussion in other chapters of this study.

---

[102] *Ibid.*, 425.
[103] See T. Komarnicki, 'The Place of Neutrality in the Modern System of International Law', 80 *RCADI* 395, 406 (1952). *Cf.* Harvard Research in International Law, Draft Convention on Rights and Duties of Neutral States in Naval and Aerial War (P. C. Jessup, Reporter), 33 *AJIL*, Sp. Supp., 167, 176 (1939) (Articles 4–5).

i.   Passage of belligerent military units and war materials As already noticed (*supra*, C, (a)), the region of war does not include the territories of neutral States, and no hostilities are permissible within neutral boundaries. A question of singular practical importance arises, however, in regard to non-violent passage of troops, weapons and supplies through neutral territory. Different legal norms have evolved in land and air warfare, as compared to maritime warfare. The general rule of land warfare, enunciated in Articles 2 and 5 of Hague Convention (V) of 1907 Respecting the Rights and Duties of Neutral Powers and Persons in Case of War on Land, is that the movement of troops or convoys of either munitions of war or supplies, across the territory of a neutral State, is forbidden.[104] The entry of belligerent military aircraft into the airspace of a neutral country is equally proscribed by Article 40 of the Rules of Aerial Warfare, formulated in 1923 by a Commission of Jurists at The Hague.[105] Contrarily, under Article 10 of Hague Convention (XIII) of 1907 Concerning the Rights and Duties of Neutral Powers in Naval War, the neutrality of a State is not impaired by the mere passage through its territorial waters of belligerent warships or prizes.[106] Subject to conditions enumerated in the Convention, belligerent warships and prizes may even enter neutral ports.[107]

The obligations outlined in Hague Convention (V) are incurred jointly by the belligerents and the neutral State. Each of the belligerents is enjoined from moving its land forces across the neutral territory (Article 2 of the Convention), and, correspondingly, the neutral State must not tolerate such movement within its territory (Article 5). If Arcadia (a belligerent) transports troops through the territory of Ruritania (a neutral) against the latter's will, Arcadia contravenes its duty towards both Ruritania and Utopia (the enemy). Should Arcadia act in complicity with Ruritania, they would both be in breach of their obligations *vis-à-vis* Utopia.

ii.   Enrolment in belligerent armed forces Articles 4 and 5 of Hague Convention (V) do not permit the formation on neutral soil of corps of combatants, or the opening of recruiting agencies, to assist the

---

[104] Hague Convention (V) Respecting the Rights and Duties of Neutral Powers and Persons in Case of War on Land, 1907, *Hague Conventions* 133, 133–4.
[105] Commission of Jurists to Consider and Report upon the Revision of the Rules of Warfare, Rules of Aerial Warfare (The Hague, 1923), 32 *AJIL*, Supp., 1, 12, 34 (1938).
[106] Hague Convention (XIII) Concerning the Rights and Duties of Neutral Powers in Naval War, 1907, *Hague Conventions* 209, 211.
[107] *Ibid.*, 211–13.

belligerents.[108] In the same vein, the neutral State must not assign military advisers to the armed forces of one of the adversaries, and, if it has sent such advisers in peacetime, it is bound to recall them once hostilities commence.[109] Yet, as stipulated in Article 6 of Hague Convention (V), the neutral State incurs no responsibility when individuals cross its frontiers offering their services to one of the belligerents.[110]

The upshot of the laws of neutrality on this point is that they countenance individual initiatives, by nationals and residents of a neutral State, to serve in the armed forces of one of the parties to the conflict.[111] The domestic legislation of the neutral State may penalize such service in a foreign army in wartime, but international law only interdicts the dispatch of organized expeditions.[112] As long as the volunteering proceeds on a purely individual basis, it is not hindered by international law (even if the overall number of volunteers is considerable).[113] Evidently, genuine volunteers must not be confused with regular troops in disguise who are falsely portrayed as 'volunteers'.[114]

iii.   *Military supplies to belligerents* The Government of a neutral State must not (directly or indirectly) furnish military supplies of whatever type to a belligerent: Article 6 of Hague Convention (XIII)[115] and Article 44 of the Hague Rules of Aerial Warfare[116] are categorical about it with respect to naval and air warfare, and incontestably this is also the rule in land warfare. As for non-governmental supplies, Article 7 of both Hague Conventions (V) and (XIII) prescribes that a neutral State is not obligated to prevent private individuals from selling and exporting arms, ammunition and war materials to belligerents.[117] The only condition, set forth in Article 9 of Hague Convention (V), is that any prohibition or limitation decided upon by the neutral State will be applied impartially to both adversaries.[118]

It follows that the neutral State is at liberty to adopt one of two contradictory policies concerning sales and exports of war materials, by private

---

[108] Hague Convention (V), *supra* note 104, at 134.
[109] See Oppenheim, *supra* note 8, at 687.
[110] Hague Convention (V), *supra* note 104, at 134.
[111] Under Article 47 of Protocol I of 1977, mercenaries (as defined therein) do not have the right to be combatants or prisoners of war. *Supra* note 31, at 112–13. But the activities of mercenaries do not compromise the neutrality of their State of origin.
[112] See I. Brownlie, 'Volunteers and the Law of War and Neutrality', 5 *ICLQ* 570, 571 (1956).
[113] See *ibid.*, 572.   [114] See *ibid.*, 578.
[115] Hague Convention (XIII), *supra* note 106, at 210.
[116] Rules of Aerial Warfare, *supra* note 105, at 37.
[117] Hague Convention (V), *supra* note 104, at 134; Hague Convention (XIII), *supra* note 106, at 211.
[118] Hague Convention (V), *supra* note 104, at 134.

individuals, to belligerents. The neutral State is entitled to impose a total embargo on such sales and exports, abolishing them altogether. Alternatively, the neutral State may erase any barrier to private trade, and afford an opportunity for the purchase of military goods by all comers in the open market. Whether the neutral State favours the one policy or the other, what is imperative is that it will apply the same yardsticks to all parties to the conflict. What the neutral State is barred from doing is establishing an embargo on individual sales of military supplies to one side, while giving a free hand to its opponent.

The neutral State may switch from one course of action to another during the war. This is what the United States did in the early days of World War II (prior to becoming a belligerent). When hostilities broke out in Europe in September 1939, the law in force in the United States was the Neutrality Act of 1935, which endorsed the embargo concept and unequivocally hamstrung the export of arms, ammunition and implements of war to belligerents.[119] In November 1939, Congress enacted a new Neutrality Act repealing the arms embargo.[120] The revised statute placed all trade with belligerents on a 'cash and carry' basis.[121] It allowed the export to belligerents of any articles or materials, provided that title would be transferred to a foreign Government or a foreign national in advance of the export, and that the transport would be effected in non-American vessels.[122]

Long before its entry into the war, the United States abandoned the semblance of traditional neutrality and openly supported the United Kingdom against Nazi Germany (see *infra*, Chapter 6, D). But one must not gloss over the fact that, even in the period preceding the transition, although in theory the United States was dealing with belligerents on an equal footing, the 'cash and carry' policy latently discriminated between them. The concept gravitated towards a preferential treatment of the belligerent (Great Britain) that ruled the waves and was actually able to pay cash and to carry, as opposed to the party (Germany) that could not avail itself of the open door owing to insurmountable obstacles in the way of transportation.

When the neutral State permits sales and exports of weapons, ammunition and war materials by private individuals to belligerents, it must be on the alert not to become a base of military operations against one of

---

[119] United States, Joint Resolution (Neutrality Act, 1935), 30 *AJIL*, Supp., 58 (1936). The term 'embargo' features *ibid.*, 59.

[120] See P. C. Jessup, 'The "Neutrality Act of 1939"', 34 *AJIL* 95, 96 (1940).

[121] See H. R. Wellman, 'The Neutrality Act of 1939', 25 *Cor.LR* 255, *id.* (1939–40).

[122] United States, Neutrality Act of 1939, 34 *AJIL*, Supp., 44, 45 (1940).

them.[123] This is primarily true of ships and aircraft. If a belligerent purchases a vessel or a plane from private individuals in a neutral country, and having obtained the craft adapts it thereafter to military purposes, no violation of neutrality occurs. However, if the craft bought by a warring party leaves the neutral territory armed and ready for action against the enemy, a breach of the laws of neutrality is committed.

Article 8 of Hague Convention (XIII)[124] and Article 46 of the Hague Rules of Aerial Warfare[125] instruct the neutral State to employ the means at its disposal to prevent within its jurisdiction the fitting out for use in war, the arming or the departure of a vessel or an aircraft, intended to engage in hostile operations against a belligerent. The progenitor of these provisions was the 1871 Washington Treaty,[126] concluded by the United States and Great Britain for the purposes of the famous Arbitration in the *Alabama* case. The 'Alabama Rules', as formulated in the Treaty, used the idiom 'due diligence' to describe the duty of prevention that has to be discharged by the neutral State.[127] Since the interpretation of the expression by the Arbitrators[128] turned out to be controversial,[129] the two clauses cited circumvent the problem by concentrating on the means at the disposal of the neutral State.

---

[123] Rules of Aerial Warfare, *supra* note 105, at 37–8 (explanatory note).

[124] Hague Convention (XIII), *supra* note 106, at 211.

[125] Rules of Aerial Warfare, *supra* note 105, at 38.

[126] Great Britain–United States, Washington Treaty for the Amicable Settlement of All Causes of Difference between the Two Countries, 1871, 143 *CTS* 145, 149.

[127] *Ibid.*, 149.

[128] *Alabama Claims* Award (1872), *History and Digest of the International Arbitrations to Which the United States Has Been a Party*, I, 653, 654 (J. B. Moore ed., 1898).

[129] See Oppenheim, *supra* note 8, at 757–8.

2   The course of war

A.   The beginning of war

(a)   War in the technical sense

War in the technical sense starts with a declaration of war. A declaration of war is a unilateral and formal announcement, issued by the constitutionally competent authority of a State, setting the exact point at which war begins with a designated enemy (or enemies). Notwithstanding its unilateral character, a declaration of war 'brings about a state of war irrespective of the attitude of the state to which it is addressed'.[1]

According to Article 1 of Hague Convention (III) of 1907 Relative to the Commencement of Hostilities:

> The contracting Powers recognize that hostilities between themselves must not commence without previous and explicit warning, in the form either of a declaration of war, giving reasons, or of an ultimatum with a conditional declaration of war.[2]

Article 1 explicitly mentions that reasons for a declaration of war must be given. But the causes of wars cannot be seriously established on the basis of a self-serving unilateral declaration. The main value of a declaration of war is derived from the fact that it pinpoints the precise time when a state of war enters into force.

An ultimatum may take one of two forms: (i) a threat that, if certain demands are not complied with, hostilities will be initiated; (ii) a warning that, unless specific conditions are fulfilled by a designated deadline, war will commence *ipso facto*.[3] Article 1 requires an ultimatum of the second type, incorporating a conditional declaration of war. An ultimatum of the

---

[1] M. Greenspan, *The Modern Law of Land Warfare* 38 (1959).

[2] Hague Convention (III) Relative to the Opening of Hostilities, 1907, *Hague Conventions* 96, *id.*

[3] See N. Hill, 'Was There an Ultimatum before Pearl Harbor?', 42 *AJIL* 355, 357–8 (1948).

first category is not deemed sufficient by itself under Article 1, and it must
be followed by a formal declaration of war. Only the subsequent declaration, rather than the preliminary threat, would be in conformity with
Hague Convention (III).[4]

A classical ultimatum of the second type (setting a deadline and
warning that war would start automatically once it lapses) was issued
by Britain and France to Germany in September 1939.[5] An ultimatum
of the first type (no specific deadline and no automatic consequences)
is exemplified in the imperative demands addressed to the Taliban
regime in Afghanistan in September 2001 – shortly after the Al-Qaeda
terrorist attacks of 9/11 – by the President of the United States, George
W. Bush. These non-negotiable demands related, primarily, to the
handing over to the US of Al-Qaeda leaders hiding in Afghanistan
and the closing down of terrorist camps.[6] The President made it clear
that 'The Taliban must act, and act immediately. They will hand over
the terrorists, or they will share in their fate'.[7] In the event, military
operations against Taliban and Al-Qaeda targets in Afghanistan
commenced on October 7th, and the President explicitly stated that the
Taliban must pay the price for failing to meet the earlier demands.[8] There
ought to be no doubt that October 7th – and not September 11th – is the
date of the beginning of the war between the United States and
Afghanistan.[9]

An ultimatum, almost by definition, entails a lapse of time (brief as it
may be) providing an opportunity for compliance with the demands
made. Hostilities are not supposed to begin unless that period has expired
and the response is considered unsatisfactory.

Insofar as an outright declaration of war is concerned, Hague
Convention (III) does not insist on any meaningful interval before combat starts.[10] Article 1 does prescribe that the declaration must be made

---

[4] See *ibid.*, 358–9. Security Council Resolution 678 (1990) (45 *RDSC* 27 (1990)) is
referred to by some commentators as an ultimatum to Iraq. M. Voelckel, 'Faut-il
Encore Déclarer la Guerre?', 37 *AFDI* 7, 21 (1991). But this is not the case, inasmuch
as the Gulf War had already been in progress since the Iraqi invasion of Kuwait in August
1990 (see *supra*, Chapter 1, A, (b), iii).

[5] See Hill, *supra* note 3, at 358.

[6] National Addresses by President Bush: 'War against Terrorism', [2001] *Digest of United
States Practice in International Law* 856, 857, 858.

[7] *Ibid.*, 858–9.

[8] Air Strikes in Afghanistan, *ibid.*, 867, 867–8.

[9] Doubts as to which of the two dates is applicable have been expressed by a number of
commentators. See, e.g., L. Condorelli, 'Les Attentats du 11 Septembre et leurs Suites:
Où Va le Droit International?', 105 *RGDIP* 829, 845–6 (2001).

[10] See E. C. Stowell, 'Convention Relative to the Opening of Hostilities', 2 *AJIL* 50, 53–4
(1908).

'previous' to the commencement of hostilities, and even refers to it (on a par with an ultimatum) as a warning. However, it is significant that a proposed amendment of the Article, to the effect that 24 hours must pass between the issuance of the declaration and the outbreak of hostilities, was defeated in the course of the Hague Conference.[11] The upshot is that fire may be opened almost immediately after the announcement has been made.[12] A declaration of war under the Convention constitutes merely a formal measure, and it does not necessarily deny the advantage of surprise to the attacking State.

Hague Convention (III) cannot be considered a reflection of customary international law.[13] Before the Convention, most wars were precipitated without a prelude in the form of a declaration of war.[14] The practice of States has not changed substantially since the conclusion of the Convention. Some hostilities are preceded by declarations of war, but this is the exception rather than the rule. There are many reasons for the contemporary reluctance to engage in a declaration of war. Some of these reasons are pragmatic, stemming for instance from a desire to avert the automatic application of the (international no less than domestic) laws of neutrality activated during war. The paucity of declarations of war at the present juncture is also linked, paradoxically, to the illegality and criminality of wars of aggression (see *infra*, Chapters 4–5). The contemporary injunction against war has not yet eliminated its incidence. Nevertheless, the prohibition has definitely created a psychological environment in which belligerents prefer using a different terminology, such as 'international armed conflict'.[15] Since States are indisposed to employ the expression 'war', they naturally eschew declarations of 'war'.

Even when a declaration of war is issued, in many instances this is done after the first strike, so that the act constitutes no more than an acknowledgement of a state of war already in progress; occasionally, the declaration is articulated by the State under attack, and it merely records that

---

[11] See A. P. Higgins, *The Hague Peace Conferences* 204 (1909).
[12] See T. J. Lawrence, *The Principles of International Law* 326 (P. H. Winfield ed., 7th ed., 1923).
[13] See G. Schwarzenberger, *The Law of Armed Conflict* (*International Law as Applied by International Courts and Tribunals*, II) 65–7 (1968).
[14] See P. M. Brown, 'Undeclared Wars', 33 *AJIL* 538, 539 (1939).
[15] The coinage 'international armed conflict', rather than war, is currently fashionable in international legal instruments meant to apply also in situations 'short of war'. A prime example is Protocol Additional to the Geneva Conventions of 12 August 1949, and Relating to the Protection of Victims of International Armed Conflicts (Protocol I), 1977, [1977] *UNJY* 95. See *supra*, Chapter 1, B, (a).

the enemy has launched war.[16] Of course, a post-attack declaration of war (by either party) is not in accordance with Hague Convention (III).

When enunciated, a declaration of war does not require 'any particular *form*', although it must be authorized by a competent organ of the State.[17] Lack of prescribed form should not be confused with rhetorical flourish. It must be appreciated that not every bellicose turn of phrase in a harangue delivered by a Head of State before a public gathering can be deemed a declaration of war. In the *Dalmia Cement* International Chamber of Commerce Arbitration of 1976, P. Lalive held that a broadcast aired by the President of Pakistan in 1965 – in which a statement was made that Pakistan and India were 'at war' – did not amount to a declaration of war pursuant to international law, inasmuch as it 'in no way was, or purported to be, a "communication" to India'.[18] The insistence on the transmittal of an official communication to the antagonist may be exaggerated, but surely a declaration of war – in whatever form – must (at the very least) be publicly announced in an explicit and lucid manner. One cannot accept the assertion by a United States Federal District Court in 1958, in the *Ulysses* case, that Egypt had declared war (consonant with international law) against Britain and France, in November 1956, in a public speech made by President Nasser before a large crowd in Cairo.[19] The Court admitted that the speech had been misunderstood or disregarded at the time, but it relied on the fact that a subsequent official Egyptian statement confirmed that it had been intended as a declaration of war.[20] However, the very misunderstanding of the purport of the speech at the point of delivery weakens the Court's position. President Nasser's speech was simply 'neither definite nor unequivocal' enough as a declaration of war.[21] If it is to have any value at all, a declaration of war must impart an unambiguous signal to all concerned.

(b)   War in the material sense

War in the material sense unfolds irrespective of any formal steps. Its occurrence is contingent only on the actual outbreak of comprehensive hostilities between two or more States. Hence, war in the material sense

---

[16] See C. Eagleton, 'The Form and Function of the Declaration of War', 32 *AJIL* 19, 32–3 (1938).

[17] E. Castrén, *The Present Law of War and Neutrality* 98 (1954).

[18] *Dalmia Cement Ltd. v. National Bank of Pakistan* (1976), 67 *ILR* 611, 616.

[19] *Navios Corporation v. The Ulysses II et al.* (1958), 161 *F. Supp.* 932, 942–3. The judgment, and the reasons given therein, were affirmed by the US Court of Appeals (4th Circuit) (260 *F. 2d* 959).

[20] *Ibid.*   [21] G. O. Fuller, 'Note', 57 *Mich.LR* 610, 612 (1958–9).

commences with an invasion or another mode of an armed attack. In the past, an air raid (*à la* Pearl Harbor) or an artillery bombardment would be emblematic. In the future, a devastating computer network attack (with massive lethal consequences) is equally likely to occur.[22] Actual hostilities may begin (i) without a declaration of war ever being made; (ii) prior to a declaration of war, which follows afterwards; (iii) simultaneously with a declaration of war; or (iv) subsequent to a declaration of war. Moreover, war in the material sense (viz. active hostilities) may not commence at all, notwithstanding a declaration of war (see *supra*, Chapter 1, A, (b), ii).

When the outbreak of comprehensive hostilities does not coincide with a declaration of war (especially when the declaration lags behind the inception of the actual fighting and, more particularly, when it is issued by the State under attack), there is likely to be some doubt as to whether war was triggered by the action or by the declaration.[23] In such a setting, it is quite possible that different dates for the outbreak of the war will be used for disparate purposes, such as the status of enemy nationals and the application of neutrality laws.[24]

Article 2 of Hague Convention (III)[25] stipulates that the existence of a state of war must be notified to neutral States without delay, and it shall not take effect in regard to them as long as the notification has not been received. All the same, the Article lays down that, if a neutral country is in fact aware of the state of war, it cannot rely on the absence of notification. Under modern conditions, since a state of war habitually gets wide coverage in the news media, any special notification to neutrals may well be redundant. Still, should there be any doubt whether the hostilities qualify as an all-out war or are 'short of war', the communication to neutral countries (or the absence thereof) is of practical importance even in the present day.

B.   The termination of war

(a)   Treaties of peace

i.   The significance of a treaty of peace The classical and ideal method for the termination of inter-State war is the conclusion of a treaty of peace between the belligerents. Traditionally, treaties of peace have had an

---

[22] On this subject, see Y. Dinstein, 'Computer Network Attacks and Self-Defense', 76 *ILS* 99, 105 (M. N. Schmitt and B. T. O'Donnell eds., 2002).
[23] *Cf.* E. Borchard, 'When Did the War Begin?', 47 *Col.LR* 742–8 (1947); C. Eagleton, '"Acts of War"', 35 *AJIL* 321, 325 (1941).
[24] See M. O. Hudson, 'The Duration of the War between the United States and Germany', 39 *Har.LR* 1020, 1021 (1925–6).
[25] Hague Convention (III), *supra* note 2, at 96.

extraordinary impact on the evolution of international law, from Westphalia (1648) to Versailles (1919). The series of treaties of peace signed at the close of World War I even encompassed, in their first part (Articles 1–26), the Covenant of the League of Nations[26] (the predecessor of the United Nations). Despite their unique political standing, treaties of peace are no different juridically from other types of inter-State agreements, and they are governed by the general law of treaties.[27]

After World War II, and as a direct consequence of the 'Cold War', no treaty of peace could be reached with the principal vanquished country (Germany), which was divided for 45 years. It was only in 1990, following a sea change in world politics, that a Treaty on the Final Settlement with Respect to Germany[28] could be formulated. The Preamble of this instrument records the fact that the peoples of the Contracting Parties (the United States, the USSR, the United Kingdom, France and the two Germanies) 'have been living together in peace since 1945'.[29] In Article 1, a united Germany (comprising the territories of the Federal Republic of Germany, the German Democratic Republic and the whole of Berlin) is established, and 'the definitive nature' of its borders – especially with Poland – is confirmed.[30] The 1990 Treaty may be deemed a final peace settlement for Germany.[31]

Treaties of Peace with five minor Axis countries – Italy, Bulgaria, Hungary, Romania and Finland – were concluded already in 1947 at Paris.[32] With Japan the Western Allied Powers arrived at a Treaty of Peace, in San Francisco, in 1951.[33] The USSR was not a Contracting Party to the latter instrument. Instead, a Joint Declaration was adopted by the USSR and Japan, in 1956, whereby the state of war between the two parties was brought to an end.[34] The Joint Declaration sets forth that negotiations aimed at a treaty of peace will continue.[35] However, since it proclaims that the state of war is ended, and that peace, friendship and good neighbourly relations are restored,[36] including diplomatic and

---

[26] Covenant of the League of Nations, 1919, 1 *Int.Leg.* 1, *id.*

[27] See G. Schwarzenberger, 'Peace Treaties before International Courts and Tribunals', 8 *IJIL* 1, *id.* (1968).

[28] Treaty on the Final Settlement with Respect to Germany, 1990, 29 *ILM* 1186, 1187 (1990).

[29] *Ibid.*   [30] *Ibid.*, 1186–9.

[31] See J. A. Frowein, 'The Reunification of Germany', 86 *AJIL* 152, 157 (1992).

[32] Paris Treaty of Peace with Bulgaria, 1947, 41 *UNTS* 21; Paris Treaty of Peace with Hungary, 1947, *ibid.*, 135; Paris Treaty of Peace with Roumania, 1947, 42 *ibid.*, 3; Paris Treaty of Peace with Finland, 1947, 48 *ibid.*, 203; Paris Treaty of Peace with Italy, 1947, 49 *ibid.*, 3.

[33] San Francisco Treaty of Peace with Japan, 1951, 136 *UNTS* 45.

[34] USSR–Japan, Joint Declaration, 1956, 263 *UNTS* 112, *id.* (Article 1).

[35] *Ibid.*, 116 (Article 9).   [36] *Ibid.*, 112 (Article 1).

consular relations,[37] the Declaration already attains most of the objectives of an ordinary treaty of peace.

The Russian–Japanese instance is a good illustration of an agreement
terminating bilaterally a war which was multilateral. Another example is
that of a bilateral British–Siamese (Thai) agreement of 1946 for the
termination of war between the parties, which constituted an integral
part of World War II.[38]

In the international armed conflicts of the post-World War II era,
States commonly try to avoid not only the term 'war' but also its corollary
'treaty of peace'. Two outstanding exceptions are the Treaties of Peace
concluded by Israel with Egypt (in 1979),[39] and with Jordan (in 1994).[40]
Another exception is the 'Peace Agreement' concluded by Ethiopia and
Eritrea in 2000.[41]

The hallmark of a treaty of peace is that it both (i) puts an end to a
pre-existing state of war, and (ii) introduces or restores amicable relations
between the parties. Two temporal matters are noteworthy in this context. The first relates to the fixed point in time in which the conclusion of
war is effected (the *terminus ad quem*). Upon signing a treaty of peace, the
parties – at their discretion – may choose to employ language indicating
that the termination of the war has either occurred already in the past; is
happening at the present moment; or will take place in the future. The
Israeli practice illustrates all three options.

In the Treaty of Peace with Egypt, Article I(1) resorts to future language:

The state of war between the Parties will be terminated and peace will be
established between them upon the exchange of instruments of ratification of
this Treaty.[42]

That is to say, the state of war between Israel and Egypt continued even
after the signature of the Treaty of Peace (in March 1979), and its
termination occurred only upon the subsequent exchange of the instruments of ratification (the following month).

A different legal technique was adopted in the case of Israel and Jordan,
delinking the end of war from the advent of peace. Article 1 of the Treaty
of Peace between the two countries (signed at the Arava in October 1994)
proclaims:

---

[37] *Ibid.*, 114 (Article 2).
[38] UK–Siam, Singapore Agreement for the Termination of the State of War, 1946, 99
UNTS 132.
[39] Egypt–Israel, Treaty of Peace, 1979, 18 *ILM* 362 (1979).
[40] Jordan–Israel, Treaty of Peace, 1994, 34 *ILM* 43 (1995).
[41] Ethiopia–Eritrea, Peace Agreement, 2000, 40 *ILM* 260 (2001).
[42] Egypt–Israel, Treaty of Peace, *supra* note 39, at 363.

Peace is hereby established between the State of Israel and the Hashemite Kingdom of Jordan (the 'Parties') effective from the exchange of the instruments of ratification of this Treaty.[43]

The onset of peace thus parallels the Israeli–Egyptian formula. But as for the state of war, the Preamble of the Israeli–Jordanian Treaty reads:

Bearing in mind that in their Washington Declaration of 25th July, 1994, they [Israel and Jordan] declared the termination of the state of belligerency between them.[44]

The Washington Declaration of July 1994 incorporates the following clause:

The long conflict between the two states is now coming to an end. In this spirit, the state of belligerency between Israel and Jordan has been terminated.[45]

The upshot is that, whereas peace between Israel and Jordan was established only upon the ratification of the Arava Treaty of October 1994, the state of war between the two countries had ended already in July of that year (the date of the Washington Declaration, which was not subject to ratification).

Unlike the future tense (used in the Treaty of Peace with Egypt) and the present tense (employed in the Washington Declaration with Jordan), there is also recourse to the past tense in the Israeli practice of ending war. This occurred in the abortive Treaty of Peace between Israel and Lebanon,[46] which was signed in May 1983 (at Qiryat Shemona and Khaldeh) but never entered into force since Lebanon declined to ratify it.[47] The instrument is significant only because it sets forth in Article 1(2):

The Parties confirm that the state of war between Israel and Lebanon has been terminated and no longer exists.[48]

It is clear that, at Khaldeh and Qiryat Shemona, Lebanon and Israel did not terminate the war between them at the moment of signature (using the present tense) or undertook to end it upon ratification (in the future): they confirmed that the state of war had already ended at some indeterminate stage (in the past), and that it therefore no longer existed. In contradistinction to the termination of war in the present or

---

[43] Jordan–Israel, Treaty of Peace, *supra* note 40, at 46.   [44] *Ibid.*, 46.

[45] Jordan–Israel, Washington Declaration, 25 July 1994, 54 *Facts on File Yearbook* 526, *id.* (1994).

[46] Lebanon–Israel, Treaty of Peace, 1983 (unratified). The text is published in 7 *Middle East Contemporary Survey* 690 (1982–3).

[47] The requirement of ratification of the instrument – as a condition precedent to its entry into force – appears in Article 10(1), *ibid.*, 692.

[48] *Ibid.*, 691. See also 43 *Facts on File Yearbook* 359, *id.* (1983).

in the future – which, in both instances, is a constitutive step – the notation that the war has already ended in the past is merely a declaratory measure.

The second temporal matter is that, apart from the lack of synchronization between the termination of war and the inauguration of peace, even peace may be introduced in stages. Thus, under Article I of the Egyptian–Israeli Treaty of Peace, while peace is established (as shown) upon ratification, 'normal and friendly relations' are to be effected only after a further interim period of three years.[49] The gradual timetable is a marginal matter. The decisive element is that a treaty of peace is not just a negative instrument (in the sense of the negation of war); it is also a positive document (regulating the normalization of friendly relations between the former belligerents).[50] Normalization produces repercussions in diverse areas, ranging from diplomatic to cultural exchanges, from navigation to aviation, and from trade to scientific cooperation. The quintessence of a treaty of peace is writing *finis* not only to the armed phase of the conflict between the parties, but to the conflict as a whole. Hence, in appropriate circumstances, the conclusion of a treaty of peace constitutes an implied recognition of a Contracting Party as a State.[51]

Patently, a treaty of peace is no guarantee of lasting peace. If the root causes of the war are not eradicated, another armed conflict may erupt in time. In addition, the same treaty of peace which closes one war can lay the foundation for the next one: the Treaty of Versailles is a prime example of this deplorable state of affairs. But notwithstanding any factual nexus linking the two periods of hostilities, the interjection of a treaty of peace signifies that legally they must be viewed as separate wars. Of course, new bones of contention, not foreseen at the point of signature of a treaty of peace, may also become catalysts to another war. When a treaty of peace is acclaimed as a 'final' settlement, and statesmen indulge in high-sounding prognostications as to its power of endurance, it is advisable to recall that most wars commence between parties that have earlier engaged themselves in treaties of peace. The life expectancy of an average treaty of peace does not necessarily exceed the span of a

---

[49] Egypt–Israel, Treaty of Peace, *supra* note 39, at 363. See also *ibid.*, 364 (Article III(3)), 367 (Annex I, Article I).

[50] On the distinction between positive and negative peace, see H. Rumpf, 'The Concepts of Peace and War in International Law', 27 *GYIL* 429, 431–3 (1984).

[51] Express recognition is specifically agreed upon in Article III of the Egyptian–Israeli Treaty of Peace, *supra* note 39, at 363–4. But there is every reason to believe that recognition would have been implied from the Treaty in any event. *Cf.* H. Lauterpacht, *Recognition in International Law* 378 (1947).

generation or two. Each generation must work out for itself a fresh formula for peaceful coexistence.

ii.   *Peace preliminaries* Prior to the entry into force of a definitive treaty of peace, the parties may agree on preliminaries of peace. Such a procedure generates the following results:

a. In the past, the peace preliminaries themselves might have brought hostilities to an end,[52] whereas the ultimate treaty of peace would focus on the process of normalizing relations between the former belligerents. Nowadays, the function of peace preliminaries of this type will usually be served by an armistice agreement (see *infra* (b)).

b. At the present time, peace preliminaries generally represent a mere *'pactum de contrahendo* on the outline of a prospective peace treaty'.[53] Unless and until the projected treaty of peace actually materializes, the final curtain is not drawn on the war. As an illustration, one can draw attention to the two Camp David Framework Agreements of 1978 for Peace in the Middle East and for the Conclusion of a Peace Treaty between Egypt and Israel.[54] Here the parties agreed on certain principles and some specifics, designed to serve as guidelines for a peace settlement. However, as mentioned, the war between Egypt and Israel was terminated only by dint of the Treaty of Peace (concluded, after further negotiations, in 1979).

iii.   *The legal validity of a treaty of peace* As long as war was regarded as a lawful course of action in international affairs, a treaty of peace was considered perfectly valid, even when imposed on the defeated party by the victor as an outcome of the use of force.[55] As soon as the use of inter-State force was forbidden by international law, some scholars began to argue that a treaty of peace dictated by an aggressor ought to be vitiated by duress.[56] This doctrinal approach has been endorsed in Article 52 of the 1969 Vienna Convention on the Law of Treaties:

A treaty is void if its conclusion has been procured by the threat or use of force in violation of the principles of international law embodied in the Charter of the United Nations.[57]

---

[52] See L. Oppenheim, *International Law*, II, 607 (H. Lauterpacht ed., 7th ed., 1952).

[53] W. G. Grewe, 'Peace Treaties', 3 *EPIL* 938, 941.

[54] Egypt–Israel, Camp David Agreements, 1978: A Framework for Peace in the Middle East, 17 *ILM* 1466 (1978); Framework for the Conclusion of a Peace Treaty between Egypt and Israel, *ibid.*, 1470.

[55] See Lord McNair, *The Law of Treaties* 207, 209 (1961).

[56] See H. Lauterpacht, *International Law*, I, 354 (E. Lauterpacht ed., 1979).

[57] Vienna Convention on the Law of Treaties, 1969, [1969] *UNJY* 140, 153.

Article 52 reflects customary international law as it stands today. In 1973, the International Court of Justice held, in a dispute between the United Kingdom and Iceland, in the *Fisheries Jurisdiction* case:

There can be little doubt, as is implied in the Charter of the United Nations and recognized in Article 52 of the Vienna Convention on the Law of Treaties, that under contemporary international law an agreement concluded under the threat or use of force is void.[58]

The International Law Commission, in its commentary on the draft of Article 52, explained that the clause does not operate retroactively by invalidating treaties of peace procured by coercion prior to the development of the modern law banning the use of force by States.[59] The Commission expressed the opinion that the provision is applicable to all treaties concluded at least since 1945 (the entry into force of the Charter of the United Nations).[60]

Article 52 does not affect equally all treaties of peace. The text makes it plain that 'only the *unlawful* use of force … can bring about the nullity of a treaty'.[61] It follows that Article 52 invalidates solely those treaties of peace that are imposed by an aggressor State on the victim of aggression. As regards the reverse situation, Article 75 of the Convention proclaims:

The provisions of the present Convention are without prejudice to any obligation in relation to a treaty which may arise for an aggressor State in consequence of measures taken in conformity with the Charter of the United Nations with reference to that State's aggression.[62]

The invalidity of a treaty of peace concluded under duress does not result from 'vitiated consent': it is a sanction against an internationally unlawful and even a criminal act (see *infra*, Chapter 5, A).[63] Hence, there is nothing legally wrong in a treaty of peace leaning in favour of a State which was the target of aggression (assuming that it has prevailed militarily).[64] One must take exception to an unqualified dictum, appearing in the 2004 Advisory Opinion of the International Court of Justice on *Legal Consequences of the Construction of a Wall in the Occupied Palestinian Territory*, as regards 'the illegality of territorial acquisition resulting from

---

[58] *Fisheries Jurisdiction* case (Jurisdiction of the Court), [1973] *ICJ Rep.* 3, 14.
[59] Report of the International Law Commission, 18th Session, [1966] II *ILC Ybk* 172, 247.
[60] *Ibid.*   [61] I. Sinclair, *The Vienna Convention on the Law of Treaties* 180 (2nd ed., 1984).
[62] Vienna Convention, *supra* note 57, at 159.
[63] P. Reuter, *Introduction to the Law of Treaties* 140 (J. Mico and P. Haggenmacher trans., 1989).
[64] See Oppenheim's *International Law*, I, 1292 (R. Jennings and A. Watts eds., 9th ed., 1992).

the threat or use of force'.[65] The illegality of such territorial acquisition is confined to the case where the beneficiary is the aggressor. In the words of Sir Humphrey Waldock, '[c]learly, there is all the difference in the world between coercion used by an aggressor to consolidate the fruits of his aggression in a treaty and coercion used to impose a peace settlement upon an aggressor'.[66]

Article 44(5) of the Vienna Convention does not permit any separation of the provisions of a treaty falling under Article 52.[67] This means that a treaty procured by coercion is void in its entirety: none of its parts may be severed from the remainder of the instrument, with a view to being saved from abrogation. The general rule would apply, *inter alia*, to a treaty of peace accepted under duress by the victim of aggression. But one must be mindful of the fact that such a treaty is not always confined to undertakings advantageous to the aggressor. Indeed, the most momentous clause in the text will presumably be the one terminating the war. If the whole juridical slate is swept clean by nullity, the section devoted to ending the war would also be wiped off. Is it to be understood that the former belligerents are put again on a war footing? The answer, as furnished by Article 43 of the Vienna Convention, is that the invalidity of a treaty does not impair duties embodied therein, if these are independently binding on the parties by virtue of general international law.[68] All States must comply with the contemporary prohibition of the use of inter-State force, and the abrogation of a particular treaty of peace does not alter this basic position.

Article 52 refers to a treaty procured by unlawful use or threat of force as 'void'. The expression is expounded by Article 69(1), which states that the 'provisions of a void treaty have no legal force'.[69] The concept underlying Article 52 is one of 'absolute nullity'.[70] It is true that a party invoking a ground for impeaching the validity of a treaty must take certain steps enumerated in Article 65.[71] The obligation to observe the procedure set out in Article 65 might suggest that, should the aggrieved party (for reasons of its own) refrain from contesting the validity of the treaty, nullification would not take place.[72] However, if that were the case, the instrument would really be voidable rather than void. If a treaty of peace dictated by an aggressor is genuinely void, it must be tainted by nullity automatically and *ab initio*. Therefore, any competent forum should be

---

[65] Advisory Opinion on *Legal Consequences of the Construction of a Wall in the Occupied Palestinian Territory*, 43 *ILM* 1009, 1034 (2004).
[66] H. Waldock, 'Second Report on the Law of Treaties', [1963] II *ILC Ybk* 36, 52.
[67] Vienna Convention, *supra* note 57, at 152.　　[68] *Ibid.*　　[69] *Ibid.*, 158.
[70] See Sinclair, *supra* note 61, at 160–1.　　[71] Vienna Convention, *supra* note 57, at 157.
[72] See C. L. Rozakis, 'The Law on Invalidity of Treaties', 16 *Ar. V.* 150, 168–9 (1973–5).

authorized to recognize the treaty as void, even if no attempt to invoke invalidity has been made by the State directly concerned.[73]

(b)   Armistice agreements

Under orthodox international law, an armistice was construed as an interlude in the fighting, interchangeable in substance with a truce or a cease-fire (see *infra*, C). It is characteristic that Articles 36 to 41 of the Hague Regulations, annexed to Hague Convention (II) of 1899 and (IV) of 1907 Respecting the Laws and Customs of War on Land, employ the expression 'armistice' when the subject under discussion is the suspension of hostilities.[74] By contrast, in the current practice of States, an armistice chiefly denotes a termination of hostilities, completely divesting the parties of the right to renew military operations under any circumstances whatever. An armistice of this nature puts an end to the war, and does not merely suspend the combat.

The transformation undergone by 'armistice' as a legal term of art had its origins in the armistices which brought about the termination of World War I.[75] A close look at the most famous armistice – that of 11 November 1918 with Germany – discloses that, although concluded at the outset for a duration of only 36 days[76] (a period later extended several times),[77] its far-reaching provisions (obligating the German armed forces, *inter alia*, to surrender their arms, to withdraw from occupied territories as well as from certain areas within Germany itself, etc.) barred the possibility of resumption of hostilities by the vanquished side. Only the victorious Allies reserved to themselves the option of resorting to force again in case of breach of the Armistice's conditions by Germany. This reading of the text is reinvigorated by the formulation of the last extension of the Armistice (without an expiry date) in February 1919.[78]

The innovative trend of terminating war by armistice continued, and became clearer, in the armistices of World War II, which resemble peace preliminaries (of the first category).[79] Significantly, in the Armistices with Romania (1944) and Hungary (1945), these two countries

---

[73] See E. Jiménez de Aréchaga, 'International Law in the Past Third of a Century', 159 *RCADI* 1, 68 (1978).

[74] Regulations Respecting the Laws and Customs of War on Land (Annexed to Hague Conventions (II) of 1899 and (IV) of 1907), *Hague Conventions* 100, 107, 121–2.

[75] The texts of all the armistices of World War I are reproduced in *A History of the Peace Conference of Paris*, I, Appendix V (H. W. V. Temperley ed., 1920).

[76] Conditions of an Armistice with Germany, 1918, *ibid.*, 459, 469 (Article XXXIV).

[77] See *ibid.*, 476–81.   [78] *Ibid.*, 480.

[79] See A. Klafkowski, 'Les Formes de Cessation de l'Etat de Guerre en Droit International', 149 *RCADI* 217, 248–50 (1976).

declared that they had 'withdrawn from the war' against the Allied Powers.[80] Romania specifically announced that it 'has entered the war and will wage war on the side of the Allied Powers against Germany and Hungary',[81] and Hungary agreed to the condition that it 'has declared war on Germany'.[82] Likewise, Italy – which concluded an Armistice with the Allies in September 1943[83] – declared war against Germany in October of that year. The Preamble to the 1947 Paris Treaty of Peace with Italy directs attention to the fact that (as a result of the declaration of war) Italy 'thereby became a co-belligerent against Germany'.[84] For a traditionalist, adhering to the notion of an armistice as a mere suspension of hostilities, 'Italy's co-belligerency created a highly anomalous situation juridically, and one which to some extent defies legal analysis and classification'.[85] After all, if the war between the Allied Powers and Italy did not end until the Treaty of Peace of 1947, Italy – the armed forces of which were fighting, after 1943, alongside Allied formations against a common foe (Germany)[86] – was the co-belligerent of its enemies! Yet, once it is perceived that an armistice signifies the termination of war, there is no anomaly in the status of Italy during World War II. Earlier, Italy was a co-belligerent with Germany against the Allies. Following the termination of its war with the Allies – by virtue of the 1943 Armistice – nothing prevented Italy from declaring war against Germany and becoming a co-belligerent with the Allies. The same is true of Romania and Hungary.

The evolution in the perception of armistice reached its zenith at a later stage, with a series of General Armistice Agreements signed in 1949 between Israel, on the one hand, Egypt, Lebanon, Jordan and Syria, on the other,[87] followed by the 1953 Panmunjom Agreement Concerning a Military Armistice in Korea.[88] These Armistice Agreements terminated the Israeli War of Independence and the Korean War, respectively,

---

[80] Armistice Agreement with Rumania, 1944, 9 *Int.Leg.* 139, 140 (Article 1); Armistice Agreement with Hungary, 1945, *ibid.*, 276, 277 (Article 1(a)).
[81] *Ibid.*, 140 (Article 1).   [82] *Ibid.*, 277 (Article 1(a)).
[83] Conditions of an Armistice with Italy, 1943, 9 *Int.Leg.* 50.
[84] Paris Treaty of Peace with Italy, *supra* note 32, at 127.
[85] G. G. Fitzmaurice, 'The Juridical Clauses of the Peace Treaties', 73 *RCADI* 259, 272 (1948).
[86] See Department of State, Commentary on the Additional Conditions of the Armistice with Italy, 1945, 40 *AJIL*, Supp., 18, *id.* (1946).
[87] Israel–Egypt, General Armistice Agreement, 1949, 42 *UNTS* 251; Israel–Lebanon, General Armistice Agreement, 1949, *ibid.*, 287; Israel–Jordan, General Armistice Agreement, 1949, *ibid.*, 303; Israel–Syria, General Armistice Agreement, 1949, *ibid.*, 327.
[88] Panmunjom Agreement Concerning a Military Armistice in Korea, 1953, 47 *AJIL*, Supp., 186 (1953).

although they did not produce peace in the full meaning of the term. Typically, the Panmunjom Agreement states as its objective the establishment of an armistice ensuring 'a complete cessation of hostilities and of all acts of armed force in Korea until a final peace settlement is achieved'.[89] The thesis (advanced in 1992) that 'the Korean War is still legally in effect',[90] is untenable.

A closer look at the Israeli Armistice Agreements may illuminate the special features and the problematics of armistice as a mechanism for ending wars. The first article of all four Agreements prescribes that, with a view to promoting the return to permanent peace in Palestine, the parties affirm a number of principles, including a prohibition of resort to military force and aggressive action.[91] In keeping with these principles, the parties are forbidden to commit any warlike or hostile act against one another.[92] The Agreements clarify that they are concluded without prejudice to the 'rights, claims and positions'[93] of the parties in the ultimate peaceful settlement of the Palestine Question.[94] The purpose of the armistice is described in terms of a transition from truce to a permanent peace[95] (in the case of Egypt, the Armistice Agreement expressly supersedes a previous General Cease-Fire Agreement).[96] Above all, the Agreements lay down that they will remain in force until a peaceful settlement between the parties is achieved.[97]

The 'without prejudice' formula (so popular among lawyers) was introduced to forestall future claims of estoppel in the course of peace negotiations. The formula must not obscure the salient point that the parties reserve only their right to reopen all outstanding issues when they eventually get to negotiate an amicable settlement of the conflict. During the intervening time, the conflict continues, but it is no longer an armed conflict. The thrust of each Agreement is that both parties waive in an unqualified manner any legal option that either of them may have had to

---

[89] *Ibid.*, 186–7 (Preamble).   [90] G. von Glahn, *Law among Nations* 727 (6th ed., 1992).

[91] General Armistice Agreements, *supra* note 87, at 252–4 (Egypt), 288–90 (Lebanon), 304–6 (Jordan), 328–30 (Syria).

[92] *Ibid.*, 254 (Egypt, Article II), 290 (Lebanon, Article III), 306 (Jordan, Article III), 330 (Syria, Article III).

[93] For the origin of this formula, *cf.* Article 40 of the UN Charter (regarding provisional measures taken by the Security Council). Charter of the United Nations, 1945, 9 *Int.Leg.* 327, 343.

[94] General Armistice Agreements, *supra* note 87, at 268 (Egypt, Article XI), 290 (Lebanon, Article II), 306 (Jordan, Article II), 330 (Syria, Article II).

[95] *Ibid.*, 268 (Egypt, Article XII), 296–8 (Lebanon, Article VIII), 318 (Jordan, Article XII), 340 (Syria, Article VIII).

[96] *Ibid.*, 270 (Egypt, Article XII(5)).

[97] *Ibid.*, 268 (Egypt, Article XII), 296–8 (Lebanon, Article VIII), 318 (Jordan, Article XII), 340 (Syria, Article VIII).

resume hostilities and to resolve the conflict by force. The Agreements can be considered transitional, inasmuch as they were intended to be ultimately replaced by definitive peace treaties; yet, there is nothing temporary about them.[98]

Article V(2) of the Agreement with Egypt avers that the Armistice Demarcation Line 'is not to be construed in any sense as a political or territorial boundary' and, again, that the line is drawn 'without prejudice'.[99] This clause is not replicated in the other Agreements, although a more diluted version has been inserted into Article VI(9) of the Agreement with Jordan[100] and Article V(l) of the Agreement with Syria[101] (there is no counterpart in the Agreement with Lebanon). Once more, the disclaimer may be taken as lip service. An analysis of the Agreements in all their aspects shows that 'the armistice demarcation lines can be regarded as equivalent to international frontiers, with all the consequences which that entails'.[102] When a line of demarcation between States is sanctioned in such a way that it can be revised only by mutual consent (and not by force), it becomes a political or territorial border.[103] The line may not be deemed 'final', but the frontiers of no country in the world are impressed with a stamp of finality. All international frontiers can be altered by mutual consent, and history shows that many of them undergo kaleidoscopic modifications through agreements.[104]

It is noteworthy that when the United Nations Security Council, in 1951, had to deal with an Israeli complaint concerning restrictions imposed by Egypt on the passage of ships through the Suez Canal, the Council adopted Resolution 95 pronouncing that the Armistice between the two countries 'is of a permanent character' and that, accordingly, 'neither party can reasonably assert that it is actively a belligerent'.[105] It emerges from the text of the Resolution, and the thorough discussion preceding it, that the Council totally rejected an Egyptian contention that a state of war continued to exist with Israel after the armistice.[106]

The Israeli Armistice Agreements carry in their titles the adjective 'General'. This was done against the backdrop of Article 37 of the

---

[98] See S. Rosenne, *Israel's Armistice Agreements with the Arab States* 82 (1951).
[99] General Armistice Agreements, *supra* note 87, at 256 (Egypt).
[100] *Ibid.*, 312 (Jordan).   [101] *Ibid.*, 332 (Syria).   [102] Rosenne, *supra* note 98, at 48.
[103] A distinction between armistice demarcation lines and other international boundaries is made in the Declaration on Principles of International Law Concerning Friendly Relations and Co-operation among States in accordance with the Charter of the United Nations. General Assembly Resolution 2625 (XXV), 25 *RGA* 121, 122 (1970). It is submitted that this distinction is no longer valid in most cases.
[104] See J. H. W. Verzijl, *International Law in Historical Perspective*, VI, 459–553 (1973).
[105] Security Council Resolution 95, 6 *RDSC* 10, 11 (1951).
[106] See N. Feinberg, *Studies in International Law* 87–92 (1979).

Hague Regulations,[107] which sets side by side a general and a local armistice (meaning suspension of hostilities (see *infra*, C)). The Panmunjom Armistice Agreement already omits the adjective. The omission is consistent with the modern meaning of an armistice agreement as an end to war, for a local termination of war is an oxymoronic figure of speech. An authentic termination of war must be general in its scope.

No doubt, an armistice agreement is never the equivalent of a treaty of peace. When it brings war to a close, an armistice is like the first category of preliminaries of peace (*supra*, (a), ii). Whereas a treaty of peace is multidimensional (both negating war and providing for amicable relations), an armistice agreement is restricted to the negative aspect of the demise of war. To the extent that a distinction is drawn between associative and dissociative peace (the latter amounting to 'the absence of war, a peace defined negatively'),[108] an armistice has to be marked as a dissociative peace.

Comparatively speaking, the negation of war is of greater import than the introduction or restoration of, say, trade or cultural relations. Still, when such relations are non-existent, a meaningful ingredient is missing from the fabric of peace. That is why the mere conclusion of an armistice agreement does not imply recognition of a new State. Furthermore, notwithstanding an armistice, diplomatic relations need not be established or reestablished. The frontiers (the Armistice Demarcation Lines) may remain closed, and, in general, relations between the former belligerents will probably be strained. After all, the armed phase of the conflict is over, but the conflict itself may continue unabated.

As a result, even after an armistice agreement, the conclusion of a treaty of peace remains a high priority item on the agenda. The armistice ends the war, but the consummation of a fully-fledged peace requires a lot more. When the advent of a treaty of peace in the post-armistice period is delayed, as has been the case both in the Arab-Israeli conflict and in Korea, the chances of another conflagration always loom large on the political horizon. Nevertheless, should any of the former belligerents plunge again into hostilities, this would be considered the unleashing of a new war and not the resumption of fighting in an on-going armed conflict.

There is entrenched resistance in the legal literature to any reappraisal of the role assigned to armistice in the vocabulary of war.[109] *Pace* this

---

[107] Hague Regulations, *supra* note 74, at 121.
[108] B. V. A. Röling, 'International Law and the Maintenance of Peace', 4 *NYIL* 1, 7 (1973).
[109] For a striking illustration, see UK Ministry of Defence, *The Manual of the Law of Armed Conflict* 264–7 (2004). *Cf.* Italian–United States Conciliation Commission, *Mergé* case (1955), 11 *RIAA* 236, 241.

doctrinal conservatism, the terminology has to be adjusted to fit the modern practice of States.[110] Scholars must open their eyes to the metamorphosis that has occurred over the years in the legal status of armistice.

(c)   Other modes of terminating war

A war may be brought to its conclusion not only in a treaty of peace or in an armistice agreement. It may also come to an end in one of the following ways.

i.   Implied mutual consent When belligerents enter into a treaty of peace or an armistice agreement, war is terminated by mutual consent expressed in the instrument. It is not requisite, however, that the mutual consent to end a war be verbalized by the parties. Such consent can also be inferred by implication from their behaviour: a state of war may come to a close thanks to a mere termination of hostilities on both sides.[111]

An examination of the legal consequences of the absence of warfare must be conducted prudently. The fact that all is quiet along the front line is not inescapably indicative of a tacit consent to put paid to hostilities. A lull in the fighting, or a formal cease-fire, may account for the military inactivity. War cannot be regarded as over unless some supplemental evidence is discernible that neither party proposes to resume the hostilities.[112] The evidence may be distilled from the establishment or resumption of diplomatic relations.[113]

To give tangible form to the scenario of a state of war continuing despite a lengthy hiatus in the fighting, one can take the case of Israel and Iraq. Iraq was one of the Arab countries that invaded Israel in 1948. Unlike its co-belligerents (Egypt, Lebanon, Jordan and Syria), Iraq took advantage of the fact that it has no common border with Israel and refused to sign an armistice agreement (simply pulling its troops out of the combat zone). After prolonged periods of avoiding a military confrontation, Iraqi and Israeli armed forces clashed again in June 1967 and in October 1973.[114] In 1981, Israeli aircraft destroyed an Iraqi nuclear reactor (under

---

[110] See J. Stone, *Legal Controls of International Conflict: A Treatise on the Dynamics of Disputes – and War – Law* 641–2, 644 (1954). *Cf.* M. W. Graham, 'Armistices – 1944 Style', 39 *AJIL* 286, 287 (1945).

[111] See C. C. Tansill, 'Termination of War by Mere Cessation of Hostilities', 38 *LQR* 26–37 (1922).

[112] See J. M. Mathews, 'The Termination of War', 19 *Mich.LR* 819, 828 (1920–1).

[113] See L. Kotzsch, *The Concept of War in Contemporary History and International Law* 251 (1956).

[114] See U. Shoham, 'The Israeli Aerial Raid upon the Iraqi Nuclear Reactor and the Right of Self-Defense', 109 *Mil.LR* 191, 206 n. 67 (1985).

construction), which had the capacity of manufacturing nuclear weapons.[115] In this writer's opinion, the only plausible legal justification for the bombing of the reactor is that the act represented another round of hostilities in an on-going armed conflict (see *infra*, Chapter 7, B, (a)). In 1991 – in the course of the Gulf War – Iraq launched dozens of Scud missiles against Israeli objectives (mostly, centres of population), despite the fact that Israel was not a member of the American-led Coalition which had engaged in combat to restore the sovereignty of Kuwait. The indiscriminate bombardment of civilians, by missiles or otherwise, is unlawful under the *jus in bello*.[116] While the *jus* is the same in every *bellum*, it is useful to single out the relevant framework of hostilities. The Iraqi missile offensive against Israel must be observed in the legal context not of the Gulf War but of the war between Iraq and Israel which started in 1948.[117] That war was still in progress in 1991, unhindered by its inordinate prolongation since 1948, for hostilities flared up intermittently. At the time of writing, it is still not clear when the war will come to an end in consequence of the occupation of Iraq by the Coalition in 2003.

ii.   *Debellatio* This is a situation in which one of the belligerents is utterly defeated, to the point of its total disintegration as a sovereign nation. Since the war is no longer inter-State in character, it is terminated by itself. Even though the extinction of an existing State as a result of war is not to be lightly assumed, there comes a time when it can no longer be denied.[118]

Debellatio necessarily involves effective military occupation of the local territory by the enemy, but it goes beyond that: all organized resistance has to disappear, and the occupied State must be 'reduced to impotence'.[119] The three basic parameters of *debellatio* are as follows: (i) the territory of the former belligerent is occupied in its entirety, no remnant being left for the exercise of sovereignty; (ii) the armed forces of the erstwhile belligerent are no longer in the field (usually there is an unconditional surrender),[120] and no allied forces carry on fighting by proxy; and (iii) the Government of the

---

[115] See *ibid.*, 191, 207–10.

[116] Protocol I, *supra* note 15, at 114 (Article 51(4)–(5)). *Cf.* P. Bretton, 'Remarques sur le *Jus in Bello* dans la Guerre du Golfe (1991)', 37 *AFDI* 139, 149 (1991).

[117] See L. R. Beres, 'After the Gulf War: Israel, Pre-Emption, and Anticipatory Self-Defense', 13 *HJIL* 259, *id.* (1990–1).

[118] See J. Crawford, *The Creation of States in International Law* 418–20 (1979).

[119] C. Phillipson, *Termination of War and Treaties of Peace* 9 (1916).

[120] An unconditional surrender (or a capitulation without condition) is a purely military measure conceding complete defeat and renouncing unreservedly the resumption of hostilities. See N. Ando, *Surrender, Occupation, and Private Property in International Law: An Evaluation of US Practice in Japan* 60–5 (1991).

former belligerent has passed out of existence, and no other Government (not even a Government in exile) continues to offer effective opposition.[121] Kuwait was saved from *debellatio* in the Gulf War, notwithstanding its total occupation by the Iraqi armed forces, because its Government went into exile and a large Coalition soon came to its aid militarily.

The phenomenon of *debellatio* has been recognized in many instances in the past.[122] Some commentators contend that a *debellatio* of Germany occurred at the end of World War II,[123] following the unconditional surrender of the Nazi armed forces.[124] However, the legal status of Germany in the immediate post-War period was exceedingly complicated.[125] The position was so intricate that, in the same Allied country (the United Kingdom), different dates were used for different legal purposes to mark the termination of the war with Germany.[126]

iii.   Unilateral declaration Just as war can – and, under Hague Convention (III), must – begin with a unilateral declaration of war, it can also end with a unilateral declaration.[127] In this way the United States proclaimed, in 1951, the termination of the state of war with Germany.[128]

The technique of a unilateral declaration can be looked upon not as an independent mode for bringing war to a close, but as an offshoot of one of the two preceding methods. As indicated (*supra*, Chapter 1, A, (b), iii), Arcadia can impose war on Utopia by a unilateral declaration or act. Just as Utopia is unable to prevent Arcadia from submerging them both in war, Utopia cannot effectively terminate the war when Arcadia is bent on continuing it. A unilateral declaration by Utopia ending the war is an inane gesture, if Arcadia is able and willing to go on fighting. 'For war can be started by one party, but its ending presupposes the consent of both parties, if the enemy state survives as a sovereign state.'[129] A unilateral declaration by Utopia promulgating that the war is over has a valid effect only if Arcadia is either completely defeated (undergoing *debellatio*) or is

[121] See Greenspan, *supra* note 1, at 600–3.
[122] See J. H. W. Verzijl, *supra* note 104, at III, 361–2 (1970).
[123] See Schwarzenberger, *supra* note 13, at 467, 730. *Cf.* H. Kelsen, 'The Legal Status of Germany according to the Declaration of Berlin', 39 *AJIL* 518–26 (1945).
[124] Act of Military Surrender of Germany, 1945, 9 *Int.Leg.* 312.
[125] See Oppenheim, *supra* note 64, at 699–700.
[126] See F. A. Mann, *Foreign Affairs in English Courts* 33 (1986).
[127] See Anonymous, 'Judicial Determination of the End of the War', 47 *Col.LR* 255, 258 (1947).
[128] This was done in a Proclamation by President Truman pursuant to a joint resolution by Congress. Termination of the State of War with Germany, 1951, 46 *AJIL*, Supp., 12 (1952).
[129] J. L. Kunz, 'Ending the War with Germany', 46 *AJIL* 114, 115 (1952).

willing to abide by the declaration.[130] If both Utopia and Arcadia exist at the end of the war, both must agree to finish it. Yet, such an agreement may consist of a formal declaration by Utopia and the tacit consent of Arcadia (or *vice versa*).[131]

C.   The suspension of hostilities

(a)   Different types of suspension of hostilities

A suspension of hostilities may evolve *de facto* when no military operations take place. A respite of this nature may endure for a long period of time. But since neither belligerent is legally committed to refrain from resuming hostilities, the fighting can break out again at any moment without warning.[132]

More importantly, belligerents may assume an obligation *de jure* to abstain from combat in the course of a war (which goes on). A number of terms are used to depict a legal undertaking to suspend hostilities: (i) truce, (ii) cease-fire, and in the past also (iii) armistice. As noted (*supra*, B, (b)), the last term – armistice – has undergone a drastic change in recent years and now principally conveys a termination, rather than a suspension, of hostilities. The current usage of the term 'cease-fire', in lieu of 'armistice', must be recalled when one examines the aforementioned Articles 36 to 41 of the Hague Regulations.[133] These clauses do not employ the phrase 'cease-fire'. Instead, they refer to 'armistice', commensurately with the vocabulary prevalent at the turn of the twentieth century. However, since their avowed aim is to govern the suspension of hostilities, they must be deemed applicable to present-day cease-fires (as opposed to modern armistices).

The expression 'truce' is embedded in tradition and history. It acquired particular resonance in the Middle Ages, in the form of the Truce of God (*Treuga Dei*). This was an ecclesiastical measure by which the Catholic Church suspended warfare in Christendom on certain days of the week, as well as during Lent and church festivals.[134] The phrase 'cease-fire' has been introduced into international legal parlance in the present (post-World War II) era. Although some scholars ascribe to truce and cease-fire

---

[130] See D. Ottensooser, 'Termination of War by Unilateral Declaration', 29 *BYBIL* 435, 442 (1952).
[131] See F. C. Balling, 'Unconditional Surrender and a Unilateral Declaration of Peace', 39 *APSR* 474, 476 (1945).
[132] See M. Sibert, 'L'Armistice', 40 *RGDIP* 657, 660 (1933).
[133] Hague Regulations, *supra* note 74, at 121–2.
[134] See 'God, Truce of', 5 *The New Encyclopaedia Britannica* 319, *id.* (15th ed., 1998).

divergent implications, the present practice of States – for the most part – treats them as synonymous.[135] As examples for an indiscriminate use of the two terms, it is possible to adduce successive resolutions adopted by the Security Council during Israel's War of Independence in 1948.[136]

A cease-fire (or truce) may be partial or total in scope. Article 37 of the Hague Regulations differentiates between a general cease-fire (originally, 'armistice') suspending all military operations everywhere, and a local cease-fire suspending such operations only between certain units at particular locations.[137]

i.   Local cease-fire agreement A cease-fire (or truce) may apply to a limited sector of the front, without impinging on the continuation of combat elsewhere. The object of such a local suspension of hostilities is to enable the belligerents to evacuate the wounded, bury the dead, conduct negotiations, and so forth. A local cease-fire may be agreed upon on the spot by military commanders (who can be relatively junior in rank), without the involvement of their respective Governments. The agreement would then be informal, and it does not have to be in writing.[138]

Article 15 of Geneva Convention (I) of 1949 for the Amelioration of the Condition of the Wounded and Sick in Armed Forces in the Field stipulates that, whenever circumstances permit, a suspension of hostilities is to be arranged (generally or locally) so as to facilitate the removal, exchange and transport of the wounded left on the battlefield or within a besieged or encircled area.[139] The Article employs the term 'armistice', but what is actually meant in current terminology is a cease-fire.

ii.   General cease-fire agreement Belligerents may enter into an agreement suspending hostilities everywhere within the region of war (see *supra*, Chapter 1, C). The duration of a general cease-fire (or truce) may be predetermined in the agreement or it may be left open.

A general cease-fire agreement is normally made in writing by (or with the approval of) the Governments concerned. In that case, it has the status of a treaty under international law.[140] The essence of a general cease-fire is

---

[135] See P. Mohn, 'Problems of Truce Supervision', 478 *Int.Con.* 51, 53–7 (1952).

[136] Security Council Resolutions 49, 50, 53, 54, 56, 59, 61 and 62 (all of 1948), 3 *RDSC* 19–30 (1948).

[137] Hague Regulations, *supra* note 74, at 121.   [138] See Oppenheim, *supra* note 52, at 550.

[139] Geneva Convention (I) for the Amelioration of the Condition of the Wounded and Sick in Armed Forces in the Field, 75 *UNTS* 31, 40–2.

[140] See R. R. Baxter, 'Armistices and Other Forms of Suspension of Hostilities', 149 *RCADI* 353, 371–2 (1976). The author did not differentiate between the terms 'cease-fire' and 'armistice'.

a detailed agreement on the conditions under which hostilities are suspended. There are two *sine qua non* specific elements: time (at which the cease-fire is due to enter into force on all fronts: there can also be different times for different geographic sectors) and place (fixing the demarcation line between the opposing military formations, with or without a buffer demilitarized zone).[141] However, nothing prevents the parties from appending to a general cease-fire agreement other clauses, which transcend the technicalities of the suspension of hostilities and relate to such matters as the immediate release of prisoners of war. Semantically, this is liable to produce a result that may sound strange. Should a general cease-fire agreement set a date for release of prisoners of war, and should a belligerent extend their detention beyond that date, the act would constitute a cease-fire violation although no fire has been opened.

iii.   Cease-fire ordered by the Security Council The Security Council, performing its functions under Chapter VII of the Charter of the United Nations,[142] may order belligerents to cease fire. Unequivocal language to that effect is contained, for example, in Resolution 54 (1948)[143] adopted at the time of Israel's War of Independence. Under Article 25 of the Charter, UN Members are legally bound to accept and carry out mandatory decisions of the Security Council (see *infra*, Chapter 10, B, (a)).[144] However, the Council does not rush to issue direct orders. Ordinarily, it shows a proclivity for milder language. In the Falkland Islands War of 1982, the Council only requested the Secretary-General 'to enter into contact with the parties with a view to negotiating mutually acceptable terms for cease-fire'.[145] On other occasions, the Council called upon the parties to cease fire,[146] and less frequently demanded a cease-fire.[147] As long as the Council is merely calling for a cease-fire, its resolution has the hallmark of a non-binding recommendation. The parties are then given an opportunity to craft a cease-fire agreement of their choosing. But if they fail to reach an agreement, the Council may be driven in time to ordain a cease-fire. In the Iran–Iraq War, the Security Council issued a call for a cease-fire in 1982,[148] demanding it only in 1987.[149] The text

---

[141] See S. Bastid, 'The Cease-Fire', 6(1) *RSIDMDG* 31, 37 (1973).
[142] Charter of the United Nations, *supra* note 93, at 343–6.
[143] Security Council Resolution 54, *supra* note 136, at 22.
[144] Charter of the United Nations, *supra* note 93, at 339. See also Article 48(1) of the Charter, *ibid.*, 345–6.
[145] Security Council Resolution 505, 37 *RDSC* 17, *id.* (1982).
[146] See, e.g., Security Council Resolution 233, 22 *RDSC* 2, *id.* (1967).
[147] See, e.g., Security Council Resolutions 234 and 235, 22 *RDSC* 3, *id.* (1967).
[148] Security Council Resolution 514, 37 *RDSC* 19, *id.* (1982).
[149] Security Council Resolution 598, 42 *RDSC* 5, 6 (1987).

and the circumstances clearly imply that 'the change in the wording from *calling* for a cease-fire to *demanding* one' conveyed a shift from a recommendation to a binding decision.[150]

The most peremptory and far-reaching cease-fire terms were imposed on Iraq following Security Council Resolution 687 (1991),[151] after the defeat of that country by an American-led Coalition in the first phase of the Gulf War (see *infra*, Chapter 9, E). Resolution 687 is 'unparalleled' in the extent to which the Security Council was prepared to go in dictating cease-fire conditions, especially where disarmament of Weapons of Mass Destruction (WMD) is concerned.[152] These disarmament obligations were based not on general international law but solely on the cease-fire regime that Iraq was forced to accept.[153] Notwithstanding its unique range, the regime established in Resolution 687 – as its text explicitly elucidates – brings into effect no more than 'a formal cease-fire'.[154] A labelling of Resolution 687 as a 'permanent cease-fire'[155] is a contradiction in terms: a cease-fire, by definition, is a transition-period arrangement. The suggestion that 'despite the terminology used in Resolution 687, it is clearly more than a mere suspension of hostilities' – for the substance 'is that of a peace treaty'[156] – is not only completely inconsistent with the plain text of the resolution: it is also counter-factual, given subsequent history (see *infra*, Chapter 10, C, (b)).

The General Assembly, too, may call upon belligerents to effect an immediate cease-fire. This is what the General Assembly did in December 1971,[157] after the outbreak of war between India and Pakistan (ultimately culminating in the creation of the independent State of Bangladesh). When such a resolution is passed by the General Assembly, it can only be issued as a recommendation and can never be binding (see *infra*, Chapter 10, E, (a)). As a non-mandatory exhortation,

---

[150] M. Weller, 'Comments: The Use of Force and Collective Security', *The Gulf War of 1980–1988* 71, 85 (I. F. Dekker and H. H. G. Post eds., 1992).
[151] Security Council Resolution 687, 46 *RDSC* 11–15 (1991).
[152] D. M. Morriss, 'From War to Peace: A Study of Cease-Fire Agreements and the Evolving Role of the United Nations', 36 *VJIL* 801, 891–2 (1995–6).
[153] See R. Wedgwood, 'The Fall of Saddam Hussein: Security Council Mandates and Preemptive Self-Defense', 97 *AJIL* 576, 579 (2003).
[154] Security Council Resolution 687, *supra* note 151, at 12.
[155] J. Lobel and M. Ratner, 'Bypassing the Security Council: Ambiguous Authorizations to Use Force, Cease-Fires and the Iraqi Inspection Regime', 93 *AJIL* 124, 148 (1999).
[156] C. Gray, 'After the Cease-Fire: Iraq, the Security Council and the Use of Force', 65 *BYBIL* 135, 144 (1994).
[157] General Assembly Resolution 2793 (XXVI), 26 *RGA* 3, *id.* (1971).

the resolution may be ignored with impunity, just as India disregarded the resolution in question.[158]

In recent years, most cease-fires have come in the wake of Security Council resolutions: either the parties carry out a mandatory decision of the Council or they arrive at an agreement at the behest of the Council. Even during the 'Cold War', as long as the Council was not in disarray owing to the exercise or the threat of a veto (see *infra*, Chapter 10, C, (a)), a cease-fire resolution became almost a conditioned reflex in response to the outbreak of hostilities. Generally speaking, the Council has tended to act as a fire-brigade, viewing its paramount task as an attempt to extinguish the blaze rather than dealing with all the surrounding circumstances.

A cease-fire, whether reached independently or on the initiative of the Council, may be limited to a predetermined time-frame. A case in point is Resolution 50 (1948), adopted in the course of Israel's War of Independence, which called upon all the parties to cease fire for a period of four weeks.[159] When the prescribed time expired, fighting recommenced. More often, the Council avoids setting specific terminal dates for cease-fires, preferring to couch them in an open-ended manner.

(b)   The nature of cease-fire

The suspension of hostilities must not be confused with their termination.[160] A termination of hostilities means that the war is over: the parties are no longer belligerents, and any subsequent hostilities between them would indicate the outbreak of a new war. Conversely, a suspension of hostilities connotes that the state of war goes on, but temporarily there is no actual warfare. Psychologically, a lengthy general cease-fire lasting indefinitely is a state of no-war and no-peace. Legally, this is a clear-cut case of war. The state of war is not terminated, despite the absence of combat in the interval.

Renewal of hostilities before a cease-fire expires would obviously contravene its provisions. Nonetheless, it must be grasped that hostilities are only continued, after an interruption, and no new war is started. For that reason, a cease-fire violation is irrelevant to the determination of armed attack and self-defence. That determination is made exclusively on the

---

[158] See P. Bretton, 'De Quelques Problèmes du Droit de la Guerre dans le Conflit Indo-Pakistanais', 18 *AFDI* 201, 211 (1972).

[159] Security Council Resolution 50, *supra* note 136, at 20.

[160] For an illustration of such confusion, see V. A. Ary, 'Concluding Hostilities: Humanitarian Provisions in Cease-Fire Agreements', 148 *Mil.LR* 186, 187–92 (1995).

basis of the beginning of a new armed conflict, and the reopening of fire in an on-going war is not germane to the issue (see *infra*, Chapter 8, A, (b)).

A cease-fire provides 'a breathing space for the negotiation of more lasting agreements'.[161] It gives the belligerents a chance to negotiate peace terms without being subjected to excessive pressure, and to turn the suspension into a termination of hostilities. But no indispensable bond ties cease-fire and peace. On the one hand, the conclusion of a treaty of peace may not be preceded by any cease-fire.[162] On the other hand, a cease-fire may break down, to be followed by further bloodshed.

The pause in the fighting, brought about by a cease-fire, is no more than a convenient juncture for direct negotiations or for efforts to be exerted by third parties to broker a peace arrangement. Even a binding cease-fire decree issued by the Security Council may prove 'too brittle to withstand the strains between the parties' over a protracted period.[163] Should the parties fail to exploit the opportunity, the period of quiescence is likely to become a springboard for additional rounds of hostilities (perhaps more intense). This is only to be anticipated. A cease-fire, in freezing the military state of affairs extant at the moment when combat is suspended, places in an advantageous position that party which gained most ground before the deadline. While the guns are silent, the opposing sides will rearm and regroup. If no peace is attained, the belligerent most interested in a return to the *status quo ante* will look for a favourable moment (militarily as well as politically) to mount an offensive, in order to dislodge the enemy from the positions acquired on the eve of the cease-fire. A cease-fire in and of itself is, consequently, no harbinger of peace. All that a cease-fire can accomplish is set the stage for negotiations or any other mode of amicable settlement of disputes. If the parties contrive to hammer out peace terms, success will be due more to the exercise of diplomatic and political skills than to the cease-fire as such.

The Arab-Israeli conflict is a classical illustration of a whole host of cease-fires, either by consensual arrangement between the parties or by fiat of the Security Council, halting hostilities without bringing them to an end. Thus, if we take as an example the mislabelled 'Six Days War' (sparked in June 1967 and proceeding through several cycles of hostilities), the Council insisted on immediate cease-fire, e.g., in June 1967[164] and in October 1973.[165] Israel and Egypt negotiated a cease-fire

[161] S. D. Bailey, 'Cease-Fires, Truces, and Armistices in the Practice of the UN Security Council', 71 *AJIL* 461, 469 (1977).
[162] See C. Rousseau, *Le Droit des Conflits Armés* 202 (1983).
[163] Morriss, *supra* note 152, at 815.
[164] Security Council Resolutions 233, 234 and 235, *supra* notes 146-7, at 2-3.
[165] Security Council Resolution 338, 28 *RDSC* 10 (1973).

agreement, e.g., in November 1973.[166] Israel and Syria agreed on a cease-fire, e.g., in May 1974.[167] In none of these cases did the cease-fire, whether initiated by the parties or by the Council, terminate the war. In the relations between Israel, on the one hand, Egypt and Jordan, on the other, the 'Six Days War' ended only in consequence (or on the eve) of the Treaties of Peace in 1979 and 1994 respectively (see *supra*, B, (a), i). In the relations between Israel and Syria, the 'Six Days War' is not over yet, after almost four decades, since the bilateral peace process (albeit started) has not yet been crowned with success. A number of rounds of hostilities between Israel and Egypt or Syria (most conspicuously, the so-called 'Yom Kippur War' of October 1973) are incorrectly adverted to as 'wars'. Far from qualifying as separate wars, these were merely non-consecutive time-frames of combat, punctuated by extended cease-fires, in the course of a single on-going war that had commenced in June 1967.

(c)   Denunciation and breach of cease-fire

Cease-fires are intrinsically fragile. Under Article 36 of the Hague Regulations, if the duration of a suspension of hostilities is not defined, each belligerent may resume military operations at any time, provided that an appropriate warning is given in accordance with the terms of the cease-fire (originally, 'armistice').[168] The language of Article 36 seems to this writer to be imprecise. It is submitted that a general cease-fire, if concluded without specifying a finite date of expiry, ought to be read in good faith as if it were undertaken for a reasonable period. Within that (admittedly flexible) stretch of time, none of the parties can be allowed to denounce the cease-fire unilaterally. Hence, it is not legitimate for a belligerent (relying on Article 36) to flout the cease-fire shortly after its conclusion. Only when a reasonable period has elapsed does the continued operation of the agreement depend on the good-will of both parties, and the cease-fire can be unilaterally denounced at will.

Article 36 contains an obligation to give advance notice to the adversary when denunciation of a cease-fire agreement occurs. But the specifics depend on what the cease-fire agreement prescribes. It appears that when the agreement is silent on this issue, hostilities may be 'recommenced at once after notification'.[169] If fire can be opened at once, the practical value of notification becomes inconsequential. Whether immediately or

---

[166] Egypt–Israel, Cease-Fire Agreement, 1973, 12 *ILM* 1312 (1973).
[167] Syria–Israel, Agreement on Disengagement between Forces, 1974, 13 *ILM* 880 (1974).
[168] Hague Regulations, *supra* note 74, at 121.   [169] Oppenheim, *supra* note 52, at 556.

after a notification, the *lex specialis of* Article 36 of the Hague Regulations clearly overrides the *lex generalis* of Article 56(2) of the Vienna Convention on the Law of Treaties, which requires a twelve months' minimum notice of the intention to denounce a treaty.[170]

A prolonged general cease-fire arrangement that fails to segue into a termination of the war is prone to charges – and counter-charges – of violations. Cease-fire (originally, 'armistice') violations are the theme of Articles 40 and 41 of the Hague Regulations. Article 41 pronounces that, should the violations be committed by private individuals acting on their own initiative, the injured party would be entitled to demand their punishment or compensation for any losses sustained.[171] Under Article 40, a serious violation of the cease-fire by one of the parties empowers the other side to denounce it and, in cases of urgency, to resume hostilities immediately.[172]

Articles 40 and 41 posit in effect a three-pronged classification of cease-fire violations: (i) ordinary violations, not justifying denunciation of the cease-fire (assuming that denunciation is not anyhow permissible under Article 36); (ii) serious violations, permitting the victim to denounce the cease-fire, but requiring advance notice before the recommencement of hostilities; and (iii) serious violations pregnant with urgency, enabling the victim to denounce the cease-fire and reopen hostilities immediately (without advance notice).[173]

The three categories of cease-fire violations are not easily applicable in reality. The question whether a breach of the cease-fire is serious, or whether any urgency is involved, seldom lends itself to objective verification. It must not be overlooked that a violation considered a minor infraction by one party may assume grave proportions in the eyes of the antagonist.[174] At the same time, the emphasis placed by Article 40 on serious cease-fire violations is consistent with the reference to a 'material breach' appearing in Article 60(1) of the Vienna Convention on the Law of Treaties (as a ground for termination or suspension of bilateral treaties).[175] The applicability of the 'material breach' criterion to general cease-fire agreements had been recognized in the international legal literature even before the Vienna Convention was crafted in its final form.[176]

---

[170] Vienna Convention on the Law of Treaties, *supra* note 57, at 154.
[171] Hague Regulations, *supra* note 74, at 122.
[172] *Ibid.*   [173] See Oppenheim, *supra* note 52, at 556.
[174] See R. Monaco, 'Les Conventions entre Belligérants', 75 *RCADI* 277, 337–8 (1949).
[175] Vienna Convention, *supra* note 57, at 155. *Cf.* Baxter, *supra* note 140, at 386.
[176] See Q. Wright, 'The Termination and Suspension of Treaties', 61 *AJIL* 1000, 1003 (1967).

The meaning of the phrase 'material breach' is not unequivocal.[177] Article 60(3) of the Vienna Convention defines a 'material breach' as either 'a repudiation of the treaty not sanctioned by the present Convention' or a 'violation of a provision essential to the accomplishment of the object or purpose of the treaty'.[178] Which provision of a treaty is to be considered 'essential'? It is generally recognized that, in the context of a 'material breach', the term covers any 'important ancillary provision' of a treaty.[179] Thus, the WMD disarmament clauses in the cease-fire agreement with Iraq were decidedly essential (albeit ancillary to the suspension of hostilities), and their violation constituted a 'material breach'.

The issue of a general cease-fire and its 'material breach' became a critical issue in the last phase of the Gulf War (in 2003). It is therefore noteworthy that, as early as August 1991 (a few months after the entry into force of the cease-fire suspending hostilities), the Security Council – acting under Chapter VII of the Charter, in Resolution 707 (1991) – already condemned Iraq's serious violation of its disarmament obligations and established that the violation 'constitutes a material breach of the relevant provisions of Resolution 687'.[180] Eleven years later, in Resolution 1441 (2002), the Security Council (again acting under Chapter VII) decided that 'Iraq has been and remains in material breach of its obligations under relevant resolutions, including Resolution 687 (1991).'[181] Some commentators believe that the concept of 'material breach' became relevant due to an alleged 'semi-treaty' character of Resolution 687.[182] But this is wrong. 'Material breach' came into the picture solely as a result of Iraq's defiance of the cease-fire agreement by which it was bound.

A determination of 'material breach' lays the ground for the resumption of hostilities by the other side to a general cease-fire agreement. In the case of Iraq, that determination need not have been made (in an objectively binding fashion) by the Security Council. Ordinarily, the adversary in the armed conflict – *i.e.* the Coalition (or even any of its component elements) – would have the prerogative of arriving at that conclusion based on a subjective assessment of the situation. However, in

---

[177] For a detailed analysis of the expression 'material breach', see M. M. Gomaa, *Suspension or Termination of Treaties on Grounds of Breach* 25–50 (1996).

[178] Vienna Convention, *supra* note 57, at 156.

[179] A. Aust, *Modern Treaty Law and Practice* 238 (2000).

[180] Security Council Resolution 707, 46 *RDSC* 22, 23 (1991).

[181] Security Council Resolution 1441 (2002), [2002–3] *RDSC* 114, 116.

[182] See M. Jacobsson, 'The Use of Force and the Case of Iraq', *Peace and Security: Current Challenges in International Law* 373, 383 (D. Amnéus and K. Svanberg-Torpman eds., 2004).

Resolution 1441, the Security Council also afforded Iraq 'a final opportunity to comply with its disarmament obligations'.[183] Consequently, the Coalition had to hold fire until it became clear that Iraq had persisted in a policy of adamant non-compliance (see *infra*, Chapter 10, C, (b), iii).

[183] Security Council Resolution 1441, *supra* note 181, at 116.

Part II

The illegality of war

3   A historical perspective of the legal status of war

A.   The 'just war' doctrine in the past

(a)   The Roman origins

The distinction between 'just war' (*bellum justum*) and 'unjust war' (*bellum injustum*) can be traced back to the *jus fetiale*. This body of law existed in ancient Rome, from the days of the kings until the late republican era.[1] The *fetiales* were a college of priests charged with a number of duties, some of which pertained to the inception of war.

Cicero stated that it may be gathered from the code of the *fetiales* that no war is considered just, unless it is preceded by an official demand for satisfaction or warning, and a formal declaration has been made.[2] It follows that two indispensable conditions of a procedural nature had to be met before the commencement of hostilities. The first requisite was that a demand be addressed to the opponent, insisting on satisfaction for the grievance caused to Rome (such satisfaction taking the form of restitution, withdrawal of forces, etc.), with a fixed time allowed for a proper response.[3] The second condition was that a formal declaration of war had to be issued. The declaration entailed an elaborate ceremony, culminating in a spear being hurled across the Roman frontier into the enemy's territory, and including the recital of ancient legal formulas recorded in detail by Livy.[4] It appears that, apart from the ritualistic and procedural aspects of their duties, the *fetiales* were also empowered to pronounce whether there were sufficient substantive grounds justifying the outbreak of hostilities (e.g., violation of a treaty or the sanctity of

---

[1] See A. Nussbaum, *A Concise History of the Law of Nations* 10–11 (1954).

[2] Cicero, *De Officiis*, Book I, § XI, 36 (Loeb Classical ed. 38–9 (W. Miller trans., 1913)). See also Cicero, *De Re Publica*, Book III, § XXIII, 35 (Loeb Classical ed. 212–13 (C. W. Keyes trans., 1928)).

[3] See C. Phillipson, *The International Law and Custom of Ancient Greece and Rome*, II, 329–39 (1911).

[4] Livy, *Ab Urbe Condita*, Book I, § XXII, 5–14 (1 Loeb Classical ed. 114–19 (B. O. Foster trans., 1919)).

ambassadors, infringement of territorial rights, or offences committed against allies).[5]

As a rule, the political powers in Rome were disallowed to go to war (during the relevant period) without the explicit and prior approval of the *fetiales*.[6] Yet, it is probably fair to observe that, to all intents and purposes, the *fetiales* were the servants of their political masters and 'practically bound to do their bidding'.[7]

(b)   Christian theology

The *bellum justum* doctrine did not disappear with the *jus fetiale*. Instead, it was espoused by Christian theology and Canon Law. As long as the Roman Emperors were pagans, the Church upheld a pacifistic posture, and even forbade Christians to enlist as soldiers.[8] But after Christianity had become the official religion of the Empire in the days of Constantine, the Church was compelled to alter its view about war: from that point onwards, Christians were expected to shed their blood for the Empire.[9] Evidently, the Church had to find theological grounds for such a radical modification of its basic concept. This was done by St. Augustine, who revived the *bellum justum* doctrine as a moral tenet. In his celebrated book *De Civitate Dei*, St. Augustine enunciated the fundamental principle that every war was a lamentable phenomenon, but the wrong suffered at the hands of the adversary imposed 'the necessity of waging just wars'.[10]

The theologians and canonists who followed St. Augustine accepted his approach and expatiated upon the theme of the just war. The most influential contribution was made by St. Thomas Aquinas, who propounded that for war to be just it had to fulfil three conditions: (i) the war had to be conducted not privately but under the authority of a prince (*auctoritas principis*); (ii) there had to be a 'just cause' (*causa justa*) for the war; and (iii) it was not enough to have a just cause from an objective viewpoint, but it was necessary to have the right intention (*intentio recta*) to promote good and to avoid evil.[11] The Thomist analysis pushed to the fore the question of the justice of causes of war. The canonists began to

---

[5] See Phillipson, *supra* note 3, at 182, 328.   [6] See *ibid.*, 328.

[7] A. S. Hershey, 'The History of International Relations during Antiquity and the Middle Ages', 5 *AJIL* 901, 920 (1911).

[8] See J. von Elbe, 'The Evolution of the Concept of the Just War in International Law', 33 *AJIL* 665, 667 (1939).

[9] See *ibid.*

[10] St. Augustine, *De Civitate Dei Contra Paganos*, Book XIX, § VII (6 Loeb Classical ed. 150–1 (W. C. Greene trans., 1960)).

[11] St. Thomas Aquinas, *Summa Theologiae*, Secunda Secundae, Quaestio 40, 1 (35 Blackfriars ed., 80–3 (1972)).

wrangle over elaborate lists of such causes, which often reflected personal and political predilections.[12]

(c)   The 'fathers' of international law

At the close of the Middle Ages, concurrently with the growth of the nation-States, modern international law came into being. The 'fathers' of international law were jurists and scholars in the sixteenth and seventeenth centuries, all Europeans – at the outset only Catholics, but at the most formative stage also Protestants – who attempted to articulate (sometimes, practically to invent) rules of conduct binding on States. Among other concepts and institutions, these eminent scholars imported into the new international legal system the well-established religious (Catholic) doctrine that only a just war is permissible. Having done that, the 'fathers' of international law, emulating the canonists, deemed it necessary to set out lists of just causes for war. These lists, too, were coloured by the bias of the respective writers.

For instance, the Spanish Dominican professor, Victoria, wrestled with the subject of his country's war against the Indians in America. Victoria rejected the premise that the Indians (as pagans) were beyond the pale of the law and bereft of any rights.[13] He maintained that, to be admissible, war against the Indians (no less than war against Christians) had to be just.[14] But ultimately Victoria justified what was happening in the New World, asserting that the Indians had violated the fundamental rights of the Spaniards to travel freely among them, to carry on trade and to propagate Christianity.[15]

The formulation of international law in a manner consistent with the personal inclinations of the author was not confined to wars against infidels in the New World. A just war could also be undertaken against Christians adhering to different political or religious creeds in Europe. Thus, the Spanish jurist Ayala, who held a position resembling that of a Judge Advocate General in the armed forces of Philip II (engaged in a struggle to put down insurrection in the Netherlands), contended that 'a prince has a most just cause of war when he is directing his arms against rebels and subjects who abjure his sovereignty'.[16]

Not only did each of the 'fathers' of international law produce his own favoured enumeration of just causes of war, but the divergent lists spread

---

[12] See A. Vanderpol, *La Doctrine Scolastique du Droit de Guerre* 63 (1925).
[13] Victoria, *De Indis et de Jure Belli Relectiones* 125 (Classics of International Law ed., J. P. Bate trans., 1917).
[14] *Ibid.*, 151–8.   [15] *Ibid.*
[16] Ayala, *De Jure et Officiis Bellicis et Disciplina Militari*, Book I, § II, 12–13 (2 Classics of International Law ed., J. P. Bate trans., 11 (1912)).

the mantle of justice over a wide variety of controversial causes. According to Suárez, 'any grave injury to one's reputation or honour' was a just cause of war.[17] Textor opined that, under certain circumstances, refusal of passage of troops *en route* to wage war against a third party 'gives a just cause, if not for declaring war against the refuser, at any rate for opening a way by sword and arms'.[18] Other jurists identified many additional just causes of war.

The expansion of the catalogue of just causes highlighted a perplexing problem. For the medieval theologians and canonists, any dispute as to the interpretation or application of the just war doctrine (or any other doctrine) could be resolved authoritatively by the Catholic Church. But when the doctrine was secularized, and absorbed into the mainstream of international law, the absence of an impartial authority – empowered to sift the evidence and appraise the justice of the cause of a concrete war – became readily apparent. Under these conditions, could war qualify as just on both sides?

Victoria argued that, even though war could really be just (from an objective standpoint) only on one side, it was not impossible that the other party acted in good faith under 'invincible ignorance' either of fact or of law, and in such a case war (subjectively speaking) was just from the latter's perspective as well.[19] A similar position was taken by Grotius.[20] Gentili carried this thought further by contending that, even in objective terms, war could be just on one side but still more just on the other side.[21] Indeed, if a broad roster of independent just causes of war is admitted, this conclusion is almost unavoidable. Should the honour of Arcadia be slighted by Ruritania, Arcadia would have a just cause for war (consistent with Suárez's thesis). Yet, if Arcadia were to attack, Ruritania might also invoke a just cause for war, *i.e.* self-defence. As a consequence, both antagonists in the same conflict would fight one another in the name of justice, and each would be entitled to do so.

The postulate that the two belligerents in war may simultaneously rely on the justice of their clashing causes, and that they will be equally right, brought the just war doctrine in international law to a *cul-de-sac*. In almost

---

[17] Suárez, *Selections from Three Works, De Triplici Virtute Theologia: Charitate*, Disputation XIII, § IV, 3 (2 Classics of International Law ed., G. L. Williams *et al.* trans., 817 (1944)).

[18] Textor, *Synopsis Juris Gentium*, § XVII, 37 (2 Classics of International Law ed., J. P. Bate trans., 178 (1925)).

[19] Victoria, *supra* note 13, at 177.

[20] Grotius, *De Jure Belli ac Pacis*, Book II, § XXIII, XIII (2 Classics of International Law ed., F. W. Kelsey trans., 565–6 (1925)).

[21] Gentili, *De Jure Belli*, Book I, § VI, 48–52 (2 Classics of International Law ed., J. C. Rolfe trans., 31–3 (1933)).

every armed conflict, justice is appealed to by all parties. If the competing claims are screened on a comparative basis, and on balance only one of them can emerge as validated by considerations of justice, the register of 'just causes' may conceivably serve as a useful guide for States in calculating future action. However, once war qualifies as objectively just on the part of both adversaries, there is scarcely a reason why any State should feel inhibited from going to war at will. Surely, when pressed, each Government can drum up some plausible justification for any policy. If that justification need not be superior to the claims of the enemy, the requirement of a just cause ceases in effect to be a hurdle on the path to war.

In the nineteenth (and early part of the twentieth) century, the attempt to differentiate between just and unjust wars in positive international law was discredited and abandoned.[22] States continued to use the rhetoric of justice when they went to war, but the justification produced no legal reverberations. Most international lawyers conceded openly that ' [w]ith the inherent rightfulness of war international law has nothing to do'.[23] Or, in the acerbic words of T. J. Lawrence, distinctions between just and unjust causes of war 'belong to morality and theology, and are as much out of place in a treatise on International Law as would be a discussion on the ethics of marriage in a book on the law of personal status'.[24]

B.   Recent concepts of 'just war'

(a)   Kelsen's theory

H. Kelsen (among others) developed the concept that war is lawful only when it constitutes a sanction against a violation of international law by the opponent.[25] According to Kelsen, war 'is permitted only as a reaction against an illegal act, a delict, and only when directed against the State responsible for this delict'.[26]

One of the central features of Kelsen's theory, as originally constructed, is that it treated war as a lawful response (a sanction) in every instance of non-compliance with international law (a delict), even if that non-compliance had not involved the use of force.[27] Once the use of inter-State force was prohibited, other than in exceptional circumstances defined by the Charter of the United Nations (see *infra*, Chapter 4, B, (a)), Kelsen adjusted the

[22] See J. L. Brierly, 'International Law and Resort to Armed Force', *4 Cam.LJ* 308, id. (1930–2).
[23] G. B. Davis, *The Elements of International Law* 272 (G. E. Sherman ed., 4th ed., 1916).
[24] T. J. Lawrence, *The Principles of International Law* 311 (P. H. Winfield ed., 7th ed., 1923).
[25] See H. Kelsen, *Principles of International Law* 33–4 (1st ed., 1952).
[26] H. Kelsen, *General Theory of Law and State* 331 (1945).   [27] *Ibid.*, 333.

theory to the evolution of international law. He still regarded war as lawful only when constituting a sanction, but the nature of the delict had changed: legitimate war now had to be a 'counterwar', waged in response to an illegal war by the other side.[28]

There is a three-fold difficulty inherent in Kelsen's theory. First, factually, war may be an inefficacious sanction. Victory in war is contingent not on right but on might, and a weak State resorting to hostilities against a strong one is apt to find it a painful and counter-productive experience. Secondly, in the absence of an impartial forum juridically competent to determine on the merits whether a specific war ought to be considered a genuine sanction, the opposing side can challenge the legality of the war. It can argue that the war, instead of amounting to a sanction (a legitimate counter-war), is actually no more than a delict (an unlawful war). Thirdly, as long as the original delict could consist of any conduct in contravention of international law (such as a failure to repay a loan), there was a distinct possibility of a glaring disproportion between the delict and the sanction. After all, war always generates inevitable destruction and suffering, and it cannot be contemplated as a proper sanction unless warranted by the gravest provocation.

Kelsen was not unaware of the obvious inadequacy immanent in the role of war as a general sanction, but he explained it away in light of the primitive nature of the international legal system.[29] Kelsen called his theory 'the *bellum justum* doctrine',[30] although he admitted that the term 'just' in the present context means 'legal'.[31] Basically, J. L. Kunz was right in stating that the concept of *bellum justum* has been replaced by that of *bellum legale*: what counts is a breach of the norms of existing international law, rather than 'the intrinsic injustice of the cause of war'.[32] This is an important corrective. Confusion between *bellum legale* and *bellum justum* can be fraught with danger, given the disparate and occasionally irreconcilable perceptions of justice, compared to the relative ascertainability of the law.[33]

(b)   'Wars of national liberation'

During the period of decolonization of former European possessions worldwide, persistent attempts were made to justify in positive international law the use of force by States in support of 'wars of national liberation', carried out by peoples in exercise of the right of self-determination (see

---

[28] Kelsen, *supra* note 25, at 28–9.   [29] *Ibid.*, 35–6.
[30] *Ibid.*, 33; Kelsen, *supra* note 26, at 331.   [31] Kelsen, *supra* note 25, at 34 n. 16.
[32] J. L. Kunz, 'Bellum Justum and Bellum Legale', 45 *AJIL* 528, 532 (1951).
[33] See Y. Dinstein, 'The Interaction of International Law and Justice', 16 *IYHR* 9, 13–17 (1986).

infra, Chapter 6, E). The real issue was not the legitimacy of the 'war of national liberation' *per se*, inasmuch as an uprising unfurling the banner of self-determination does not amount to an inter-State war (liberation or statehood being the contested goal). The focal question was whether a foreign State – embracing the cause of the 'national liberation movement' – was entitled to intervene actively in the hostilities, in order to assist in the overthrow of the 'yoke of colonialism'. Those answering the question in the affirmative believed that colonialism is 'a purely evil state and one which it is legal and just to fight against'.[34] Thus, whereas traditional international law permitted a foreign State to lend its support only to the central Government against insurgents (see *infra*, Chapter 4, G, (a)), 'under the new theory of just wars' the reverse was true: military intervention from the outside would be lawful solely when directed against the central Government on behalf of a 'national liberation movement'.[35]

Usually, the rationale offered (principally by the former Soviet Union and Third World countries) in sustaining the legitimacy of the use of inter-State force when extended in aid of 'wars of national liberation' was that these are just wars.[36] The obstacle confronting the interventionist school of thought was that the Charter of the United Nations does not incorporate support of 'wars of national liberation' among the licit exceptions to the general prohibition of recourse to inter-State force (see *infra*, Chapter 4, B, (b)).

In his Dissenting Opinion in the *Nicaragua* case of 1986, Judge Schwebel criticized the majority of the International Court of Justice because a brief dictum in its judgment 'may be understood as inferentially endorsing' the legality of forcible 'intervention in the promotion of so-called "wars of liberation"'.[37] In fact, the Court's dictum[38] is no more than a faint hint in that direction, and Judge Schwebel may have overreacted.

Nevertheless, important milestones on the path pursued by advocates of foreign intervention in 'wars of national liberation' were set in two consensus resolutions adopted by the General Assembly: the 1970 Declaration on Principles of International Law Concerning Friendly

---

[34] A. Shaw, 'Revival of the Just War Doctrine?', 3 *Auck.ULR* 156, 170 (1976–9).

[35] D. J. Scheffer, 'Use of Force after the Cold War: Panama, Iraq, and the New World Order', *Right v. Might: International Law and the Use of Force* 109, 137 (L. Henkin *et al.* eds., 2nd ed., 1991).

[36] See the statement of Chairman Khrushchev: 'Moral, material and other assistance must be given so that the sacred and just struggle of the peoples for their independence can be brought to its conclusion', cited by R. E. Gorelick, 'Wars of National Liberation: *Jus ad Bellum*', 11 *CWRJIL* 71, 81 (1979).

[37] *Case Concerning Military and Paramilitary Activities in and against Nicaragua* (Merits), [1986] *ICJ Rep.* 14, 350–1.

[38] 'The Court is not here concerned with the process of decolonization; this question is not in issue in the present case.' *Ibid.*, 108.

Relations and Co-operation among States in accordance with the Charter of the United Nations,[39] and Article 7 of the 1974 Definition of Aggression.[40] These texts are not free of doubt as to their exact meaning (in regard to Article 7 of the Definition of Aggression, see *infra*, Chapter 5, B). But the driving force behind them cannot be dismissed lightly.

The alleged licence of one State to use force against another in abetting a 'war of national liberation' is predicated not on legal norms but on claims of justice (as perceived by the claimants). Because a people striving for independence from alien domination is the *soi-disant* beneficiary of a just cause, a State endorsing that cause is purportedly authorized by international law to go to war against another State. The long and short of it is that, in the name of justice, the existing legal proscription of the use of inter-State force is corroded by political motivations.[41]

The principal drawback in the endorsement of 'wars of national liberation' is that, as in the heyday of the *bellum justum* doctrine, just causes of war happen to coincide with the political and ideological slant of whoever is invoking them.[42] In the words of Judge Schwebel, 'the lack of beauty is in the eyes of the beholder'.[43] Over the years – with the process of decolonization of European possessions overseas largely accomplished, and following the collapse of the Soviet Union – the pressure to support 'wars of national liberation' has subsided.[44] But it is the irony of fate that the most sanguinary 'war of national liberation' waged at the outset of the twenty-first century has been the civil war in Chechnya, in which the heirs of the USSR are still engaged at the time of writing in ruthlessly quelling an attempt to secede from the Russian Federation by a people invoking the right to self-determination.[45]

(c)   'Humanitarian intervention'

Towards the end of the twentieth century, the recrudescence of the just war doctrine has taken a new turn. The rhetoric of justice shifted from

[39] General Assembly Resolution 2625 (XXV), 25 *RGA* 121, 123 (1970).

[40] General Assembly Resolution 3314 (XXIX), 29(1) *RGA* 142, 144 (1974).

[41] See D. E. Graham, 'The 1974 Diplomatic Conference on the Law of War: A Victory for Political Causes and a Return to the "Just War" Concept of the Eleventh Century', 32 *WLLR* 25, 44 (1975).

[42] See W. D. Verwey, 'Humanitarian Intervention', *The Current Legal Regulation of the Use of Force* 57, 69–70 (A. Cassese ed., 1986).

[43] *Nicaragua* case, *supra* note 37, at 351.

[44] See L. Henkin, 'Use of Force: Law and U.S. Policy', *Right v. Might, supra* note 35, at 37, 43.

[45] On the ethnic animosities underlying the turbulence in the North Caucasus, see R. Menon and G. E. Fuller, 'Russia's Ruinous Chechen War', 79 *For.Aff.* 32, 33–5 (2000).

those oppressed by European colonialists to those persecuted by their own Government anywhere. Strong doctrinal support developed in favour of legitimizing forcible measures of 'humanitarian intervention', employed by Atlantica for the sake of compelling Patagonia to cease and desist from massive violations of international human rights.[46] Nothing in the Charter of the United Nations substantiates a unilateral right of one State to use force against another under the guise of securing the implementation of human rights.[47] Yet, the advocates of 'humanitarian intervention' emphasize the significance of several allusions in the Charter to the need to promote and encourage respect for human rights and fundamental freedoms, as well as stress the significance of the 1948 Genocide Convention.[48] In addition, they rely on State practice of intervention on behalf of downtrodden minorities and individuals in the nineteenth (and early twentieth) century.[49] Commentators have drawn comparisons between 'humanitarian intervention' and medieval just war criteria, and have accordingly dubbed the intervenors 'knights of humanity'.[50] As a rule, interventionists believe that they are pursuing a higher goal: 'the ideal of justice backed by power'.[51] The trouble is that there can be contradictory subjective opinions as to whether a course of action is just, and there is too much room to abuse the law in the name of justice. Indeed, the human rights record of the intervening country itself (flying the banner of humanitarianism) can be distressing: the intervention may prove a mere 'opportunity to redeem its own failings in the eyes of the international community'.[52]

This writer believes that the arguments in support of unilateral 'humanitarian intervention' do not stand up to close scrutiny. The examples evoked from State practice of the nineteenth (and early twentieth) century have no resonance in the present era, bearing in mind that at the time international law did not hinder the use of force for whatever reason, good or bad[53] (see *infra*, D). By virtue of the law of the Charter, only the Security

[46] See M. S. McDougal and W. M. Reisman, 'Response', 3 *Int.Law.* 438–45 (1968–9).
[47] See T. M. Franck and N. S. Rodley, 'After Bangladesh: The Law of Humanitarian Intervention by Military Force', 67 *AJIL* 275, 299–302 (1973).
[48] See McDougal and Reisman, *supra* note 46, at 442–4.
[49] See M. Reisman and M. S. McDougal, 'Humanitarian Intervention to Protect the Ibos', *Humanitarian Intervention and the United Nations* 167, 179–83 (R. B. Lillich ed., 1973).
[50] O. Ramsbotham and T. Woodhouse, *Humanitarian Intervention in Contemporary Conflict: A Reconceptualization* 228–9 (1996).
[51] M. J. Glennon, 'The New Interventionism: The Search for a Just International Law', 78 *For.Aff.* 2, 7 (1999).
[52] K. Nowrot and E. W. Schabacker, 'The Use of Force to Restore Democracy: International Legal Implications of the ECOWAS Intervention in Sierra Leone', 14 *AUILR* 321, 411 (1998–9).
[53] See R. R. Baxter, 'Comments', *Humanitarian Intervention and the United Nations, supra* note 49, at 14–15.

Council is empowered to take forcible action against a State which is in breach of its international undertakings to respect human rights (see *infra*, Chapter 10, D, (c)). In 1986, the International Court of Justice rejected the notion that the United States could employ force against Nicaragua in order to ensure respect for human rights in that country.[54] It is almost impossible to avoid the conclusion that this ruling 'unmistakably places the Court in the camp of those who claim that the doctrine of humanitarian intervention is without validity'.[55] Yet, despite the conspicuously broad range of the Court's pronouncement, attempts have been made to 'read [it] narrowly'.[56] The *Nicaragua* Judgment has certainly not curbed the enthusiasm of commentators seeking to disencumber the preservation of human rights from the heavy weight of the provisions of the Charter.[57]

As for the Genocide Convention, it prescribes in Article I:

The Contracting Parties confirm that genocide, whether committed in time of peace or in time of war, is a crime under international law which they undertake to prevent and to punish.[58]

The International Court of Justice, in its 1951 Advisory Opinion on *Reservations to the Genocide Convention*, confirmed that 'the principles underlying the Convention are principles which are recognized by civilized nations as binding on States, even without any conventional obligation'.[59]

The question is, what remedies are available to a State desirous of precluding or terminating the perpetration of genocide on foreign soil? Article VIII of the Convention sets forth:

Any Contracting Party may call upon the competent organs of the United Nations to take such action under the Charter of the United Nations as they consider appropriate for the prevention and suppression of acts of genocide.[60]

Article IX establishes the compulsory jurisdiction of the International Court of Justice in case of disputes relating to the application or interpretation of the Convention (including the issue of State responsibility for genocide).[61] It follows that no State acting alone (or even jointly with

---

[54] *Nicaragua* case, *supra* note 37, at 134–5.

[55] N. S. Rodley, 'Human Rights and Humanitarian Intervention: The Case Law of the World Court', 38 *ICLQ* 321, 332 (1989).

[56] See F. R. Tesón, *Humanitarian Intervention: An Inquiry into Law and Morality* 270 (2nd ed., 1997).

[57] See, e.g., A. D'Amato, 'The Invasion of Panama Was a Lawful Response to Tyranny', 84 *AJIL* 516, 520 (1990).

[58] Convention on the Prevention and Punishment of the Crime of Genocide, 1948, 78 *UNTS* 277, 280.

[59] Advisory Opinion on *Reservations to the Convention on the Prevention and Punishment of the Crime of Genocide*, [1951] *ICJ Rep.* 15, 23.

[60] Genocide Convention, *supra* note 58, at 282.   [61] *Ibid.*

like-minded allies) has a legal option of resorting to force against another State, with a view to averting genocide or bringing it to an end. 'Knights of humanity' are out of time and out of place in the contemporary world. Those wishing to take effective action against genociders must turn to the competent (political or judicial) organs of the United Nations. The competent organs – the Security Council and the International Court of Justice – have the authority to redress the situation (by ordaining the measures necessary in their discretion), but no 'general licence' for the use of force is provided to 'vigilantes and opportunists'.[62]

C. The extra-legality of war

War occurs in human history so repetitively that there is a tendency to take it for granted. For many centuries, war was discerned with resignation as a perennial fact of life. The popular outlook was that war is tantamount to a 'providential visitation to be compared with plague or flood or fire'.[63] In similarity to these and other natural disasters (such as earthquakes and volcanic eruptions), war was expected to inflict itself on mankind in cyclical frequency. Like the plague, war would appear every once in a while, leave death and devastation in its wake, and temporarily pass away to return at a later date.[64]

The analogy between war and catastrophes decreed by nature influenced lawyers, who have occasionally suggested that war falls into the same 'category of events, considered incapable of legal control but entailing legal consequences'.[65] Just as no legal system can forbid thunderbolts or droughts, it has been assumed that international law cannot possibly interdict war. War has been deemed beyond the reach of international law and, therefore, 'neither legal nor illegal'.[66] As A. Nussbaum put it, '[t]he "outbreak" of war is a metajuristic phenomenon, an event outside the range and control of the law'.[67] The Italian–American Conciliation Commission, in its decision of 1953 in the *Armstrong Cork* case, also adverted to the state of war as an 'extra-juridical regime'.[68]

This line of approach proved particularly attractive in the nineteenth (and early twentieth) century, although most international lawyers were

---

[62] I. Brownlie, 'Thoughts on Kind-Hearted Gunmen', *Humanitarian Intervention and the United Nations, supra* note 49, at 139, 147–8.

[63] C. Eagleton, *International Government* 455 (3rd ed., 1957).

[64] See W. R. Harris, *Tyranny on Trial* 514 (Rev. ed., 1999).

[65] Q. Wright, 'Changes in the Conception of War', 18 *AJIL* 755, 756 (1924). The author modified his position at a later date. See Q. Wright, *A Study of War*, II, 891–3 (1942).

[66] J. L. Brierly, *The Outlook for International Law* 22 (1944).

[67] A. Nussbaum, 'Just War – A Legal Concept', 42 *Mich.LR* 453, 477 (1943–4).

[68] *Armstrong Cork Company* case (1953), 14 *RIAA* 159, 163.

not prepared to follow the proposition to its logical conclusion. J. Westlake held that '[i]nternational law did not institute war, which it found already existing, but regulates it with a view to its greater humanity'.[69] In somewhat different terms, W. E. Hall commented that '[i]nternational law has ... no alternative but to accept war, independently of the justice of its origin, as a relation which the parties to it may set up if they choose, and to busy itself only in regulating the effects of the relation'.[70] The latest (seventh) edition (dated 1952) of the second volume of L. Oppenheim's *International Law*, edited by Sir Hersch Lauterpacht, still includes the statement that '[w]ar is a fact recognised, and with regard to many points regulated, but not established, by International Law'.[71]

The phraseology typical of those who represent war as an extra-legal phenomenon is that international law only 'finds' or 'accepts' war as a *fait accompli*. It is universally acknowledged that, once war begins, international law can and does regulate the relations between belligerents (as well as between them and neutrals).[72] However, the exponents of the extra-legality of war believe that, while there is plenty of room for a *jus in bello* (governing conduct in warfare), there can be no real *jus ad bellum* (imposing normative limitations on the unleashing of hostilities). 'Law cannot say *when*, but only *how* war is to be waged.'[73]

The proposition that war is a meta-juridical occurrence may be tempting, but it is devoid of foundation. The assimilation of war to events taking place in nature is artificial and delusive.[74] Unlike earthquakes and epidemics, war is caused by human beings. Every form of human behaviour is susceptible of regulation by law. No category of human behaviour is excluded *a priori* from the range of application of legal norms (actual or potential). At bottom, the undisputed ability of international law to control the conduct of combatants in the course of war (*jus in bello*) proves that it can also restrict the freedom of action of belligerents in the generation of war (*jus ad bellum*). When an epidemic is raging, law is utterly unable to dictate to the virus not only when (and if) to mount an assault upon the human body, but also how to go about it. From a

---

[69] J. Westlake, *International Law*, II, 3 (2nd ed., 1913).
[70] W. E. Hall, *A Treatise on International Law* 82 (A. P. Higgins ed., 8th ed., 1924).
[71] L. Oppenheim, *International Law*, II, 202 (H. Lauterpacht ed., 7th ed., 1952).
[72] See Y. Dinstein, *The Conduct of Hostilities under the Law of International Armed Conflict passim* (2004).
[73] C. A. Pompe, *Aggressive War an International Crime* 140 (1953). This is a summation of the legal position taken by D. Anzilotti and others.
[74] See R. W. Tucker, 'The Interpretation of War under Present International Law', 4 *ILQ* 11, 13 (1951).

jurisprudential standpoint, there is no real difference between governing the 'when' and the 'how' of war.

Certainly, international law does not 'establish' war. For that matter, domestic law does not 'establish' murder or robbery. War, as a form of human conduct, resembles murder or robbery more than flood or drought. In the same way that murder and robbery are prohibited by domestic law, war can be forbidden by international law.

For a long time international law did refrain from obtruding upon the liberty of States to go to war (see *infra*, D). Yet, this forbearance did not mean that international law had a built-in impediment depriving it of the power to ban war. In reality, by not prohibiting recourse to war, international law indicated that war was tolerated and, therefore, permitted. War can be legal or illegal, but it is misleading to suggest that it is extra-legal.[75]

Upon analysis, the theory of the extra-legality of war is of far greater potential moment than the concept of its legality. Moving from the legality to the extra-legality of war is a transition from bad to worse.[76] If war is lawful in a given era, it can still be disallowed afterwards. But if war is extra-legal, it can never be made unlawful. Consequently, the prohibition of aggressive war in the twentieth century (see *infra*, Chapter 4) implies (i) a denial of the doctrine of its extra-legality; as well as (ii) a confirmation of the hypothesis that, prior to the interdiction, war used to be legal.

D.   The legality of war

Subsequent to the virtual demise of the just war doctrine, the predominant conviction in the nineteenth (and early twentieth) century was that every State had a right – namely, an interest protected by international law – to embark upon war whenever it pleased. The discretion of States in this matter was portrayed as unfettered. States could 'resort to war for a good reason, a bad reason or no reason at all'.[77] Among the legitimate reasons for war would figure the desire to use it as a sanction against non-compliance with international law (as perceived by Kelsen, *supra*, B, (a)). Equally, war could be employed as a means to challenge and upset the

---

[75] See *ibid*.

[76] See J. N. Moore, 'Strengthening World Order: Reversing the Slide to Anarchy', 4 *AUJILP* 1, 5 (1989).

[77] H. W. Briggs, *The Law of Nations* 976 (2nd ed., 1952). It has been suggested that 'even before the League of Nations any war in Europe had to have a justifying cause or reason'. S. Verosta, 'The Unlawfulness of Wars of Aggression before 1914', *Essays in Honour of Judge Taslim Olawale Elias*, I, 117, 124 (E. G. Bello and B. A. Ajibola eds., 1992). But the evidence produced (the Greek–Turkish War of 1897) is not persuasive.

international legal *status quo*.[78] At one and the same time, war 'had a static as well as a dynamic function': to enforce existing rights and to defy them.[79]

War came to be characterized as 'a right inherent in sovereignty itself'.[80] Moreover, the war-making right was thought of as the paramount attribute of sovereignty.[81] When the statehood of a specific political entity was in doubt, the best litmus test comprised of checking whether the prerogative of launching war at will was vested in it.[82] The international legal freedom to wage war for whatever reason even impacted upon the constitutions and basic laws of quite a few countries. Some of these instruments, when spelling out to which branch of Government the war-making power was entrusted, overtly applied different procedures to the initiation of offensive and defensive wars.[83]

When observed through the lens of legal theory, the freedom to indulge in war without thereby violating international law seemed to create an egregious anomaly. It did not make much sense for the international legal system to be embedded in respect for the sovereignty of States, while each State had a sovereign right to destroy the sovereignty of others.[84] On the one hand, it was incumbent on every State to defer to a plethora of rights accorded to other States under both customary and treaty law. On the other hand, each State was at liberty to attack any other State whenever it pleased. J. L. Brierly termed this state of affairs 'a logical impossibility'.[85]

The apparent incongruity may be examined from a somewhat different point of departure. In the final analysis, every legal system has to protect the vital interests of its subjects. States are the primary subjects of international law. Hence, it is arguable that '[a] system of international law must premise the right of states to exist'.[86] When international law recognized the privilege of States to engage in war at their discretion, the net result was that the right of the target State to exist could be repudiated

---

[78] See J. L. Kunz, 'The Law of Nations, Static and Dynamic', 27 *AJIL* 630, 634 (1933).
[79] *Ibid.*
[80] A. S. Hershey, *The Essentials of International Public Law* 349 (1912).
[81] See M. Virally, 'Panorama du Droit International Contemporain', 183 *RCADI* 9, 99 (1983).
[82] For that reason, some writers maintained that States like Switzerland – subjected to a regime of permanent neutrality (*supra*, Chapter 1, C, (a)) – could not 'be said to possess complete external sovereignty', since they were deprived of 'the right to engage in any except strictly defensive warfare'. H. Taylor, *A Treatise on International Public Law* 174 (1901).
[83] See E. D. Dickinson, *The Equality of States in International Law* 202–4 (1920).
[84] See C. De Visscher, *Theory and Reality in Public International Law* 286 (P. E. Corbett trans., 1957).
[85] Brierly, *supra* note 66, at 21.
[86] Q. Wright, 'The Present Status of Neutrality', 34 *AJIL* 391, 399 (1940).

at any moment.[87] What emerged was a deep-rooted inconsistency in the international legal order, which 'both asserts and denies the right of states to exist'.[88] Some scholars even reasoned that the inconsistency was calamitous to international law. To their minds, by not restraining war and thus failing to protect the fundamental interests of its principal subjects (the States), international law was not true law.[89]

This was by no means the prevalent opinion. Many writers totally disavowed the notion that the freedom of war was not in harmony with the existence of a genuine international legal system.[90] Others simply sidestepped the issue. In any event, irrespective of any scholarly bafflement, States and statesmen in the nineteenth (and early twentieth) century did not consider the freedom of war to be a fatal flaw in the structure of international law. Nor did they find it inconceivable that, by invoking its own sovereignty, each State was empowered to challenge the sovereignty of other States. The practice of States in that period was 'dominated by an unrestricted right of war',[91] and conceptual criticisms were largely ignored.

E.   Exceptions to the general liberty to go to war

(a)   Special arrangements

Precisely because the liberty to go to war was regarded by States as the general rule, there is no dearth of bilateral treaties in the nineteenth (and early twentieth) century, in which the Contracting Parties assumed an obligation not to resort to war in their reciprocal relations. Concomitantly, the parties consented to seek an amicable settlement (e.g., mediation or arbitration) whenever a dispute might arise between them. Such a treaty was applicable, however, only *inter partes*, without diminishing from the freedom of action of signatories *vis-à-vis* third States. In addition, the treaty was usually limited to a fixed time, although frequently subject to extension. When the prescribed period expired, every Contracting Party had the right to terminate the treaty on notice. Once the treaty was no longer in force, all States concerned regained the option to commence hostilities against one another.

As an illustration, we may take a treaty concluded between Honduras and Nicaragua in 1878, in which these two countries agreed that 'there shall in no case be war' between them and, in the event of a dispute,

---

[87] *Ibid.*, 399–400.   [88] *Ibid.*, 400.
[89] See Kelsen, *supra* note 26, at 340.
[90] See, e.g., L. Oppenheim, *International Law*, II, 55 (1st ed., 1906).
[91] I. Brownlie, *International Law and the Use of Force by States* 19 (1963).

undertook to turn to arbitration by a friendly nation.[92] Each party was entitled to give notice after four years, so as to terminate the treaty.[93]

The trend of concluding bilateral treaties of this kind continued well into the post-World War I era. But in the 1920s and 1930s, States preferred to couch their obligations in terms of 'non-aggression pacts' (thereby clearly retaining the right to wage wars of self-defence). A good example is a 1926 treaty between Persia (present-day Iran) and Turkey, wherein the parties committed themselves 'not to engage in any aggression against the other' and 'not to participate in any hostile action whatsoever directed by one or more third Powers against the other Party'.[94]

Occasionally, a non-aggression pact had more than two Contracting Parties. The most important non-aggression instrument of the period was the 1925 Locarno Treaty of Mutual Guarantee, in which Germany and France, and also Germany and Belgium, were mutually bound not to 'resort to war against each other'.[95]

A different approach was reflected in a series of bilateral agreements, known as the Bryan treaties (after the American Secretary of State who originated them), concluded between the United States and dozens of other countries on the eve of World War I.[96] In these treaties, the Contracting Parties agreed to submit all disputes to investigation by an International Commission, and the Commission was instructed to complete its report within one year.[97] Pending the investigation and the ensuing report, the parties pledged 'not to declare war or begin hostilities'.[98]

The Bryan treaties did not negate the right of any State to start war eventually. What the treaties sought to accomplish was the introduction of a 'cooling-off period' of one year to enable passions to subside.[99] The underlying supposition was that delay as such (or the gaining of time) would be advantageous, since the parties were expected to become progressively more amenable to reason.[100] As a matter of fact, reliance on lapse of time as a factor allaying suspicions and fears is not empirically corroborated in all instances. Some international disputes are easier to

---

[92] Honduras–Nicaragua, Tegucigalpa Treaty of Friendship, Commerce and Extradition, 1878, 152 *CTS* 415, 416 (Article II).
[93] *Ibid.*, 423 (Article XXXV).
[94] Persia–Turkey, Teheran Treaty of Friendship and Security, 1926, 106 *LNTS* 261–3.
[95] Locarno Treaty of Mutual Guarantee, 1925, 54 *LNTS* 289, 293 (Article 2).
[96] See Anonymous, 'The Bryan Peace Treaties', 7 *AJIL* 823, 824–5 (1913).
[97] See, e.g., Guatemala–United States, Washington Treaty for the Establishment of a Permanent Commission of Enquiry, 1913, 218 *CTS* 373, 373–4.
[98] *Ibid.*, 373 (Article I).
[99] See A. Zimmern, *The League of Nations and the Rule of Law 1918–1935* 129 (1939).
[100] See J. F. Williams, *Some Aspects of the Covenant of the League of Nations* 136–8 (1934).

tackle, and to settle, at an earlier stage. Passage of time, far from cooling off hot tempers, may only exacerbate incipient tensions.

(b)   The Hague Conventions

The first steps, designed to curtail somewhat the freedom of war in general international law (through multilateral treaties), were taken in the two Hague Peace Conferences of 1899 and 1907. Under Article 2 of Hague Convention (I) of both 1899 and 1907 for the Pacific Settlement of International Disputes, Contracting Parties agreed that in case of a serious dispute, before making 'an appeal to arms', they would resort ('as far as circumstances allow') to good offices or mediation of friendly States.[101] The liberty to go to war was circumscribed here in an exceedingly cautious way, leaving to the discretion of the parties the determination whether to employ force or to search for amicable means of settling the dispute.

Article 1 of Hague Convention (II) of 1907 Respecting the Limitation of the Employment of Force for the Recovery of Contract Debts – often called the Porter Convention (after the American delegate who had proposed it) – obligated Contracting Parties 'not to have recourse to armed force' for the recovery of contract debts (claimed from one Government by another as being due to its nationals), unless the debtor State refused an offer of arbitration, prevented agreement on a *compromis* or rejected an arbitral award.[102] Hague Convention (II) echoed the Drago Doctrine (named after an Argentinian Foreign Minister), which had denied the justification of war as a mode of compelling payment of a public debt.[103] The scope of the limitation on the freedom of war, as formulated in the Convention, was quite narrow. First, war was still permissible if the debtor State refused to go through the process of arbitration or abide by its results. Secondly, the Convention did not apply to direct inter-Governmental loans and was confined to contractual debts to foreign nationals (whose claims were espoused by their respective Governments).[104] Still, it is arguable that, from this modest beginning, 'a shift in the notion of the *jus ad bellum*' started to take place.[105]

---

[101] Hague Convention (I) of 1899 and 1907 for the Pacific Settlement of International Disputes, *Hague Conventions* 41, 43.

[102] Hague Convention (II) of 1907 Respecting the Limitation of the Employment of Force for the Recovery of Contract Debts, *Hague Conventions* 89, id.

[103] See A. S. Hershey, 'The Calvo and Drago Doctrines', 1 *AJIL* 26, 28–30 (1907).

[104] See G. W. Scott, 'Hague Convention Restricting the Use of Force to Recover on Contract Claims', 2 *AJIL* 78, 90 (1908).

[105] C. R. Rossi, '*Jus ad Bellum* in the Shadow of the 20th Century', 15 *NYLSJICL* 49, 60 (1994–5).

(c)   The Covenant of the League of Nations

The Covenant of the League of Nations qualified the right to go to war in a more comprehensive way. In Article 10, Members of the League pledged 'to respect and preserve as against external aggression the territorial integrity and existing political independence of all Members of the League'.[106] This was an abstract provision, which lent itself to more than one interpretation. Hence, Article 10 had to be read in conjunction with, and subject to, the more specific stipulations following it.[107]

Article 11 enunciated that any war or threat of war was a matter of concern to the entire League.[108] Pursuant to Article 12, if any dispute likely to lead to rupture arose between Members of the League, they were required to submit it to arbitration, judicial settlement or inquiry by the League's Council.[109] Members were bound 'in no case to resort to war until three months after the award by the arbitrators or the judicial decision, or the report of the Council'. The award of the arbitrators or the judicial decision had to be rendered 'within reasonable time'. The Council's report had to be arrived at no later than six months after the submission of the dispute.

Article 13 specified which subject-matters were 'generally suitable' for submission to either arbitration or judicial settlement.[110] Members were obligated to carry out in good faith any arbitral award or judicial decision. They agreed that they 'will not resort to war' against another Member complying with the award or decision.

In accordance with Article 15, disputes between Members, when not submitted to arbitration or judicial settlement, had to be brought before the Council.[111] The Council's role was restricted to issuing recommendations, as distinct from binding decisions. However, under paragraph 6 of the Article, if the Council's report was carried unanimously (excluding the parties to the dispute), Members consented 'not to go to war with any party to the dispute which complies with the recommendations of the report'. If the Council failed to reach a unanimous report (apart from the parties to the dispute), paragraph 7 reserved the right of Members to take any action that they considered necessary for the maintenance of right and justice. Paragraph 8 precluded the Council from making any recommendation if it thought that the dispute had arisen out of a matter 'which

---

[106] Covenant of the League of Nations, 1919, 1 *Int.Leg.* 1, 7.
[107] See A. V. Levontin, *The Myth of International Security* 23 (1957).
[108] Covenant of the League of Nations, *supra* note 106, at 7.
[109] *Ibid.*, 7–8 (original version), 25 (amended text).
[110] *Ibid.*, 8 (original version), 26–7 (amended text).
[111] *Ibid.*, 9–10 (original version), 28–9 (amended text).

by international law is solely within the domestic jurisdiction of that party'. Article 15 also enabled referral of the dispute from the Council to the Assembly of the League, in which case it was the Assembly that was empowered to make recommendations. An Assembly report, if adopted by the votes of all the Members of the Council and a majority of the other Members (again not counting the parties to the dispute), had the same force as a unanimous report of the Council.

In all, the Covenant did not abolish the right of States to resort to war. Subject to specific prohibitions, detailed in the Articles cited, war remained lawful.[112] If looked at from a complementary angle of vision, one could easily discern a number of 'gaps' in the legal fence installed by the Covenant around the right of States to resort to war. The 'gaps' opened the legal road to war in the following circumstances:[113]

a. The most blatant case in which the liberty to plunge into war was kept intact resulted from Article 15(7). In the absence of unanimity in the Council or a proper majority in the Assembly, excluding the votes of parties to the dispute, the parties retained their freedom of action.

b. In light of Article 15(8), the Council (or the Assembly) was incompetent to reach a recommendation if in its judgment the matter came within the domestic jurisdiction of a party to the dispute. Since no recommendation would be adopted, the parties preserved their freedom of action. Thus, paradoxically, an international war could be triggered by a dispute that was ostensibly non-international in character.

c. It was implied in Article 12 that, if the Council (or the Assembly) did not arrive at a recommendation within six months – or, alternatively, if either an arbitral award or a judicial decision was not delivered within reasonable time – the parties would be free to take any action that they deemed fit.

d. Articles 13 and 15 forbade going to war against a State complying with an arbitral award, a judicial decision, a unanimous recommendation of the Council or an Assembly recommendation based on the required majority. In conformity with Article 12, no war could be undertaken within three months of the award, decision or recommendation. The upshot was that, after three months, war could be started against a State failing to comply with the award, decision or recommendation.

---

[112] See A. Möller, *International Law in Peace and War*, II, 88 (H. M. Pratt trans., 1935).
[113] See J. B. Whitton, 'La Neutralité et la Société des Nations', 17 *RCADI* 453, 479–90 (1927).

e. Naturally, all the limitations on the freedom of war applied to the relations between League Members *inter se*. The Covenant did not, and could not, curtail that freedom in the relations between non-Members and Members (and *a fortiori* between non-Members among themselves). Article 17 provided that, in the event of a dispute between a Member and a non-Member or between non-Members, the non-Member(s) should be invited to accept the obligations of membership for the purposes of the dispute, and then the stipulations of Articles 12 *et seq.* would apply.[114] It goes without saying that non-Members had an option to accede to such an invitation or to decline it.

Shortly after the entry into force of the Covenant, initiatives were taken to close these 'gaps'. The most famous attempt was made in the Geneva Protocol on the Pacific Settlement of International Disputes, which was adopted by the Assembly of the League in 1924, but never entered into force.[115] The capstone of the Protocol was Article 2, whereby the Contracting Parties agreed 'in no case to resort to war', except in resistance to aggression or with the consent of the League's Council or Assembly.[116] Article 2 was intended to abolish the general right to go to war.[117] Yet, since the Protocol remained abortive, war did not become illegal in principle until the Kellogg–Briand Pact of 1928.

---

[114] Covenant of the League of Nations, *supra* note 106, at 12.
[115] Geneva Protocol on the Pacific Settlement of International Disputes, 1924, 2 *Int.Leg.* 1378, 1379.
[116] *Ibid.*, 1381.   [117] See P. J. Noel Baker, *The Geneva Protocol* 29–30 (1925).

4   The contemporary prohibition
of the use of inter-State force

A.   The Kellogg–Briand Pact

1928 was a watershed date in the history of the legal regulation of the use
of inter-State force. That was when the General Treaty for Renunciation
of War as an Instrument of National Policy, known as the Kellogg–Briand
Pact (after the American Secretary of State and the French Foreign
Minister), was signed in Paris.[1] Before the outbreak of World War II,
the Pact had 63 Contracting Parties,[2] a record number for that period.

The Kellogg–Briand Pact comprised only three Articles, including one
of a technical nature. In Article 1, the Contracting Parties solemnly
declared that 'they condemn recourse to war for the solution of international controversies, and renounce it as an instrument of national
policy in their relations with one another'.[3] In Article 2, they agreed
that the settlement of all disputes with each other 'shall never be sought
except by pacific means'.[4]

With the Kellogg–Briand Pact, international law progressed from *jus ad
bellum* to *jus contra bellum*.[5] But although generally prohibited under the
Pact, war remained lawful in the following circumstances:

a. A war of self-defence. No provision pertaining to this vitally important
subject was incorporated in the text of the Pact. Nevertheless, formal
notes reserving the right of self-defence were exchanged between the
principal signatories prior to the conclusion of the Pact,[6] and there
never was any doubt that the renunciation of war had to be construed

---

[1] General Treaty for Renunciation of War as an Instrument of National Policy
(Kellogg–Briand Pact of Paris), 1928, 94 *LNTS* 57.
[2] A list of the 63 States that ratified or adhered to the Pact by the end of 1938 appears in 33
AJIL, Sp. Supp., 865 (1939).
[3] Kellogg–Briand Pact, *supra* note 1, at 63.   [4] *Ibid.*
[5] See M. Howard, '*Temperamenta Belli*: Can War Be Controlled?', *Restraints on War* 1, 11
(M. Howard ed., 1979).
[6] Identic Notes of the United States to other Governments in relation to the Pact are
reproduced in 22 *AJIL*, Supp., 109–13 (1928). Replies appear in 23 *ibid.*, Supp., 1–13
(1929).

accordingly. In any event, under the Preamble of the Pact, any Contracting Party 'which shall hereafter seek to promote its national interests by resort to war should be denied the benefits furnished by this Treaty'.[7] In other words, if Arcadia went to war against Utopia in violation of the Pact, Arcadia could no longer benefit from the renunciation of war. Consequently, Utopia was allowed to mount a war of self-defence against Arcadia. It appears from the way the Preamble was phrased that permission to embark upon hostilities, in response to the violation of the Pact by Arcadia, was granted not only to Utopia (the State under attack) but also to Ruritania (any other country). This is akin to the current concept of collective self-defence in response to an armed attack (see *infra*, Chapter 9, A).

Since the topic of self-defence was not expressly regulated in the Pact, its parameters were not set out. In addition, no competent body was established to determine whether a State employing force was acting in self-defence or in breach of the Pact.

b. War as an instrument of international policy. Inasmuch as Article 1 of the Pact forbade war only as an instrument of national policy, war remained lawful as an instrument of international policy. That made recourse to war legitimate, primarily, under the aegis of the League of Nations (see *infra*, Chapter 10, A, (b)). But the 'national policy' formula gave rise to the interpretation that other wars – in pursuit of religious, ideological and similar (not strictly national) goals – were also permitted.[8] J. H. W. Verzijl developed the thesis that a Contracting Party was entitled to resort to armed action if there was no other way to carry out an arbitral award or judicial decision, for that did not fall under the heading of war as an instrument of national policy.[9] H. Kelsen, in keeping with the perception of war as a sanction (see *supra*, Chapter 3, B, (a)), argued that 'a war which is a reaction against a violation of international law, and that means a war waged for the maintenance of international law, is considered an instrument of international and hence not of national policy'.[10] Yet, to the extent that war was undertaken in response to an ordinary violation of international law, the analysis could not be harmonized with the requirement in Article 2 of the Pact that the settlement of all disputes 'shall never be sought except by pacific means'.[11]

---

[7] Kellogg–Briand Pact, *supra* note 1, at 59–61.

[8] See H. Wehberg, *The Outlawry of War* 76 (1931).

[9] J. H. W. Verzijl, *International Law in Historical Perspective*, VIII, 109–10, 600 (1976).

[10] H. Kelsen, *Principles of International Law* 43 (1st ed., 1952).

[11] On the import of Article 2 in the interpretation of the Pact, see J. L. Brierly, 'Some Implications of the Pact of Paris', 10 *BYBIL* 208, *id.* (1929).

c. War outside the span of the reciprocal relations of the Contracting Parties. The renunciation of war in Article 1 was circumscribed to the relations between Contracting Parties *inter se*. Therefore, the freedom of war was preserved as between Contracting and non-Contracting Parties (and, obviously, among non-Contracting Parties).

Additionally, the limitation of the Pact to the renunciation of 'war' elicited much criticism in the international legal literature. Apart from the fact that the term 'war' seemed to some commentators to be ambiguous, the disturbing implication was that the use of force 'short of war' was left to the discretion of each State.[12]

In brief, the *jus ad bellum* engendered by the Kellogg–Briand Pact was flawed in four ways: (i) the issue of self-defence was not clearly addressed in the text; (ii) no agreed upon limits were set on the legality of war as an instrument of international policy; (iii) the abnegation of war did not embrace the entire international community; and (iv) forcible measures 'short of war' were eliminated from consideration.

B.   The Charter of the United Nations

(a)   *The prohibition of the use of inter-State force*

When the Charter of the United Nations was drafted in San Francisco, in 1945, one of its aims was redressing the shortcomings of the Kellogg–Briand Pact. The pivot on which the present-day *jus ad bellum* hinges is Article 2(4) of the Charter, which proclaims:

All Members shall refrain in their international relations from the threat or use of force against the territorial integrity or political independence of any state, or in any other manner inconsistent with the Purposes of the United Nations.[13]

Article 2(4) avoids the term 'war'. The use of force in international relations, proscribed in the Article, includes war. But the language transcends war and covers also forcible measures 'short of war'. On the other hand, the use or threat of force is abolished in Article 2(4) only in the 'international relations' of Member States. Intra-State clashes therefore are out of the reach of the Charter's provision.

The expression 'force' in Article 2(4) is not preceded by the adjective 'armed',[14] whereas the full phrase 'armed force' appears elsewhere in the

---

[12] See C. H. M. Waldock, 'The Regulation of the Use of Force by Individual States in International Law', 81 *RCADI* 455, 471–4 (1952).

[13] Charter of the United Nations, 1945, 9 *Int.Leg.* 327, 332.

[14] See M. Virally, 'Article 2 Paragraph 4', *La Charte des Nations Unies* 113, 120 (J.-P. Cot and A. Pellet eds., 1985).

Charter (in the Preamble as well as in Articles 41 and 46).[15] As a result, over the years, there have been many 'acrimonious' debates (for example, in the context of the codification of the law of treaties) about the scope of the 'force' to which Article 2(4) adverts, and, in particular, whether it extends to economic pressure.[16] However, when studied in context, the term 'force' in Article 2(4) must denote armed – or military – force.[17] Psychological or economic pressure (including economic boycott) as such does not come within the purview of the Article, unless coupled with the use or at least the threat of force.[18]

Article 2(4) goes beyond actual recourse to force, whether or not reaching the level of war, and interdicts mere threats of force. As expounded by the International Court of Justice in the 1996 Advisory Opinion on the *Legality of the Threat or Use of Nuclear Weapons*:

The notions of 'threat' and 'use' of force under Article 2, paragraph 4, of the Charter stand together in the sense that if the use of force itself in a given case is illegal – for whatever reason – the threat to use such force will likewise be illegal.[19]

In other words, for a threat of force to be illicit, the force itself must be unlawful. Hence, if a State declares its readiness to use force in conformity with the Charter, this is not an illegal 'threat' but a legitimate warning and reminder.[20] As well, a threat of force must not be confused with an ultimatum (see *supra* Chapter 2, A, (a)). Usually, a threat of force is viewed as 'a form of coercion'.[21] But Article 2(4) does not require that an illegal threat be accompanied with any concrete demands. A threat of force, not in compliance with the Charter, is unlawful as such.[22]

Two specific objectives, against which the use or threat of inter-State force is forbidden in Article 2(4), are the territorial integrity and the political independence of States. These dual idioms, when standing alone, may invite a rigid interpretation blunting the edge of Article 2(4). Thus, it has been suggested that the use of force within the boundaries of a foreign State does not constitute a violation of its territorial integrity,

---

[15] Charter of the United Nations, *supra* note 13, at 330, 343, 345.

[16] R. D. Kearney and R. E. Dalton, 'The Treaty on Treaties', 64 *AJIL* 495, 534–5 (1970).

[17] See A. Randelzhofer, 'Article 2(4)', *The Charter of the United Nations: A Commentary*, I, 112, 117–18 (B. Simma ed., 2nd ed., 2002).

[18] See H. Wehberg, 'L'Interdiction du Recours à la Force. Le Principe et les Problèmes qui se Posent', 78 *RCADI* 1, 69 (1951).

[19] Advisory Opinion on *Legality of the Threat or Use of Nuclear Weapons*, [1996] *ICJ Rep.* 226, 246.

[20] See *ibid.*   [21] R. Sadurska, 'Threats of Force', 82 *AJIL* 239, 241 (1988).

[22] See N. D. White and R. Cryer, 'Unilateral Enforcement of Resolution 687: A Threat Too Far?', 29 *CWILJ* 243, 253 (1998–9).

unless a portion of the State's territory is permanently lost.[23] While the argument is not particularly persuasive, it should spotlight the consequences likely to flow from a restrictive reading of Article 2(4). If the injunction against resort to force in international relations is confined to specific situations affecting only the territorial integrity and the political independence of States, a legion of loopholes will inevitably be left open.[24]

In emphasizing the reference to the territorial integrity and the political independence of States, the restrictive construction of Article 2(4) fails to give proper account to the conjunctive phrase 'or in any other manner inconsistent with the Purposes of the United Nations'. In the present writer's opinion, these words form the centre of gravity of Article 2(4), because they create 'a residual "catch-all" provision'.[25] Indeed, the *travaux préparatoires* of the Charter indicate that the expressions 'territorial integrity' and 'political independence' had not originally been included in the text and were added later for 'particular emphasis', there being no intention to restrict the all-embracing prohibition of force inconsistent with the Purposes of the United Nations.[26]

The first and foremost Purpose of the United Nations is enshrined in Article 1(1) of the Charter:

To maintain international peace and security, and to that end: to take effective collective measures for the prevention and removal of threats to the peace, and for the suppression of acts of aggression or other breaches of the peace.[27]

Already the first paragraph of the Preamble of the Charter expounds the *raison d'être* of the Organization in enunciating the determination 'to save succeeding generations from the scourge of war'[28] (interestingly, here the term 'war' is not dispensed with). Moreover, Article 2(3) prescribes:

All Members shall settle their international disputes by peaceful means in such a manner that international peace and security, and justice, are not endangered.[29]

Article 2(4) is 'inseparable' from Article 2(3), and these two consecutive paragraphs must be perused together.[30]

The correct interpretation of Article 2(4), given such stipulations as a background, is that any use of inter-State force by Member States for

---

[23] See A. D'Amato, *International Law: Process and Prospect* 58–9 (1987).
[24] See J. Stone, *Aggression and World Order: A Critique of United Nations Theories of Aggression* 43 (1958).
[25] *Cf.* M. Lachs, 'The Development and General Trends of International Law in Our Time', 169 *RCADI* 9, 162 (1980).
[26] See Randelzhofer, *supra* note 17, at 123.
[27] Charter of the United Nations, *supra* note 13, at 331.   [28] *Ibid.*, 330.   [29] *Ibid.*, 332.
[30] Virally, *supra* note 14, at 114.

whatever reason is banned, unless explicitly allowed by the Charter.[31] It is noteworthy that, in its 1986 Judgment in the *Nicaragua* case, the International Court of Justice pronounced that Article 2(4) articulates the 'principle of the prohibition of the use of force' in international relations.[32] The principle was presented by the Court in a non-restrictive fashion, and a careful dissection of the Judgment will disclose that this is no accident.

The sweeping exclusion of recourse to inter-State force, under Article 2(4), is subject to exceptions. But these are laid down in other provisions of the Charter. Not counting the licence to take action against the enemy States of World War II (Articles 53 and 107),[33] there are only two enduring settings in which the Charter permits the use of inter-State force: collective security (Articles 39 *et seq.*)[34] and self-defence (Article 51).[35] The exact range of application of these exceptional situations will be discussed in detail *infra*, Part III.

(b)   Attempts to limit the scope of the prohibition

Ever since the entry into force of the Charter, strenuous efforts have been made to portray special types of inter-State armed action, not amounting to either self-defence or collective security, as exempt from the general obligation established in Article 2(4).

One assertion along these lines is that, if a State does not comply with a judgment rendered by the International Court of Justice, the aggrieved party is entitled to seek execution through the use of force.[36] But the claim must be rejected.[37] The aggrieved party may only turn to the Security Council which, under Article 94(2) of the Charter, is empowered to recommend or decide what measures should be taken 'to give effect to the judgment'.[38] The Council can determine that non-compliance with the judgment forms a threat to the peace and, by dint of this decision, activate the collective security system[39] (see *infra*, Chapter 10,

---

[31] See J. Mrazek, 'Prohibition of the Use and Threat of Force: Self-Defence and Self-Help in International Law', 27 *CYIL* 81, 90 (1989).
[32] *Case Concerning Military and Paramilitary Activities in and against Nicaragua* (Merits), [1986] *ICJ Rep.* 14, 100.
[33] Charter of the United Nations, *supra* note 13, at 347–8, 362–3.
[34] *Ibid.*, 343 ff.   [35] *Ibid.*, 346.
[36] See C. Vulcan, 'L'Exécution des Décisions de la Cour Internationale de Justice d'après la Charte des Nations Unies', 51 *RGDIP* 187, 195 (1947).
[37] See O. Schachter, 'The Enforcement of International Judicial and Arbitral Decisions', 54 *AJIL* 1, 15–16 (1960).
[38] Charter of the United Nations, *supra* note 13, at 359.
[39] *Cf.* M.E. O'Connell, 'The Prospects for Enforcing Monetary Judgments of the International Court of Justice: A Study of Nicaragua's Judgment against the United States', 30 *VJIL* 891, 908–9 (1989–90).

A, (c)). In contradistinction to the Council, no State is authorized by the Charter to unilaterally undertake forcible measures in order to execute a judgment.

It is also propounded that resort to force by Carpathia would be concordant with Article 2(4), if the purpose of the military operation is the recovery of a territory allegedly belonging to that State and 'illegally occupied' by Numidia, because in such circumstances there is supposedly no infringement of Numidian territorial integrity (the Indian invasion of Goa in 1961 and the Argentine invasion of the Falkland Islands in 1982 are leading examples).[40] This position, too, cannot be sustained.[41] The argument was carried to an incongruous length when, in 1990, Iraq deigned to annex the entire territory of a sovereign neighbouring State (Kuwait) by reviving flimsy historical claims. The international community categorically rejected the transparent attempt by Iraq to circumvent Article 2(4). In Resolution 662, the Security Council decided that the 'annexation of Kuwait by Iraq under any form and whatever pretext has no legal validity, and is considered null and void'.[42]

Other attempts to slip through the tight net of Article 2(4) are reflected in constant endeavours to revive the just war doctrine in contemporary international law (see *supra*, Chapter 3, B, (b)–(c)). As long as European decolonization was at issue, the contention – largely characteristic of the former Soviet bloc and Third World countries – was that inter-State force is excluded from the ambit of Article 2(4) when marshalled on behalf of the just cause of self-determination[43] (see *infra*, Chapter 6, E). It was averred that military support lent by Pacifica to a 'war of national liberation', conducted against Apollonia by a people exercising the right of self-determination, does not contradict Article 2(4). Laborious explanations were offered, with a view to developing a legal rationale that would legitimize the use of force by Pacifica against Apollonia despite Article 2(4). Foremost among them was the proposition that, since at its inception a colonial regime had been installed by armed force, the continued denial of the right of self-determination amounts to 'permanent' aggression.[44] Yet, this impressionistic picture is 'surely a distortion'.[45] Unless the condition of self-defence or collective security is satisfied, there is no way to reconcile Article 2(4) with recourse to

[40] See O. Schachter, 'The Right of States to Use Armed Force', 82 *Mich.LR* 1620, 1627 (1984).
[41] See *ibid.*, 1627–8.   [42] Security Council Resolution 662, 45 *RDSC* 20, *id.* (1990).
[43] See J. Zourek, 'Enfin une Définition de l'Agression', 20 *AFDI* 9, 24 (1974).
[44] R. E. Gorelick, 'Wars of National Liberation: *Jus ad Bellum*', 11 *CWRJIL* 71, 77 (1979).
[45] L. Henkin, *How Nations Behave* 144 (2nd ed., 1979).

force by one State against another, even if the target is a colonial Power.[46] In the words of Judge Schwebel (in his Dissenting Opinion in the *Nicaragua* case):

> it is lawful for a foreign State ... to give to a people struggling for self-determination moral, political and humanitarian assistance; but it is not lawful for a foreign State ... to intervene in that struggle with force.[47]

We shall return to the question in the context of the definition of aggression (*infra*, Chapter 5, B).

By the same token, notwithstanding fervent pleadings to the contrary,[48] should Atlantica use force unilaterally in order to overthrow a despotic (even genocidal) regime in Patagonia, it would also run afoul of Article 2(4).[49] Claims for the legitimacy of forcible measures taken on behalf of the victims of violations of human rights are also premised on the underlying assumption that, because no change is sought in the territorial integrity of Patagonia and no challenge is posed to its political independence, a 'humanitarian intervention' by Atlantica does not come within the bounds of Article 2(4).[50] There is a cognate question, whether Atlantica may protect its own nationals against an attack upon them by Patagonia under the rubric of self-defence. That issue will be examined separately (*infra*, Chapter 8, A, (a), iii). However, the exponents of the putative right of 'humanitarian intervention' minimize the link of nationality and focus on the protection of individuals or minority groups from oppression by their own Government.[51] Most commentators who favour 'humanitarian intervention' studiously avoid the terminology of self-defence and insist that the forcible measures taken are legitimate, not by virtue of compatibility with Article 51 (the exception clause) but as a result of being compatible with Article 2(4) (the general rule).[52]

This is a misreading of the Charter. No individual State (or group of States) is authorized to act unilaterally, in the domain of human rights or

---

[46] See O. Schachter, 'Just War and Human Rights', 1 *PYIL* 1, 8 (1989).

[47] *Nicaragua* case, *supra* note 32, at 351.

[48] See W. M. Reisman, 'Coercion and Self-Determination: Construing Charter Article 2(4)', 78 *AJIL* 642–5 (1984).

[49] See O. Schachter, 'The Legality of Pro-Democratic Invasion', 78 *AJIL* 645–50 (1984).

[50] See J.-P. L. Fonteyne, 'The Customary International Law Doctrine of Humanitarian Intervention: Its Current Validity under the U.N. Charter', 4 *CWILJ* 203, 253–4 (1973–4).

[51] See R. B. Lillich, 'Forcible Self-Help by States to Protect Human Rights', 53 *Io.LR* 325, 332 (1967–8).

[52] See J. R. D'Angelo, 'Resort to Force by States to Protect Nationals: The U.S. Rescue Mission to Iran and Its Legality under International Law', 21 *VJIL* 485, 496 (1980–1).

in any other sphere, as if it were the policeman of the world.[53] Pursuant to the Charter, the Security Council – and the Security Council alone – is legally competent to undertake or to authorize forcible 'humanitarian intervention'.[54] The subject will be addressed again when the powers of the Council are examined (*infra*, Chapter 10, D, (c)).

C.   Customary international law

(a)   The general prohibition of the use of inter-State force

At the present time, membership in the United Nations spans almost the entire international community. Still, what about non-Member States? Article 2(4) forbids the use of force by UN Members against 'any state', viz. either a fellow Member or a non-Member. Recourse to force by a non-Member State (against either a Member or another non-Member State) is the fulcrum of Article 2(6):

The Organization shall ensure that states which are not Members of the United Nations act in accordance with these Principles so far as may be necessary for the maintenance of international peace and security.[55]

The Principles of the United Nations are enumerated in Article 2 in its entirety. Indisputably, the most pertinent Principle is the one embodied in Article 2(4).

Some scholars maintain that Article 2(6) is a 'revolutionary' stipulation, in that it indirectly imposes on non-Member States the legal regime of Article 2(4).[56] If Article 2(6) purported to do that, it would indeed be revolutionary. One of the basic tenets of international law is that no treaty can bind third States without their consent. Article 35 of the 1969 Vienna Convention on the Law of Treaties promulgates that an obligation may arise for a third State from a provision of a treaty only if the third State accepts the obligation expressly and in writing.[57] Article 35 'is so worded as to make it clear that the juridical basis of the obligation for the third

---

[53] It is submitted that this is not only the law as it is, but also the law as it should be. Consequently, proposals to amend the Charter, with a view to introducing 'humanitarian intervention' as an exception to the rule laid down in Article 2(4) (see M. J. Levitin, 'The Law of Force and the Force of Law: Grenada, the Falklands, and Humanitarian Intervention', 27 *HILJ* 621, 652–5 (1986)), are not only unrealistic; they are also undesirable.

[54] See B. Simma, 'NATO, the UN and the Use of Force: Legal Aspects', 10 *EJIL* 1, 5 (1999).

[55] Charter of the United Nations, *supra* note 13, at 332.

[56] H. Kelsen, *The Law of the United Nations* 106–7, 110 (1950).

[57] Vienna Convention on the Law of Treaties, 1969, [1969] *UNJY* 140, 150.

State is not the treaty itself but the collateral agreement whereby the third State has accepted the obligation'.[58]

It is not required to regard Article 2(6) as a deviation from the fundamental precept concerning treaty obligations and third States. As the text of Article 2(6) clearly indicates, the duty established therein devolves not on non-Member States but on the Organization itself.[59] What the Article says is that the Organization is obligated to take the necessary steps against non-Member States, if they undermine international peace and security. Palpably, when the Organization discharges its duty *vis-à-vis* a non-Member State, any steps taken must be in keeping with general customary international law.[60] But using force against an aggressor non-Member State is not at variance with that law.

Logically, there are two possibilities here. The first is that the liberty of States to go to war has survived intact in customary international law. If that were the case, freedom of action would be a double-edged argument. Should a non-Member State unleash war invoking such freedom, the UN Organization would be equally entitled to use counter-force in the name of the self-same privilege. If lack of restraint characterizes international relations, the Organization can use the argument of the sword no less than the aggressor non-Member State.

The second logical possibility is that the unbridled prerogative of States to indulge in war has been effaced from customary international law. In that case, a breach of the peace by the aggressor (be it a Member or a non-Member) is in contravention of the new norm. If so, the UN Organization may take counter-action against a flagrant violation of international law.

In reality, the rules of the game have changed radically in the post-Charter era. The licence to venture into war, and generally to employ inter-State force, is obsolete. Nowadays, the prohibition of the use of inter-State force, as articulated in Article 2(4) of the Charter, has become an integral part of customary international law. As such, it obligates all States, whether or not Members of the United Nations. The current state of customary international law in this field was authoritatively canvassed by the International Court of Justice in the *Nicaragua* case.[61]

Customary international law comes into being when there is 'evidence of a general practice accepted as law' (to repeat the well-known formula appearing in Article 38(1)(b) of the Statute of the International Court of

---

[58] I. Sinclair, *The Vienna Convention on the Law of Treaties* 101 (2nd ed., 1984).

[59] See R. L. Bindschedler, 'La Délimitation des Compétences des Nations Unies', 108 *RCADI* 307, 404–5 (1963).

[60] See G. G. Fitzmaurice, 'Fifth Report on Law of Treaties', [1960] II *ILC Ybk* 69, 88.

[61] *Nicaragua* case, *supra* note 32, at 99–101.

Justice).[62] Two elements are condensed here: the (objective) practice of States and (the subjective) *opinio juris sive necessitatis* (*i.e.* 'a belief that this practice is rendered obligatory by the existence of a rule of law requiring it').[63]

In the *Nicaragua* proceedings, both parties were in agreement that 'the principles as to the use of force incorporated in the United Nations Charter correspond, in essentials, to those found in customary international law'.[64] All the same, the Court deemed it necessary to confirm the existence of a general *opinio juris* about the binding character of the customary prohibition of inter-State force.[65]

In determining the tenor of customary international law, the Court relied *inter alia* on the Declaration on Principles of International Law Concerning Friendly Relations and Co-operation among States in accordance with the Charter of the United Nations, unanimously adopted in 1970 by the UN General Assembly.[66] The Declaration, in its first Principle, reiterates the wording of Article 2(4) of the Charter, except that the duty to refrain from the use of force is imposed on '[e]very State' instead of '[a]ll Members'.[67] This was done deliberately, on the ground that all States are now subject to the same rule.[68]

While the Court in the *Nicaragua* case stressed the *opinio juris* of States, it did not strive to investigate 'the ways in which governments actually behave' where the use of force is concerned.[69] The omission is not unrelated to the incontrovertible fact that recourse to force continues to permeate international relations. The incidence of inter-State force is so widespread that T. M. Franck argued in 1970 that its proscription is totally eroded in world affairs, and that Article 2(4) 'mocks us from its grave'.[70] In 2002, the same author (while challenging the strict application of the black-letter law of Article 2(4) which leaves no allowance for exceptional situations) seems to have shied away from such a harsh conclusion.[71] However, a year later he asserted that 'Article 2(4) has died again, and, this time, perhaps for good'.[72]

---

[62] Statute of the International Court of Justice, Annexed to the Charter of the United Nations, 1945, 9 *Int.Leg.* 510, 522.

[63] *North Sea Continental Shelf* cases, [1969] *ICJ Rep.* 3, 44.

[64] *Nicaragua* case, *supra* note 32, at 99.   [65] *Ibid.*, 99–100.

[66] General Assembly Resolution 2625 (XXV), 25 *RGA* 121 (1970).   [67] *Ibid.*, 122.

[68] See R. Rosenstock, 'The Declaration of Principles of International Law Concerning Friendly Relations: A Survey', 65 *AJIL* 713, 717 (1971).

[69] F. L. Kirgis, Jr., 'Custom on a Sliding Scale', 81 *AJIL* 146, 147 (1987).

[70] T. M. Franck, 'Who Killed Article 2(4)? Or: Changing Norms Governing the Use of Force by States', 64 *AJIL* 809, *id.*, 835 (1970).

[71] See T. M. Franck, *Recourse to Force: State Action against Threats and Armed Attacks* 174–91 (2002).

[72] T. M. Franck, 'What Happens Now? The United Nations after Iraq', 97 *AJIL* 607, 610 (2003).

Irrespective of these vacillations, an assault upon Article 2(4) – predicated on the record of (real or perceived) multiple violations of its strictures – hardly turns this key provision of the Charter into a dead letter. As pointed out by L. Henkin, in a response to Franck, the persistence of inter-State force need not suggest the disappearance of the legal norm expressed in Article 2(4).[73] The criminal codes of all States are constantly trampled underfoot by countless criminals, yet the unimpaired legal validity of these codes is universally conceded.

To be sure, if it could be proved that Article 2(4) is generally ignored by States, no rules of customary international law might conceivably be germinated by this (supposedly barren) clause. The question whether Article 2(4) is brazenly disregarded in international relations is, therefore, of immense import. Nevertheless, in providing an answer to the question, the uppermost consideration should be that – in spite of the frequent roar of guns – States involved in armed conflicts uniformly profess their fidelity to Article 2(4).[74]

When resorting to force, States ordinarily invoke the right of self-defence (see *infra*, Chapter 7, A, (a)). Sometimes, Governments misrepresent the law or apply incorrect legal terminology to label their action (see *infra*, Chapter 7, D, (c)). But the telling point is that Governments, however they understand or misunderstand the *jus ad bellum*, are not prepared – in this day and age – to endorse the proposition that there are no legal restraints whatever on the employment of inter-State force. 'No State has ever suggested that violations of article 2(4) have opened the door to free use of force.'[75] When Governments charge each other with infringements of Article 2(4), as happens all too frequently, such accusations are always contested. The plea that Article 2(4) is dead has never been put forward by any Government.

The Court in the *Nicaragua* case commented on the way that States behave and account for their behaviour:

It is not to be expected that in the practice of States the application of the rules in question should have been perfect, in the sense that States should have refrained, with complete consistency, from the use of force ... The Court does not consider that, for a rule to be established as customary, the corresponding practice must be in absolutely rigorous conformity with the rule. In order to deduce the existence of

---

[73] L. Henkin, 'The Reports of the Death of Article 2(4) Are Greatly Exaggerated', 65 *AJIL* 544, 547 (1971).

[74] For an expression of this fidelity, see the consensus Declaration on the Enhancement of the Effectiveness of the Principle of Refraining from the Threat or Use of Force in International Relations, General Assembly Resolution 42/22, 42(1) *RGA* 287, 288 (1987).

[75] O. Schachter, 'In Defense of International Rules on the Use of Force', 53 *UCLR* 113, 131 (1986).

customary rules, the Court deems it sufficient that the conduct of States should, in general, be consistent with such rules, and that instances of State conduct inconsistent with a given rule should generally have been treated as breaches of that rule, not as indications of the recognition of a new rule. If a State acts in a way prima facie incompatible with a recognized rule, but defends its conduct by appealing to exceptions or justifications contained within the rule itself, then whether or not the State's conduct is in fact justifiable on that basis, the significance of that attitude is to confirm rather than to weaken the rule.[76]

The discrepancy between what States say and what they do may be due to pragmatic reasons, militating in favour of a choice of the line of least exposure to censure.[77] Even so, a disinclination to challenge the validity of a legal norm has a salutary effect in that it shows that the norm is accepted, if only reluctantly, as the rule. There is a common denominator between those who try (even disingenuously) to take advantage of the refinements of the law, and those who rigorously abide by its letter and spirit. They all share a belief in the authority of the law.

(b)   The relationship between customary and treaty law

The injunction against the use of inter-State force is the cornerstone of present-day customary international law. When inspected through an analytical prism, the current prohibition of the use of inter-State force, under customary international law, is seen to be embedded in the Kellogg–Briand Pact and in the Charter of the United Nations. As Article 38 of the Vienna Convention on the Law of Treaties sets forth, treaty norms may become binding on third States as rules of customary international law.[78] Customary international law and treaty law are not kept apart in 'sealed compartments',[79] and there is a lot of cross-fertilization between them. In extreme cases, the general practice and *opinio juris* of States may virtually clone norms originally created by treaty.

When treaty law crystallizes as customary international law, the norm which has its genesis in a treaty is binding on a third State *post hoc* although not *propter hoc*.[80] Historically, the duties incurred by the third State 'owe their origin to the fact that the treaty supplied the basis for the growth of a customary rule of law'.[81] Yet, legally, these duties are

---

[76] *Nicaragua* case, *supra* note 32, at 98.
[77] See T. Meron, 'The Geneva Conventions as Customary Law', 81 *AJIL* 348, 369 (1987).
[78] Vienna Convention on the Law of Treaties, *supra* note 57, at 150.
[79] E. Jiménez de Aréchaga, 'International Law in the Past Third of a Century', 159 *RCADI* 1, 13 (1978).
[80] See J. L. Brierly, 'Règles Générales du Droit de la Paix', 58 *RCADI* 5, 223–4 (1936).
[81] R. F. Roxburgh, *International Conventions and Third States* 74 (1917).

assumed by third States *qua* customary law, and the treaty (which has a 'stimulating function' in the formative process of customary law) continues to be binding only on Contracting Parties.[82] From the standpoint of non-Contracting Parties, it is not the treaty that counts but the relevant customary law norm.[83]

In the *Nicaragua* proceedings, there was disagreement whether the customary and treaty (Charter) prohibitions of the use of inter-State force are identical, and whether the customary rule can still be operative in the relations between UN Member States.[84] The Court arrived at three conclusions:

i. The two sources of international law do not coincide exactly in regulating the use of force in international relations; there are variations between them on a number of points, especially insofar as the right of self-defence is concerned (see *infra*, Chapter 7, B).[85]

ii. Even if the customary and treaty norms did overlap in every respect, customary law would retain its separate identity – and continue to exist side by side with treaty law – so that it might be applied between the parties when, for some reason, an adjudication could not rest on the law of the Charter (as transpired in the case before the Court).[86]

iii. No conflicting standards of conduct have evolved in treaty (Charter) and customary law on the use of inter-State force.[87] Charter and customary norms in this area are not completely identical. But at bottom there is no marked divergence between them, for customary international law has solidified under the influence of the Charter.[88]

There is every reason to affirm the Court's finding that a great deal of similarity, if no identity, exists between contemporary customary and treaty (Charter) *jus ad bellum*. However, the Court did not examine in detail whether any difference of degree might exist between customary international law and Article 2(4) (as distinct from Article 51 relating to self-defence). It can be taken for granted that pre-Charter customary international law was swayed by the Charter and that, *grosso-modo*, customary and Charter *jus ad bellum* have converged. But did the process of change in customary international law come to a stop in the post-Charter era?

---

[82] M. E. Villiger, *Customary International Law and Treaties* 181–2, 186 (2nd ed., 1997).
[83] It is necessary, for that reason, to pay special attention to the particular practice and *opinio juris* of non-Contracting Parties. See M. H. Mendelson, 'The *Nicaragua Case* and Customary International Law', *The Non-Use of Force in International Law* 85, 95–6 (W. E. Butler ed., 1989).
[84] *Nicaragua* case, *supra* note 32, at 92–3, 96.   [85] *Ibid.*, 93–4.   [86] *Ibid.*, 94–6.
[87] *Ibid.*, 96–7.   [88] *Ibid.*

There is no ground to maintain that the congruence of Charter and customary international law in the prohibition of the use of inter-State force has disintegrated – or even diminished – since the *Nicaragua* Judgment has been delivered. But despite the fact that, at the present time, customary international law can be looked upon substantially as a replica of Article 2(4), it is hard to believe that the exact correlation of the two will 'freeze' indefinitely.[89] By its very nature, customary international law alters over the years, albeit incrementally. Will the general practice of States (accepted as law) remain steadfast in its faith in every aspect of Article 2(4)? As pointed out (*supra*, B, (b)), efforts are frequently made to limit the scope of the overall prohibition of the use of inter-State force. Such attempts cannot override the text of Article 2(4), but they may leave their imprint on customary international law. It seems logical to aver that an eventual dissonance between Article 2(4) and customary international law can be anticipated (subject to the problem of modifying *jus cogens*; see *infra*, E, (b)).

D.   Treaties other than the Pact and the Charter

The interdiction of the use of inter-State force has been reiterated in numerous international treaties subsequent to the Kellogg–Briand Pact and the Charter of the United Nations. Strictly speaking, there is no need to repeat the language of the Charter. Nonetheless, in some political settings, a reminder of the prohibition of recourse to force in international relations may serve a useful purpose.

Occasionally, this is done in general multilateral treaties governing a certain branch of international law. For instance, Article 301 of the 1982 United Nations Convention on the Law of the Sea stipulates that, '[i]n exercising their rights and performing their duties under this Convention, States Parties shall refrain from any threat or use of force against the territorial integrity or political independence of any State, or in any other manner inconsistent with the principles of international law embodied in the Charter of the United Nations'.[90] It is noteworthy that Article 301 largely reiterates the language of Article 2(4) of the Charter, except that – after the words 'or in any other manner inconsistent with' – it uses the phrase 'the principles of international law embodied in the Charter of the United Nations', in lieu of the original terminology ('the Purposes of the United Nations'). Apparently, the recast formulation is intended to highlight that 'Article 301 refers not only to Chapter I of the UN Charter

---

[89] See A. D'Amato, 'Trashing Customary International Law', 81 *AJIL* 101, 104 (1987).
[90] United Nations Convention on the Law of the Sea, 1982, Official Text, 104.

(Purposes and Principles) but to other parts too, such as Chapter VII, which includes Article 51 (right of self-defence)'.[91]

For the most part, clauses recapitulating the proscription of the use of force in international relations feature in treaties concluded either on a regional or on a bilateral basis. In the context of regional cooperation, examples may be drawn from the American continent. As early as 1933, in the Rio de Janeiro Anti-War Treaty (Non-Aggression and Conciliation) – commonly designated, after an Argentine Foreign Minister, the Saavedra Lamas Treaty – the American States, joined by several European countries, condemned wars of aggression and undertook to settle all disputes through pacific means.[92] The 1947 Rio de Janeiro Inter-American Treaty of Reciprocal Assistance also includes a formal condemnation of war, bolstered by a general undertaking not to resort to force in any manner inconsistent with the UN Charter.[93]

The American continent is not the only part of the world where recurrent commitments are made to refrain from the use of inter-State force. The language of Article 2(4) of the Charter is reproduced in the 1975 Helsinki Final Act, adopted by the Conference on Security and Co-operation in Europe.[94] Although the Helsinki Final Act does not form a treaty, the International Court of Justice cited it in the *Nicaragua* case as evidence for the emergence of customary international law banning the use of inter-State force.[95] Upon the demise of the 'Cold War', in the 1990 Charter of Paris for a New Europe, the States participating in the Helsinki process renewed their pledge to refrain from the threat or use of force.[96]

In the bilateral relations between States, quite a few non-aggression pacts were made after the Kellogg–Briand Pact, with a view to 'confirming and completing' it.[97] This is no longer common practice today. Yet, some bilateral or trilateral treaties of political and military cooperation restate the duty not to employ force in any way contrary to the UN

---

[91] R. Wolfrum, 'Military Activities on the High Seas: What Are the Impacts of the U.N. Convention on the Law of the Sea?', 71 *ILS* 501, 505 (M. N. Schmitt and L. C. Green eds., 1998).

[92] Rio de Janeiro Anti-War Treaty (Non-Aggression and Conciliation), 1933, 163 *LNTS* 393, 405 (Article 1).

[93] Rio de Janeiro Inter-American Treaty of Reciprocal Assistance, 1947, 21 *UNTS* 77, 95 (Article 1).

[94] Conference on Security and Co-operation in Europe, Helsinki Final Act, 1975, 14 *ILM* 1292, 1294 (1975).

[95] *Nicaragua* case, *supra* note 32, at 100. See also *ibid.*, 133.

[96] Conference on Security and Co-operation in Europe, Charter of Paris for a New Europe, 1990, 30 *ILM* 190, 196 (1991).

[97] See, e.g., Finland–USSR, Helsinki Treaty of Non-Aggression and Pacific Settlement of Disputes, 1932, 157 *LNTS* 393, 395 (Preamble).

Charter.[98] The impulse to reaffirm the prohibition of the use or threat of force is strongest among countries ascending from war with each other. That explains the texts of the 1966 Indian–Pakistani Tashkent Declaration,[99] the 1988 Afghan–Pakistani Agreement,[100] the two Israeli Treaties of Peace – the one with Egypt (1979),[101] and the other with Jordan (1994)[102] – as well as the Ethiopian–Eritrean Peace Agreement of 2000.[103]

E. The prohibition of the use of inter-State force as *jus cogens*

(a) *The significance of* jus cogens

Article 53 of the 1969 Vienna Convention on the Law of Treaties,[104] as its title indicates, addresses the subject of *jus cogens*. Under the Article, '[a] treaty is void if, at the time of its conclusion, it conflicts with a peremptory norm of general international law'. For a norm to qualify as peremptory, it has to be one 'accepted and recognized by the international community of States as a whole as a norm from which no derogation is permitted and which can be modified only by a subsequent norm of general international law having the same character.'

Article 53 applies to those cases in which a treaty is invalidated upon conclusion owing to a clash with a pre-existing peremptory norm. A complementary provision appears in Article 64 of the Vienna Convention, whereby '[i]f a new peremptory norm of general international law emerges, any existing treaty which is in conflict with that norm becomes void and terminates'.[105] What it comes down to is that a treaty, although valid at the time of its conclusion, may be invalidated thereafter, as a result of the evolution of a conflicting *jus cogens* in the meantime.[106]

Articles 53 and 64 do not specify when a norm of general international law is to be considered peremptory in nature. But the International Law

---

[98] See, e.g., Greece–Turkey–Yugoslavia, Bled Treaty of Alliance, Political Co-operation and Mutual Assistance, 1954, 211 *UNTS* 237, 241 (Article I).

[99] India–Pakistan, Tashkent Declaration, 1966, 5 *ILM* 320, id. (1966).

[100] Afghanistan–Pakistan, Agreement on the Principles of Mutual Relations, in Particular on Non-Interference and Non-Intervention, 1988, 27 *ILM* 581, 582 (1988) (Article II (3)).

[101] Egypt–Israel, Treaty of Peace, 1979, 18 *ILM* 362, 363–4 (1979) (Article III).

[102] Jordan–Israel, Treaty of Peace, 1994, 34 *ILM* 43, 46 (1995) (Article 2).

[103] Ethiopia–Eritrea, Peace Agreement, 2000, 40 *ILM* 260, id. (2001) (Article 1).

[104] Vienna Convention on the Law of Treaties, *supra* note 57, at 154.   [105] *Ibid.*, 157.

[106] See Draft Articles on the Law of Treaties, Report of the International Law Commission, 18th Session, [1966] II *ILC Ybk* 172, 173, 248–9, 261.

Commission, in its commentary on the draft of the Vienna Convention, identified the Charter's prohibition of the use of inter-State force as 'a conspicuous example' of *jus cogens*.[107] The Commission's position was quoted by the International Court in the 1986 *Nicaragua* case.[108] In his Separate Opinion, President Singh underscored that 'the principle of non-use of force belongs to the realm of *jus cogens*'.[109] Judge Sette-Camara, in another Separate Opinion, also expressed the firm view that the non-use of force can be recognized as a peremptory rule.[110] In 2001, when concluding its work on State Responsibility, the International Law Commission pronounced that 'it is generally agreed that the prohibition of aggression is to be regarded as peremptory'.[111]

What is it that marks out peremptory norms (constituting *jus cogens*), as compared to ordinary norms of general international law (amounting to mere *jus dispositivum*)? The special standing of *jus cogens* is manifested less in enjoining States from contrary behaviour (violations), and more in aborting attempted derogations from the general norms.[112] Violations of all laws, however characterized (be they *jus cogens* or *jus dispositivum*), are forbidden. If Arcadia and Numidia were to conclude today a pact of aggression against Utopia, the action envisaged would plainly be in breach of general (Charter as well as customary) international law. For a breach of the Charter to be perpetrated, it is immaterial whether Member States act jointly or severally. Neither Arcadia nor Numidia, when acting on its own, is permitted to wage an aggressive war against Utopia. What each is disallowed to do separately, the two of them are forbidden to do together.

When an international legal norm is classified as *jus cogens*, what is meant is not just that a particular pattern of State conduct is interdicted. The peremptory nature of the injunction signifies that the contractual freedom of States is curtailed. Two major conclusions ensue:

i. A pact of aggression concluded between Arcadia and Numidia against Utopia will not only be stigmatized as a violation of the Charter, as well as general customary international law, but it will also be void *ab initio*[113] (on the meaning of the term 'void' under the Vienna Convention, see *supra*, Chapter 2, B, (a), iii). It must be appreciated that the rule does not apply to all treaties projecting recourse to inter-State force. There is an intrinsic difference between a pact aimed at an

[107] *Ibid.*, 247.   [108] *Nicaragua* case, *supra* note 32, at 100.
[109] *Ibid.*, 153.   [110] See *ibid.*, 199.
[111] Draft Articles on Responsibility of States for Internationally Wrongful Acts, Report of the International Law Commission, 53rd session, 43, 283 (mimeographed, 2001).
[112] See J. Sztucki, *Jus Cogens and the Vienna Convention on the Law of Treaties* 67–8 (1974).
[113] See G. G. Fitzmaurice, 'Third Report on Law of Treaties', [1958] II *ILC Ybk* 20, 40.

unlawful use of force (aggression) and a treaty for the organization of legitimate measures of counter-force (collective self-defence) in the event of an armed attack[114] (see *infra*, Chapter 9, B). Only the former instrument, and not the latter, will be annulled. Should a dispute arise whether a specific treaty is invalid on the ground of conflict with *jus cogens*, the International Court of Justice would be vested with compulsory jurisdiction in the matter under Article 66(a) of the Vienna Convention.[115]

A pact of aggression ought not to be confused with a treaty, concluded between Arcadia and Numidia, colliding with ordinary rights of Utopia (*i.e.* rights derived from *jus dispositivum*). The validity of an ordinary treaty between Arcadia and Numidia is not affected by the infringement of Utopia's rights. Arcadia and Numidia will bear international responsibility towards Utopia, but their treaty remains in force.[116] By contrast, a pact of aggression, being in conflict with *jus cogens*, would be invalid. It is perhaps easier to understand the need for the distinction between these two categories of instruments when it is perceived that a pact of aggression is an agreement to commit a crime[117] (see *infra*, Chapter 5, A). Even without waiting for the actual consummation of the crime, the preparatory act contemplating it – namely, the treaty – is invalidated as a conspiracy to commit a crime.[118]

ii. Arcadia and Numidia are not allowed to conclude a treaty derogating from *jus cogens*, even in their mutual relations *inter se*. Thus, they cannot enter into a valid agreement in which they absolve each other from the prohibition of the use of inter-State force and decide to settle a dispute by war, nor will such an agreement be saved by an express pledge to safeguard the rights of non-Contracting Parties.[119] All States have an interest, currently protected by international law, that no war will break out anywhere (be it in the most distant part of the globe), lest the conflagration spread to other countries far and near. A treaty initiating war by consent is abrogated, although its impact is allegedly limited to the relations *inter partes*, because of its potential deleterious effects on the international community. There is no contracting out from *jus cogens* obligations.

[114] See Sinclair, *supra* note 58, at 216.
[115] Vienna Convention on the Law of Treaties, *supra* note 57, at 157.
[116] See Draft Articles on the Law of Treaties, *supra* note 106, at 217.
[117] See G. Gaja, '*Jus Cogens* beyond the Vienna Convention', 172 *RCADI* 271, 301 (1981).
[118] See Jiménez de Aréchaga, *supra* note 79, at 65.
[119] *Cf.* Fitzmaurice, *supra* note 113, at 40.

It has been argued that 'if two States enter into a treaty sanctioning the use of force by one of them against the other, use of force is a misnomer and the treaty is not contrary to Article 2(4)'.[120] However, this is a misrepresentation of the current *jus ad bellum*. Utopia can validly express its consent to the use of force by Arcadia against non-State actors operating within Utopian territory (see *infra*, G). Conversely, Utopia has no legal competence to sanitize the illegality of the use of force by Arcadia either against itself or against any other State.

(b)   *How can* jus cogens *be modified?*

As the International Law Commission observed, 'it would clearly be wrong to regard even rules of *jus cogens* as immutable and incapable of modification in the light of future developments'.[121] But any modification of a peremptory norm must be brought about (through general custom or treaty) in the same way that the original norm was established. Whereas two States cannot validly agree to release themselves from the prohibition of recourse to force in international relations, the international community as a whole is in a more advantageous position. Having constructed the peremptory norm, the international community may amend it (by narrowing or broadening its scope), supersede it with another rule or even rescind it altogether.

A modification of an existing peremptory norm through the emergence of a conflicting general custom may prove hard to accomplish, since custom usually consists of a series of unilateral acts which in the setting of an incompatible *jus cogens* could be judged as lacking any legal effect.[122] Arguably, a declaratory resolution, adopted by consensus by the United Nations General Assembly, may be of help.[123] But can such a resolution, not supported by valid State practice, create so-called 'instant custom' (an immensely controversial concept at the best of times)[124] powerful enough to intrude upon and reshape *jus cogens*? The idea is flatly repudiated by several scholars.[125]

---

[120] O. Spiermann, 'Humanitarian Intervention as a Necessity and the Threat or Use of *Jus Cogens*', 71 *NJIL* 523, 535 (2002).
[121] Draft Articles on the Law of Treaties, *supra* note 106, at 248.
[122] On this problem, see C. L. Rozakis, *The Concept of Jus Cogens in the Law of Treaties* 89–90 (1976).
[123] See L. Hannikainen, *Peremptory Norms (Jus Cogens) in International Law: Historical Development, Criteria, Present Status* 266 (1988).
[124] Consensus resolutions of the General Assembly can provide important evidence as regards the emergence of a new customary rule. See Advisory Opinion on *Nuclear Weapons*, *supra* note 19, at 254–5.
[125] See, e.g., G. M. Danilenko, *Law-Making in the International Community* 252 (1993).

The modification of *jus cogens* should be easier to attain through a general (multilateral) treaty terminating or amending prior obligations. However, the process of concluding a general treaty, intended to modify a pre-existing *jus cogens*, is not free of difficulties. Sir Ian Sinclair regards the process as 'enigmatic', because the modifying treaty 'would, *at the time of its conclusion*, be in conflict with the very rule of *jus cogens* which it purports to modify'.[126] The present writer is inclined to think that the enigma is more apparent than real, provided that, 'at the time of its conclusion', the modifying treaty has gained the backing of the international community as a whole. General support for the treaty would demonstrate that (in the words of Article 53 of the Vienna Convention) it constitutes 'a subsequent norm of general international law having the same character' as the original *jus cogens*.

What is the proper manner of manifesting general support by the international community for a treaty modifying *jus cogens*? T. Meron seems to adhere to the view that the mere formulation of the modifying treaty by a large majority of States indicates the emergence of a new *jus cogens*, 'even before the entry into force' of that treaty.[127] This probably goes too far. The required support for the novel peremptory norm is expressed only by the consent of States to be bound by the modifying treaty. Hence, the entry into force of the modifying treaty has to be conditioned on ratification or accession by the bulk of the international community. If the modifying treaty – negotiated, and perhaps signed, by almost all States – stipulates that it will enter into force following the deposit of a relatively small number of ratifications or accessions, the treaty is likely to be considered void, at the point of ostensible entry into force, due to an unequal clash with the very *jus cogens* which it tries to revise. But if the modifying treaty obtains an impressive number of ratifications and accessions prior to entry into force, it manages to overcome the hurdle of the pre-existing *jus cogens* and gain validity. In becoming a valid and binding instrument, it alters the obsolete peremptory norm.

The problem of modifying *jus cogens* is further complicated by the interaction of customary and treaty law. This is epitomized by a hypothetical amendment of the UN Charter. Such an amendment is permissible when a certain procedure, prescribed in Article 108,[128] is complied with. The amending power covers every single clause in the Charter, bar none. At some indefinite time in the future, Member States may theoretically avail themselves of the existing mechanism to amend even Article 2(4).

[126] Sinclair, *supra* note 58, at 226.
[127] T. Meron, *Human Rights Law-Making in the United Nations* 184 n.150 (1986).
[128] Charter of the United Nations, *supra* note 13, at 363.

Yet, it must not be forgotten that the current prohibition of the use of inter-State force derives its peremptory nature not only from Article 2(4), but also from an independently valid general customary law. The quandary is whether an amendment of Article 2(4), unaccompanied by a corresponding change in the general practice of States, may be considered a sufficient lever for modifying the existing customary *jus cogens*.

F.   State responsibility

(a)   *Application of general rules of State responsibility*

As the International Law Commission phrased it, in 2001, in Article 1 of the finalized Draft Articles on Responsibility of States for Internationally Wrongful Acts:

> Every internationally wrongful act of a State entails the international responsibility of that State.[129]

In conformity with this general rule, recourse to inter-State force – in breach of the United Nations Charter and customary international law – gives rise to State responsibility. As will be shown (*infra*, Chapter 5, C), the planning or waging of a war of aggression may also lead to the imposition of penal sanctions on certain individuals who acted as organs of the aggressor State. But individual liability (for war of aggression) and State responsibility (whether for war of aggression or for any other unlawful use of inter-State force) exist cumulatively rather than alternatively: one does not detract from the other.

What is the essence of State responsibility? The International Law Commission stated, in Article 31(1), that '[t]he responsible State is under an obligation to make full reparation for the injury caused by the internationally wrongful act'.[130] This is based on the holding of the Permanent Court of International Justice, in the *Chorzów Factory* case of 1928, that 'it is a principle of international law, and even a general conception of law, that any breach of an engagement involves an obligation to make reparation'.[131] The Court went on to say that 'reparation must, as far as possible, wipe out all the consequences of the illegal act and reestablish the situation which would, in all probability, have existed if that act had not been committed'.[132] The aspiration to bring about a *restitutio in integrum*

---

[129] Draft Articles on State Responsibility, *supra* note 111, at 43.   [130] *Ibid.*, 51
[131] *Case Concerning the Factory at Chorzów* (Claim for Indemnity) (Merits) (A/17, 1928), 1 *WCR* 646, 664.
[132] *Ibid.*, 677–8.

may be frustrated by the fact that restoring the *status quo ante* is not feasible in realistic terms.[133] If restitution in kind is ruled out, the duty to make reparation becomes a duty to pay financial compensation for the damage caused.[134] When the injury sustained cannot be made good by either restitution or compensation, reparation may take the shape of 'satisfaction'.[135] Satisfaction denotes 'an acknowledgement of the breach, an expression of regret, a formal apology or another appropriate modality'.[136]

Satisfaction (which is a remedy for injuries 'not financially assessable')[137] will usually not suffice in circumstances of State responsibility arising for an unlawful use of inter-State force (particularly for waging war of aggression). Restitution in kind is possible when property which has been taken away by the aggressor State is traceable[138] (a prospect of the utmost importance in connection with spoliation of treasures of art). Yet, on the whole, since war causes death and irreversible destruction on a vast scale, restitution in kind cannot be considered a pragmatic remedy. Payment of compensation must be looked upon as the most effective mode of reparation. In principle, the compensation should relate to all losses and injuries suffered by the victim States and their nationals as a result of the unlawful use of force.[139]

The parties to a conflict may conclude a special agreement turning over the appraisal of compensation to judges, arbitrators or assessors. But the International Court of Justice may acquire jurisdiction in the matter even without a special agreement. In the *Nicaragua* case of 1986, having rejected an American challenge to its jurisdiction and having determined that the United States employed unlawful force against Nicaragua (thus incurring an obligation to make reparation for all injuries caused), the Court decided to settle the form and amount of such reparation at a later stage.[140] Eventually, in 1991, Nicaragua renounced its right of action and the Court recorded the discontinuance of the proceedings.[141]

The obligation of an aggressor State to indemnify the victim of aggression (for the violation of the *jus ad bellum*) must not be confused with the independent liability of a belligerent party to pay compensation for a

---

[133] See Draft Articles on State Responsibility, *supra* note 111, at 52 (Article 35).

[134] *Ibid.* (Article 36). *Cf. Factory at Chorzów* case, *supra* note 131, at 678.

[135] Draft Articles on State Responsibility, *supra* note 111, at 52 (Article 37(1)).

[136] *Ibid.* (Article 37(2)).   [137] *Ibid.*, 264.

[138] See, e.g., Article 238 of the Versailles Treaty of Peace with Germany, 1919, *Peace Treaties*, II, 1265, 1394; Article 75 of the Paris Treaty of Peace with Italy, 1947, 49 *UNTS* 3, 157–8.

[139] See Q. Wright, 'The Outlawry of War and the Law of War', 47 *AJIL* 365, 372 (1953).

[140] *Nicaragua* case, *supra* note 32, at 142–3, 146–9.

[141] *Case Concerning Military and Paramilitary Activities in and against Nicaragua* (Order), [1991] *ICJ Rep.* 47, 48.

breach of the laws of warfare (the *jus in bello*). The latter duty is spelt out in Article 3 of Hague Convention (IV) of 1907 Respecting the Laws and Customs of War on Land,[142] and in Article 91 of Protocol I of 1977 (Additional to the Geneva Conventions of 1949).[143] There is no guarantee that, if infractions of the *jus in bello* are committed, the armed forces of the aggressor will turn out to be the culpable party. It is entirely plausible that the victim of aggression will be responsible for some, if not all, such contraventions. Should this come to pass, a set-off (reducing the amount of compensation which the aggressor ought to pay to its victim) might be called for.

The pecuniary losses borne by a victim of aggression may also be fixed, in the form of a lump sum, in a peace treaty. Once such a procedure is followed, much depends on policy considerations. The lump sum may reflect the principle that 'the burdens of war are to be placed on the belligerents who spawn them', but it may also mirror the opposing goal of post-war reconstruction and reconciliation.[144] Another factor, not to be overlooked, is that a State emerging from a debilitating war will scarcely be in condition to carry a heavy financial load. An extended war is so devastating that any fair evaluation of the damages to be paid may end up with staggering amounts, in excess of the economic capacity of the State to which responsibility is attributed. This is especially true if remote (or indirect) losses, causally linked to the war, are to be taken into account.[145] Excessive war reparations are liable to famish a country in a manner that may be regarded as incompatible with the basic human rights of its civilian population.[146]

The issue of excessive war reparations always brings to mind the case of Germany in the wake of World War I. In Article 231 of the 1919

---

[142] Hague Convention (IV) Respecting the Laws and Customs of War on Land, 1907, *Hague Conventions* 100, 103.

[143] Protocol Additional to the Geneva Conventions of 12 August 1949, and Relating to the Protection of Victims of International Armed Conflicts (Protocol I), 1977, [1977] *UNJY* 95, 132.

[144] R. B. Lillich and B. H. Weston, *International Claims: Their Settlement by Lump Sum Agreements*, I, 167 (1975).

[145] The Mixed Claims Commission, United States-Germany, held (per E. B. Parker, Umpire): 'It matters not whether the loss be directly or indirectly sustained as long as there is a clear, unbroken connection between Germany's act and the loss complained of. It matters not how many links there may be in the chain of causation connecting Germany's act with the loss sustained, provided there is no break in the chain and the loss can be clearly, unmistakably, and definitely traced, link by link, to Germany's act.' *Administrative Decision No. II* (1923), 7 *RIAA* 23, 29–30. *Cf.* G. Cottereau, 'De la Responsabilité de l'Iraq selon la Résolution 687 du Conseil de Sécurité', 37 *AFDI* 99, 113–14 (1991).

[146] See F. Domb, 'Human Rights and War Reparation', 23 *IYHR* 77, 94–5 (1993).

Peace Treaty of Versailles, Germany accepted responsibility (shared with its allies)[147] 'for causing all the loss and damage to which the Allied and Associated Governments and their nationals have been subjected as a consequence of the war imposed upon them by the aggression of Germany and her allies'.[148] Article 232 recognized that the resources of Germany were not sufficient to make complete reparation for all such loss and damage, and the compensation was limited to damage done to the civilian population of the Allied and Associated Powers and their property.[149] To determine the amount, an Inter-Allied Reparation Commission was set up in Article 233.[150] German resentment of these clauses soured international relations in the post-War era. Ultimately, the actual indemnities remitted fell far short of the levels of expectations of the architects of the Treaty of Versailles, and, according to some calculations, Germany may have paid no net reparations at all.[151] In retrospect, J. M. Keynes, the prominent economist, proved right in his admonition that a 'Carthagenian peace is not *practically* right or possible'.[152]

After the outbreak of the Gulf War, the Security Council – in Resolution 674 (1990) – reminded Iraq that 'under international law it is liable for any loss, damage or injury arising in regard to Kuwait and third States, and their nationals and corporations, as a result of the invasion and illegal occupation of Kuwait by Iraq'.[153] The Council further invited States 'to collect relevant information regarding their claims, and those of their nationals and corporations, for restitution or financial compensation by Iraq'.[154] In Resolution 687 (1991), laying down the terms of the cease-fire, the Council reiterated Iraq's liability under international law and decided that a fund to pay compensation for the ensuing claims would be created.[155] The Compensation Fund and a Compensation Commission were established in Resolution 692.[156]

Millions of claims by and on behalf of individuals, as well as several governmental claims, have been filed with the Compensation Commission. By July 2002, the Commission has awarded more than 42 billion

---

[147] Parallel provisions appeared in St. Germain Treaty of Peace with Austria, 1919, *Peace Treaties*, III, 1535, 1598 ff. (Articles 177 *et seq.*); Neuilly Treaty of Peace with Bulgaria, 1919, *ibid.*, 1727, 1769 ff. (Articles 121 *et seq.*); Trianon Treaty of Peace with Hungary, 1920, *ibid.*, 1863, 1923 ff. (Articles 161 *et seq.*).
[148] Versailles Treaty of Peace, *supra* note 138, at 1391.   [149] *Ibid.*   [150] *Ibid.*, 1392.
[151] See D. Thomson, *Europe since Napoleon* 566–8 (2nd ed., 1962).
[152] J. M. Keynes, *The Economic Consequences of the Peace* 23 (2 *Collected Writings of J. M. Keynes*, 1971).
[153] Security Council Resolution 674, 45 *RDSC* 25, 26 (1990).   [154] *Ibid.*
[155] Security Council Resolution 687, 46 *RDSC* 11, 14 (1991).
[156] Security Council Resolution 692, 46 *RDSC* 18, *id.* (1991).

dollars, of which approximately 15 billion dollars have been made available to claimants.[157] These astounding figures 'dwarf all previous efforts in the area of international claims resolution'.[158]

(b)   State responsibility for international crimes

The general rules of State responsibility are not attuned to the tremendous implications of an aggressive war as a violation of *jus cogens* and an international crime. The conundrum of the criminal responsibility of States is not easy to resolve. In 1996, when the International Law Commission adopted the Draft Code of Crimes against the Peace and Security of Mankind, it explicitly referred (in Article 16) to the fact that a crime of aggression must be 'committed by a State'.[159] Yet, the Draft Code is confined to individual criminal responsibility,[160] and the Commission clarified (in Article 4) that this is 'without prejudice to any question of the responsibility of States under international law'.[161] It has been suggested that the Commission 'tergiversates' when it requires a determination that a crime of aggression is committed by a State but separates the issue from any connection with State responsibility.[162]

In its separate and independent study of State Responsibility (which went on for decades), the International Law Commission – on the initiative of its Special Rapporteur, R. Ago[163] – was for many years inclined to address the specific legal consequences of international crimes[164] (although the practical connotations spelt out in the Draft Articles were not dramatic).[165] The Commission's approach to the subject of international crimes underwent a radical change when the Draft Articles were brought to their conclusion (under the guidance of a new Special Rapporteur, J. Crawford). In its final text, the Commission dropped

---

[157] See V. Heiskanen, 'The United Nations Compensation Commission', 296 *RCADI* 255, 386 (2002).

[158] D. D. Caron, 'Introductory Note', 35 *ILM* 939, *id.* (1996).

[159] Draft Code of Crimes against the Peace and Security of Mankind, Report of the International Law Commission, 48th Session, [1996] II (2) *ILC Ybk* 17, 42–3.

[160] *Ibid.*, 18 (Article 2).   [161] *Ibid.*, 23.

[162] J. Allain and J. R. W. D. Jones, 'A Patchwork of Norms: A Commentary on the 1996 Draft Code of Crimes against the Peace and Security of Mankind', 8 *EJIL* 100, 108 (1997).

[163] See R. Ago, 'Fifth Report on State Responsibility', [1976] II (1) *ILC Ybk* 3, 32–5.

[164] For the latest text, see Chapter IV (Articles 51–3) of the tentative Draft Articles on State Responsibility, 37 *ILM* 440, 458–9 (1998).

[165] On the effect of the text, see D. W. Bowett, 'Crimes of State and the 1996 Report of the International Law Commission on State Responsibility', 9 *EJIL* 163, 172 (1998); C. Tomuschat, 'International Crimes by States: An Endangered Species', *International Law: Theory and Practice (Essays in Honour of Eric Suy)* 253, 256–8 (K. Wellens ed., 1998).

altogether the reference to international crimes,[166] replacing it (in Articles 40–1) with rather anodyne provisions dealing with serious breaches of obligations under peremptory norms of general international law[167] (see *infra*, i).

Nonetheless, three observations are apposite:

   i. Ordinarily, when Patagonia (through an act of commission or omission) is in breach of an international obligation, there is a particular State (Atlantica) or group of States (Atlantica, Numidia *et al.*) vested with the right correlative to that obligation. Hence, only Atlantica, Numidia etc. will have a *jus standi* to institute an international claim against Patagonia. If Ruritania does not possess a right corresponding to the Patagonian obligation, it has no *jus standi* in the dispute. In political, economic and other terms, Ruritania may have a genuine interest in any Atlantican or Numidian initiative challenging Patagonian behaviour. However, that interest is not protected by international law.

     In the 1970 *Barcelona Traction* case, the International Court of Justice held that there are some obligations in contemporary international law (the Court specifically referred, as an illustration, to those derived 'from the outlawing of acts of aggression'), and these obligations – which arise 'towards the international community as a whole' – are 'obligations *erga omnes*', for all States have 'a legal interest' in the protection of the rights involved.[168] The concept of *erga omnes* obligations has since been reaffirmed by the Court in diverse contexts, ranging from self-determination[169] to genocide.[170]

     In the exceptional circumstances of *erga omnes* obligations, international law protects the interests not merely of a specific State or group of States, but of all the States in the world. Each State is vested with rights corresponding to *erga omnes* obligations, thus obtaining a *jus standi* in the matter.[171] All the same, the status of other States cannot

---

[166] For an explanation, see Draft Articles on State Responsibility, *supra* note 111, at 277–82.

[167] *Ibid.*, 53–4.

[168] *Case Concerning the Barcelona Traction, Light and Power Company, Limited*, [1970] *ICJ Rep.* 3, 32.

[169] See *Case Concerning East Timor*, [1995] *ICJ Rep.* 90, 102. See also Advisory Opinion on *Legal Consequences of the Construction of a Wall in the Occupied Palestinian Territory*, 2004, 43 *ILM* 1009, 1034 (2004).

[170] See *Application of the Convention on the Prevention and Punishment of the Crime of Genocide* (Preliminary Objections), [1996] *ICJ Rep.* 595, 616.

[171] See Y. Dinstein, 'The Erga Omnes Applicability of Human Rights', 30 *Ar.V.* 16, 18–19 (1992).

be equated with that of the direct victim of the international crime. It is quite obvious that only the direct victim – and not all other States – will be entitled to demand monetary compensation.[172]

In Article 41 of its Draft Articles on State Responsibility, the International Law Commission laid down that when a serious breach of an obligation under peremptory norms of general international law takes place, States must cooperate to bring it to an end through lawful means and no State shall recognize as lawful a situation created by such a serious breach.[173]

ii. An allusion has already been made to the existence of individual criminal responsibility for waging aggressive war (a matter that will command attention *infra*, Chapter 5, C). Can a State, too, bear criminal responsibility for such an act? Calls for the recognition of the penal responsibility of States have been made since the 1920s.[174] Then as now, quite a few scholars,[175] as well as representatives of States,[176] have flatly denied that there is any merit in the idea. At times, writers take contradictory positions on this issue. Thus, G. I. Tunkin declared in one context that 'the concept of criminal responsibility of a state is wholly unfounded'.[177] Further on, in the same book, he registered the emergence in international law of a new phenomenon of 'sanctions relating to the international crimes of a State', including 'measures having the character of preventive punishment' (like the treatment of Germany after World War II).[178]

It is elementary that a State, as an artificial legal person, cannot actually be subjected to certain penal sentences (like imprisonment). However, from the outset of the debate, it has been argued that military, diplomatic and economic measures may serve as penal sanctions against States.[179] More recently, actions such as those taken against Germany and Japan after World War II (e.g., 'the destruction of factories capable of increasing the military potential') have been

---

[172] See B. Simma, 'International Crimes: Injury and Countermeasures. Comments on Part 2 of the ILC Work on State Responsibility', *International Crimes of States* 283, 301 (J. H. H. Weiler, A. Cassese and M. Spinedi eds., 1989).

[173] Draft Articles on State Responsibility, *supra* note 111, at 53.

[174] For a brief summary, see V. V. Pella, 'Towards an International Criminal Court', 44 *AJIL* 37, 50–1 (1950).

[175] See K. Marek, 'Criminalizing State Responsibility', 14 *RBDI* 460, 483 (1978–9). See also P.-M. Dupuy, 'Observations sur le "Crime International de l'Etat"', 84 *RGDIP* 449–86 (1980).

[176] See L. Henkin, R. C. Pugh, O. Schachter and H. Smit, *International Law Cases and Materials* 559 (3rd ed., 1993).

[177] G. I. Tunkin, *Theory of International Law* 402 (1974).   [178] *Ibid.*, 422.

[179] See V. V. Pella, 'Plan d'Un Code Répressif Mondial', 12 *RIDP* 348, 369 (1935).

offered for consideration as penal sanctions available against States.[180]
G. Schwarzenberger even advocated the policy of treating States like
Nazi Germany, which deliberately plan and pursue 'wholesale aggression' (to be distinguished from an ordinary case of resorting to unlawful
force), in the manner of 'outlaws': such States should 'forfeit their
international personality and put themselves beyond the pale of international law'.[181] These are far-fetched and not very attractive proposals. After all, when penal sanctions are inflicted on a State (an
incorporeal juristic person), they are tantamount to the collective
punishment of the State's population, striking at the innocent together
with the guilty.[182] Modern conceptions of international human rights
exclude the possibility of exposing the civilian population of a State to
indiscriminate collective punishment.[183]

iii. It has been noted (*supra*, (a)) that compensation, as a measure of
reparation, is supposed to cover the actual damage caused.
Additionally, a proposal has been raised, in the course of the deliberations of the International Law Commission, to impose on the
perpetrators of international crimes – as an exceptional measure –
'severe punitive damages'.[184] Of course, if punitive damages could be
meted out to the aggressor State, they would constitute a monetary
punishment (like a fine in national criminal law).[185] At a certain
point, the Commission resolved that 'damages reflecting the gravity
of the infringement' should be paid in the case of gross breaches.[186]
However, this text encountered opposition by Governments on the
ground that 'damages reflecting the gravity of the breach' are 'scarcely
different from "punitive damages"'.[187] Ultimately, the Commission
arrived at the categorical conclusion that 'the award of punitive
damages is not recognized in international law even in relation to
serious breaches of obligations arising under peremptory norms'.[188]

One reason for the reluctance to pursue the path of imposing punitive
damages on aggressor States is that, if the economic burden of paying
ordinary compensation for war losses is liable to be too onerous to bear,

---

[180] Pella, *supra* note 174, at 52.
[181] G. Schwarzenberger, 'The Judgment of Nuremberg', 21 *Tul.LR* 329, 351 (1946–7).
[182] See P. N. Drost, *The Crime of State*, I, 292 (1959).
[183] *Cf.* I. Brownlie, *International Law and the Use of Force by States* 153 (1963).
[184] Summary Records of the International Law Commission, 46th Session, [1994] I *ILC Ybk* 135.
[185] See F. Malekian, *International Criminal Responsibility of States* 179–80, 196 (1985).
[186] Draft Articles on State Responsibility, *supra* note 164, at 456 (Article 45(2)(c)).
[187] See C. J. Tams, 'Do Serious Breaches Give Rise to Any Specific Obligations of the Responsible State?', 13 *EJIL* 1161, 1169 (2002).
[188] Draft Articles on State Responsibility, *supra* note 111, at 279.

the chances of collecting punitive damages from the responsible State is *a fortiori* slim. Should that State default, there would be no point in driving it to bankruptcy. In the first place, a bankrupt State will surely lack the capacity to discharge its war debts. Besides, ability to pay punitive damages cannot conceivably serve as an exclusive yardstick when the future of a State is at stake. A State cannot be equated with a commercial concern threatened with bankruptcy, inasmuch as there are essential governmental functions which must continue to be exercised no matter what.[189]

G.   Consent

(a)   Ad hoc *consent*

Article 20 of the Draft Articles on State Responsibility sets forth:

Valid consent by a State to the commission of a given act by another State precludes the wrongfulness of that act in relation to the former State to the extent that the act remains within the limits of that consent.[190]

This Article 'reflects the basic international law principle of consent'.[191] Accordingly, military assistance may be 'rendered by one State to another at the latter's request and with its consent, which may be given *ad hoc* or in advance by treaty'.[192] Military assistance from the outside against non-State actors, being 'consensual' rather than 'coercive', is not forbidden by Article 2(4) of the Charter of the United Nations.[193]

Contemporary international practice is replete with instances of detachments of armed forces sent by one State to another, at the latter's request, in order to help in safeguarding law and order in the face of intractable domestic turmoil.[194] A prime example is that of the Regional Assistance Mission to the Solomon Islands (RAMSI), created by the Pacific Islands Forum and led by Australia, sent in 2003 to the Solomon Islands – at the request of that country – with a view to restoring internal security.

It is true that, under Article 2 of the 1975 Resolution of the *Institut de Droit International* on 'The Principle of Non-Intervention in Civil

---

[189] See J. F. Williams, 'A Legal Footnote to the Story of German Reparations', 13 *BYBIL* 9, 31 (1932).

[190] Draft Articles on State Responsibility, *supra* note 111, at 48.   [191] *Ibid.*, 173.

[192] Oppenheim's *International Law*, I, 435 (R. Jennings and A. Watts eds., 9th ed., 1992).

[193] A. Abass, 'Consent Precluding State Responsibility: A Critical Analysis', 53 *ICLQ* 211, 224 (2004).

[194] See Oppenheim, *supra* note 192, at 435–6.

Wars', it is forbidden to extend foreign assistance to any party in a civil war.[195] However, this prohibition is inconsistent both with traditional international law[196] and with the modern practice of States.[197] International law draws a sharp distinction between the central (legitimate) Government, on the one hand, and rebel groups, on the other. Unless the civil war gains such scope that the rebels are granted recognition of belligerency (implying that foreign States must remain neutral in the internal armed conflict),[198] intervention from the outside is permissible against the rebels at the request of the central Government. Differently put, under ordinary circumstances (absent recognition of belligerency), when a rebellion is raging within Ruritanian territory, Atlantica is allowed to lend military assistance to the Ruritanian Government (if requested to do so) with a view to stamping out the uprising. Since Atlantica and Ruritania are then using force jointly against non-State actors (the Ruritanian rebels), there is no inter-State clash, and Article 2(4) of the Charter does not come into play. Conversely, Pacifica is legally barred from extending any military aid to the rebels against the central Government of Ruritania. In the *Nicaragua* case, the International Court of Justice firmly concluded that forcible intervention from the outside, 'in support of an opposition within another State', constitutes a breach of the prohibition of the use of inter-State force.[199]

The trouble is that it may be easier to maintain this sharply delineated dichotomy in theory than in practice. Ruritania may plunge into chaotic turbulence, with several claimants to constitutional legitimacy or none at all ('failed State' is a locution occasionally used).[200] Should Atlantica contemplate forcible intervention at the request of one of the feuding parties, it may be incapable of identifying any remnants of the legitimate Ruritanian Government and determining who has rebelled against whom.[201] The *Institut*'s position would definitely be corroborated in such a situation. Otherwise, the result may be that a civil war would

---

[195] *Institut de Droit International*, Resolution, 'The Principle of Non-Intervention in Civil Wars', 56 *AIDI* 545, 547 (Wiesbaden, 1975).

[196] See J. W. Garner, 'Questions of International Law in the Spanish Civil War', 31 *AJIL* 66, 67–9 (1937).

[197] *Cf.* L. Doswald-Beck, 'The Legal Validity of Military Intervention by Invitation of the Government', 56 *BYBIL* 189–252 (1985).

[198] See Oppenheim, *supra* note 192, at 165.

[199] *Nicaragua* case, *supra* note 32, at 110–11.

[200] See D. Thürer, 'The "Failed State" and International Law', 81 *IRRC* 731, 733–4 (1999).

[201] See R. R. Baxter, 'Ius in Bello Interno: The Present and Future Law', *Law and Civil War in the Modern World* 518, 525 (J. N. Moore ed., 1974).

turn into an international armed conflict, since Atlantica and Pacifica may intervene in support of two opposing factions (each claiming that it is the true Ruritanian Government).[202]

Another major problem relating to consent is the possibility of abuse. Ruritanian consent to (and request for) military assistance by Atlantica must be genuine and free of 'fabrication'.[203] As was pointed out, in the context of the Soviet military intervention in Hungary in 1956 (allegedly by request), '[t]he consent of a state cannot be deduced from the request of a puppet government acting in its name but set up by foreign intervention'.[204] The same statement of the law could apparently be made also in the setting of the Soviet military intervention in Afghanistan in 1979 (ostensibly at the invitation of the Kabul Government).[205] But it is not necessary to go to extremes. The international record abounds with consents and invitations of doubtful validity. A case in point is that of the US military intervention in Panama, in 1989, partly predicated on the 'tacit consent' of a democratically elected President of Panama – whose election had been set aside by the incumbent Government of General Noriega – sworn in only as a result of the American military intervention.[206] Plainly, all invitations of military assistance from abroad must be subjected to a thorough scrutiny.

The growing incidence of terrorism in recent times raises another possibility, namely, that Ruritania will grant its consent to the use of force within its territory by Atlantica against terrorists who are using Ruritania as a base of operations against Atlantica.[207] In such a scenario, Atlantica's intervention is not carried out at the request of Ruritania, with a view to quashing a rebellion against the central authority of the latter country. Atlantica is acting to defend itself against the terrorists, and the Ruritanian consent to the Atlantican military operation may be given rather reluctantly. Indeed, Ruritania may give its consent only because it is aware of the fact that, in extreme cases, Atlantica might otherwise act within Ruritanian territory even non-consensually, as part of an extra-territorial law enforcement (see *infra*, Chapter 8, B).

---

[202] See C. Gray, *International Law and the Use of Force* 81 (2nd ed., 2004).

[203] Oppenheim, *supra* note 192, at 436.

[204] Q. Wright, 'Intervention, 1956', 51 *AJIL* 257, 275 (1957).

[205] See W. M. Reisman and J. Silk, 'Which Law Applies to the Afghan Conflict?', 82 *AJIL* 459, 472–4, 485 (1988).

[206] Oppenheim, *supra* note 192, at 436–7 n. 14.

[207] See M. N. Schmitt, 'Counter-Terrorism and the Use of Force in International Law', 32 *IYHR* 53, 111 (2002).

(b)   Consent by treaty

It has been suggested that consent to forcible intervention must be given *ad hoc* and 'no blanket authorization for the future' may be given.[208] But, as noted (*supra*, (a)), Ruritania may express its consent to accept military assistance from Atlantica not only *ad hoc* but also 'in advance by treaty' (which can be either bilateral or multilateral). One example is a treaty of guarantee (see *infra*, Chapter 9, B, (c)). Moreover, there is a growing tendency in the African continent to allow by treaty regional military intervention in internal armed conflicts and in other grave situations. This is epitomized in Article 25 of the 1999 Lomé Protocol Relating to the ECOWAS Mechanism for Conflict Prevention, Management and Resolution, Peace-Keeping and Security.[209] Even prior to the Lomé Protocol, ECOWAS (the Economic Community of West African States) had already intervened militarily through ECOMOG (Cease-Fire Monitoring Group) in a number of civil wars, mainly in Liberia (1990) and Sierra Leone (1997).[210] However, in both instances, appeals to ECOWAS for intervention were issued by crumbling central Governments.[211]

The African tendency to allow by treaty a forcible intervention in the affairs of Member States has reached its apogee in the 2002 Durban Protocol (which, at the time of writing, was on the verge of entry into force).[212] The Durban Protocol established a 'Peace and Security Council of the African Union' (AUPSC) and conferred upon it extensive powers, including the deployment of forces.[213] 'It is expected to consider the right to intervene when the situation so warrants and make appropriate recommendations to the Assembly of the Union for possible intervention', even without the *ad hoc* consent of the Member State concerned.[214]

---

[208] A. Cassese, *International Law* 318 (2001).

[209] Lomé Protocol Relating to the ECOWAS Mechanism for Conflict Prevention, Management, Resolution, Peace-Keeping and Security, 1999, *Africa: Selected Documents on Constitutive, Conflict and Security, Humanitarian, and Judicial Issues* 261, 274 (J. I. Levitt ed., 2003).

[210] See J. Levitt, 'African Interventionist States and International Law', *African Interventionist States* 15–50 (O. Furley and R. May eds., 2001).

[211] See J. Levitt, 'Humanitarian Intervention by Regional Actors in Internal Conflicts: The Cases of ECOWAS in Liberia and Sierra Leone', 12 *TICLJ* 333, 343, 365 (1998).

[212] Durban Protocol Relating to the Establishment of the Peace and Security Council of the African Union (AUPSC), 2002, *Africa: Selected Documents*, *supra* note 209, at 161, 163.

[213] *Ibid.*, 169 (Article 7).

[214] B. Kioko, 'The Right of Intervention under the African Union's Constitutive Act: From Non-Interference to Non-Intervention', 85 *IRRC* 807, 817 (2003).

It goes without saying that a treaty like the Lomé or the Durban Protocol can apply only between Contracting Parties. No forcible intervention can be undertaken by ECOWAS or the African Union except within the consensual sphere of application of the respective Protocol. Consent is also valid only as long as it lasts. Assuming that a central Government is in place, it can always withdraw the State's consent (even if such conduct would be in breach of the treaty). Yet, naturally, if conditions have deteriorated to the point that there is no central authority in control of the country (which has become a 'failed State'), no group or *junta* is vested with the competence to withdraw the consent previously expressed in the treaty.

Any attempt by a regional treaty to impose a different legal regime, purporting to authorize a regional body like ECOWAS or the African Union to intervene forcibly notwithstanding the clear wishes of an established central Government, would run counter to Article 2(4) of the Charter. It must be recalled that, given the *jus cogens* nature of Article 2(4) (see *supra*, E, (a)), a regional treaty cannot contract out of the general prohibition of the use of force.[215] Pursuant to Article 53(1) of the Charter,[216] regional organizations can use force against a State only under the authority of the Security Council (see *infra*, Chapter 10, D, (c)).

---

[215] Article 26 of the Draft Articles on State Responsibility expressly subjects the provision regarding consent to the obligation of compliance with peremptory norms: *supra* note 111, at 50.

[216] Charter of the United Nations, *supra* note 13, at 347.

5   The criminality of war of aggression

A.   War of aggression as a crime against peace

The paucity of meaningful sanctions calculated to enforce respect for legal norms is a pervasive problem in every branch of international law, but nowhere is the need for such sanctions more evident than in the domain of the *jus ad bellum*. Even at the embryonic stage of the process culminating in the imposition of a legal ban on the use of inter-State force, it was generally recognized that, unless coupled with effective sanctions, the interdiction of aggressive war was liable to be chimerical. To be effective, sanctions in this context must go beyond the bounds of State responsibility (see *supra*, Chapter 4, F, (b)). Only if it dawns on the actual decision-makers that when they carry their country along the path of war in contravention of international law they expose themselves to individual criminal liability, are they likely to hesitate before taking the fateful step.

Already at the end of World War I (prior to the proscription of war by positive international law), plans were made to prosecute the German Kaiser, Wilhelm II, on account of his personal responsibility for the War. In Article 227 of the Versailles Treaty of Peace, the Allied and Associated Powers charged the Kaiser with 'a supreme offence against international morality and the sanctity of treaties'.[1] As the language of the Article suggests, the Kaiser's acts were looked upon as an offence not against international law but against international morality[2] (and the sanctity of treaties, a phrase with a religious more than a legal connotation). In any event, the Kaiser found asylum in the Netherlands, not a Contracting Party to the Treaty of Versailles, and that country refused to extradite him on the ground that it was not obligated by international law to do so.[3]

---

[1] Versailles Treaty of Peace with Germany, 1919, *Peace Treaties*, II, 1265, 1389.
[2] See L. C. Green, 'Superior Orders and Command Responsibility', 27 *CYIL* 167, 191–2 (1989).
[3] For the text of the Dutch note, see J. B. Scott, 'The Trial of the Kaiser', *What Really Happened at Paris* 231, 243–4 (E. M. House and C. Seymour eds., 1921).

In the era between the two World Wars, the criminality of aggressive war was heralded in several international instruments, none of which was legally binding. Thus, the Preamble of the unratified 1924 Geneva Protocol on the Pacific Settlement of International Disputes, crafted as a device to close the 'gaps' in the Covenant of the League of Nations (see *supra*, Chapter 3, E, (c)), enunciated that 'a war of aggression constitutes ... an international crime'.[4]

The criminalization of aggressive war in a treaty in force was attained only in the aftermath of World War II, upon the conclusion of the Charter of the International Military Tribunal annexed to an Agreement done in London in 1945.[5] Article 6 of the Charter[6] establishes the jurisdiction of the Tribunal over crimes against peace, war crimes and crimes against humanity. Paragraph (a) of the Article defines crimes against peace as follows:

planning, preparation, initiation or waging of a war of aggression, or a war in violation of international treaties, agreements or assurances, or participation in a common plan or conspiracy for the accomplishment of any of the foregoing.

Article 6 specifically adds:

Leaders, organizers, instigators and accomplices participating in the formulation or execution of a common plan or conspiracy to commit any of the foregoing crimes are responsible for all acts performed by any persons in execution of such plan.

The London Agreement originally had as signatories the four dominant Powers – the United States, the USSR, the United Kingdom and France – but later it was adhered to by 19 additional Allied nations.[7] The Charter of the International Military Tribunal served as the fulcrum for the *Nuremberg* trial of the major German war criminals.

Article 6(a) of the London Charter represented a singular advance in the evolution of international law. The gist of the clause was soon reiterated, with some variations, in Article II(1)(a) of Control Council Law No. 10 (forming the legal foundation of the so-called Subsequent Proceedings at Nuremberg, in which other German war criminals were tried by American Military Tribunals),[8] and in Article 5(a) of the Charter of the International Military Tribunal for the Far East (issued in a

---

[4] Geneva Protocol on the Pacific Settlement of International Disputes, 1924, 2 *Int.Leg.* 1378, 1380.
[5] Charter of the International Military Tribunal, Annexed to the London Agreement for the Establishment of an International Military Tribunal, 1945, 9 *Int.Leg.* 632, 637.
[6] *Ibid.*, 639–40.   [7] *Ibid.*, 632.
[8] Control Council Law No. 10, 1945, 1 *NMT* xvi, xvii.

Proclamation by General D. MacArthur, in his capacity as Supreme Commander of the Allied Powers in the region, and designed for the trial of the major Japanese war criminals).[9]

In its Judgment of 1946, the International Military Tribunal at *Nuremberg* held that Article 6(a) of the London Charter is declaratory of modern international law, which regards war of aggression as a grave crime.[10] Hence, the Tribunal rejected the argument that the provision of the Article amounted to *ex post facto* criminalization of the acts of the defendants, in breach of the *nullum crimen sine lege* principle.[11] The Tribunal relied heavily on the renunciation of war in the Kellogg–Briand Pact.[12] The Pact established the illegality of war as an instrument of national policy, and from that the Judgment inferred that 'those who plan and wage such a war, with its inevitable and terrible consequences, are committing a crime in so doing'.[13]

The Tribunal conceded that the Pact had neither expressly promulgated that war is a crime nor set up courts to try offenders.[14] But this is also true of Hague Convention (IV) of 1907 Respecting the Laws and Customs of War on Land.[15] Hague Convention (IV) – through its Regulations – prohibits certain practices in warfare, such as the maltreatment of prisoners of war, the employment of poisoned weapons and the improper use of flags of truce.[16] These forbidden acts have been viewed as war crimes, at least after 1907, notwithstanding the fact that the Convention does not designate them as criminal and does not introduce penal sanctions.[17] The Tribunal considered the criminality of war as analogous and even more compelling.[18] The Judgment adduced diverse non-binding instruments (like the Geneva Protocol of 1924), whereby aggressive war had been stigmatized as a crime, finding in them evidence for the dynamic development of customary international law.[19] The linch-pin of the Tribunal's position was that:

Crimes against international law are committed by men, not by abstract entities, and only by punishing individuals who commit such crimes can the provisions of international law be enforced.[20]

In other words, the banning of war is devoid of any practical significance, unless international law is prepared to mete out real

[9] Charter of the International Military Tribunal for the Far East, 1946, 14 *DSB* 361, 362 (1946).
[10] International Military Tribunal (*Nuremberg* trial), Judgment (1946), 1 *IMT* 171, 219–23.
[11] *Ibid.*, 219.   [12] *Ibid.*, 219–20.   [13] *Ibid.*, 220.   [14] *Ibid.*
[15] Hague Convention (IV) of 1907 Respecting the Laws and Customs of War on Land, *Hague Conventions* 100.
[16] *Nuremberg* trial, *supra* note 10, at 220.
[17] *Ibid.*, 220–1.   [18] *Ibid.*, 221.   [19] *Ibid.*, 221–2.   [20] *Ibid.*, 223.

penalties to flesh-and-blood offenders acting on behalf of the artificial legal person that is the State.

The *Nuremberg* decision concerning crimes against peace has instigated harsh criticism,[21] which cannot be pretermitted. No doubt, the weakest link in the chain constructed by the International Military Tribunal is the certitude that the illegality of war (under the Kellogg–Briand Pact) ineluctably leads to its criminality.[22] International law renders many an act of State unlawful, yet in most instances that does not mean that the interdicted conduct becomes a crime. Why is the injunction against war different from other international legal prohibitions? A reply to the question may be gleaned in another section of the Judgment:

War is essentially an evil thing. Its consequences are not confined to the belligerent States alone, but affect the whole world.

To initiate a war of aggression, therefore, is not only an international crime; it is the supreme international crime differing only from other war crimes in that it contains within itself the accumulated evil of the whole.[23]

The decisive point is that war is a cataclysmic event. There is no way in which war can be waged as if it were a chess game. In the nature of things, blood and fire, suffering and pain, are the concomitants of war. As a result, war simply must be a crime.

The stand taken by the International Military Tribunal is not invulnerable. If wars by their very nature (because of the devastation associated with them) are viewed as *mala in se*,[24] it is incomprehensible how they could have retained their legality in the centuries preceding the Kellogg–Briand Pact. If, for most of its duration, international law managed to adapt itself to the lawfulness of war, surely the proscription of war may be deemed an achievement that is sufficient unto itself. Why are criminal sanctions, directed against the individual organs of the State, assumed to be *sine qua non* to such an extent that they have to be looked upon as implicit in the Pact?

These and other difficulties were hotly debated in the late 1940s. It seems only fair to state that when the London Charter was concluded, Article 6(a) was not really declaratory of pre-existing customary international law.[25] The *Nuremberg* Judgment was innovative when it ingested the criminality of

[21] See, e.g., F. B. Schick, 'The Nuremberg Trial and the International Law of the Future', 41 *AJIL* 770, 783–4 (1947).
[22] See C. A. Pompe, *Aggressive War an International Crime* 245 (1953).
[23] *Nuremberg* trial, *supra* note 10, at 186. This well-known dictum is based on a passage from Lord Wright, 'War Crimes under International Law', 62 *LQR* 40, 47 (1946).
[24] See Q. Wright, 'The Law of the Nuremberg Trial', 41 *AJIL* 38, 63 (1947).
[25] See L. Gross, 'The Criminality of Aggressive War', 41 *APSR* 205, 218–20 (1947).

war into general international law.[26] However, the issue is no longer of great importance. It is virtually irrefutable that present-day positive international law reflects the Judgment. War of aggression currently constitutes a crime against peace. Not just a crime, but the supreme crime under international law.

The *Nuremberg* criminalization of aggressive war was upheld, in 1948, by the International Military Tribunal for the Far East at *Tokyo*.[27] It was also endorsed in other trials against criminals of World War II, most conspicuously in the *Ministries* case, in 1949, the last of the Subsequent Proceedings.[28] However, no indictment for crimes against peace (in violation of the *jus ad bellum*) has followed the multiple armed conflicts of the post-World War II era.[29] The idea of charging Saddam Hussein with a long list of international offences, above all the crime of waging a war of aggression against Kuwait, was advanced in the early 1990s.[30] But, after his apprehension in the final phase of the Gulf War, Saddam Hussein was handed over for trial by domestic Iraqi courts.

In 1993, the Security Council – in Resolution 827 – decided to establish an *ad hoc* international tribunal for prosecuting persons responsible for serious violations of international humanitarian law in the territory of the former Yugoslavia since 1991.[31] The Council approved a report submitted by the UN Secretary-General (pursuant to an earlier resolution),[32] which incorporated a Statute of the International Tribunal.[33] The Statute limits the subject-matter jurisdiction of the Yugoslav Tribunal to grave breaches of the Geneva Conventions of 1949, violations of the laws and customs of war, genocide and crimes against humanity.[34] Crimes against peace are not listed.

In 1994, a second *ad hoc* tribunal was established by the Security Council – in Resolution 955 – this time with respect to crimes committed in Rwanda.[35] Here the subject-matter jurisdiction covers genocide,

---

[26] See G. A. Finch, 'The Nuremberg Trial and International Law', 41 *AJIL* 20, 33–4 (1947).

[27] *In re Hirota and Others* (International Military Tribunal for the Far East, *Tokyo* trial, 1948), [1948] *AD* 356, 362–3.

[28] *USA v. Von Weizsaecker et al.* ('the *Ministries* case') (Nuremberg, 1949), 14 *NMT* 314, 318–22.

[29] See J. F. Murphy, 'Crimes against Peace at the Nuremberg Trial', *The Nuremberg Trial and International Law* 141, 153 (G. Ginsburgs and V. N. Kudriavtsev eds., 1990).

[30] See A. M. Warner, 'The Case against Saddam Hussein – The Case for World Order', 43 *Mer.LR* 563, 598–601 (1991–2).

[31] Security Council Resolution 827, 48 *RDSC* 29, *id.* (1993).

[32] Security Council Resolution 808, 48 *RDSC* 28, *id.* (1993).

[33] Report of the Secretary-General Pursuant to Paragraph 2 of Security Council Resolution 808 (1993), 32 *ILM* 1163 (1993).

[34] *Ibid.*, 1170–4 (Articles 2–5).

[35] Security Council Resolution 955, 49 *RDSC* 15, *id.* (1994).

crimes against humanity and violations of Article 3 common to the Geneva Conventions and of Additional Protocol II.[36] Once more, crimes against peace are not included.

In addition to the two *ad hoc* tribunals – the International Criminal Tribunal for Yugoslavia (ICTY) and the International Criminal Tribunal for Rwanda (ICTR), seated at The Hague and Arusha, respectively – there is now a permanent International Criminal Court (ICC), established in 2002 after the entry into force of a special treaty: the Rome Statute of 1998.[37] Article 5 of the Rome Statute confers on the ICC subject-matter jurisdiction with respect to genocide, crimes against humanity, war crimes and the crime of aggression.[38] What substantially detracts from the significance of the explicit reference to the crime of aggression is that – unlike the other offences subjected to the jurisdiction of the ICC – this particular crime was not defined in Rome. Article 5(2) defers action to a future time:

> The Court shall exercise jurisdiction over the crime of aggression once a provision is adopted in accordance with articles 121 and 123 defining the crime and setting out the conditions under which the Court shall exercise jurisdiction with respect to this crime. Such a provision shall be consistent with the relevant provisions of the Charter of the United Nations.[39]

Articles 121 and 123 of the Statute pertain to amendment and review procedures that will commence seven years after the entry into force of the Statute.[40] In accordance with Article 121(5), should an amendment to Article 5 be adopted in the future, any State Party may refuse to accept the amendment, in which case 'the Court shall not exercise its jurisdiction regarding a crime covered by the amendment when committed by that State Party's nationals or on its territory'.[41] The proviso applies also to the review procedure under Article 123(3).[42] This safeguard was added in order to allay misgivings of Contracting Parties about possible future trends relating to the configuration of the crime of aggression.[43]

The Rome decision to postpone the elucidation of the meaning of the crime of aggression reflects a divergence of opinions as to the precise scope of the definition and the manner of its drafting.[44] Above all,

---

[36] *Ibid.*, 16 (Articles 2–4).

[37] Rome Statute of the International Criminal Court, 1998, 37 *ILM* 1002 (1998).

[38] *Ibid.*, 1003–4.   [39] *Ibid.*, 1004.   [40] *Ibid.*, 1067–8.   [41] *Ibid.*, 1067.   [42] *Ibid.*, 1068.

[43] See D. Sarooshi, 'The Statute of the International Criminal Court', 48 *ICLQ* 387, 401 (1999).

[44] See H. von Hebel and D. Robinson, 'Crimes within the Jurisdiction of the Court', *The International Criminal Court: The Making of the Rome Statute – Issues, Negotiations, Results* 79, 82–5 (R. S. Lee ed., 1999).

the Rome conference was unable to reach an agreement as to whether the ICC would be empowered to exercise jurisdiction in the absence of a Security Council determination that an act of aggression has occurred.[45] This is an issue of potentially grave consequences, since – in theory at least – the ICC (if acting independently of the Security Council) might convict a person of the crime of aggression, even though the Council has ruled that the other side is the aggressor in the war.[46] The last sentence of Article 5(2) 'was understood as a reference to the role the Council may or should play in relation to this crime'.[47]

The controversies attending the formulation of the Rome Statute must not be minimized. One may even conclude that, pending the entry into force of the projected amendment, 'the crime of aggression is *de facto* not included in the Statute'.[48] However, there is no indication that States regard as anachronistic the concept of wars of aggression as a crime under international law. On the contrary, support for this concept has been manifested consistently in international fora. The best testimony is afforded by a string of uncontested UN General Assembly resolutions, complemented by studies undertaken by the International Law Commission.

As early as 1946, the General Assembly affirmed the principles of international law recognized by the Charter and the Judgment of the International Military Tribunal.[49] In 1947, the General Assembly instructed the International Law Commission to formulate these principles and also to prepare a Draft Code of Offences against the Peace and Security of Mankind.[50] The Commission composed the 'Nürnberg Principles' in 1950. The text recites the Charter's definition of crimes against peace, emphasizing that offenders bear responsibility for such crimes and are liable to punishment.[51]

The first phase of the Commission's work on the Draft Code of Offences against the Peace and Security of Mankind was completed in 1954.[52] Article 2(1) of the Draft Code characterized as an offence any act

[45] See M. H. Arsanjani, 'The Rome Statute of the International Criminal Court', 93 *AJIL* 22, 29–30 (1999).
[46] See A. Zimmermann, 'The Creation of a Permanent International Criminal Court', 2 *MPYUNL* 169, 203 (1998).
[47] Von Hebel and Robinson, *supra* note 44, at 85.
[48] A. Zimmermann, 'Article 5', *Commentary on the Rome Statute of the International Criminal Court* 97, 102 (O. Triffterer ed., 1999).
[49] General Assembly Resolution 95 (I), 1(2) *RGA* 188, *id.* (1946).
[50] General Assembly Resolution 177 (II), 2 *RGA* 111, 112 (1947).
[51] Principles of International Law Recognized in the Charter of the Nürnberg Tribunal and in the Judgment of the Tribunal, Report of the International Law Commission, 2nd Session, [1950] II *ILC Ybk* 364, 374, 376.
[52] Draft Code of Offences against the Peace and Security of Mankind, Report of the International Law Commission, 6th Session, [1954] II *ILC Ybk* 140, 149.

of 'aggression'.[53] Article 1 laid down that the offences incorporated in the Draft Code 'are crimes under international law, for which the responsible individuals shall be punished'.[54]

A serious examination of the 1954 Draft Code was suspended until a definition of aggression could be agreed upon.[55] It took quite some time before the impetus favouring such a definition overcame resistance that, initially, was considerable. For two decades, the Draft Code remained dormant. Finally, in 1974, the General Assembly produced a consensus Definition of Aggression, stating unequivocally in Article 5(2) that 'war of aggression is a crime against international peace'.[56] In the wake of the formulation of the Definition, the work on the Draft Code was restarted.[57] In 1996, the International Law Commission, having pondered no less than thirteen reports submitted by a Special Rapporteur (D. Thiam), adopted the final text of a new Draft Code of Crimes against the Peace and Security of Mankind[58] (the term Crimes having replaced Offences). The crime of aggression is contained in Article 16 of the Code:

An individual who, as leader or organizer, actively participates in or orders the planning, preparation, initiation or waging of aggression committed by a State shall be responsible for a crime of aggression.[59]

In the commentary, the Commission stressed that the branding of aggression as a crime against the peace and security of mankind is drawn from the London Charter as interpreted and applied by the International Military Tribunal.[60]

Irrespective of the codification undertaken by the International Law Commission, the General Assembly – in the 1970 Declaration on Principles of International Law Concerning Friendly Relations and Co-operation among States in accordance with the Charter of the United Nations – proclaimed that 'war of aggression constitutes a crime against peace, for which there is responsibility under international law'.[61]

In all, the criminality of aggressive war has entrenched itself in an impregnable position in contemporary international law. It is true that the full consequences of this criminality are not always agreed upon (see *infra*, Chapter 6). But it cannot be denied that responsibility for

---

[53] *Ibid.*, 151.   [54] *Ibid.*, 150.
[55] See L. Gross, 'Some Observations on the Draft Code of Offences against the Peace and Security of Mankind', 13 *IYHR* 9, 20 (1983).
[56] General Assembly Resolution 3314 (XXIX), 29(1) *RGA* 142, 144 (1974).
[57] See Gross, *supra* note 55, at 26 ff.
[58] Draft Code of Crimes against the Peace and Security of Mankind, Report of the International Law Commission, 48th Session, [1996] II (2) *ILC Ybk* 17.
[59] *Ibid.*, 42–3.   [60] *Ibid.*, 43.
[61] General Assembly Resolution 2625 (XXV), 25 *RGA* 121, 122 (1970).

international crimes, as distinct from responsibility for ordinary breaches of international law, entails the punishment of individuals. The criminality of war of aggression means the accountability of human beings, and not merely of abstract entities.

B.   The definition of aggression

The General Assembly consensus Definition of Aggression, adopted in 1974, relates to 'aggression' in a generic way. Article 5(2) of the Definition differentiates between aggression (which 'gives rise to international responsibility') and war of aggression (which is 'a crime against international peace').[62] The drafters of the Definition thereby signalled clearly that not every act of aggression constitutes a crime against peace: only war of aggression does.[63] That is to say, an act of aggression 'short of war' – as distinct from a war of aggression – would not result in individual criminal responsibility,[64] although it would bring about the application of general rules of State responsibility (see *supra*, Chapter 4, F, (a)).

The inseparability of crimes against peace from aggressive wars is in conformity with the definition of crimes against peace appearing in Article 6(a) of the London Charter of the International Military Tribunal (see *supra*, A). By contrast, the International Law Commission has expanded the scope of the crimes. In the 1954 Draft Code, the Commission defined '[a]ny act' of aggression as an offence against the peace and security of mankind.[65] Article 16 of the 1996 Draft Code (quoted *supra*, A) equally deals with acts of aggression in general, rather than merely wars of aggression.[66] Article 5(2) of the Rome Statute (also quoted *ibid.*) – at least tentatively – goes in the same direction.[67]

Admittedly, the International Law Commission, in its commentary, cautiously noted that individual criminal responsibility for the crime of aggression is contingent on 'a sufficiently serious violation of the prohibition contained in Article 2, paragraph 4, of the Charter of the United Nations'.[68] However, a serious violation of the Charter's prohibition of the use of inter-State force may still constitute an act of aggression

---

[62] See G. Gilbert, 'The Criminal Responsibility of States', 39 *ICLQ* 345, 360 (1990).

[63] See B. Broms, 'The Definition of Aggression', 154 *RCADI* 299, 357 (1977).

[64] See J. Hogan-Doran and B. T. van Ginkel, 'Aggression as a Crime under International Law and the Prosecution of Individuals by the Proposed International Criminal Court', 43 *NILR* 321, 335 (1996).

[65] Draft Code of Offences against the Peace and Security of Mankind, *supra* note 52, at 151 (Article 2(1)).

[66] Draft Code of Crimes against the Peace and Security of Mankind, *supra* note 58, at 42–3.

[67] Rome Statute, *supra* note 37, at 1004.

[68] Draft Code of Crimes against the Peace and Security of Mankind, *supra* note 58, at 43.

'short of war'. The extension of the range of crimes against peace to acts of aggression 'short of war' represents a striking departure from the law as perceived in the London Charter and in the consensus Definition of Aggression. It remains to be seen whether the practice of States, and the future definition to be incorporated in the revised Statute of the ICC, will confirm the broadening of criminal liability in this sphere.

While Article 5(2) of the Definition of Aggression pronounces war of aggression to be a crime against international peace, the Definition as a whole is not engrossed in the criminal ramifications of aggressive war. The Resolution, to which the Definition of Aggression is annexed, makes it plain that the primary intention of the General Assembly was to recommend the text as a guide to the Security Council when the latter is called upon to determine (within its mandate under the UN Charter) the existence of an act of aggression[69] (see *infra*, Chapter 10, A, (c)). It should be borne in mind that aggression may appear in a different light when inspected by the Security Council for political purposes and when a judicial inquiry is made into criminal liability.[70]

On balance, the main value of any definition of aggression lies in the criminal field. The reason is that a tribunal vested with jurisdiction to try crimes against peace cannot possibly gloss over the theme of aggression, which is the gravamen of the charge: unless a war is aggressive in nature, no crime has been committed. By contrast, under Chapter VII of the Charter, the Security Council's powers are identical in the face of aggression, breach of the peace or any threat to the peace.[71] It is not imperative for the Council to determine specifically that aggression has been perpetrated. Irrespective of the exact classification of activities examined by the Council – as long as they can be categorized either as aggression or as a breach of, or a threat to, the peace – the Council is authorized to put in effect the same measures of collective security (see *infra*, Chapter 10, A, (d)). Nevertheless, since the General Assembly largely de-emphasized the criminal aspect of its formulation, and brought to the fore the political dimension, the Definition of Aggression is less useful in its penal implications.

Having said that, it must be acknowledged that the General Assembly's Definition of Aggression is the most recent and the most widely (albeit not universally)[72] accepted. At least one paragraph of the Definition,

---

[69] General Assembly Resolution 3314, *supra* note 56, at 143.
[70] See J. I. Garvey, 'The U.N. Definition of "Aggression": Law and Illusion in the Context of Collective Security', 17 *VJIL* 177, 193–4 (1976–7).
[71] Charter of the United Nations, 1945, 9 *Int.Leg.* 327, 343–6.
[72] For a scathing criticism of the Definition, see J. Stone, 'Hopes and Loopholes in the 1974 Definition of Aggression', 71 *AJIL* 224–46 (1977).

namely, Article 3(g) (to be quoted *infra*), has been held by the International Court of Justice, in the *Nicaragua* case of 1986, to mirror customary international law.[73] Even Judge Schwebel, who cautioned in his Dissenting Opinion not to magnify the significance of the Definition, admitted that it cannot be discarded.[74] Other definitions of aggression assuredly exist, some of them in treaty form (particularly in agreements concluded by the USSR with neighbouring countries in 1933).[75] But these definitions are not applicable to non-Contracting Parties, and they are no more apposite to the contours of crimes against peace. *Faute de mieux*, the essence of crimes against peace has to be extracted from the General Assembly's wording.

Au fond, the General Assembly utilized the technique of a composite definition, combining general and enumerative elements: it started with an abstract statement of what aggression means, and appended a non-exhaustive catalogue of specific illustrations.[76] The general part of the Definition is embodied in Article 1:

Aggression is the use of armed force by a State against the sovereignty, territorial integrity or political independence of another State, or in any other manner inconsistent with the Charter of the United Nations, as set out in this Definition.[77]

In an explanatory note, the framers of the Definition commented that the term 'State' includes non-UN Members, embraces a group of States and is used without prejudice to questions of recognition.[78]

Article 1 of the Definition repeats the core of the wording of Article 2(4) of the Charter (quoted *supra*, Chapter 4, B, (a)), subject to a number of variations: (i) the mere threat of force is excluded; (ii) the adjective 'armed' is interposed before the noun 'force'; (iii) 'sovereignty' is mentioned together with the territorial integrity and the political independence of the victim State; (iv) the victim is described as 'another' (rather than 'any') State; (v) the use of force is forbidden whenever it is inconsistent with the UN Charter as a whole, and not only with the Purposes of the United Nations; (vi) a linkage is created with the rest of the Definition. Some of these points are of peripheral, if not nominal, significance. Others are of greater consequence. Thus, the allusion

---

[73] *Case Concerning Military and Paramilitary Activities in and against Nicaragua* (Merits), [1986] *ICJ Rep.* 14, 103.
[74] *Ibid.*, 345.
[75] London Conventions for the Definition of Aggression, 1933, 147 *LNTS* 67; 148 *ibid.*, 211.
[76] See S. M. Schwebel, 'Aggression, Intervention and Self-Defence in Modern International Law', 136 *RCADI* 411, 443–4 (1972).
[77] General Assembly Resolution 3314, *supra* note 56, at 143.   [78] *Ibid.*

to inconsistency with the Charter in its entirety (rather than just the Purposes of the United Nations) may imply that even technical provisions of the Charter have to be observed, so that the breach of procedures detailed in the Charter may turn the use of armed force into an unlawful aggression.[79] The cardinal divergence from Article 2(4) is, however, the first: the threat of force *per se* does not qualify as aggression, since an actual use of armed force is absolutely required.

Article 2 of the Definition sets forth that '[t]he first use of armed force by a State in contravention of the Charter shall constitute *prima facie* evidence of an act of aggression', but the Security Council may determine otherwise 'in the light of other relevant circumstances, including the fact that the acts concerned or their consequences are not of sufficient gravity'.[80] The 'other relevant circumstances' leave a broad margin for interpretation; apparently, they include the intent and purposes of the acting State.[81] Whereas Article 2 is oriented towards the Security Council, its nucleus is equally germane to the issue of penal responsibility. First use of armed force is no conclusive evidence of the commission of a crime against peace. At most, the opening of fire creates a rebuttable presumption of culpability.[82] When all the facts are weighed, it may be the other side that will be held accountable for commencing a war of aggression.

The *de minimis* clause in Article 2 clarifies that 'a few stray bullets across a boundary' cannot be invoked as an act of aggression.[83] In the same vein, slight incidents are outside the ambit of a crime against peace. Indeed, responsibility for a war of aggression may be incurred by the target State, should it resort to comprehensive force in over-reaction to trivial incidents.

The enumeration of specific acts of aggression appears in Article 3. Under the Article, the following amount to acts of aggression ('regardless of a declaration of war'):

(a) The invasion or attack by the armed forces of a State of the territory of another State, or any military occupation, however temporary, resulting from such invasion or attack, or any annexation by the use of force of the territory of another State or part thereof;

(b) Bombardment by the armed forces of a State against the territory of another State or the use of any weapons by a State against the territory of another State;

---

[79] See B. B. Ferencz, 'A Proposed Definition of Aggression: By Compromise and Consensus', 22 *ICLQ* 407, 416 (1973).

[80] General Assembly Resolution 3314, *supra* note 56, at 143.

[81] See B. B. Ferencz, *Defining International Aggression*, II, 31 (1975).

[82] See P. Rambaud, 'La Définition de l'Agression par l'Organisation des Nations Unies', 80 *RGDIP* 835, 872 (1976).

[83] See Broms, *supra* note 63, at 346.

(c) The blockade of the ports or coasts of a State by the armed forces of another State;

(d) An attack by the armed forces of a State on the land, sea or air forces, or marine and air fleets of another State;

(e) The use of armed forces of one State which are within the territory of another State with the agreement of the receiving State, in contravention of the conditions provided for in the agreement or any extension of their presence in such territory beyond the termination of the agreement;

(f) The action of a State in allowing its territory, which it has placed at the disposal of another State, to be used by that other State for perpetrating an act of aggression against a third State;

(g) The sending by or on behalf of a State of armed bands, groups, irregulars or mercenaries, which carry out acts of armed force against another State of such gravity as to amount to the acts listed above, or its substantial involvement therein.[84]

These seven paragraphs identify flagrant instances of aggression, and several of them will be reexamined in subsequent chapters. Obviously, some of the acts of aggression itemized in Article 3 may consist of measures 'short of war', which are not crimes against peace under the Definition. Yet, as observed, the current trend (at least in theory) is to broaden crimes against peace to acts of aggression in general.

The fact that paragraph (g) has been pronounced by the International Court of Justice to be declaratory of customary international law is possibly indicative that other portions of Article 3 may equally be subsumed under the heading of true codification. But whatever the legal status of its sundry paragraphs, Article 3 was not intended to exhibit the entire spectrum of aggression. According to Article 4, the acts inscribed in Article 3 do not exhaust the definition of that term, and the Security Council may determine what other acts are tantamount to aggression.[85]

Under Articles 10 and 11(1) of the Charter, the General Assembly (which adopted the Definition) is authorized to make recommendations to the Security Council.[86] Although the General Assembly is incompetent to dictate a definition of aggression to the Security Council, it is empowered to offer guidelines in the form of a recommendation for the benefit of the Council. In actuality, after existing for three decades, the Definition of Aggression has had 'no visible impact' on the deliberations of the Security Council.[87] The Council is free to devise novel categories of aggression. All the same, should it do so – ignoring the General

---

[84] General Assembly Resolution 3314, *supra* note 56, at 143.   [85] *Ibid.*

[86] Charter of the United Nations, *supra* note 71, at 334–5.

[87] M. C. Bassiouni and B. B. Ferencz, 'The Crime against Peace', 1 *International Criminal Law* 313, 334 (M. C. Bassiouni ed., 2nd ed., 1999). There has been no change in the situation in the last few years.

Assembly's Definition as well as past precedents – no criminal responsibility would necessarily ensue, since the principle *nullum crimen sine lege* is now enshrined in general international law.[88] Article 15(1) of the 1966 International Covenant on Civil and Political Rights prescribes: 'No one shall be held guilty of any criminal offence on account of any act or omission which did not constitute a criminal offence, under national or international law, at the time when it was committed.'[89]

Article 5(1) of the Definition of Aggression states that '[n]o consideration of whatever nature, whether political, economic, military or otherwise, may serve as a justification for aggression'.[90] This clause underscores that the motive does not count: even 'a good motive does not prevent an act from being illegal'.[91]

Article 6 adds a proviso that '[n]othing in this Definition shall be construed as in any way enlarging or diminishing the scope of the Charter, including its provisions concerning cases in which the use of force is lawful'.[92] Thus, if an act itemized in Article 3 can legitimately be classified as either self-defence or collective security (see *infra*, Part III), it will automatically be removed from the roster of aggression.

The most controversial stipulation in the Definition is that of Article 7:

Nothing in this Definition, and in particular article 3, could in any way prejudice the right to self-determination, freedom and independence, as derived from the Charter, of peoples forcibly deprived of that right and referred to in the Declaration on Principles of International Law concerning Friendly Relations and Co-operation among States in accordance with the Charter of the United Nations, particularly peoples under colonial and racist regimes or other forms of alien domination; nor the right of these peoples to struggle to that end and to seek and receive support, in accordance with the principles of the Charter and in conformity with the above-mentioned Declaration.[93]

Textually, the veiled terms of Article 7 reflect a compromise between irreconcilable views.[94] Politically, the adoption of the clause gives a boost to the concept that a 'war of national liberation' is a just war (see *supra*, Chapter 3, B, (b)). Legally, the right to receive (and presumably to give)

---

[88] *Cf.* Article 13 of the 1996 Draft Code of Crimes against the Peace and Security of Mankind, *supra* note 58, at 71; Article 22 of the 1998 Rome Statute, *supra* note 37, at 1015.
[89] International Covenant on Civil and Political Rights, 1966, [1966] *UNJY* 178, 183.
[90] General Assembly Resolution 3314, *supra* note 56, at 143.
[91] A. V. W. Thomas and A. J. Thomas, *The Concept of Aggression in International Law* 52 (1972).
[92] General Assembly Resolution 3314, *supra* note 56, at 144.   [93] *Ibid.*
[94] See B. B. Ferencz, 'The United Nations Consensus Definition of Aggression: Sieve or Substance', 10 *JILE* 701, 714 (1975).

support from the outside for a 'national liberation' war is subordinated to the Principles of the Charter. Such subordination is implicit in every General Assembly resolution, which – if clashing with the Principles of the Charter – may be deemed *ultra vires*. But in any event, the superiority of the Charter is spelt out, both in the general proviso of Article 6 and (lest there be any misunderstanding as to how Articles 6 and 7 mesh, considering that both start with the same caveat that '[n]othing in this Definition' can be construed as diminishing from the effect of either clause) more concretely in Article 7 itself. The Charter does not permit the use of inter-State force, except in the exercise of self-defence or collective security (see *supra*, Chapter 4, B, (a)). If Article 7 is understood as permitting recourse to armed force by one State against another for the sake of fortifying the right of peoples to self-determination, in circumstances exceeding the bounds of self-defence or collective security, the dispensation would be inconsistent with the Charter.[95]

C.   Individual responsibility for crimes against peace

(a)   *The scope of the crimes*

Having scanned the General Assembly's Definition of Aggression, it is necessary to explore the applicability of crimes against peace *ratione materiae, ratione personae* and *ratione temporis*.

i.   Ratione materiae Attention has already been called to the exclusion of the threat of force from Article 1 of the General Assembly's Definition (*supra*, B). It may be argued on that basis that a threat of aggression, even one that 'causes capitulation without a fight', does not amount to a crime.[96] Such a limitation would run counter to the case law of the Subsequent Proceedings at Nuremberg, where it was held that a crime against peace may be committed by mere threat of aggression, if the weaker country 'succumbs without the necessity of a "shooting war"'.[97] However, there is no contradiction between Article 1 and the case law: the Definition simply does not come to grips with the problematics of crimes against peace. The question whether crimes against peace are restricted to certain manifestations of aggression in the context of war, or cover also related acts, must find an answer elsewhere.

---

[95] *Cf.* the Dissenting Opinion of Judge Schwebel in the *Nicaragua* case, *supra* note 73, at 351.

[96] See Ferencz, *supra* note 94, at 713.

[97] See T. Taylor, 'The Nuremberg War Crimes Trials', 450 *Int.Con.* 243, 340–1 (1949).

In the seminal provision of Article 6(a) of the London Charter of the International Military Tribunal (quoted *supra*, A), crimes against peace include the 'planning, preparation, initiation or waging' of war of aggression, 'participation in a common plan or conspiracy' and complicity.[98]

A person charged with crimes against peace may be guilty cumulatively of planning, preparation, initiation and waging of war of aggression. In the event, it may not be easy to determine the exact point at which, say, planning ends and preparation begins. But the different terms used in Article 6(a) relate to separate (albeit successive) stages of the criminal course of action, each having a texture of its own. Planning consists of 'the formulation of a design or scheme for a specific war of aggression', whereas preparation is spawned by 'the various steps taken to implement the plan' before the actual outbreak of hostilities.[99] Initiation is linked to the commencement of the war, while waging continues as long as the war is not terminated.

Conspiracy is the least precise term used in Article 6(a). Had the English common law definition of conspiracy been applied to crimes against peace, it would have cast a wide net.[100] The International Military Tribunal was not prepared to go that far.[101] In its Judgment, the Tribunal pronounced that 'the conspiracy must be clearly outlined in its criminal purpose. It must not be too far removed from the time of decision and of action.'[102] To qualify as a conspirator, a person must be shown to have participated in a concrete and criminal common plan. It is not enough for this purpose that a person had supported a vague political programme, even if it ultimately led to a war of aggression.[103]

In the 1954 Draft Code, the preparation of the employment of armed force against another State constituted an offence against the peace and security of mankind.[104] Conspiracy, direct incitement, complicity and attempts to commit any act of aggression also amounted to such offences.[105] The 1996 Draft Code encompasses the concepts of planning, preparation, initiation or waging of aggression.[106]

---

[98] See H. Donnedieu de Vabres, 'Le Procès de Nuremberg devant les Principes Modernes du Droit Pénal International', 70 *RCADI* 481, 540–1 (1947).

[99] M. Greenspan, *The Modern Law of Land Warfare* 455 (1959).

[100] See A. L. Goodhart, 'The Legality of the Nuremberg Trials', 58 *Jur.R.* 1, 10–11 (1946).

[101] See F. Biddle, 'Le Procès de Nuremberg', 19 *RIDP* 1, 14 (1948).

[102] *Nuremberg* trial, *supra* note 10, at 225.

[103] See H. Wechsler, 'The Issues of the Nuremberg Trial', 62 *PSQ* 11, 20 (1947).

[104] Draft Code of Offences against the Peace and Security of Mankind, *supra* note 52, at 151 (Article 2(3)).

[105] *Ibid.*, 152 (Article 2(13)).

[106] Draft Code of Crimes against the Peace and Security of Mankind, *supra* note 58, at 42–3.

In the *Nuremberg* trial, conspiracy, planning and preparation to wage war of aggression were all scrutinized with the advantage of hindsight, after aggression had actually been carried out and finally crushed. However, conspiracy, planning and preparation for aggression constitute crimes against peace as soon as they are committed. In theory, their perpetrators may be brought to trial and punishment even if no war materializes. In practice, of course, it is not easy to contemplate indictment and prosecution of persons accused only of conspiracy, planning and preparation for aggression, when the war is a matter of conjecture and not of historical record.[107]

ii.   *Ratione personae* The waging of war of aggression forms the kernel of crimes against peace. Yet, what does 'waging' mean? If the word is given a broad interpretation *ratione personae*, extending to every person who contributed to the fighting in whatever capacity, all combatants in the armed forces of the aggressor State become criminals automatically; and most civilians may be convicted, as well, on the ground of complicity. This was one of the foremost criticisms levelled at the London Charter and the *Nuremberg* trial by their detractors.[108] Indeed, the broad interpretation was subscribed to in a Separate Opinion by the President of the International Military Tribunal for the Far East (W. F. Webb) in the *Tokyo* trial.[109]

Contrarily, in the *High Command* case of 1948, an American Military Tribunal ruled that the criminality of aggressive war attaches only to 'individuals at the policy-making level'.[110] Another Tribunal, in the *I. G. Farben* case of the same year, declared that only those persons in the political, military or industrial spheres who bear responsibility for the formulation and execution of policies are to be held liable for crimes against peace; a departure from this concept would lead to incongruous results: the entire population could then be charged with the crimes, including the private soldier on the battlefield, the farmer who supplied the armed forces with foodstuffs, and even the housewife who conserved essential commodities for the military industry.[111]

Notwithstanding some dicta weakening it, the general principle that can be derived from the Subsequent Proceedings at Nuremberg is that

---

[107] See P. C. Jessup, 'The Crime of Aggression and the Future of International Law', 62 *PSQ* 1, 8 (1947).
[108] See Viscount Maugham, *U.N.O. and War Crimes* 18–39, 52–8 (1951).
[109] *Tokyo* trial, *supra* note 27, at 373.
[110] *USA v. Von Leeb et al.* ('the *High Command* case') (Nuremberg, 1948), 11 *NMT* 462, 486.
[111] *USA v. Krauch et al.* ('the *I. G. Farben* case') (Nuremberg, 1948), 8 *NMT* 1081, 1124–5.

liability for crimes against peace is limited to the policy-making level.[112] The International Law Commission in 1950 arrived at the similar conclusion that only 'high-ranking military personnel and high State officials' can be guilty of waging war of aggression.[113] In its 1996 Draft Code, the Commission strictly defined the crime of aggression as limited to leaders or organizers.[114]

This is not to say that responsibility for crimes against peace is reduced, even in a dictatorship, to one or two individuals at the pinnacle of power. As the Tribunal in the *High Command* case asseverated: 'No matter how absolute his authority, Hitler alone could not formulate a policy of aggressive war and alone implement that policy by preparing, planning and waging such a war.'[115]

The Tribunal declined to fix a distinct line, somewhere between the private soldier and the Commander-in-Chief, where liability for crimes against peace begins.[116] The Judgment did articulate that criminality hinges on the actual power of an individual 'to shape or influence' the war policy of his country.[117] Those acting as instruments of the policy-makers 'cannot be punished for the crimes of others'.[118] On the whole, it is necessary to sift the evidence concerning the personal contributions to the decision-making process by all those who belong to leadership echelons.

Relevant leadership echelons are by no means curtailed to the military. Crimes against peace may equally be committed by civilians.[119] The most obvious example relates to members of the cabinet or senior government officials whose input is apt, at times, to outweigh that of generals and admirals. But even when a civilian is not a minister or a civil servant, he may be held accountable for crimes against peace (especially for complicity, conspiracy or preparation), if he holds an influential position in public affairs or in the economy.[120]

iii.   Ratione temporis The Tribunal in the *High Command* case remarked that the nature of war as aggressive or otherwise is determined by factors linked to its initiation.[121] This does not mean that persons who

---

[112] See G. Brand, 'The War Crimes Trials and the Laws of War', 26 *BYBIL* 414, 420–1 (1949).

[113] Nürnberg Principles, *supra* note 51, at 376.

[114] Draft Code of Crimes against the Peace and Security of Mankind, *supra* note 58, at 42–3.

[115] *High Command* case, *supra* note 110, at 486.   [116] *Ibid.*, 486–7.   [117] *Ibid.*, 488–9.

[118] *Ibid.*, 489.   [119] See Greenspan, *supra* note 99, at 455–6.

[120] Yet, in the Subsequent Proceedings at Nuremberg, industrialists and financiers were acquitted from charges of aggressive war. See Taylor, *supra* note 97, at 309–10, 339.

[121] *High Command* case, *supra* note 110, at 486.

steer an aggressor State during an advanced stage of the war (without being involved in the outbreak of hostilities) cannot be arraigned. Waging war of aggression is a continuous offence. Periodic reviews of the changing situation are inevitable in the course of every prolonged war. Those who mould a decision to persist in the illegal use of force may be charged with waging aggressive war, although they had nothing to do with the inception of the fighting.

The identification of the aggressor State on the basis of the commencement of war means that subsequent events do not affect the legal analysis. The aggressor, satisfied with the immediate territorial or other gains, may assume a defensive posture. The victim State, desiring to dislodge the aggressor from its positions, may be operationally on the offensive. These shifting military strategies do not remove the legal stamp of aggression, which is irreversibly attached to the opening of war by one of the parties. The relative standing of the belligerents as aggressor and victim States is not eroded by the tide of war, nor is it altered by the means and methods of warfare. If the victim State violates a cease-fire suspending hostilities (see *supra*, Chapter 2, C), it still does not trade places with the aggressor. Even if the aggressor State conducts hostilities in perfect harmony with the *jus in bello*, while the armed forces of the victim State commit war crimes and crimes against humanity,[122] the legal position under the *jus ad bellum* remains the same as regards responsibility for crimes against peace.

A temporal issue arising after the commission of a crime is that of possible prescription. The statutory limitation of crimes is not a principle recognized by all States in their internal legislation, and it has certainly not crystallized as an international legal norm.[123] The issue is whether crimes against peace are exempt from the operation of general statutes of limitation obtaining within the domestic legal system of the prosecuting State. There are two international conventions promulgating the non-applicability of statutory limitations to war crimes and crimes against humanity: one drafted in 1968 by the General Assembly,[124] the other concluded in 1974 under the auspices of the Council of Europe.[125] Neither instrument is relevant to crimes against peace. The exemption of crimes against peace from national statutes of limitations was discussed

---

[122] War crimes and crimes against humanity are defined in Article 6(b)-(c) of the London Charter, *supra* note 5, at 639–40.

[123] See F. Weiss, 'Time Limits for the Prosecution of Crimes against International Law', 53 *BYBIL* 163, 165, 185 (1982).

[124] Convention on the Non-Applicability of Statutory Limitations to War Crimes and Crimes against Humanity, 1968, [1968] *UNJY* 160.

[125] European Convention on the Non-Applicability of Statutory Limitation to Crimes against Humanity and War Crimes, 1974, 13 *ILM* 540 (1974).

in the context of the UN instrument, but ultimately the General Assembly decided (for political and practical reasons, without prejudging the legal question) not to deal with the matter.[126] On the other hand, the Rome Statute of 1998 promulgates in Article 29:

> The crimes within the jurisdiction of the Court shall not be subject to any statute of limitations.[127]

As noted (*supra*, A), aggression is one of the crimes within the jurisdiction of the ICC.

(b)   Mens rea

All existing international crimes have two constituent elements: the criminal act (*actus reus*), and a criminal intent or at least a criminal consciousness (*mens rea*).[128] The indispensability of *mens rea* as an essential component of international crimes is proclaimed in Article 30 of the Rome Statute:

1. Unless otherwise provided, a person shall be criminally responsible and liable for punishment for a crime within the jurisdiction of the Court only if the material elements are committed with intent and knowledge.
2. For the purposes of this article, a person has intent where:
   (a) In relation to conduct, that person means to engage in the conduct;
   (b) In relation to a consequence, that person means to cause that consequence or is aware that it will occur in the ordinary course of events.
3. For the purposes of this article, 'knowledge' means awareness that a circumstance exists or a consequence will occur in the ordinary course of events. 'Know' and 'knowingly' shall be construed accordingly.[129]

The Definition of Aggression, adopted by the General Assembly, does not go beyond the *actus reus*.[130] However, a crime against peace is not completed unless the *actus reus* is accompanied by *mens rea*, often termed *animus agressionis*.[131] The significance of criminal intent as an essential ingredient of crimes against peace was brought into relief by the

---

[126] See N. Lerner, 'The Convention on the Non-Applicability of Statutory Limitations to War Crimes', 4 *Is.LR* 512, 519–20 (1969).

[127] Rome Statute, *supra* note 37, at 1018.

[128] See Y. Dinstein, 'Defences', *Substantive and Procedural Aspects of International Criminal Law: The Experience of International and National Courts*, I, 371, 371–2 (G. K. McDonald and O. Swaak-Goldman eds., 2000).

[129] Rome Statute, *supra* note 37, at 1018.

[130] See R. Mushkat, 'When War May Justifiably Be Waged: An Analysis of Historical and Contemporary Legal Perspectives', 15 *BJIL* 223, 235–8 (1989).

[131] See S. Glaser, 'Culpabilité en Droit International Pénal', 99 *RCADI* 467, 504–5 (1960).

Judgment in the *High Command* case.[132] The Tribunal noted that almost all nations, including even a traditionally neutral country like Switzerland, arm and prepare for the eventuality of war.[133] 'As long as there is no aggressive intent, there is no evil inherent in a nation making itself militarily strong.'[134] The International Military Tribunal at *Nuremberg*, in acquitting Schacht of the crimes with which he had been charged, emphasized that a rearmament programme by itself is not criminal: to qualify as a crime against peace, rearmament must be undertaken as part of a plan to wage aggressive war.[135] Indeed, insofar as a rearmament programme is concerned, the element of intent is so predominant in the composition of a crime against peace that its absence precludes the consolidation of the *actus reus* itself.

The manufacture or purchase of armaments is not the only course of action which may appear in a different light, depending on the intention. In most countries, staff officers[136] devote a lot of time and energy to the production of contingency plans for a host of hypothetical scenarios,[137] especially war. Provided that these are genuine contingency plans, and that they are premised on the assumption of self-defence, their authors cannot be regarded as criminals. The high command may even simulate 'war games', and carry out manoeuvres to test operational concepts for combat readiness. Once more, in the absence of aggressive designs, these actions are not criminal.

The intent to undertake war of aggression may be formed by only one or few individuals at the helm of a State. Others at the policy-making level need not be personally guided by the same intent. The acid test is whether, in assisting the preparations for war, they actually know of the aggressive schemes.[138] If they know that aggression is planned, this may suffice to establish the requisite *mens rea*.[139] The obverse side of the coin is that when a person (who actively participates in honing the military machinery) does not possess personal knowledge as to aggressive plans, he cannot be convicted of crimes against peace.

Lack of *mens rea* can be translated into assorted defences. The principal defences which are relevant to crimes against peace are:

[132] *High Command* case, *supra* note 110, at 486. [133] *Ibid.*, 487–8. [134] *Ibid.*, 488.
[135] *Nuremberg* trial, *supra* note 10, at 309.
[136] On the distinction between ordinary staff officers and the *Nuremberg* defendants, see Lord Justice Lawrence (Lord Oaksey), 'The Nuremberg Trial', 23 *Int.Aff.* 151, 157 (1947).
[137] *Cf.* H. Meyrowitz, 'The Function of the Laws of War in Peacetime', 251 *IRRC* 77, 83 (1986).
[138] See *Nuremberg* trial, *supra* note 10, at 310. [139] *Cf. ibid.*, 282–4.

i. Mistake of fact The defence of mistake of fact is starkly recognized in Article 32(1) of the Rome Statute:

1. A mistake of fact shall be a ground for excluding criminal responsibility only if it negates the mental element required by the crime.[140]

In other words, an act which would otherwise be an international crime may be excused should the Court be satisfied that the accused committed it under an honest but mistaken belief in the existence of facts which, if true, would have made his conduct legal. The defence rests on the well-established principle *ignorantia facti excusat*, and is corroborated by several judicial decisions delivered in war crimes trials (relating to violations of the *jus in bello*).[141] There is no reason to exclude crimes against peace from the general rule. Thus, if it can be factually determined that – when launching hostilities against Atlantica (subsequently condemned as an aggressive war) – policy-makers in Patagonia mistakenly believed *bona fide* that they were acting in self-defence against an armed attack (see *infra*, Chapter 7, B),[142] this absence of *mens rea* should exonerate them from individual criminal responsibility.

ii. Mistake of law The defence of mistake of law is also accepted, under certain circumstances, by Article 32(2) of the Rome Statute:

2. A mistake of law as to whether a particular type of conduct is a crime within the jurisdiction of the Court shall not be a ground for excluding criminal responsibility. A mistake of law may, however, be a ground for excluding criminal responsibility if it negates the mental element required by such a crime, or as provided for in article 33.[143]

The implication is that the rule *ignorantia juris non excusat* – widely upheld by national legal systems – has not been espoused by international criminal law. Several scholars take the view that, owing to the relative uncertainty of many rules of international criminal law (as compared to the prohibitions of national law), there is no room for a false presumption that every person is acquainted with the international normative scheme.[144] The war crimes trials of the post-World War II period seem to disclose a tendency to admit ignorance of international law as an excuse, particularly when the relevant norms are disputable.[145]

---

[140] Rome Statute, *supra* note 37, at 1019.
[141] See United Nations War Crimes Commission, 15 *LRTWC* 184 (1949).
[142] The question has been posed by R. Lapidoth, 'Book Review' [of the first edition of this volume], 23 *Is.LR* 557, 559 (1989).
[143] Rome Statute, *supra* note 37, at 1019. Article 33 of the Statute will be examined *infra*, (c), ii.
[144] See Dinstein, *supra* note 128, at 377.
[145] See United Nations War Crimes Commission, *supra* note 141, at 182–3.

The allegation of mistake of law may be less potent in the context of crimes against peace than in other situations, since policy-makers are more likely than plain soldiers to be knowledgeable about international law. Even high-ranking officers and civilians may invoke *ignorantia juris* when the more subtle points of legitimate self-defence are at issue (see *infra*, Chapters 7–9). But the penumbra of uncertainty, which is characteristic of some segments of the contemporary *jus ad bellum*, should not be exaggerated. In most cases, the claim of mistake of law will not be credible when made by top-level functionaries who perpetrated a crime against peace. If the subjective knowledge of such persons with respect to specific norms of international law cannot be ascertained by direct evidence, the task can be facilitated through the use of objective criteria (such as the manifest illegality of the action taken).[146]

iii. Duress The definition of the defence of duress appears in Article 31(1)(d) of the Rome Statute:

1. In addition to other grounds for excluding criminal responsibility provided for in this Statute, a person shall not be criminally responsible if, at the time of that person's conduct:

. . .

(d) The conduct which is alleged to constitute a crime within the jurisdiction of the Court has been caused by duress resulting from a threat of imminent death or of continuing or imminent serious bodily harm against that person or another person, and the person acts necessarily and reasonably to avoid this threat, provided that the person does not intend to cause a greater harm than the one sought to be avoided. Such a threat may either be:

(i) Made by other persons; or
(ii) Constituted by other circumstances beyond that person's control.[147]

The defence of duress means that an act which would otherwise be an international offence may be excused, if the Court is satisfied that the accused committed it in the absence of moral choice (that is to say, that the choice available to him was morally vitiated by the constraints of the situation). As the International Military Tribunal at *Nuremberg* phrased it, the 'true test' of criminal responsibility is 'whether moral choice was in fact possible'.[148]

In principle, duress has been expressly accepted as an admissible defence in international judicial proceedings, subject to stringent

[146] See Y. Dinstein, *The Defence of 'Obedience to Superior Orders' in International Law* 28–9 (1965).
[147] Rome Statute, *supra* note 37, at 1018–19.
[148] *Nuremberg* trial, *supra* note 10, at 224.

conditions.[149] But empirically, when the leaders of a nation deliberate the pros and cons of embarking upon an aggressive war against a foreign country, the decision is seldom (if ever) motivated by coercion in the full legal sense of the term.

iv. Insanity Article 31(1)(a) of the Rome Statute excludes criminal responsibility when:

(a) The person suffers from a mental disease or defect that destroys that person's capacity to appreciate the unlawfulness or nature of his or her conduct, or capacity to control his or her conduct to conform to the requirements of law.[150]

This denotes that an accused will not be held criminally responsible for a crime against peace if he acted as a result of insanity (the presumption being that every person is of sound mind).

(c)   Inadmissible defence pleas

There are a number of spurious defence pleas, typical of war crimes trials, which must be dismissed:

i. Obedience to national law When international criminal law directly imposes obligations on individuals, any provisions of national law colliding head-on with these obligations are annulled by international law. In the words of the Tribunal in the *High Command* case:

International common law must be superior to and, where it conflicts with, take precedence over national law or directives issued by any national governmental authority. A directive to violate international criminal common law is therefore void and can afford no protection to one who violates such law in reliance on such a directive.[151]

The logic of the general rule is enhanced when the defendants are leading statesmen and military commanders who bear responsibility for crimes against peace. If the national policy-makers could seek refuge behind national enactments (often products of their own efforts), the prohibitions of international law might have an evanescent existence. Even in a dictatorship, the despot must rely on some key individuals to assist him in expounding and administering the national policy. As the International Military Tribunal at *Nuremberg* held:

Hitler could not make aggressive war by himself. He had to have the co-operation of statesmen, military leaders, diplomats, and business men. ... They are not to

---

[149] See Dinstein, *supra* note 128, at 374–5.
[150] Rome Statute, *supra* note 37, at 1018.
[151] *High Command* case, *supra* note 110, at 508.

be deemed innocent because Hitler made use of them, if they knew what they were doing.[152]

Offenders are not relieved of responsibility only because their State failed to incorporate crimes against peace (or other international crimes) in the domestic penal code. This is one of the Nürnberg Principles, as formulated by the International Law Commission.[153]

ii. Obedience to superior orders When superior orders are issued, they may be illegal from the perspective of national law as much as international law. Should that be the case, no clash between the two legal systems would be fuelled by the unlawful orders. Nevertheless, a doctrine was developed by L. Oppenheim[154] and others, whereby commanders alone incur responsibility for the war crimes of their subordinates (*respondeat superior*), so that obedience to superior orders is an admissible defence *per se*. The usual expectation is that the shield of *respondeat superior* will be raised by lower echelons. Yet, senior German officials, who wielded immense power in the Nazi hierarchy, also tried to shift their responsibility to the dead *Führer*.

Under Article 8 of the London Charter, the fact that a defendant acted pursuant to orders does not free him from responsibility although it may be considered in mitigation of punishment.[155] The proper meaning of this provision is that the fact of obedience to superior orders must not play any part at all in the evaluation of criminal responsibility (in connection with any defence whatever), and it is only relevant in the assessment of punishment.[156] The International Military Tribunal at *Nuremberg* fully endorsed the provision of Article 8, while adding in a somewhat improper context the 'moral choice' test.[157] The International Law Commission introduced the element of moral choice into the Nürnberg Principles,[158] whereas it employed different terminology in the 1954 Draft Code.[159] In 1996, the Commission followed in the footsteps of the London Charter when it prescribed in Article 5:

The fact that an individual charged with a crime against the peace and security of mankind acted pursuant to an order of a Government or a superior does not

---

[152] *Nuremberg* trial, *supra* note 10, at 226.
[153] Nürnberg Principles, *supra* note 51, at 374–5 (Principle II and Commentary).
[154] See L. Oppenheim, *International Law*, II, 264–5 (lst ed., 1906).
[155] Charter of the International Military Tribunal, *supra* note 5, at 640.
[156] See Dinstein, *supra* note 146, at 117.
[157] *Nuremberg* trial, *supra* note 10, at 224.
[158] Nürnberg Principles, *supra* note 51, at 375 (Principle IV).
[159] Draft Code of Offences against the Peace and Security of Mankind, *supra* note 52, at 152 (Article 4).

relieve him of criminal responsibility, but may be considered in mitigation of punishment if justice so requires.[160]

Article 33(1) of the Rome Statute employs different language:

1. The fact that a crime within the jurisdiction of the Court has been committed by a person pursuant to an order of a government or of a superior, whether military or civilian, shall not relieve that person of responsibility unless:
(a) The person was under a legal obligation to obey orders of the government or the superior in question;
(b) The person did not know that the order was unlawful; and
(c) The order was not manifestly unlawful.[161]

The basic precept of the Rome Statute is the same as that enshrined in the London Charter: obedience to superior orders is no defence. However, the Statute recognizes an exception related to the defence of mistake of law (defined in Article 32(2)). When three cumulative conditions are met (the existence of a legal obligation to obey the order, the lack of knowledge of the order's illegality and the fact that it is not manifestly unlawful), criminal responsibility can be relieved. This text provides a fragmented solution to a wide-ranging problem. There is nothing wrong with the reference to knowledge of the law and manifest illegality.[162] But by focusing exclusively on obedience to superior orders as an element in the context of the defence of mistake of law, the framers of Article 33(1) disregarded possible combinations between obedience to superior orders and the defences of mistake of fact and duress.

In the opinion of the present writer, there is no difference in this respect between mistake of law, mistake of fact and duress, which in practice are often intertwined with obedience to superior orders. When the evidence shows that the accused in the dock obeyed orders under duress (within the legitimate scope of that defence), or without being aware of the true state of affairs or the illegality of the order (within the permissible bounds of the dual defence of mistake), he ought to be relieved of criminal responsibility.

It is submitted that the correct legal position should be set forth as follows: the fact that a defendant acted in obedience to superior orders

---

[160] Draft Code of Crimes against the Peace and Security of Mankind, *supra* note 58, at 23.
[161] Rome Statute, *supra* note 37, at 1019.
[162] The reference to manifest illegality in Article 33(1) has been criticized on the ground that all crimes enumerated in the Rome Statute are serious and consequently all orders to commit them are manifestly unlawful. See P. Gaeta, 'The Defence of Superior Orders: The Statute of the International Criminal Court *versus* Customary International Law', 10 *EJIL* 172, 190–1 (1999). However, the definitions of the gravest of crimes may be surrounded by a periphery of uncertainty (see *supra*, (b), ii).

cannot constitute a defence *per se*, but is a factual element which may be taken into account – in conjunction with other circumstances – within the compass of an admissible defence based on lack of *mens rea* (specifically, duress or mistake). This statement of the law, first advanced by the present writer,[163] has been adopted by Judges McDonald and Vohrah in their Joint Separate Opinion in the Judgment of the Appeals Chamber of the International Criminal Tribunal for the Former Yugoslavia (ICTY) in the *Erdemovic* case.[164]

Even when a plea of obedience to superior orders is deemed inadmissible as a reason for relieving a defendant of responsibility, it may nevertheless be considered in mitigation of punishment where the circumstances of the case warrant such a conclusion. As indicated, Article 8 of the London Charter – which utterly removes obedience to superior orders from the purview of any defence whatever – allows weighing that fact in mitigation of punishment 'if the Tribunal determines that justice so requires'.[165] Obviously, when alleviation of punishment is permitted, it is not mandatory but merely within the discretion of the Court. In the *Erdemovic* case, the ICTY Trial Chamber observed that 'tribunals have tended to show more leniency in cases where the accused arguing a defence of superior orders held a low rank in the military or civilian hierarchy'.[166] It is self-evident that high-ranking policy-makers held responsible for crimes against peace can scarcely expect mitigation of punishment, notwithstanding evidence that they have complied with orders.

iii. Acts of State According to H. Kelsen and others, the crime of aggressive war is imputed by international law to the State, and no criminal responsibility can be attached to individuals acting in their capacity as organs of that State.[167] Approval of the acts of State doctrine would have totally obstructed the goal of punishing crimes against peace, inasmuch as the perpetrators of these crimes are almost always organs of the State.

---

[163] See Dinstein, *supra* note 146, at 88, 214, 252.

[164] 'We subscribe to the view that obedience to superior orders does not amount to a defence *per se* but is a factual element which may be taken into consideration in conjunction with other circumstances of the case in assessing whether the defences of duress or mistake of fact are made out.' *Prosecutor v. Erdemovic*, Sentencing Appeal, ICTY Case No. IT-96–22-A, Appeals Chamber, 1997, 111 *ILR* 298, 333.

[165] Charter of the International Military Tribunal, *supra* note 5, at 640.

[166] *Prosecutor v. Erdemovic*, Sentencing Judgment, ICTY Case No. IT-96–22-T, Trial Chamber, 1996, 108 *ILR* 180, 199.

[167] See H. Kelsen, 'Collective and Individual Responsibility for Acts of State in International Law', [1948] *JYIL* 226, 238–9.

In conformity with Article 7 of the London Charter, the official position of a defendant (even as Head of State) does not free him from responsibility, nor will it mitigate his punishment.[168] The International Military Tribunal at *Nuremberg* flatly repudiated the concept underlying Kelsen's thesis:

> The principle of international law, which under certain circumstances, protects the representatives of a state, cannot be applied to acts which are condemned as criminal by international law. The authors of these acts cannot shelter themselves behind their official position in order to be freed from punishment in appropriate proceedings.[169]

The rejection of the theory that the official position of a person can relieve him of responsibility figures prominently in the Nürnberg Principles,[170] as well as in the two Draft Codes of 1954[171] and 1996.[172] Article 27(1) of the Rome Statute is more detailed than other texts:

> 1. This Statute shall apply equally to all persons without any distinction based on official capacity. In particular, official capacity as a Head of State or government, a member of a government or parliament, an elected representative or a government official shall in no case exempt a person from criminal responsibility under this Statute, nor shall it, in and of itself, constitute a ground for reduction of sentence.

Undeniably, the attribution of an act to the State, while generating State responsibility (see *supra*, Chapter 4, F, (a)), does not negate today the criminal liability of individuals.

(d)   The penal proceedings

How is an individual to be held responsible for crimes against peace? Rudimentary considerations of due process require that this be done only by a court of law, and not by a political body (such as the Security Council). One of the Nürnberg Principles is that a person charged with crimes against peace (or other offences) 'has the right to a fair trial on the facts and law'.[173] Judicial guarantees for a fair trial are incorporated in the

---

[168] Charter of the International Military Tribunal, *supra* note 5, at 640.
[169] *Nuremberg* trial, *supra* note 10, at 223.
[170] Nürnberg Principles, *supra* note 51, at 375 (Principle III).
[171] Draft Code of Offences against the Peace and Security of Mankind, *supra* note 52, at 152 (Article 3).
[172] Draft Code of Crimes against the Peace and Security of Mankind, *supra* note 58, at 26 (Article 7).
[173] Nürnberg Principles, *supra* note 51, at 375 (Principle V).

1996 Draft Code.[174] Detailed provisions about the rights of the accused appear in the Rome Statute.[175]

Two International Military Tribunals with jurisdiction over crimes against peace functioned successfully, at *Nuremberg* and at *Tokyo*, after World War II. However, those judicial bodies were set up by the victors in that war – for the *ad hoc* prosecution of the major enemy war criminals – and, having discharged their duties, they were dismantled.[176] As mentioned (*supra*, A), the two *ad hoc* International Tribunals operating at the present moment (ICTY and ICTR) have no jurisdiction over crimes against peace. The recently established permanent International Criminal Court (ICC) does, under the rubric of the crime of aggression. But in the absence of a definition of the crime, the ICC will not be able to exercise that jurisdiction until the Rome Statute is amended (see *supra*, A). At the moment, there is no international penal tribunal competent to deal with the perpetrators of crimes against peace. By default, offenders can solely be tried and punished by domestic tribunals.

The rationale for entrusting an international criminal court with jurisdiction over crimes against peace is palpable. Trials of other international crimes (principally, war crimes and crimes against humanity) have a lot of merit even when conducted before domestic courts. But the nature of crimes against peace is such that no domestic proceedings can conceivably dispel doubts regarding the impartiality of the judges. As a matter of law, jurisdiction over crimes against peace is probably universal,[177] although the Joint Separate Opinion of Judges Higgins, Kooijmans and Buergenthal in the 2002 *Case Concerning the Arrest Warrant of 11 April 2000* (adjudicated by the International Court of Justice) expressed a certain hesitation about the range of application of the exercise of universal jurisdiction.[178] In any event, only enemy (or former enemy) States, rather than neutrals, are likely to convict and sentence offenders charged with crimes against peace. Any panel of judges comprised exclusively of enemy (or former enemy) nationals will be suspected of irrepressible bias. There is no escape from the conclusion that the present state of affairs is lamentable, giving rise as it does to assertions of 'victor's justice'.[179] The flaw in the system cannot be redressed until the Rome Statute is amended in a satisfactory fashion.

[174] Draft Code of Crimes against the Peace and Security of Mankind, *supra* note 58, at 33 (Article 11).
[175] Rome Statute, *supra* note 37, at 1040–1 (Articles 66–7).
[176] See R. K. Woetzel, *The Nuremberg Trials in International Law* 40 (1962).
[177] See M. Akehurst, 'Reprisals by Third States', 44 *BYBIL* 1, 18 (1970).
[178] *Case Concerning the Arrest Warrant of 11 April 2000*, [2002] *ICJ Rep.* 3, 76–9.
[179] See, e.g., R. H. Minear, *Victor's Justice: The Tokyo War Crimes Trial* 180 (1971).

(e)   Immunities from jurisdiction

Article 27(2) of the Rome Statute prescribes:

Immunities or special procedural rules which may attach to the official capacity of a person, whether under national or international law, shall not bar the Court from exercising its jurisdiction over such a person.[180]

Irrespective of immunities existing under national law, there is no doubt that – under customary international law – certain individuals benefit from at least some jurisdictional immunity when they go abroad. The immunity can apply either *ratione personae* (to wit, as regards any act that they commit, whether in an official or in a private capacity) or *ratione materiae* (namely, with respect only to acts committed in an official capacity).

i. Diplomatic and consular agents   The most obvious jurisdictional immunity is enjoyed by diplomatic agents. A foreign diplomatic agent benefits from full immunity *ratione personae* from the criminal jurisdiction of the domestic courts of the country to which he is accredited. This jurisdictional immunity – applicable to any type of criminal prosecution in the receiving State – is deeply rooted in customary international law,[181] and is reconfirmed in Article 31(1) of the 1961 Vienna Convention on Diplomatic Relations.[182] Since diplomatic immunity is all-embracing – relating, as it does, to any criminal prosecution in the receiving State – it covers also international crimes, such as crimes against peace.

As an American Military Tribunal held, in 1949, in the *Ministries* case, the immunity *ratione personae* of diplomatic agents 'continues only so long as the diplomatic agent is accredited to the country, plus such additional time as may be necessary to permit him to leave its boundaries'.[183] Thereafter, under Article 39(2) of the Vienna Convention, diplomatic immunity 'shall continue to subsist', but only 'with respect to acts performed by such a person in the exercise of his functions as a member of the mission'.[184] This is an immunity *ratione materiae*, strictly confined in its application to official acts performed in the discharge of diplomatic functions.[185] Diplomatic functions are defined in Article 3 of the Vienna Convention.[186] Inasmuch as crimes against peace clearly exceed the

---

[180] Rome Statute, *supra* note 37, at 1017.
[181] See Y. Dinstein, 'Diplomatic Immunity from Jurisdiction *Ratione Materiae*', 15 *ICLQ* 76, 76–8 (1966).
[182] Vienna Convention on Diplomatic Relations, 1961, 500 *UNTS* 96, 112.
[183] *Ministries* case, *supra* note 28, at 661.
[184] Vienna Convention on Diplomatic Relations, *supra* note 182, at 118.
[185] See Dinstein, *supra* note 181, at 81–9.
[186] Vienna Convention on Diplomatic Relations, *supra* note 182, at 98.

range of diplomatic functions, they are not cloaked by immunity *ratione materiae*.

For the same reason, consular immunity from jurisdiction is irrelevant to international crimes. Under Article 43(1) of the 1963 Vienna Convention on Consular Relations, consular jurisdictional immunity applies (even during the tenure of the consular officer) only 'in respect of acts performed in the exercise of consular functions'.[187] Consular functions are defined in Article 5 of the Convention,[188] and an act committed beyond their scope does not qualify for immunity.[189] It follows that the perpetration of crimes against peace can never be shielded by consular immunity.

ii. Heads of States Incontrovertibly, when a serving Head of State is sued in the domestic courts of a foreign country, he enjoys a jurisdictional immunity *ratione personae* comparable to diplomatic immunity.[190] The construct that a Head of State while in office is protected by immunity *ratione personae* was underscored by Lord Hope in the *Pinochet* case of 1999.[191] The *Institut de Droit International*, in a resolution adopted in Vancouver in 2001, stated the rule categorically:

In criminal matters, the Head of State shall enjoy immunity from jurisdiction before the courts of a foreign State for any crime he or she may have committed, regardless of its gravity.[192]

The real issue about Heads of States relates to their position once they step down from their lofty position. Nobody can deny that some degree of jurisdictional immunity *ratione materiae* applies *sine die* in respect of acts performed by the Head of State while he was in office. As pointed out by Lord Millett in the *Pinochet* case, this immunity is confined to official acts performed in the representative capacity of a Head of State.[193] But the question is whether the immunity covers all official acts. The answer given in the *Pinochet* case is that the immunity *ratione materiae* of former Heads of States is subject to exceptions in respect of war crimes and other serious international crimes.[194] The *Pinochet* case served as the main

---

[187] Vienna Convention on Consular Relations, 1963, [1963] *UNJY* 109, 122.
[188] *Ibid.*, 111–12.
[189] See Y. Dinstein, *Consular Immunity from Judicial Process* 48–61 (1966).
[190] See Oppenheim's *International Law*, I, 1038 (R. Jennings and A. Watts eds., 9th ed., 1992).
[191] *Ex parte Pinochet Ugarte* (No. 3) (House of Lords), [1999] 2 *All ER* 97, 152.
[192] *Institut de Droit International*, Resolution, 'Immunities from Jurisdiction and Execution of Heads of State and of Government in International Law', 69 *AIDI* 743, 753 (Vancouver, 2001) (Article 13(2)).
[193] *Pinochet* case, *supra* note 191, at 172. Lord Millett relied on an analogy from diplomatic immunity *ratione materiae*, citing the present writer (*supra* note 181, at 82).
[194] See, e.g., *ibid.*, 152 (Lord Hope).

ground[195] for the *Institut de Droit International* pronouncing that a former Head of State 'may be prosecuted and tried when the acts alleged constitute a crime under international law'.[196] However, as we shall see (*infra*, iv), in the *Arrest Warrant* case of 2002, the International Court of Justice made no overt reference to international crimes as exceptions to the jurisdictional immunities of former Heads of States charged before domestic courts. Hence, the apparent implication is that (where domestic courts are concerned) the *Arrest Warrant* Judgment 'effectively overrules the House of Lords decision in the *Pinochet* case'.[197]

iii. Certain high-ranking office-holders   In the *Arrest Warrant* case, the International Court of Justice pronounced:

in international law it is firmly established that, as also diplomatic and consular agents, certain holders of high-ranking office in a State, such as the Head of State, Head of Government and Minister for Foreign Affairs, enjoy immunities from jurisdiction in other States, both civil and criminal.[198]

In this case, Belgium – invoking universal jurisdiction – sought to prosecute the incumbent Foreign Minister of the Congo for the commission of war crimes and crimes against humanity. The Court held that, in order to ensure the effective performance of his functions, customary international law grants a Foreign Minister – throughout the duration of his office – full immunity from the criminal jurisdiction of another State.[199] The Court stressed:

In this respect, no distinction can be drawn between acts performed by a Minister for Foreign Affairs in an 'official' capacity, and those claimed to have been performed in a 'private capacity', or, for that matter, between acts performed before the person concerned assumed office as Minister for Foreign Affairs and acts committed during the period of office.[200]

Moreover, the Court concluded that – under customary international law – there is no exception to this full immunity rule even where war crimes and crimes against humanity are concerned.[201] The Court did not regard provisions like Article 7 of the London Charter and Article 27 of the Rome Statute – which concern international criminal tribunals – as relevant to the rule of customary international law applicable to proceedings before national courts.[202] Presumably, the same sweeping immunity

---

[195] See H. Fox, 'The Resolution of the Institute of International Law on the Immunities of Heads of State and Government', 51 *ICLQ* 119, 121 (2002).
[196] *Institut de Droit International, supra* note 192 , at 753 (Article 13(2)).
[197] C. Wickremasinghe, 'Arrest Warrant of 11 April 2000', 52 *ICLQ* 775, 781 (2003).
[198] *Arrest Warrant* case, *supra* note 178, at 20–1.   [199] *Ibid.*, 22–3.   [200] *Ibid.*, 23.
[201] *Ibid.*, 24.   [202] *Ibid.*

ratione personae would cover crimes against peace (which are not mentioned in the Judgment).

   iv. The limits of jurisdictional immunities In 1948, the International Military Tribunal for the Far East declared in the *Tokyo* trial:

Diplomatic privilege does not import immunity from legal liability, but only exemption from trial by the Courts of the State to which an Ambassador is accredited.[203]

In 2002, the International Court of Justice, in the *Arrest Warrant* case, emphasized that 'jurisdictional immunity is procedural in nature' and must not be confused with criminal responsibility (which is a matter of substantive law).[204] As the Court put it, immunity does not mean impunity.[205] Accordingly, the Court held that there is no bar to prosecution of a Foreign Minister (or any other high-ranking office-holder) enjoying jurisdictional immunity in four sets of circumstances:[206]

(1) When the prosecution is conducted under domestic law in the home country of the Foreign Minister.

(2) When the State represented by the Foreign Minister waives his immunity from the jurisdiction of another State.

(3) When a person ceases to serve as a Foreign Minister and he is prosecuted before the domestic court of another State (provided that the court has jurisdiction under international law) in respect of acts committed by him – even during his period of office – in his private capacity.

(4) When the Foreign Minister is prosecuted before an international criminal court vested with jurisdiction (the Court specifically quoted Article 27(2) of the Rome Statute).

These points deserve a few comments. A prosecution of the office-holder by his own State indisputably goes beyond the realm of international law. Waiver can be 'explicit or implied, provided it is certain',[207] and it can be effected either *ad hoc* or in advance by treaty.[208] The narrow formulation of the law as regards the possibility of putting a former office-holder on trial for acts committed in his private capacity raises doubts whether all official acts are excluded without exception (see *supra*, ii).

When the constitutive instrument of an international criminal tribunal explicitly negates jurisdictional immunities – in the vein of Article 27(2)

---

[203] *Tokyo* trial, *supra* note 27, at 372.
[204] *Arrest Warrant* case, *supra* note 178, at 25.   [205] *Ibid.*   [206] *Ibid.*, 25–6.
[207] *Institut de Droit International, supra* note 192, at 749 (Article 7(1)).
[208] See A. Orakhelashvili, 'Arrest Warrant of 11 April 2000', 96 *AJIL* 677, 681 (2002).

of the Rome Statute – this is conclusive for Contracting Parties. Each Contracting Party may be deemed to have waived thereby the jurisdictional immunity of any office-holder representing it. Yet, a two-fold issue arises:

(i) What would be the legal position if a new international penal tribunal is established without addressing the matter of jurisdictional immunities? Is there by now a rule of customary international law that automatically removes any immunity of Utopian office-holders brought before an international penal tribunal whose overall jurisdiction has been accepted by Utopia?

(ii) Surely, even Article 27(2) of the Rome Statute affects only Contracting Parties. However, Article 12(2)(a) of the Statute[209] vests the International Criminal Court with jurisdiction in respect of international crimes (including, in the future, the crime of aggression) committed in the territories of Contracting Parties, 'regardless of the nationality of the offender'.[210] The following question consequently arises: if Arcadia is a Contracting Party to the Statute but Utopia is not, can John Doe – a Utopian high-ranking office-holder – be denied by the Court immunity pursuant to customary international law, having committed an international crime on Arcadian territory? It stands to reason that the answer to the question is negative.[211] If Utopia is not a Contracting Party to the Rome Statute, no waiver by treaty of John Doe's immunity is effected by the only State capable of issuing that waiver, i.e. the State whom he represents (as a rule, the State of nationality).

---

[209] Rome Statute, *supra* note 37, at 1010.
[210] W. A. Schabas, *An Introduction to the International Criminal Court* 62 (2001).
[211] A. Cassese, 'When May Senior State Officials Be Tried for International Crimes? Some Comments on the *Congo v. Belgium* Case', 13 *EJIL* 853, 875 (2002).

6   Controversial consequences of the change in the legal status of war

The profound change that has gripped the international legal system, as a result of the prohibition of the use of inter-State force and the criminalization of aggressive war, raises searching questions in regard to a number of concepts and institutions rooted in the obsolete axiomatic postulate that States are free to commence hostilities at will. It is true that, in some measure, the international community has already adjusted itself to the new legal environment. This is manifest, for instance, in the current invalidity of peace treaties dictated by the aggressor to the victim of aggression (see *supra*, Chapter 2, B, (a), iii). But modification of time-honoured doctrines encounters intractable difficulties in many areas.

The need for adaptation of the law to the present status of inter-State force is adumbrated against the silhouette of the antiquated perception of the two antagonists in war (aggressor and victim) as intrinsically equal in legal standing. It is noteworthy that, as pointed out already by Grotius, the Latin word *bellum* is derived from the more ancient term *duellum*.[1] For centuries, international law treated war in the same manner that domestic law used to deal with the duel. War, like a duel, was viewed with toleration. The parity of the contenders was taken for granted, and the sole concern was about adherence to criteria of 'fair play'. Yet, just as the duel is no longer permitted by national legal systems, war is now forbidden by international law.[2] The criminalization of aggressive war is incompatible with the idea of the equality of belligerents, inasmuch as by definition one

---

[1] Grotius, *De Jure Belli ac Pacis*, Book I, § I, II (2 Classics of International Law ed., F. W. Kelsey trans., 33 (1925)).

[2] In fact, it was the prohibition of the duel that largely guided and encouraged the proponents of the outlawry of war in lobbying for the Kellogg–Briand Pact. 'They were thinking in terms of generations, not of decades.' It is obvious that the frequency of war has not yet been sharply reduced, despite its proscription. But there was also a lengthy interval between the formal banning of the duel and its virtual disappearance. What really counts today is that duelling has been all but eliminated. It is hoped that the fate of war will ultimately be the same. See Q. Wright, 'The Outlawry of War and the Law of War', 47 *AJIL* 365, 369 (1953).

of the parties is a criminal while the other is either the victim of the crime or whoever comes to the victim's rescue.

The discussion in this chapter will focus on the repercussions of the illegality and criminality of war of aggression. The problem to be confronted (in several different ways) is whether the ground has not been cut from under certain norms relevant to the status of war under international law.[3]

A.   War in the technical sense

Can a formal state of war, in the technical sense, be warranted today? Evidently, full-scale hostilities may break out *de facto* in breach of international law. When that happens, the reality of conflict must be acknowledged, and the *jus in bello* will apply (subject to possible reservations as to the mode and extent of its application, to be considered *infra*, C). But do States retain the capacity to initiate *de jure* a state of war? A number of scholars deny that war can 'now lawfully exist as a technical condition', maintaining that a wrongdoer should not be allowed 'to assert belligerent rights arising out of his own wrongdoing'.[4]

Assuming that large-scale hostilities are actually raging, and that the *jus in bello* ought to be applied in its plenitude, a negation of the existence of a state of war appears to be no more than a hollow semantic gesture. Why alter the terminology if no tangible consequences emanate from the change? The argumentation against recognition of a state of war is more compelling in those situations where the war breaks out only in the technical, and not in the material, sense (see *supra*, Chapter 1, A, (b), ii). In such circumstances, the state of war is brought about by a mere declaration. Without resorting to hostilities, conceivably without even running any risk, the country issuing the declaration is allowed to take steps seriously impinging on the rights of individuals (e.g., the sequestration of the property of enemy nationals).[5] The time may have come to eliminate this opportunity to use a state of war, existing essentially on paper, for what may be viewed as curtailment of domestic due process of law and even unjust enrichment by Governments at the expense of individuals.

If (as seems to be the case) a state of war in the material sense can still be triggered today, another issue comes to the fore. N. Feinberg and others

---

[3] See H. Lauterpacht, 'The Limits of the Operation of the Law of War', 30 *BYBIL* 206, 208–11 (1953).

[4] E. Lauterpacht, 'The Legal Irrelevance of the "State of War"', 62 *PASIL* 58, 63–5 (1968). *Cf.* Wright, *supra* note 2, at 365.

[5] See L. Kotzsch, *The Concept of War in Contemporary History and International Law* 248–9 (1956).

ask whether the state of war can continue to exist *de jure* subsequent to the *de facto* cessation of hostilities.[6] Feinberg opines that, upon the actual cessation of hostilities, the relationship between the two opposing sides must revert from war to peace.[7] This is an attractive idea, but it is not borne out by the practice of States. Suffice it to cite Article I of the Treaty of Peace, concluded by Egypt and Israel in 1979, which provides for the termination of the state of war (and the establishment of peace) between the parties upon ratification[8] (see *supra*, Chapter 2, B, (a), i). For several years prior to the ratification of the Treaty of Peace, Israel and Egypt were not engaged in hostilities. Nevertheless, the state of war continued until it was explicitly ended by consent of the parties.

B.   Inconclusive 'police action'

Is it possible that an international force – carrying out enforcement action by virtue of a binding decision, adopted by the Security Council under Article 42 of the Charter of the United Nations[9] (see *infra*, Chapter 10, A, (c)) – will desist from its operations before they are crowned with complete success? The question has not yet arisen in its full dimensions, since so far no enforcement action has been taken by the Security Council under Article 42 (see *infra*, Chapter 10, D, (a)). However, a comparison between World War II and the Korean War will make the dilemma more vivid.

During World War II, the Allied nations expressed their determination to continue the fighting until the Axis Powers 'have laid down their arms on the basis of unconditional surrender'.[10] The policy of unconditional surrender was tenaciously adhered to, and hostilities did not come to a close until the total collapse of the enemy States. All that happened in the pre-Charter era and in a war conducted by the Allies on the legal basis of collective self-defence (see *infra*, Chapter 9), rather than collective security (see *infra*, Chapter 10).

The position was remarkably different at the time of the Korean War. When hostilities commenced, in June 1950, the United Nations Organization had already been functioning. The Security Council formally determined that the armed attack by North Korea against the Republic of Korea constituted a breach of the peace.[11] It further recommended that Member States render assistance to the victim State, in

---

[6] N. Feinberg, *Studies in International Law* 96 (1979).   [7] *Ibid.*, 97.
[8] Egypt–Israel, Treaty of Peace, 1979, 18 *ILM* 362, 363 (1979).
[9] Charter of the United Nations, 1945, 9 *Int.Leg.* 327, 343–4.
[10] Moscow Declaration on General Security, 1943, 9 *Int.Leg.* 82, 83.
[11] Security Council Resolution 82, 5 *RDSC* 4, *id.* (1950).

order to repel the armed attack and to restore the peace.[12] Such assistance was promptly extended by the United States and other nations. In July 1950, the Security Council welcomed this development, recommended to all Members providing military forces that they put their contingents under a unified command, and permitted the use of the UN flag in the course of operations against North Korea.[13] By flying the UN flag, troops from various countries – under American command – appeared to constitute a United Nations force,[14] although strictly speaking this was a coalition of the willing fighting in collective self-defence (see *infra*, Chapter 9, E).

Security Council recommendations have merely a hortatory effect, and are not legally binding (see *infra*, Chapter 10, B, (a)). Hence, the military action in Korea, pursued by UN Member States in compliance with the Council's recommendations, was permissive in nature. The Council, having determined the existence of a breach of the peace, could in theory adopt a mandatory decision ordaining enforcement measures by UN Members. In opting for a recommendation, the Council did not exploit the maximal powers which it possesses under the Charter. But the critical factor is that, in Korea, a multinational force was fighting under the moral aegis of the United Nations.

The force fighting under the banner of the UN managed to save South Korea from being crushed by the aggressor. However, the force did not contrive to achieve unadulterated victory, due to massive intervention by the People's Republic of China (through so-called 'volunteers'). Ultimately, in 1953, an Armistice Agreement was concluded in Panmunjom[15] (see *supra*, Chapter 2, B, (b)). The Agreement provided for the termination of hostilities between the 'United Nations Command' and the North Korean/Chinese forces, along a line not radically swerving from the original 38th parallel (the springboard of the North Korean armed attack in 1950). This was a far cry from what had transpired in 1945. In lieu of unconditional surrender, the co-existence of the two Koreas (aggressor and victim alike) has been confirmed. In 1991, both North and South Korea were admitted as Members of the United Nations.[16]

Will the Panmunjom formula serve as a satisfactory precedent if and when the Security Council activates, in a binding resolution, the full

---

[12] Security Council Resolution 83, 5 *RDSC* 5, *id.* (1950).
[13] Security Council Resolution 84, 5 *RDSC* 5, 6 (1950).
[14] See D. W. Bowett, *United Nations Forces* 45–7 (1964).
[15] Panmunjom Agreement Concerning a Military Armistice in Korea, 1953, 47 *AJIL*, Supp., 186 (1953).
[16] See 45 *Yearbook of the United Nations* 96, *id.* (1991).

panoply of the collective security system under Article 42? As far as the text of the Charter goes, since the task assigned to the Council is that of maintaining or restoring international peace and security – rather than the punishment of aggressors – there cannot be any fault in a post-hostilities settlement which satisfies the Council. But considering the criminalization of aggressive war in international law, it is legitimate to query whether a genuine United Nations force, charged with a mandatory enforcement mission, can limit itself to merely rebuffing an aggressor without scoring a total victory.

Several factors have to be put in balance here. On the one hand, the international functions of a veritable United Nations force (established by the Security Council with a view to carrying out enforcement action against an aggressor) roughly correspond to the role played by an internal police force.[17] If the analogy is pursued to its logical conclusion, always keeping in mind that an aggressor is a criminal, it ensues that the goal of the United Nations force must be the unconditional surrender of the opposing side. In other words, the international 'police' ought to impose law and order by suppressing the crime, and it must refrain from making a 'live and let live' type of a deal with the criminal. 'The police do not negotiate with the law breaker but arrest him and subject him to judicial process.'[18]

On the other hand, the analogy between a United Nations force and a modern police cannot be stretched to extreme lengths.[19] As long as international relations are dominated by the fundamental concept of the sovereignty of States, there is an element of wishful thinking in ascribing to any international force the authority or the sheer power of the national police. The operation of an authentic police presupposes conditions of subjection to societal restraints that are alien to the international community as presently composed.

It is also useful to remember that the domestic police is inclined to be indulgent when confronted with mass movements of lawbreakers. An aggressor State constitutes a single juristic entity, but in reality – owing to the vast numbers of people who are taking up arms when a State embarks upon war – aggression is more reminiscent of a hard-to-quell domestic disturbance of the peace than of an offence committed by an individual criminal. Besides, the internal police finds it occasionally necessary to make deals even with individual criminals (such as hostage takers).

---

[17] See F. Seyersted, *United Nations Forces in the Law of Peace and War* 208 (1966).
[18] See Q. Wright, 'Law and Politics in the World Community', *Law and Politics in the World Community* 3, 9 (G. A. Lipsky ed., 1953).
[19] See Seyersted, *supra* note 17, at 208–9.

On the whole, whereas the settlement reached at the conclusion of hostilities in Korea leaves a lot to be desired, entertaining great expectations of heroic feats to be accomplished by robust United Nations forces is likely to prove anticlimactic. The overriding problem with international 'police' forces is not that they fail in attaining their objectives, but that they are not established in the first place (see *infra*, Chapter 10, C). Setting unrealizable goals for UN forces will not expedite the process of their creation.

C.   Equal application of the *jus in bello*

(a)   Self-defence

The most troubling problem, stemming from the drastic modification of the *jus ad bellum*, relates to the application of the *jus in bello* on an equal footing between the opponents (the aggressor State and the State exercising self-defence). Historically, the notion of equality between belligerents has formed the underpinning of the *jus in bello*. It was unchallenged as long as States were at liberty to go to war against each other.[20] However, once war of aggression became proscribed and criminalized, voices were raised in support of a policy of applying the *jus in bello* in a discriminatory fashion, adversely affecting the aggressor State.

Two main arguments are adduced against the construct of equality between the aggressor State and the victim of aggression in the operation of the *jus in bello*:

(i) The first line of approach was taken up by the prosecution in the *Nuremberg* trial.[21] The contention rests on the reasoning that every war inevitably consists of a series of acts that are criminal in nature (murder, assault, deprivation of liberty, destruction of property, and the like).[22] When a combatant kills an enemy soldier on the battlefield, he is immune from criminal prosecution for murder (viz. he benefits from a 'justification'), because – and to the extent that – the war is lawful.[23] 'Stripped of the mantle of such legality, the act in question stands out starkly as an unjustifiable and inexcusable killing of a human being.'[24] That is to say,

---

[20] The principle of equality was not easily reconcilable with the just war doctrine (discussed *supra*, Chapter 3, A). See G. I. A. D. Draper, 'Wars of National Liberation and War Criminality', *Restraints on War* 135, 136, 158 (M. Howard ed., 1979).

[21] See R. H. Jackson, 'Opening Address', 2 *IMT* 98, 146–7; F. De Menthon, 'Opening Address', 5 *ibid.*, 368, 387; H. Shawcross, 'Closing Address', 19 *ibid.*, 433, 458.

[22] See Jackson, *ibid.*, 146.

[23] See S. Glueck, 'The Nuernberg Trial and Aggressive War', 59 *Har.LR* 396, 455 (1945–6).

[24] *Ibid.*

when the war loses its legality, an umbrella protecting combatants from penal proceedings must be folded. Their immunity is removed, and no justification for premeditated homicide (or any other crime) is admissible as a defence.[25] In a sense, the killing ceases to have the juridical character of an act of war.[26] The act is indistinguishable from any other murder.[27]

All this leads up to the assertion that, since under contemporary international law war is lawful in exercise of self-defence but is unlawful as an act of aggression, there is no place for equality in the treatment of soldiers committing acts of war. Soldiers participating in a lawful war should be accorded the status of prisoners of war (which guarantees their lives and a humane treatment in captivity). Yet, no such privilege ought to be accessible to soldiers taking part in an unlawful war. The latter must be prosecuted and severely punished for any death or other injury that they have caused in the course of the war.

(ii) The second train of thought is linked to the general principle *ex injuria jus non oritur*, whereby he who acts contrary to the law cannot acquire rights as a result of his transgression.[28] The thesis advocated is that no new powers (*i.e.* powers beyond those available in peacetime) may be gained by a State waging an unlawful war.[29] Hence, the aggressor State may not benefit from any rights bestowed by the *jus in bello*. Contrastingly, when a State is engaged in a lawful war (in response to aggression), it is entitled to the whole spectrum of belligerent rights.[30]

From a practical perspective, it is evident that acceptance of either of these two conceptual analyses would have led to a complete collapse of the *jus in bello*. The proposition of equality between the belligerents is, first and foremost, a precept of common sense. The *jus in bello* has in the past succeeded in curbing excesses, notwithstanding the pervasive animosity towards the enemy that is characteristic of every war, only because it has generated mutual advantages for both sides. No State (least of all a State which, through its aggression, has already perpetrated the supreme crime against international law) would abide by the strictures of the *jus in bello* if it knew that it was not going to derive reciprocal benefits from the application of the norms.[31] Moreover, no aggressor is ever willing to concede that it has indeed acted in breach of the *jus ad bellum*. The Security Council, vested by the UN Charter with the authority to

---

[25] See B. D. Meltzer, 'A Note on Some Aspects of the Nuremberg Debate', 14 *UCLR* 455, 461 (1946–7).
[26] See De Menthon, *supra* note 21, at 387.
[27] See Shawcross, *supra* note 21, at 458.
[28] See Lauterpacht, *supra* note 3, at 212.
[29] See Wright, *supra* note 2, at 370–1.   [30] See *ibid.*, 371.
[31] See R. R. Baxter, 'The Role of Law in Modern War', 47 *PASIL* 90, 96 (1953).

determine in a binding way who the aggressor is, rarely issues such a verdict. Each belligerent, consequently, feels free to charge that its opponent has committed aggression. If every belligerent were given a licence to deny the enemy the benefits of the *jus in bello* on the ground that it is the aggressor State, there is reason for scepticism whether any country would ever pay heed to international humanitarian law.[32] Mankind might simply slide back to the barbaric cruelty of war in the style of Genghis Khan.

Even when the position is looked at from a theoretical standpoint, it is necessary to remember that the *jus in bello* confers rights (and imposes duties) not only on the belligerent States but also on human beings.[33] A right afforded by international law to an individual, such as the right of a lawful combatant to be treated in a humane way when captured by the enemy, is not rescinded just because his State has acted in contravention of international law.[34] The individual who does not himself violate the rules of warfare is entitled to profit from these rules, irrespective of the criminal conduct of the country to which he belongs.

When considered *in abstracto*, there may be some merit in subdividing the *jus in bello* into several legal layers. Such a stratification might enable a restrictive application of the principle of equality to norms creating human rights, excluding it from operation when rights accruing solely for belligerent States are established. As early as 1939, the Harvard Research in International Law offered for consideration a differentiation between humanitarian rules governing the conduct of hostilities and other rules (especially those concerning titles to property).[35]

Similar proposals, with somewhat diverse emphases, have been put forward since then. For instance, H. Lauterpacht – in admitting that the principle of equality must continue to prevail in the actual conduct of hostilities – suggested *de lege ferenda* that the principle be inoperative, at least after the end of the war, as regards the acquisition of title over property (so that such an acquisition, albeit consistent with the *jus in bello*, would be invalidated in the case of an aggressor State).[36]

However, any attempt to restrict the range of application of the concept of equality in the *jus in bello* is highly controversial.[37] A thorough study of

[32] See Lauterpacht, *supra* note 3, at 212–13.
[33] See Y. Dinstein, *The Conduct of Hostilities under the Law of International Armed Conflict* 20–2 (2004).
[34] See Wright, *supra* note 2, at 373.
[35] Harvard Research in International Law, Draft Convention on Rights and Duties of States in Case of Aggression (P. C. Jessup, Reporter), 33 *AJIL*, Sp. Supp., 819, 828, 830 (1939) (Articles 2–4, 14).
[36] Lauterpacht, *supra* note 3, at 224–32.
[37] See H. Meyrowitz, *Le Principe de l'Egalité des Belligérants devant le Droit de la Guerre* 106–40 (1970).

the question, with all its ramifications, was conducted by the *Institut de Droit International*.[38] The study culminated, in 1963, with the *Institut* declining to endorse specific recommendations by its Rapporteur (J. P. A. François) to deviate in a meaningful way from the standard of equality.[39] The *Institut* accepted the basic premise that 'there cannot be complete equality' in the operation of the rules of warfare when the competent organ of the United Nations determines that one of the belligerents has resorted to armed force unlawfully.[40] All the same, it was resolved that rules restraining the horrors of war must be equally observed by all belligerents.[41] The *Institut* did decide to explore the conditions under which 'inequality must be accepted'.[42] But in the event, the sequel study was limited to United Nations forces (see *infra*, (b)).

The actual practice of States discloses no diminution in the validity of the principle of the equal application of the *jus in bello* to all belligerents. The four Geneva Conventions of 1949 for the Protection of War Victims – drafted after the Charter of the United Nations and the *Nuremberg* trial, that is, subsequent to the prohibition of the use of inter-State force and the criminalization of aggressive war – apply (under common Article 2) in 'all cases' of war or any other international armed conflict[43] (see *supra*, Chapter l, A, (b), ii). Nothing in the text may be construed as a permission to discriminate between the aggressor and its victim.[44] Protocol I of 1977, Additional to the Geneva Conventions, proclaims explicitly in its Preamble:

the provisions of the Geneva Conventions of 12 August 1949 and of this Protocol must be fully applied in all circumstances to all persons who are protected by those instruments, without any adverse distinction based on the nature or origin of the

---

[38] *Institut de Droit International*, 45 (I) *AIDI* 555–8 (Aix-en-Provence, 1954); 47 (I) *ibid.*, 323–606 (Amsterdam, 1957); 48 (II) *ibid.*, 178–263, 389–90 (Neuchâtel, 1959); 50 (I) *ibid.*, 5–127 (Bruxelles, 1963); 50 (II) *ibid.*, 306–56, 376 (Bruxelles, 1963); 51 (I) *ibid.*, 353–56 (Varsovie, 1965).

[39] J. P. A. François, 'Rapport Définitif ', 50 (I) *AIDI* 111–27 (Bruxelles, 1963).

[40] *Institut de Droit International*, Resolution, 'Equality of Application of the Rules of the Law of War to Parties to an Armed Conflict', 50 (II) *AIDI* 376 (Bruxelles, 1963).

[41] *Ibid.*   [42] *Ibid.*

[43] Geneva Convention (I) for the Amelioration of the Condition of the Wounded and Sick in Armed Forces in the Field, 1949, 75 *UNTS* 31, 32; Geneva Convention (II) for the Amelioration of the Condition of Wounded, Sick and Shipwrecked Members of Armed Forces at Sea, 1949, *ibid.*, 85, 86; Geneva Convention (III) Relative to the Treatment of Prisoners of War, 1949, *ibid.*, 135, 136; Geneva Convention (IV) Relative to the Protection of Civilian Persons in Time of War, 1949, *ibid.*, 287, 288.

[44] See F. Bugnion, 'Just Wars, Wars of Aggression and International Humanitarian Law', 84 *IRRC* 523, 541 (2002).

armed conflict or on the causes espoused by or attributed to the Parties to the conflict.[45]

The judgments delivered in the war crimes trials of the post-World War II period demonstrate that the equal reach of the *jus in bello* to all belligerents was not lessened by the aggression of Nazi Germany (branded as a crime against peace). There are a number of precedents for the rejection of an attempt to undermine the principle of equality. In the *Justice* case, in 1947, an American Military Tribunal responded to the argument that the criminality of the Nazi aggression taints as crimes all the acts of the defendants committed in the course of World War II:

If we should adopt the view that by reason of the fact that the war was a criminal war of aggression every act which would have been legal in a defensive war was illegal in this one, we would be forced to the conclusion that every soldier who marched under orders into occupied territory or who fought in the homeland was a criminal and a murderer. The rules of land warfare ... would not be the measure of conduct and the pronouncement of guilt in any case would become a mere formality.[46]

The Tribunal refused to reach that conclusion.[47] In the *Hostage* case, in 1948, it was held:

international law makes no distinction between a lawful and an unlawful occupant in dealing with the respective duties of occupant and population in occupied territories. There is no reciprocal connection between the manner of the military occupation of territory and the rights and duties of the occupant and population to each other after the relationship has in fact been established. Whether the invasion was lawful or criminal is not an important factor in the consideration of this subject.[48]

Dutch courts followed the same path in several instances. Thus, in the *Christiansen* case, a Special Court enunciated in 1948:

The rules of international law, in so far as they regulate the methods of warfare and the occupation of enemy territory, make no distinction between wars which have been started legally and those which have been started illegally.[49]

In the *Zuhlke* case, the Court of Cassation, also in 1948, stated (in over-ruling a lower tribunal):

it would be going too far to consider as war crimes all war-like acts, including those which were in accordance with the laws and customs of war, performed against

---

[45] Protocol Additional to the Geneva Conventions of 12 August 1949, and Relating to the Protection of Victims of International Armed Conflicts (Protocol I), 1977, [1977] *UNJY* 95, 96.

[46] *USA v. Altstoetter et al.* ('the *Justice* case') (Nuremberg, 1947), 3 *NMT* 954, 1027.

[47] *Ibid.*

[48] *USA v. List et al.* ('the *Hostage* case') (Nuremberg, 1948), 11 *NMT* 1230, 1247.

[49] *Re Christiansen* (Holland, Special Court, Arnhem, 1948), [1948] *AD* 412, 413.

Holland or against Dutch subjects by Germany's military forces or other State organs on the sole ground of the illegality of her war of aggression.[50]

In light of all these weighty authorities, the principle of the equal application in war of the *jus in bello* – irrespective of the merits of the case under the *jus ad bellum* – has been treated by many scholars as 'absolute dogma'.[51] However, the issue has been reopened to some extent as a result of the 1996 Advisory Opinion of the International Court of Justice on the *Legality of the Threat or Use of Nuclear Weapons*.[52] Here the Court pronounced by the barest of majorities (seven votes to seven, with the President's casting vote):

> It follows from the above-mentioned requirements that the threat or use of nuclear weapons would generally be contrary to the rules of international law applicable in armed conflict, and in particular the principles and rules of humanitarian law;
> However, in view of the current state of international law, and of the elements of fact at its disposal, the Court cannot conclude definitively whether the threat or use of nuclear weapons would be lawful or unlawful in an extreme circumstance of self-defence, in which the very survival of a State would be at stake.[53]

The last sentence implies a *non-liquet*, since the Court could not conclude definitively whether the action alluded to is lawful or unlawful.[54] Yet, it is usually understood that if international law does not prohibit a certain conduct, that conduct is lawful.[55] It follows that, according to the majority of the Court, the use of nuclear weapons would be lawful when undertaken by the party acting in extreme self-defence, provided that the very survival of the State is at stake. But patently, in the Court's opinion, the adversary of that party – the aggressor – cannot employ nuclear weapons no matter what: not even if its survival is at stake.[56]

The entire reference to a special case of 'extreme circumstance of self-defence, in which the very survival of a State would be at stake' is enigmatic and vexing. Letting aside the pertinent question, '[w]ho is to judge if the very survival of a State is at stake',[57] it is not clear from what

---

[50] *In re Zuhlke* (Holland, Special Court of Cassation, 1948), [1948] *AD* 415, 416.
[51] L. Doswald-Beck, 'International Humanitarian Law and the Advisory Opinion of the International Court of Justice on the Legality of the Threat or Use of Nuclear Weapons', 37 *IRRC* 35, 53 (1997).
[52] Advisory Opinion on the *Legality of the Threat or Use of Nuclear Weapons*, [1966] *ICJ Rep.* 226.
[53] *Ibid.*, 266.
[54] See the Dissenting Opinion of Vice-President Schwebel, *ibid.*, 322–3.
[55] See the Dissenting Opinion of Judge Shahabuddeen, *ibid.*, 389–90.
[56] See R. Müllerson, 'Missiles with Non-Conventional Warheads and International Law', 27 *IYHR* 225, 241 (1997).
[57] S. Rosenne, 'The Nuclear Weapons Advisory Opinions of 8 July 1996', 27 *IYHR* 263, 296 (1997).

legal angle the Court was addressing the anomalous factual circumstances. One conceivable interpretation of the passage is that the use of
nuclear weapons is contrary to international humanitarian law, but a
breach of that law is nevertheless excused *in extremis* while exercising
self-defence.[58] If this is the correct rendering of the Court's view, one
may ask why other breaches of the *jus in bello* by a State invoking self-
defence are not equally glossed over *in extremis*, 'in particular by a State
whose survival hangs in the balance but which does not possess nuclear
weapons'.[59] The second (and more likely) construction of the text is that
recourse to nuclear weapons is not incompatible with the *jus in bello*, but it
is solely reserved to a State in perilous conditions of self-defence.[60] If so,
'one is forced to wonder whether the Court, indeed, tangled up *ius ad
bellum* and *ius in bello*'.[61] The Court's ruling may be construed as a
dangerous departure from the concept that the *jus in bello* applies equally
to all belligerents, irrespective of their status pursuant to the *jus ad bellum*.
Granted, the scope of the departure is limited by the unique attributes of
nuclear weapons. Still, the precedent is alarming.

(b)   Collective security

The issue of the equal application of the *jus in bello* to all parties in wartime
becomes more complex when one of the opposing sides is a United Nations
force. UN forces consist of national contingents provided by Member
States. The UN Organization as such is not a Contracting Party to the
1949 Geneva Conventions or to any other treaties governing international
humanitarian law. Given the almost universal acceptance of the Geneva
Conventions, it is virtually certain that they are binding on Member States
participating in the peacekeeping operation.[62] But it could be argued that
the UN Organization is not bound by 'these instruments *per se* or *in toto*'.[63] It
is therefore noteworthy that in August 1999, on the Jubilee of the Geneva

---

[58] Apparently, this is the way in which Dissenting Judge Higgins understood the Court's
pronouncement. Advisory Opinion on *Nuclear Weapons, supra* note 52, at 590.

[59] L. Condorelli, 'Nuclear Weapons: A Weighty Matter for the International Court of
Justice: *Jura Non Novit Curia?*', 37 *IRRC* 9, 19 (1997).

[60] See C. Greenwood, '*Jus ad Bellum* and *Jus in Bello* in the *Nuclear Weapons* Advisory
Opinion', *International Law, the International Court of Justice and Nuclear Weapons* 247,
264 (L. Boisson de Chazournes and P. Sands, 1999).

[61] W. Verwey, 'The International Court of Justice and the Legality of Nuclear Weapons:
Some Observations', *International Law: Theory and Practice (Essays in Honour of Eric Suy)*
751, 760 (K. Wellens ed., 1998).

[62] See Y. Sandoz, 'The Application of Humanitarian Law by the Armed Forces of the
United Nations Organization', 206 *IRRC* 274, 283 (1978).

[63] B. D. Tittemore, 'Belligerents in Blue Helmets: Applying International Humanitarian
Law to United Nations Peace Operations', 33 *SJIL* 61, 97 (1997).

Conventions, the UN Secretary-General promulgated a Bulletin setting forth that the fundamental principles and rules of international humanitarian law are applicable to UN forces when engaged as combatants in situations of armed conflict, whether these are enforcement actions or 'peacekeeping' operations[64] (on the difference between the two categories of UN forces, see *infra*, Chapter 10, D). The Secretary-General's Bulletin conclusively shows that UN forces – of whatever type – do not really differ in their legal standing from ordinary (national) armed forces, insofar as the application of the *jus in bello* is concerned.

The Secretary-General's Bulletin only confirmed previous doctrinal views that UN forces must comply with the *jus in bello*.[65] It is true that some divergent positions were advocated prior to the promulgation of the Secretary-General's Bulletin, particularly as regards the scenario of enforcement actions mounted by the Security Council in a mandatory way.[66] However, the *Institut de Droit International* – after an examination of the topic on the basis of a report submitted by P. De Visscher[67] – arrived in 1971 at the conclusion that all the humanitarian rules of the law of armed conflict must be observed without fail by United Nations forces.[68] In 1975, the *Institut* addressed the issue of the application of other (non-humanitarian) rules of armed conflict to United Nations forces (the Rapporteur on this occasion was E. Hambro), and it was resolved that in general these rules, too, must be respected in hostilities in which United Nations forces are engaged.[69]

D.   Impartial neutrality

Neutrality as a policy (see *supra*, Chapter 1, D) is far from *passé*, even under the law of the UN Charter.[70] As the International Court of Justice

[64] UN Secretary-General's Bulletin on the Observance by United Nations Forces of International Humanitarian Law, 1999, 38 *ILM* 1656, *id.* (1999).

[65] See D. Schindler, 'United Nations Forces and International Humanitarian Law', *Studies and Essays on International Humanitarian Law and Red Cross Principles in Honour of J. Pictet* 521, 523 (C. Swinarski ed., 1984).

[66] See, especially, Report of Committee on Study of Legal Problems of the United Nations, 'Should the Laws of War Apply to United Nations Enforcement Action?' (C. Eagleton, Chairman), 46 *PASIL* 216, 220 (1952).

[67] *Institut de Droit International*, 54 (I) *AIDI* 1–228 (Zagreb, 1971); 54 (II) *ibid.*, 149–288, 465–70 (Zagreb, 1971).

[68] *Institut de Droit International*, Resolution, 'Conditions of Application of Humanitarian Rules of Armed Conflict to Hostilities in which United Nations Forces May Be Engaged', 54 (II) *AIDI* 465, 466 (Zagreb, 1971) (Article 2).

[69] *Institut de Droit International*, Resolution, 'Conditions of Application of Rules, Other than Humanitarian Rules, of Armed Conflict to Hostilities in which United Nations Forces May Be Engaged', 56 *AIDI* 541, 543 (Wiesbaden, 1975) (Article 2).

[70] See M. Torrelli, 'La Neutralité en Question', 96 *RGDIP* 5, 29 (1992).

held in its 1996 Advisory Opinion on the *Legality of the Threat or Use of Nuclear Weapons*:

> The Court finds that ... international law leaves no doubt that the principle of neutrality, whatever its content, which is of a fundamental character similar to that of the humanitarian principles and rules, is applicable (subject to the relevant provisions of the United Nations Charter), to all international armed conflict.[71]

A UN Member State is still entitled to remain neutral in a war between other States, as long as the Security Council does not specifically impose on it (in a binding fashion) the obligation to take part in measures of collective security.[72]

Neutrality in the traditional meaning of the term – as a concept based on the principle of impartiality and non-discrimination among belligerents – may be assimilated to the position of a spectator in a duel who is enjoined from rendering assistance to one of the antagonists. But how can impartiality be harmonized with the criminality of war of aggression? How can a third State retain its equanimity, and remain completely above the fray, when it is witnessing a crime against peace?

At the outset, Article 2(5) of the Charter of the United Nations has to be considered:

> All Members shall give the United Nations every assistance in any action it takes in accordance with the present Charter, and shall refrain from giving assistance to any state against which the United Nations is taking preventive or enforcement action.[73]

What this clause denotes is that when measures of collective security are carried out by the UN in conformity with the Charter, Member States must help one side (the UN force) and refrain from aiding and abetting the other (the aggressor State). This, to say the least, is 'not neutrality in the old established sense'.[74]

There are those who believe that even a non-Member of the UN must not treat a UN force (discharging collective security duties) as if it were equal to the aggressor.[75] While it is doubtful that non-Members are subject to any obligation in the matter (an obligation that can apply to them only on the basis of customary international law), it is a safe assumption that they have a right to discriminate between a UN force

---

[71] Advisory Opinion on *Nuclear Weapons*, *supra* note 52, at 261.
[72] See D. Schindler, 'Aspects Contemporains de la Neutralité', 121 *RCADI* 221, 248–9 (1967).
[73] Charter of the United Nations, *supra* note 9, at 332.
[74] C. G. Fenwick, 'Is Neutrality Still a Term of Present Law?', 63 *AJIL* 100, 101 (1969).
[75] See H. J. Taubenfeld, 'International Actions and Neutrality', 47 *AJIL* 377, 395–6 (1953).

and an aggressor State. The *Institut de Droit International*, in its Resolution of 1975, declared that (i) every State (*i.e.* not only a Member State) is entitled to assist a United Nations force when requested to do so; (ii) Member States may not depart from the rules of neutrality for the benefit of the party opposing the UN force; (iii) Member States may not take advantage of the general rules of neutrality in order to evade their obligation to carry out a binding decision of the Security Council.[76]

Article 2(5) deals only with action taken by the United Nations in circumstances of collective security (see *infra*, Chapter 10), and it is not directly apposite to the case of individual or collective self-defence against an armed attack (see *infra*, Chapters 7–9). Yet, the rationale of Article 2(5) militates in favour of a similar solution in both situations, provided that the Security Council has determined who the aggressor is. As a criminal, the duly identified aggressor should not be treated by UN Member States on the basis of equality with whoever is opposing it. One may in fact contend that, once the identity of the aggressor has authoritatively been established by the Council, all Member States must do whatever they can to foil the aggressor's designs and to assist the party resisting it.[77]

During the first phase of the Gulf War, the Security Council – having determined in Resolution 660 (1990) that the Iraqi invasion of Kuwait constituted a breach of the peace[78] – called upon all States in Resolution 661 to act in accordance with the decision to impose economic sanctions on Iraq, and expressly addressed also non-Member States of the United Nations.[79] Similar calls to non-Member States have been made by the Council without any hesitation, even subsequent to a determination of a mere threat to the peace. This is exemplified in Resolution 748 (1992) relating to Libya,[80] Resolution 757 (1992) pertaining to Yugoslavia,[81] and Resolution 917 (1994) regarding Haiti[82] (the latter case being an intra-State affair). Although not strictly germane to the issue of neutrality, such resolutions display an expectation that non-Member States would follow the lead of the Council in all matters of peace and security.

[76] *Institut de Droit International*, Resolution, *supra* note 69, at 543 (Articles 3–4).
[77] See G. Scelle, 'Quelques Réflexions sur l'Abolition de la Compétence de Guerre', 58 *RGDIP* 5, 16 (1954).
[78] Security Council Resolution 660, 45 *RDSC* 19, *id.* (1990).
[79] Security Council Resolution 661, 45 *RDSC* 19, 20 (1990).
[80] Security Council Resolution 748, 47 *RDSC* 52, 53 (1992).
[81] Security Council Resolution 757, 47 *RDSC* 13, 15 (1992).
[82] Security Council Resolution 917, 49 *RDSC* 47, 48 (1994).

In Resolution 678 (1990), which authorized the Coalition cooperating with Kuwait in the Gulf War to 'use all necessary means' (viz. resort to force) to secure full Iraqi compliance with its decisions, the Security Council requested all States to provide appropriate support for the actions undertaken.[83] Since the Council had earlier determined the existence of a breach of the peace, an old-fashioned posture of neutrality – failing to distinguish between Iraq and the Coalition – would have been beset by formidable juridical difficulties. Even non-Member States of the United Nations discontinued the policy of impartial neutrality. Thus, Switzerland (not, at the time, a Member State) fully participated in the economic sanctions against Iraq, as well as in subsequent trade and air embargoes imposed by the Security Council on Libya and Yugoslavia.[84] Moreover, in 1991, Switzerland overcame initial reluctance and allowed overflights by Coalition military transport aircraft (thereby facilitating logistical support for combat missions against Iraq),[85] despite the general rule prohibiting the entry of such aircraft into neutral airspace (see *supra*, Chapter 1, D, (b), i).

When the Security Council determines in an authoritative way who the aggressor is, it is easy for States to justify the abandonment of their neutrality. Yet, the question arises whether – in the absence of such determination – a neutral State, relying on its own judgment in the matter, is entitled to forsake the time-honoured principle of impartiality. A precedent for such conduct may be discerned in the policy of the United States in the early stages of World War II (obviously, prior to the adoption of the UN Charter).

Almost from the start of hostilities in Europe, the neutrality of the United States was more benevolent towards one belligerent (Great Britain) than the other (Nazi Germany) (see *supra*, Chapter 1, D, (b), iii). As the war progressed, the balance tilted increasingly in the same direction. In September 1940, the United States transferred to the United Kingdom 50 old destroyers in consideration for a lease of naval and air bases in British colonies.[86] In March 1941, Congress approved the 'Lend-Lease' Act, which made it possible to sell, lend or

---

[83] Security Council Resolution 678, 45 *RDSC* 27, 27–8 (1990).
[84] See G. P. Politakis, *Modern Aspects of the Laws of Naval Warfare and Maritime Neutrality* 392–4 (1998).
[85] US Department of Defense Report to Congress on the Conduct of the Persian Gulf War, 1992, 31 *ILM* 612, 640 (1992). But see D. Schindler, 'Transformations in the Law of Neutrality since 1945', *Humanitarian Law of Armed Conflict: Challenges Ahead: Essays in Honour of Frits Kalshoven* 367, 372–3 (A. J. M. Delissen and G. J. Tanja eds., 1991).
[86] United Kingdom–United States, Exchange of Notes, 1940, 34 *AJIL*, Supp., 184–6 (1940).

lease weapons, ammunition and supplies to a country the defence of which was deemed vital to the defence of the United States.[87] Following the new legislation, all barriers to the provision of military supplies to Britain were lifted. In May 1941, US naval forces even began to help in ensuring the delivery of the supplies to the British Isles, and, in September of that year, instructions were issued to the US fleet to open fire at sight on any German or Italian submarine or surface vessel entering a sector of the high seas the protection of which was considered necessary for American defence.[88] In December, after Pearl Harbor, the United States itself became a belligerent.

The legal philosophy underlying the far-reaching measures, taken by the United States before its entry into World War II, was expounded by the then Attorney-General (later Associate Justice of the Supreme Court and Chief American Prosecutor at the *Nuremberg* trial), R. H. Jackson, in an address delivered in 1941.[89] According to Jackson, the classical doctrine of impartial neutrality was founded on the assumption of the legality of war, whereas discrimination among belligerents has become permissible as a result of the prohibition of war in the Kellogg–Briand Pact.[90] Jackson traced his thesis back to Grotius,[91] who had stated that a neutral State must not hinder the party waging a just war or strengthen its adversary.[92] Lauterpacht, too, read into Grotius's words a whole concept of 'qualified neutrality'.[93] Support for this concept may be found in other scholarly contributions since Grotius, for example in the Budapest Articles of Interpretation of the Kellogg–Briand Pact, adopted in 1934 by the International Law Association.[94]

It has been suggested that the idea of qualified neutrality should be explained in terms of reprisals (see *infra*, Chapter 8, A, (a), ii) undertaken by third States; meaning that a neutral State may invoke an act of aggression, directed against another country, as a legitimate ground for treating the law-breaker in a manner which would normally be illegal.[95] But this rationalization is not widely shared.

Qualified neutrality is so dissociated from orthodox neutrality that some scholars prefer using the term 'non-belligerency' to depict the status

---

[87] An Act to Promote the Defense of the United States, 1941, 35 *AJIL*, Supp., 76–9 (1941).
[88] See L. Oppenheim, *International Law*, II, 640–1 (H. Lauterpacht ed., 7th ed., 1952).
[89] R. H. Jackson, 'Address', 35 *AJIL* 348–59 (1941).   [90] *Ibid.*, 349–50, 354.
[91] Grotius, *supra* note 1, at Book III, § XVII, III (p. 786).
[92] Jackson, *supra* note 89, at 351.
[93] H. Lauterpacht, 'The Grotian Tradition in International Law', 23 *BYBIL* 39–41 (1946).
[94] International Law Association, *Report of the Thirty-Eighth Conference* 66, 67 (Budapest, 1934) (Article 4).
[95] See M. Akehurst, 'Reprisals by Third States', 44 *BYBIL* 1, 6 (1970).

of a third State discriminating between the two belligerents.[96] Under whatever name, the pitfall is that qualified neutrality is tantamount to a '"half-way house" between neutrality and belligerency'.[97] The belligerent suffering from adverse treatment by a neutral State may not bow to that State's subjective determination as to who the aggressor is, and bilateral relations are liable to deteriorate until the two countries drift into open hostilities.

E.   Territorial changes

Can a State produce territorial changes by resorting to illegal force (or the threat of force)? The issue has already been partly raised, with respect to the legal effect of a peace treaty ceding territory from one party to another (*supra*, Chapter 2, B, (a), iii). As indicated, the validity of such a peace treaty depends on who the beneficiary is. If the cession is from the aggressor to the victim of aggression, there is nothing inherently wrong in the transaction; whereas if the reverse happens, the treaty is null and void.

What is the legal effect of a territorial change brought about without recourse to treaty, in consequence of belligerent occupation and unilateral annexation? The rule that has emerged in international law (well before the prohibition of war and regardless of which State is the aggressor) is that belligerent occupation, by itself, cannot produce a transfer of title over territory to the occupying State.[98] As early as 1917, L. Oppenheim enunciated that '[t]here is not an atom of sovereignty in the authority of the occupant'.[99] An American Military Tribunal reiterated the rule, in 1948, in the *RuSHA* case:

Any purported annexation of territories of a foreign nation, occurring during the time of war and while opposing armies were still in the field, we hold to be invalid and ineffective.[100]

---

[96] See F. R Coudert, 'Non-Belligerency in International Law', 29 *Vir.LR* 143, *id.* (1942–3). For a more recent presentation of the dichotomy between neutrality and so-called non-belligerency, see D. Schindler, 'Neutral Powers in Naval War: Commentary', *The Law of Naval Warfare* 211, 213 (N. Ronzitti ed., 1988).

[97] See T. Komarnicki, 'The Problem of Neutrality under the United Nations Charter', 38 *TGS* 77, 79 (1952).

[98] See the Arbitral Award in *Affaire de la Dette Publique Ottoman* (1925), 1 *RIAA* 529, 555 (per E. Borel).

[99] L. Oppenheim, 'The Legal Relations between an Occupying Power and the Inhabitants', 33 *LQR* 363, 364 (1917).

[100] *USA v. Greifelt et al.* ('the *RuSHA* case') (Nuremberg, 1948), 5 *NMT* 88, 154.

Article 4 of Protocol I, Additional to the Geneva Conventions, reaffirms the principle that the occupation of a territory does not affect its legal status.[101] No territory under belligerent occupation can be validly annexed by the occupying Power acting unilaterally.

While the invalidity of a unilateral annexation subsequent to belligerent occupation is undisputed, the position is not so simple when the annexation takes place after the *debellatio* of the enemy State (see *supra*, Chapter 2, B, (c), ii). Belligerent occupation posits the existence of the enemy as a State and the continuation of the war.[102] *Debellatio* signifies the disintegration of the enemy State and the termination of the war. Under classical international law, if a process of *debellatio* occurred, the victorious State could annex unilaterally the occupied territory of the former enemy.[103] Nowadays, the legal position must be reconsidered on two grounds:

(i) It is necessary to take into account the modern right of self-determination vested in the people (or peoples) inhabiting the conquered territory. Self-determination is referred to in many recent international instruments.[104] Preeminently, common Article 1(1) of the twin 1966 Covenants on human rights prescribes:

All peoples have the right of self-determination. By virtue of that right they freely determine their political status.[105]

The International Court of Justice even held, in the *East Timor* case of 1995, that the assertion that the right of peoples to self-determination has an *erga omnes* character 'is irreproachable'.[106]

If the local people is truly at liberty to determine its political status, a post-*debellatio* annexation by the victorious State must clearly be precluded. The obliteration of the sovereignty of the defeated State does not extinguish the right of self-determination conferred on the people living in the territory overrun by the victorious State. On the contrary, this is the most appropriate moment for that right to assert itself.

---

[101] Protocol I, *supra* note 45, at 97.

[102] See Y. Dinstein, 'The International Law of Belligerent Occupation and Human Rights', 8 *IYHR* 104, 105 (1978).

[103] See M. Greenspan, *The Modern Law of Land Warfare* 600–1 (1959).

[104] The principle of self-determination is mentioned in the UN Charter in two places: Articles 1(2) and 55 (*supra* note 9, at 331, 348). The right derived from this principle is elucidated in the Declaration on Principles of International Law Concerning Friendly Relations and Co-operation among States in accordance with the Charter of the United Nations, General Assembly Resolution 2625 (XXV), 25 *RGA* 121, 123 (1970).

[105] International Covenant on Economic, Social and Cultural Rights, 1966, [1966] *UNJY* 170, 171; International Covenant on Civil and Political Rights, 1966, *ibid.*, 178, 179.

[106] *Case Concerning East Timor*, [1995] *ICJ Rep.* 90, 102. See also the Advisory Opinion on *Legal Consequences of the Construction of a Wall in the Occupied Palestinian Territory*, 2004, 43 *ILM* 1009, 1034 (2004).

It must be appreciated, however, that the legal existence of a right is no guarantee of its implementation. The victorious State may refuse to heed the right of self-determination, annexing the conquered territory notwithstanding the wishes of the local population. This would not be the only instance in which self-determination is frustrated by the facts of life, and the Covenants do not specify how the right expressed in Article 1(1) is to be safeguarded in the absence of cooperation on the part of the State in actual control of the territory.[107]

(ii) Even irrespective of the issue of self-determination, a post-*debellatio* annexation of the territory of the erstwhile enemy by the victorious State may not be easily reconcilable with basic contemporary tenets. As long as the annexation is accomplished by the victim of aggression, benefiting at the expense of the former aggressor State, the process is not without its legal logic: let the aggressor pay for its crimes. But should the annexation expand the territory of the aggressor State, the upshot would be that might creates rights in defiance of the legal system in which these rights are embedded.[108]

As noted, the prohibition of aggressive war constitutes *jus cogens* (see *supra*, Chapter 4, E, (a)). In light of the principle *ex injuria jus non oritur*, many scholars subscribe to the view that a unilateral State action, just like a treaty, can have no legal force when it is in contravention of *jus cogens*.[109] However, the notion of nullity of unilateral acts inconsistent with *jus cogens* is problematic.[110] As Sir Gerald Fitzmaurice put it, even if international law refuses to validate an act conflicting with *jus cogens*, it may be forced to recognize the situation brought about by that (illegal) act.[111]

Article 5(3) of the General Assembly's Definition of Aggression, adopted in 1974 (see *supra*, Chapter 5, B), proclaims that no territorial acquisition resulting from aggression 'is or shall be recognized as lawful'.[112] This clause echoes the text of the 1970 General Assembly Declaration on Principles of International Law Concerning Friendly Relations and Co-operation among States in accordance with the Charter of the United Nations.[113] As mentioned (*supra* Chapter 4, F, (b)), in Article 41(2) of its

---

[107] See Y. Dinstein, 'Self-Determination Revisited', *International Law in an Evolving World (Liber Amicorum Eduardo Jiménez de Aréchaga)*, I, 241, 250–1 (M. Rama-Montaldo ed., 1994).

[108] See Wright, *supra* note 2, at 366.

[109] See T. Meron, 'On a Hierarchy of International Human Rights', 80 *AJIL* 1, 19–21 (1986).

[110] See *ibid.*, 21.

[111] G. Fitzmaurice, 'The General Principles of International Law Considered from the Standpoint of the Rule of Law', 92 *RCADI* 1, 120 (1957).

[112] General Assembly Resolution 3314 (XXIX), 29(1) *RGA* 142, 144 (1974).

[113] General Assembly Resolution 2625, *supra* note 104, at 123.

Draft Articles on State Responsibility – adopted in 2001 – the International Law Commission laid down that, when a serious breach of an obligation under peremptory norms of general international law takes place, no State shall 'recognize as lawful' a situation created by such a serious breach.[114] There are also treaties in which the Contracting Parties undertook not to recognize territorial acquisition brought about by armed force, such as the 1933 Saavedra Lamas Anti-War Treaty (Non-Aggression and Conciliation),[115] and the 1948 Charter of the Organization of American States.[116]

It is not entirely certain what non-recognition of territorial acquisition means in practice.[117] But probably the gist of non-recognition is that, despite a continuous and effective control over the annexed territory, no prescriptive rights[118] evolve in favour of the aggressor. In I. Brownlie's words, 'prescription cannot purge this type of illegality'.[119]

The trouble with non-recognition is that it is 'a device which works well for a limited time-span'.[120] If the *de facto* control of the territory annexed by the aggressor continues uninterrupted for generations, the non-prescription rule may have to give way in the end. International law must not be divorced from reality. When a post-*debellatio* annexation is solidly entrenched over many decades, there may be no escape from the conclusion that new rights (valid *de jure*) have crystallized, although they flow from a violation of international law in the remote past.[121] Even if the initial act of annexation was invalid, the prolonged (and undisturbed) exercise of sovereignty in the territory will finally create prescriptive rights, independently of the originally defective title. There comes a point at which the international legal system has 'to capitulate' to facts: that stage is postponed as far as possible in the case of the extinction of States, but it cannot be completely avoided.[122] The most ardent

---

[114] Draft Articles on Responsibility of States for Internationally Wrongful Acts, Report of the International Law Commission, 53rd session, 43, 53 (mimeographed, 2001).

[115] Rio de Janeiro Anti-War Treaty (Non-Aggression and Conciliation), 1933, 163 *LNTS* 405, *id.* (Article II).

[116] Bogotá Charter of the Organization of American States, 1948, 119 *UNTS* 48, 56 (Article 17).

[117] See H. M. Blix, 'Contemporary Aspects of Recognition', 130 *RCADI* 587, 662–5 (1970).

[118] On the concept of prescription, see Oppenheim's *International Law*, I, 706 (R. Jennings and A. Watts eds., 9th ed., 1992).

[119] I. Brownlie, *Principles of Public International Law* 490 (6th ed., 2003).

[120] C. Tomuschat, 'International Crimes by States: An Endangered Species', *International Law: Theory and Practice, supra* note 61, at 253, 259.

[121] See R. W. Tucker, 'The Principle of Effectiveness in International Law', *Law and Politics in the World Community, supra* note 18, at 31, 44.

[122] K. Marek, *Identity and Continuity of States in Public International Law* 579 (2nd ed., 1968).

supporters of the application of the principle *ex injuria jus non oritur* in international law concede that this maxim 'often yields to the rival principle, *ex factis jus oritur*'.[123] There is really 'little practical alternative ... in the long run'.[124]

These remarks are merely tentative and speculative, for they concern a theme that has not yet been earnestly debated in a concrete setting. The criminalization of aggressive war has been a part of positive international law only since the *Nuremberg* Judgment. In the relatively short time that has elapsed, the international community has not been called upon to resolve, in a specific case of post-aggression annexation, a clash between the legal principles of non-prescription and self-determination, on the one hand, and the gravitational pull of the facts, on the other.[125] It is impossible to forecast, with any degree of confidence, what direction the future practice of States will take with respect to this subject-matter.

[123] Lauterpacht, *supra* note 3, at 212.   [124] Oppenheim, *supra* note 118, at 186.
[125] The long-term effects of non-recognition of a situation created by an unlawful use of force are discussed in the Dissenting Opinion of Judge *ad hoc* Skubiszewski in the *Case Concerning East Timor*, *supra* note 106, at 262–5. But the majority of the Court did not address the issue.

Part III

Exceptions to the prohibition of the use
of inter-State force

7   The concept of self-defence

A.   The right of self-defence

(a)   The meaning of self-defence

In its 1996 Advisory Opinion on the *Legality of the Threat or Use of Nuclear Weapons*, the International Court of Justice stated:

> Furthermore, the Court cannot lose sight of the fundamental right of every State to survival, and thus its right to resort to self-defence, in accordance with Article 51 of the Charter, when its survival is at stake.[1]

The implication is that the right of self-defence is engendered by, and embedded in, the fundamental right of States to survival. However, the Court itself acknowledged that 'the very survival of a State would be at stake' only 'in an extreme circumstance of self-defence'.[2] Extreme circumstances of self-defence – when the very survival of a State is imperilled – do arise from time to time, but the exercise of self-defence is by no means confined to such catastrophic scenarios. The reality of self-defence in inter-State relations is much more prosaic: it transcends life-or-death existential crises and impinges on a host of commonplace situations involving the use of counter-force.

The essence of self-defence is self-help: under certain conditions set by international law, a State acting unilaterally – perhaps in association with other countries – may respond with lawful force to unlawful force (or, minimally, to the imminent threat of unlawful force). The reliance on self-help, as a remedy available to States when their rights are violated, is and always has been one of the hallmarks of international law.[3] Self-help

---

[1] Advisory Opinion on the *Legality of the Threat or Use of Nuclear Weapons*, [1996] *ICJ Rep.* 226, 263.

[2] *Ibid.*, 266. For the full quotation and its context, see *supra*, Chapter 6, C, (a).

[3] See H. Kelsen, *General Theory of Law and State* 339 (1945).

is a characteristic feature of all primitive legal systems, but in international law it has been honed to art form.[4]

Self-help under international law may be displayed in a variety of ways. In the first place, an aggrieved State may resort to non-forcible measures, such as severing diplomatic relations with another State or declaring a foreign diplomat *persona non grata*.[5] Additionally, legitimate self-help in the relations between States may take the shape of forcible measures, in which case these measures must nowadays meet the requirements of self-defence. Occasionally, international legal scholars regard the concepts of self-help and self-defence as related yet separate.[6] However, the proper approach is to view self-defence as a species subordinate to the genus of self-help. In other words, self-defence is a permissible form of 'armed self-help'.[7]

The legal notion of self-defence has its roots in inter-personal relations, and is sanctified in domestic legal systems since time immemorial. From the dawn of international law, writers sought to apply this concept to inter-State relations, particularly in connection with the just war doctrine[8] (see *supra*, Chapter 3 A, (c)). But when the freedom to wage war was countenanced without reservation (in the nineteenth and early twentieth centuries), concern with the issue of self-defence was largely a meta-juridical exercise. As long as recourse to war was considered free for all, against all, for any reason on earth – including territorial expansion or even motives of prestige and grandeur – States did not need a legal justification to commence hostilities. The plea of self-defence was relevant to the discussion of the legality of forcible measures 'short of war', such as extra-territorial law enforcement (see *infra*, Chapter 8, B, (b)).[9] Still, logically as well as legally, it had no role to play in the international arena as regards the cardinal issue of war.[10] Up to the point of the

---

[4] See Y. Dinstein, 'International Law as a Primitive Legal System', 19 *NYUJILP* 1, 12 (1986–7).

[5] See B. Sen, *A Diplomat's Handbook of International Law and Practice* 218, 232 (3rd ed., 1988).

[6] See T. R. Krift, 'Self-Defense and Self-Help: The Israeli Raid on Entebbe', 4 *BJIL* 43, 55–6 (1977–8).

[7] Report of the International Law Commission, 32nd Session, [1980] II (2) *ILC Ybk* 1, 54.

[8] See M. A. Weightman, 'Self-Defense in International Law', 37 *Vir.LR.* 1095, 1099–1102 (1951).

[9] Owing to these historical roots, the customary law relating to self-defence is often viewed as 'best expressed' in D. Webster's formula in the *Caroline* incident (examined *infra*, Chapter 8, B, (c)). M. A. Rogoff and E. Collins, 'The *Caroline* Incident and the Development of International Law', 16 *BJIL* 493, 506 (1990).

[10] See E. Giraud, 'La Théorie de la Légitime Défense', 49 *RCADI* 687, 715 (1934); J. L. Kunz, 'Individual and Collective Self-Defense in Article 51 of the Charter of the United Nations', 41 *AJIL* 872, 876 (1947).

prohibition of war, to most intents and purposes, 'self-defence was not a legal concept but merely a political excuse for the use of force'.[11] Only when the universal liberty to go to war was eliminated, could self-defence emerge as a right of signal importance in international law.[12] Indeed, on the eve of the renunciation of war (and, subsequently, upon the proscription of all forms of inter-State force), the need for regulating the law of self-defence became manifest (see *supra*, Chapter 4, A). The evolution of the idea of self-defence in international law goes 'hand in hand' with the prohibition of aggression.[13]

The right of self-defence is enshrined in Article 51 of the Charter of the United Nations, which proclaims:

> Nothing in the present Charter shall impair the inherent right of individual or collective self-defense if an armed attack occurs against a Member of the United Nations, until the Security Council has taken the measures necessary to maintain international peace and security. Measures taken by Members in the exercise of this right of self-defense shall be immediately reported to the Security Council and shall not in any way affect the authority and responsibility of the Security Council under the present Charter to take at any time such action as it deems necessary in order to maintain or restore international peace and security.[14]

The provision of Article 51 has to be read in conjunction with Article 2(4) of the Charter (see *supra*, Chapter 4, B, (a)).[15] Article 2(4) promulgates the general obligation to refrain from the use of inter-State force. Article 51 introduces an exception to this norm by allowing Member States to employ force in self-defence in the event of an armed attack.

Article 51 describes the right of self-defence as both 'individual' and 'collective' in nature. The meaning of these two adjectives in the context of self-defence will be examined *infra* (Chapter 9, A). Interestingly enough, the legislative history shows that, at its inception, the whole clause governing self-defence was inserted in the Charter with a view to confirming the legitimacy of regional security arrangements (notably, the inter-American system).[16] In actuality, Article 51 has become the main pillar of the law of self-defence in all its forms, individual as well as collective.

This chapter will deal with common questions pertaining to self-defence of whatever category. The next two chapters will be devoted to specific problems relating to the two distinct types of self-defence.

---

[11] E. Jiménez de Aréchaga, 'International Law in the Past Third of a Century', 159 *RCADI* 1, 96 (1978).
[12] See J. Verhoeven, 'Les "Etirements" de la Légitime Défense', 48 *AFDI* 49, 52 (2002).
[13] Report of the International Law Commission, *supra* note 7, at 52.
[14] Charter of the United Nations, 1945, 9 *Int.Leg.* 327, 346.   [15] *Ibid.*, 332.
[16] L. M. Goodrich, E. Hambro and A. P. Simons, *Charter of the United Nations* 342–4 (3rd ed., 1969).

(b)   Self-defence as a right

Article 51 explicitly refers to a 'right' of self-defence. A State subjected to an armed attack is thus legally entitled to resort to force. The argument has been made that self-defence connotes only a *de facto* condition, rather than a veritable right.[17] But since it is conceded that the State exercising self-defence is 'exonerated' from the duty to refrain from the use of force against the other side (the aggressor),[18] the difference between that and a *de jure* right is purely nominal.

The thesis of self-defence as a legitimate recourse to force by Utopia is inextricably linked to the antithesis of the employment of unlawful force by Arcadia (its opponent). Under no circumstances can the actual use of force by both parties to a conflict be lawful simultaneously. If Utopia is properly exercising the right of self-defence, Arcadia must be in violation of the corresponding duty to abstain from an illegal resort to force. Should Arcadia be using force against Utopia legitimately – as an exercise of collective security decreed or authorized by the Security Council (see *infra*, Chapter 10, A–B) – Utopia would not be able to invoke against Arcadia the right of self-defence.[19] By the same token, as an American Military Tribunal (following Wharton) held in the 1949 *Ministries* case, 'there can be no self-defense against self-defense'.[20]

In practice, when inter-State force is employed, both parties usually invoke the right of self-defence.[21] But such contradictory claims are mutually exclusive: only one of the antagonists can possibly be acting in an authentic exercise of the right of self-defence, whereas the other must be dissembling. When each persists in its posture, an authoritative determination is required to establish who is legally in the right (see *infra*, D, (a)). Even where no binding decision is made by a competent forum, it must be borne in mind that one of the parties is using force under false pretences of legality.

Self-defence, in conformity with general international law, is a right and not a duty. Vattel, like many others before and after his time, propounded that '[s]elf-defence against an unjust attack is not only a

---

[17] See R. Ago, 'Addendum to Eighth Report on State Responsibility', [1980] II (1) *ILC Ybk* 13, 53.

[18] *Ibid.*

[19] K. Nagy, *Le Problème de la Légitime Défense en Droit International* 55 (1992).

[20] *USA v. Von Weizsaecker et al.* ('the *Ministries* case') (Nuremberg, 1949), 14 *NMT* 314, 329.

[21] See O. Schachter, 'In Defense of International Rules on the Use of Force', 53 *UCLR* 113, 131 (1986).

right which every Nation has, but it is a duty, and one of its most sacred duties'.[22] Although the statement may reflect morality or theology, it does not comport with international law. As a rule, international law does not lay down any obligation to exercise self-defence.[23] A State subjected to an armed attack is vested with a right, hence an option, to resort to counterforce. A prudent State may decline to exercise this right, on the ground that a political compromise is preferable to a clash of arms. The indubitable military supremacy of the adversary may have a sobering effect on the target State, inhibiting it from steps that would transmute a theoretical right into a practical disaster. The idea that a State must sacrifice realism at the altar of conceptualism, and risk defeat while prodded on by a 'sacred duty', is incongruous.

The status of self-defence as a right, and not a duty, is embedded in general international law. There is no impediment to the assumption by a State of a special obligation (through a bilateral or multilateral treaty) to exercise self-defence, should an armed attack occur.[24] The duty of individual self-defence is usually incurred by a State when binding itself in a permanent neutrality regime[25] (see *supra*, Chapter 1, C, (a)). The obligation of collective self-defence is formulated in several treaty forms, such as military alliances, to be discussed in detail *infra* (Chapter 9, B).

Self-defence as a duty may also be incorporated in national instructions to armed forces. Thus, the United States Rules of Engagement establish a commander's obligation to use force in self-defence.[26] Still, this obligation must be understood in the context of 'unit' self-defence (see *infra*, Chapter 8, A, (a), i), and – bearing in mind the distinct possibility of escalation – it is a privilege that only the strong can afford.

(c)   Self-defence as an 'inherent' right

Article 51 of the UN Charter pronounces self-defence to be an 'inherent' right. In the French text of the Article, the phrase 'inherent right' is rendered '*droit naturel*'.[27] The choice of words has overtones of *jus naturale*, which appears to be the fount of the right of self-defence. However,

---

[22] Vattel, *The Law of Nations or the Principles of Natural Law*, Book III, § III, 35 (3 Classics of International Law ed., C. G. Fenwick trans., 246 (1916)).

[23] See J. Zourek, 'La Notion de Légitime Défense en Droit International', 56 *AIDI* 1, 51 (Wiesbaden, 1975).

[24] See *ibid.*, 51.

[25] See A. Verdross, 'Austria's Permanent Neutrality and the United Nations Organization', 50 *AJIL* 61, 63 (1956).

[26] United States Army, Judge Advocate General's Legal Center and School, *Operational Law Handbook* 75 (2004).

[27] Charter of the United Nations, *supra* note 14, at 346.

a reference to self-defence as a 'natural right' or a right generated by 'natural law' – although common in popular and even some official pronouncements[28] – is unwarranted.[29] It may be conceived as an anachronistic residue from an era in which international law was dominated by ecclesiastical doctrines. At the present time, there is not much faith in transcendental truths professed to be derived from nature. A legal right is an interest protected by law, and it must be validated within the framework of a legal system. Self-defence, as an international legal right, must be proved to exist within the compass of positive international law.

It may be contended that the right of self-defence is inherent not in *jus naturale*, but in the sovereignty of States. This construct finds support in a series of identical notes, sent in 1928 by the Government of the United States to a number of other Governments (inviting them to become Contracting Parties to the Kellogg–Briand Pact), where it was stated:

There is nothing in the American draft of an antiwar treaty which restricts or impairs in any way the right of self-defense. That right is inherent in every sovereign state and is implicit in every treaty.[30]

Yet, the principle of State sovereignty sheds no light on the theme of self-defence.[31] State sovereignty has a variable content, which depends on the stage of development of the international legal order at any given moment.[32] The best index of the altered perception of sovereignty is that, in the nineteenth (and early twentieth) century, the liberty of every State to go to war as and when it pleased was also considered 'a right inherent in sovereignty itself'[33] (see *supra*, Chapter 3, D). Notwithstanding the abolition of this liberty in the last century, the sovereignty of States did not crumble. The contemporary right to employ inter-State force in self-defence is no more 'inherent' in sovereignty than the discredited right to resort to force at all times.

It is advisable to take with a grain of salt the frequently made assertion that, in the language of the Judgment of the International Military Tribunal for the Far East (delivered at *Tokyo* in 1948):

---

[28] See S. Sims and K. Van der Borght, 'The Advisory Opinion on the Legality of the Threat or Use of Nuclear Weapons', 27 *GJICL* 345, 367 (1998–9).
[29] See H. Kelsen, *The Law of the United Nations* 791–2 (1950).
[30] United States, Identic Notes, 1928, 22 *AJIL*, Supp., 109, *id.* (1928).
[31] See G. Schwarzenberger, 'The Fundamental Principles of International Law', 87 *RCADI* 191, 339–40 (1955).
[32] See M. Virally, 'Panorama du Droit International Contemporain', 183 *RCADI* 9, 79 (1983).
[33] See A. S. Hershey, *The Essentials of International Public Law* 349 (1912).

Any law, international or municipal, which prohibits recourse to force, is necessarily limited by the right of self-defence.[34]

This postulate may have always been true in regard to domestic law, and it is currently accurate also in respect of international law. But it is safer to avoid axiomatic propositions purporting to cover future eventualities for all time. Even if the right of self-defence will never be abolished in the relations between flesh-and-blood human beings, there is no guarantee of a similar immobility in international law. Self-defence exercised by States (legal entities) is not to be equated with self-defence carried out by physical persons (see *infra*, Chapter 8, A, (b), iii). It is not beyond the realm of the plausible that a day may come when States will agree to dispense completely with the use of force in self-defence, exclusively relying thenceforth on some central authority wielding an effective international police force. The allegation that the prerogative of self-defence is inherent in the sovereignty of States to such an extent that no treaty can derogate from it,[35] cannot be accepted. It is by no means clear whether the right of self-defence may be classified as *jus cogens*[36] (thus curtailing the freedom of States to contract out of it), and, in any event, even *jus cogens* is susceptible of modification (see *supra*, Chapter 4, E, (b)). Far be it from us to suggest that, at this juncture, the right of self-defence is receding or that its significance is abating. On the contrary, if anything, self-defence is gaining ground in the practice of States. Nevertheless, what is – and was – is not always what will be.

In its Judgment in the *Nicaragua* case, in 1986, the International Court of Justice gave a different meaning to self-defence as an 'inherent right'. The Court construed the expression as a reference to customary international law.[37] According to the Court, the framers of the Charter thereby acknowledged that self-defence was a pre-existing right of a customary nature, which they desired to preserve (at least in essence).[38] This is a sensible interpretation of Article 51, rationalizing the employment of the adjective 'inherent' without ascribing to it far-fetched (and insupportable) consequences.

Article 51 addresses only the right of self-defence of UN Member States. After all, these are also the subjects of the duty, set out in Article 2(4),

---

[34] *In re Hirota and Others* (International Military Tribunal for the Far East, *Tokyo* trial, 1948), [1948] *AD* 356, 364.
[35] See Ago, *supra* note 17, at 67 n. 263.
[36] But see A. P. Rubin, 'Book Review', 81 *AJIL* 254, 255–8 (1987).
[37] *Case Concerning Military and Paramilitary Activities in and against Nicaragua* (Merits), [1986] *ICJ Rep.* 14, 94.
[38] *Ibid.*

to refrain from the use of force (see *supra*, Chapter 4, B, (a)). The existence of the right of self-defence under general customary international law denotes that it is conferred on every State. Contemporary customary international law forbids the use of inter-State force by all States, whether or not they are UN Members (see *supra*, Chapter 4, C, (a)). In the same vein, any State (even if not a UN Member) is entitled to the right of self-defence under existing customary international law. Both the general prohibition of the use of inter-State force and the exception to it (the right of self-defence) are part and parcel of customary international law, as well as the law of the Charter.[39]

B.   Self-defence as a response to an armed attack

Since the right of self-defence arises under Article 51 only 'if an armed attack occurs', it is clear that the use of force in self-defence is contingent on demonstrating that an armed attack has taken place. As the International Court of Justice pronounced in 2003, in the *Case Concerning Oil Platforms* (between Iran and the United States), 'the burden of proof of the facts showing the existence' of an armed attack rests on the State justifying its own use of force as self-defence.[40]

(a)   Armed attack and preventive war

The United States has traditionally taken the position that a State may exercise 'anticipatory' self-defence,[41] in response not only to a 'hostile act' but even to a 'hostile intent' (a dichotomy elevated to the level of doctrine by the US Rules of Engagement).[42] In the past, the US was careful to underscore that anticipatory self-defence – or response to a hostile intent – must nevertheless relate to the 'threat of *imminent* use of force'.[43] The emphatic use of the qualifying adjective 'imminent' is of great import. As we shall see (*infra*, (b), (aa), i), the imminence of an armed attack (provided that it is no longer a mere threat) does indeed justify an early response by way of interceptive self-defence. However, after the heinous terrorist attacks of 11 September 2001 (9/11), a well-known statement of policy on preemptive action in self-defence was

---

[39] See *ibid.*, 102–3.
[40] *Case Concerning Oil Platforms*, 2003, 42 *ILM* 1334, 1356 (2003).
[41] *Annotated Supplement to the Commander's Handbook on the Law of Naval Operations*, 73 *ILS* 263 (A. R. Thomas and J. C. Duncan eds., 1999).
[42] *Operational Law Handbook*, *supra* note 26, at 75 (2004).
[43] *Ibid.* See also *Annotated Supplement*, *supra* note 41, at 263.

issued as part of the US National Security Strategy.[44] The new policy, often referred to as the 'Bush Doctrine' (after President G. W. Bush), appears to push the envelope by claiming a right to preemptive self-defence countering pure threats, especially by terrorists and in particular when the potential use of weapons of mass destruction (WMD) comes into the equation.[45] It is not yet clear what practical effects the new policy will have in the future: contrary to what many commentators believe, it was not applied in Iraq in 2003 (see *infra*, Chapter 10, C, (b), iii). But to the extent that it will actually bring about a preventive use of force in response to sheer threats, it will not be in compliance with Article 51 of the Charter.[46]

Since Article 51 permits self-defence solely when an 'armed attack' occurs, the question arises whether there exists – independently of the Charter – a broader customary international law right of anticipatory self-defence. The International Court of Justice, in the *Nicaragua* case, based its decision on the norms of customary international law concerning self-defence as a sequel to an armed attack.[47] Yet, the Court stressed that this was due to the circumstances of the case, and it passed no judgment on the issue at hand.[48]

On the other hand, Judge Schwebel – in his Dissenting Opinion – did take a clear-cut position on the subject. In conformity with a scholarly school of thought maintaining that Article 51 only highlights one form of self-defence (viz. response to an armed attack), without negating other patterns of legitimate action in self-defence vouchsafed by customary international law,[49] Judge Schwebel rejected a reading of the text which would imply that the right of self-defence under Article 51 exists 'if, and only if, an armed attack occurs'.[50]

In the opinion of the present writer, precisely such a restrictive reading of Article 51 is called for. Any other interpretation of the Article would be counter-textual, counter-factual and counter-logical:

---

[44] Preemptive Action in Self-Defense: National Security Strategy, [2002] *Digest of United States Practice in International Law* 947.
[45] See, e.g., A. E. Wall, 'International Law and the Bush Doctrine', 34 *IYHR* 193, 196–7, 212 (2004).
[46] See D. Rezac, 'President Bush's Security Strategy and Its "Pre-Emptive Strikes Doctrine" – A Legal Basis for the War against Iraq?', 7 *ARIEL* 223, 227 (2002).
[47] See *Nicaragua* case, *supra* note 37, at 102–6.   [48] See *ibid.*, 103.
[49] See D. W. Bowett, *Self-Defence in International Law* 187–92 (1958); M. S. McDougal and F. P. Feliciano, *Law and Minimum World Public Order* 232–41 (1961); J. Stone, *Aggression and World Order: A Critique of United Nations Theories of Aggression* 44 (1958).
[50] *Nicaragua* case, *supra* note 37, at 347.

(i) A different interpretation of Article 51 would be counter-textual because the use of the phrase 'armed attack' in Article 51 is not inadvertent. The expression should be juxtaposed with comparable locutions in other provisions of the Charter. It is particularly striking that the framers of the text preferred in Article 51 the coinage 'armed attack' to the term 'aggression', which appears in the Charter in several contexts (the Purposes of the United Nations (Article 1(1)), collective security (Article 39) and regional arrangements (Article 53(1))).[51] The choice of words in Article 51 is deliberately confined to a response to an armed attack.

An armed attack is, of course, a type of aggression. Aggression in its generic meaning may be stretched to include mere threats (*cf. supra*, Chapter 5, C, (a), i), although it is interesting that the consensus Definition of Aggression, adopted by the General Assembly in 1974 – while not pretending to be exhaustive – does not cover the threat of force[52] (see *supra*, Chapter 5, B). Yet, only a special form of aggression amounting to an armed attack justifies self-defence under Article 51. The French version of the Article sharpens its thrust by speaking of '*une agression armée*'.[53] Under the Article, a State is permitted to use force in self-defence only in response to aggression which is armed.

(ii) The idea that one can go beyond the text of Article 51 and find support for a broad concept of preventive self-defence in customary international law is counter-factual. When did such customary international law evolve and what evidence in the practice of States (as distinct from scholarly writings) do we have for it? As mentioned (*supra*, A, (a)), the right of self-defence consolidated only upon the prohibition of the use of force between States. That prohibition was first evinced in the Kellogg–Briand Pact of 1928 and reiterated, in clearer and broader terms, in Article 2(4) of the Charter in 1945. What preventive war of self-defence was unleashed between 1928 and 1945?

It is frequently stated that the concept of anticipatory self-defence goes back to the 1837 *Caroline* incident[54] (examined *infra*, Chapter 8, B, (c)). However, reliance on that incident in the context of anticipatory self-defence is misplaced. There was nothing anticipatory about the British action against the *Caroline* steamboat on US soil, inasmuch as use of the *Caroline* for transporting men and materials across the Niagara River – in

[51] Charter of the United Nations, *supra* note 14, at 331, 343, 347.
[52] General Assembly Resolution 3314 (XXIX), 29(1) *RGA* 142, 143 (1974) (Articles 2–4).
[53] Charter of the United Nations, *supra* note 14, at 346.
[54] See, e.g., T. M. Franck, *Recourse to Force: State Action against Threats and Armed Attacks* 97 (2002).

support of an anti-British rebellion in Canada – had already been in progress.[55] No less significantly, the issue addressed at the time related exclusively to the use of force by Britain 'short of war'. The question was not whether Britain had a right to go to war against the US in the exercise of self-defence (since any State then had a right to go to war against another State for any reason). The question, rather, was whether Britain could use forcible measures of self-defence within US territory without plunging into war.

(iii) The reliance on an extra-Charter customary right of self-defence is also counter-logical. After all, the authors of Article 51 introduced significant limitations on the exercise of self-defence (which is subject to the overriding powers of the Security Council (see *infra*, D)). Does it make sense that the most obvious case of self-defence – conducted in response to an armed attack – is subordinated to confining conditions, whereas self-defence putatively invoked in other circumstances (on a preventive basis) is absolved of those conditions? What is the point in stating the obvious (*i.e.* that an armed attack gives rise to the right of self-defence), while omitting any reference whatever to the ambiguous circumstances of an allegedly permissible preventive war? Preventive war in self-defence (if legitimate under the Charter) would require regulation by *lex scripta* more acutely than a response to an armed attack, since the opportunities for abuse are incomparably greater. Surely, if preventive war in self-defence is justified (on the basis of 'probable cause' rather than an actual use of force), it ought to be exposed to no less – if possible, even closer – supervision by the Security Council. In all, is this not an appropriate case for the application of the maxim of interpretation *expressio unius est exclusio alterius*?

When pressed, the advocates of the legitimacy of a broad anticipatory concept of self-defence are forced to frown upon the strict language of Article 51 as 'an inept piece of draftsmanship'.[56] However, the draftsmanship appears to be quite satisfactory once it is recognized that the right of self-defence is deliberately circumscribed to counter-force stimulated by an armed attack. The leading opinion among scholars is in harmony with the view expressed here.[57]

---

[55] See J. P. Paust, 'Post-9/11 Overreaction and Fallacies Regarding War and Defense, Guantanamo, the Status of Persons, Treatment, Judicial Review of Detention, and Due Process in Military Commissions', 79 *NDLR* 1335, 1345 (2003–4).

[56] McDougal and Feliciano, *supra* note 49, at 234.

[57] See Ago, *supra* note 17, at 64–7; W. E. Beckett, *The North Atlantic Treaty, the Brussels Treaty and the Charter of the United Nations* 13 (1950); Kelsen, *supra* note 29, at 797–8; Kunz, *supra* note 10, at 877–8; L. Oppenheim, *International Law*, II, 156 (H. Lauterpacht ed., 7th ed., 1952); K. Skubiszewski, 'Use of Force by States. Collective Security. Law of

The proposition that UN Member States are barred by the Charter from exercising self-defence, in response to a mere threat of force, is applicable in every situation. It is sometimes put forward that '[t]he destructive potential of nuclear weapons is so enormous as to call into question any and all received rules of international law regarding the trans-boundary use of force'.[58] But the inference that Article 51 is only operative under conditions of conventional warfare cannot be substantiated.

Hence, when the United States imposed a 'quarantine' on Cuba in 1962, subsequent to the installation of Soviet missiles on the island, this could not be reconciled with the provision of Article 51,[59] notwithstanding valiant attempts by some writers to do so.[60] The installation of the missiles so close to American shores did pose a certain threat to the United States. Yet, in the absence of an armed attack, no recourse could be made to the exceptional right of self-defence, and the general interdiction of the use of inter-State force prevailed.

When Israeli aircraft raided an Iraqi nuclear reactor (under construction) in 1981, the legal justification of the act should have rested on the state of war which characterized the relations between the two countries (see *supra*, Chapter 2, B, (c), i). Had Israel been at peace with Iraq, the bombing of the site would have been prohibited, since (when examined in itself and out of the context of an on-going war) it did not qualify as a legitimate act of self-defence consonant with Article 51. This is the position *de lege lata*, despite the understandable apprehension existing at the time that nuclear devices, if produced by Iraq, might ultimately be delivered against Israeli targets.[61]

The requirement of an armed attack as a condition of legitimate self-defence, in accordance with Article 51, precludes not only threats. Recourse to self-defence under the Article is not vindicated by any violation of international law other than an armed attack. Even declarations of war, if it is evident to all that they are unaccompanied by deeds, are not enough.[62] The contention that mere mobilization or 'bellicose

---

War and Neutrality', *Manual of Public International Law* 739, 767 (M. Sørensen ed., 1968); H. Wehberg, 'L'Interdiction du Recours à la Force. Le Principe et les Problèmes qui se Posent', 78 *RCADI* 1, 81 (1951).

[58] A. D'Amato, 'Israel's Air Strike upon the Iraqi Nuclear Reactor', 77 *AJIL* 584, 588 (1983).

[59] See Q. Wright, 'The Cuban Quarantine', 57 *AJIL* 546, 560–2 (1963).

[60] See M. S. McDougal, 'The Soviet-Cuban Quarantine and Self-Defense', 57 *AJIL* 597–604 (1963).

[61] *Per contra*, see T. L. H. McCormack, *Self-Defense in International Law: The Israeli Raid on the Iraqi Nuclear Reactor* 295–302 (1996).

[62] A declaration of war patently unaccompanied by deeds may be deemed 'an overt threat of the use of force'. E. Myjer, 'Book Review' [of the first edition of this volume], 2 *LJIL* 278, 283 (1989). But such a threat *per se* does not constitute an armed attack.

utterances' as such may justify self-defence within the framework of Article 51,[63] has no foundation.

At bottom, self-defence consistent with Article 51 implies resort to counter-force: it comes in reaction to the use of force by the other party. When a country feels menaced by the threat of an armed attack, all that it is free to do – in keeping with the Charter – is make the necessary military preparations for repulsing the hostile action should it materialize, as well as bring the matter forthwith to the attention of the Security Council (hoping that the latter will take collective security measures in the face of a threat to the peace (see *infra*, Chapter 10, A, (c)).[64] Either course of action may fail to inspire confidence in the successful resolution of the crisis. The military preparations can easily prove inadequate, whether as a deterrence or as a shock absorber. The Council, for its part, may proceed in a nonchalant manner.[65] Regardless of the shortcomings of the system, the option of a preventive use of force is excluded by Article 51.

Having said that, it is the considered opinion of the present writer that the right to self-defence can be invoked in response to an armed attack as soon as it becomes evident to the victim State (on the basis of hard intelligence available at the time) that the attack is in the process of being mounted. There is no need to wait for the bombs to fall – or, for that matter, for fire to open – if it is morally certain that the armed attack is under way (however incipient the stage of the attack is). The victim State can lawfully (under Article 51) intercept the armed attack with a view to blunting its edge (see *infra*, (b), (aa), i).

(b)   The nature and scope of an armed attack

An armed attack can be conducted by a foreign State. It can also be conducted by non-State actors from within a foreign State. This section will be divided into two parts dealing with the two disparate sets of circumstances.

(aa)   An armed attack by a State
i.   *The beginning of an armed attack and interceptive self-defence* Since self-defence (under Article 51) is linked to an armed attack, it is important to pinpoint the exact moment at which an armed attack begins to take

---

[63] See E. Miller, 'Self-Defence, International Law, and the Six Day War', 20 *Is.LR* 49, 58–60 (1985).

[64] See J. Zourek, *L'Interdiction de L'Emploi de la Force en Droit International* 106 (1974).

[65] For a case in point, see R. Lapidoth, 'The Security Council in the May 1967 Crisis: A Study in Frustration', 4 *Is.LR* 534–50 (1969).

place: this is also the moment when forcible counter-measures become legitimate as self-defence. In practice, the issue acquires another dimension as a result of the proclivity of both parties, once hostilities break out, to charge each other with the initiation of an armed attack. Verification of the precise instant at which an armed attack commences is well-nigh equivalent to an identification of the aggressor and the victim State respectively.

When confronted with contradictory claims of self-defence (and attendant charges of armed attack), the international community is generally confounded by effusions of disinformation pouring forth from dubious sources. Given that there may be meagre opportunity for impartial observers to investigate what really happened, the public tends to search for deceptively uncomplicated criteria designed to establish the starting point of the armed attack. The most simplistic touchstone is that of the 'first shot', namely, finding out which State (through its armed forces) was the first to open fire.

Article 2 of the General Assembly's consensus Definition of Aggression refers to the first use of force as only *prima facie* evidence of aggression[66] (see *supra*, Chapter 5, B). This is a judicious approach that relegates the opening of fire to the level of a presumption of an armed attack. While the burden of proof shifts to the State firing the first shot, that State is not estopped from demonstrating that the action came in response to steps taken by the opponent, which were far and away more decisive as a turning point in the process leading from peace to war (or from quiescence to an international armed conflict 'short of war').

In many instances, the opening of fire is an unreliable test of responsibility for an armed attack. The most elementary example pertains to an invasion of one country by another. An invasion constitutes the foremost case of aggression enumerated in Article 3(a) of the General Assembly's Definition.[67] It may start when massive Arcadian armoured or infantry divisions storm, with blazing guns, a Utopian line of fortifications. But an invasion may also be effected when a smaller military Numidian force crosses the Ruritanian frontier and then halts, positioning itself in strategic outposts well within the Ruritanian territory (the movement of Pakistani troops into Indian Kashmir in 1999 is a good case in point).[68] If the invasion takes place in a tract of land not easily accessible and lightly guarded, it is entirely conceivable that some time would pass before the competent authorities of Ruritania grasp what has actually transpired. In these circumstances, it may very well ensue that the armed forces of

---

[66] General Assembly Resolution 3314, *supra* note 52, at 143.   [67] *Ibid.*
[68] For the Kashmir incident, see 45 Keesing's *Record of World Events* 42997 (1999).

Ruritania would be instructed to dislodge from their positions the invading contingents belonging to Numidia, and that fire be opened first by soldiers flying the Ruriutanian colours against Numidian military units. Nevertheless, Numidia cannot relieve itself of responsibility for an armed attack. When a country sends armed formations across an international frontier, without the consent of the local Government, it must be deemed to have triggered an armed attack. The opening of fire by the other side would amount to a legitimate measure of self-defence.

Another rudimentary illustration for the need to gaze beyond the first shot relates to circumstances in which Atlantican military forces are stationed by permission, for a limited space of time, on Patagonian soil. When the agreed-upon period comes to an end, and Patagonia is unwilling to prolong the stay within its territory of the Atlantican troops, Atlantica must pull them out. If Atlantica fails to do so, its refusal to withdraw from Patagonia amounts to an act of aggression under Article 3(e) of the General Assembly's Definition.[69] The factual situation may be legally analyzed as a constructive armed attack.[70] When the armed forces of Patagonia open fire first, with a view to compelling the evacuation of Atlantican troops from Patagonian territory, they are exercising the right of self-defence.[71]

These are open-and-shut cases, inasmuch as the first shot fired by the Ruritanian or Patagonian armed forces is plainly provoked, either by a Numidian invasion or by an unauthorized Atlantican military presence within Patagonian territory. But a State may resort to force in self-defence, even before its territory is penetrated by another State. Suppose that Carpathia launches inter-continental ballistic missiles against Apollonia on the other side of the planet. The Apollonian radar immediately detects the launching. In the few minutes left prior to impact (and before the missiles draw near the Apollonian frontier), Apollonia activates its armed forces and an Apollonian submarine torpedoes a Carpathian warship cruising in the ocean. Although a Carpathian target

[69] General Assembly Resolution 3314, *supra* note 52, at 143.
[70] See W. Wengler, 'L'Interdiction de Recourir à la Force. Problèmes et Tendances', [1971] *RBDI* 401, 408.
[71] It must be emphasized that the scenario of a constructive armed attack relates to a non-consensual extension by Atlantica of the stay of its troops on Patagonian soil. Article 3(e) of the Definition of Aggression also pertains to the use of Atlantican forces, during their agreed-upon stay in Patagonia, in contravention of the conditions provided for in agreement. There is no doubt that Atlantican troops may commence an armed attack against Patagonia in the course of their consensual stay there (see *infra*, iii). But minor breaches of the conditions of an unexpired agreement, allowing the stationing of foreign forces on local soil, cannot be considered an armed attack. See A. Randelzhofer, 'Article 51', *The Charter of the United Nations: A Commentary*, I, 788, 799 (B. Simma ed., 2nd ed., 2002).

is the first to be hit, one can scarcely deny that Carpathia (having launched its missiles previously) should be regarded as the initiator of an armed attack, whereas Apollonia ought to be able to invoke self-defence.

It may be contended that what ultimately counts in the last script is the launching of the missiles, which resembles the firing of a gun: once a button is pressed, or a trigger is pulled, the act is complete (while impact is a mere technicality). However, suppose that the radar of a Carpathian aircraft locks on to an objective in Apollonia or that the aircraft illumi-nates (*i.e.* aims laser beams at) the target. While no missile has been fired yet – and no laser-homing bomb has been dropped – an armed attack is clearly in the process of being unleashed. A timely response would merely constitute interceptive self-defence.

The best way to illustrate what interceptive self-defence signifies is to hypothesize that the Japanese Carrier Striking Force, *en route* to the point from which it mounted the notorious attack on Pearl Harbor in December 1941, had been destroyed by American forces before a single Japanese naval aircraft got anywhere near Hawaii.[72] If that were to have happened, and the Americans would have succeeded in aborting an onslaught which in one fell swoop managed to change the balance of military power in the Pacific, it would have been preposterous to look upon the United States as answerable for inflicting an armed attack upon Japan.

The proper analysis of the case should be based on three disparate scenarios (all linked to a counter-factual premise that the Americans knew exactly what the Japanese were up to):

(1) The easiest scenario relates to the hypothetical shooting down by the Americans of the Japanese aircraft – following detection by radar or other means – in the relatively short time-frame between launch from the air carriers and the actual execution of the attack mission. Once the launch was completed, there can be no doubt that (although theoretically the mission could still be called off) the US as the target State had every right to regard the Japanese armed attack as having commenced and to intercept it.

(2) The more difficult scenario pertains to a hypothetical sinking of the Japanese fleet once poised for the attack on Pearl Harbor but prior to the launch of the aircraft. In the opinion of the present writer, the turning point in the unfolding events was the sailing of the tasked Japanese fleet towards its fateful destination (again, notwithstanding the possibility of its being instructed to turn back). Had the

---

[72] The Pearl Harbor example was adduced in debates in the United Nations. See M. M. Whiteman, *Digest of International Law*, V, 867–8 (1965).

Americans – perhaps through the breaking of Japanese naval codes – been in possession of conclusive evidence as to the nature of the mission in which the Japanese Striking Force was already engaged, and had the Americans located the whereabouts of the Japanese fleet, they need not have relinquished the opportunity to intercept.

(3) On the other hand, had the Americans sought to destroy the Japanese fleet before it sailed – while it was still training for its mission, war-gaming it or otherwise making advance preparations – this would not have been an interceptive (hence, lawful) response to an armed attack but an (unlawful) preventive use of force in advance of the attack, which had not yet commenced. As and of themselves, training, war-gaming and advance preparations do not cross the red line of an armed attack.

The crux of the issue, therefore, is not who fired the first shot but who embarked upon an apparently irreversible course of action, thereby crossing the legal Rubicon. The casting of the die, rather than the actual opening of fire, is what starts the armed attack. It would be absurd to require that the defending State should sustain and absorb a devastating (perhaps a fatal) blow, only to prove an immaculate conception of self-defence. As Sir Humphrey Waldock phrased it:

Where there is convincing evidence not merely of threats and potential danger but of an attack being actually mounted, then an armed attack may be said to have begun to occur, though it has not passed the frontier.[73]

Interceptive self-defence is lawful, even under Article 51 of the Charter,[74] for it takes place after the other side has committed itself to an armed attack in an ostensibly irrevocable way. Whereas a preventive strike anticipates a latent armed attack that is merely 'foreseeable' (or even just 'conceivable'), an interceptive strike counters an armed attack which is in progress, even if it still is incipient: the blow is 'imminent' and practically 'unavoidable'.[75] To put it in another way, there is nothing preventive about nipping an armed attack in the bud. But the real (in contradistinction to the suspected) existence of that bud is an absolute requirement. Self-defence cannot be exercised merely on the ground of assumptions, expectations or fear. It has to be demonstrably apparent

---

[73] C. H. M. Waldock, 'The Regulation of the Use of Force by Individual States in International Law', 81 *RCADI* 451, 498 (1952).

[74] For support of this view, see M. N. Shaw, *International Law* 1030 (5th ed., 2003).

[75] *Cf.* C. C. Joyner and M. A. Grimaldi, 'The United States and Nicaragua: Reflections on the Lawfulness of Contemporary Intervention', 25 *VJIL* 621, 659–60 (1984–5). See also I. Pogany, 'Book Review' [of the first edition of this volume], 38 *ICLQ* 435, *id.* (1989).

that the other side is already engaged in carrying out an armed attack (even if the attack has not yet fully developed).

An in-depth study of the background may be required before a decision is made regarding the classification of the first shot as either preventive (namely, unlawful) or interceptive (*i.e.* a legitimate exercise of self-defence). Thus, in the 'Six Days War' of June 1967, Israel was the first to open fire. Nevertheless, a careful analysis of the events surrounding the actual outbreak of the hostilities (assuming that the factual examination was conducted, in good faith, at the time of action) would lead to the conclusion that the Israeli campaign amounted to an interceptive self-defence, in response to an incipient armed attack by Egypt (joined by Jordan and Syria). True, no single Egyptian step, evaluated alone, may have qualified as an armed attack. But when all of the measures taken by Egypt (especially the peremptory ejection of the United Nations Emergency Force from the Gaza Strip and the Sinai Peninsula; the closure of the Straits of Tiran; the unprecedented build-up of Egyptian forces along Israel's borders; and constant sabre-rattling statements about the impending fighting) were assessed in the aggregate, it seemed to be crystal-clear that Egypt was bent on an armed attack, and the sole question was not whether war would materialize but when.[76]

That, at least, was the widely shared perception (not only in Israel) in June 1967, based on sound judgement of events. Hindsight knowledge, suggesting that – notwithstanding the well-founded contemporaneous appraisal of events – the situation may have been less desperate than it appeared, is immaterial.[77] The invocation of the right of self-defence must be weighed on the ground of the information available (and reasonably interpreted) at the moment of action, without the benefit of *post factum* wisdom.[78] In the circumstances, as perceived in June 1967, Israel did not have to wait idly by for the expected shattering blow (in the military manner of the October 1973 'Yom Kippur' offensive), but was entitled to resort to self-defence as soon as possible.

---

[76] See Y. Dinstein, 'The Legal Issues of "Para-War" and Peace in the Middle East', 44 *SJLR* 466, 469–70 (1970).

[77] 'Hindsight can be 20/20; decisions at the time may be clouded with the fog of war.' G. K. Walker, 'Anticipatory Collective Self-Defense in the Charter Era: What the Treaties Have Said', 72 *ILS* 365, 393 (M. N. Schmitt ed., 1998). Although the statement is made about anticipatory action (which is inadmissible in the opinion of the present writer), it is equally applicable to interceptive self-defence.

[78] This rule works both for and against the State invoking self-defence. Thus, it cannot base its recourse to forcible measures on information unavailable at the time of action and acquired only subsequently. See International Military Tribunal (*Nuremberg* trial), Judgment (1946), 1 *IMT* 171, 207–8.

ii.   *A small-scale armed attack* There is no doubt that, for an illegal use of force to acquire the dimensions of an armed attack, a minimal threshold has to be reached. Since Article 2(4) of the Charter forbids 'the threat or use of force' and Article 51 allows taking self-defence measures only against an 'armed attack', a gap is discernible between the two stipulations.[79] Even leaving aside mere threats of force (discussed *supra*, (a)), it is clear that one State may employ some illegal force against another without unleashing a full-fledged armed attack. Thus, agents of Arcadia – without inflicting any casualties or much damage – may break into a Utopian diplomatic bag or detain a Ruritanian ship in circumstances disallowed by international law. In both instances, a modicum of force must be posited, yet no armed attack can be alleged to have occurred. In the absence of an armed attack, self-defence is not an option available to the victim State, so that neither Utopia nor Ruritania can respond with self-defence.

Logically and pragmatically, the gap between Article 2(4) ('use of force') and Article 51 ('armed attack') ought to be quite narrow, inasmuch as 'there is very little effective protection against States violating the prohibition of the use of force, as long as they do not resort to an armed attack'.[80] If Utopia and Ruritania are barred from invoking the right of self-defence against Arcadia, notwithstanding the use of some force against them, this is so merely because of the applicability of the principle *de minimis non curat lex*. That is to say, a use of force not tantamount to an armed attack is simply not of 'sufficient gravity' (in the words of Article 2 of the consensus Definition of Aggression,[81] *supra*, Chapter 5, B). An armed attack presupposes a use of force producing (or liable to produce) serious consequences, epitomized by territorial intrusions, human casualties or considerable destruction of property. When no such results are engendered by (or reasonably expected from) a recourse to force, Article 51 does not come into play.

In the *Nicaragua* case, the International Court of Justice alluded to 'measures which do not constitute an armed attack but may nevertheless involve a use of force',[82] and found it 'necessary to distinguish the most grave forms of the use of force (those constituting an armed attack) from other less grave forms'[83] (a differentiation reiterated in the *Oil Platforms* case of 2003).[84] The Judgment in the *Nicaragua* case envisaged legitimate counter-measures, 'analogous' to but less grave than self-defence, in

---

[79] See Randelzhofer, *supra* note 71, at 790.   [80] *Ibid.*, 791.
[81] General Assembly Resolution 3314, *supra* note 52, at 143.
[82] *Nicaragua* case, *supra* note 37, at 110.   [83] *Ibid.*, 101.
[84] *Case Concerning Oil Platforms*, *supra* note 40, at 1355.

response to use of force which is less grave than an armed attack.[85] What emerges is a quadruple structure of (i) self-defence versus (ii) armed attack, and (iii) counter-measures analogous to but short of self-defence versus (iv) forcible measures short of an armed attack. This construct is entirely satisfactory, provided that it is understood that the counter-measures coming within the framework of rubric (iii) cannot entail the use of force, because – however 'analogous' to self-defence – in the absence of an armed attack, they cannot constitute self-defence. Unfortunately, the Court carefully refrained from ruling out the possibility that such counter-measures may involve the use of force by the victim State.[86] Indeed, it was 'strongly suggested' in the Judgment that these counter-measures may include acts of force.[87] The notion that 'an unlawful use of force "short of" an armed attack' can prompt in response 'defensive action – by force also "short of" Article 51' – is expressly developed by Judge Simma in his Separate Opinion in the *Oil Platforms* case decided by the Court in 2003.[88] Yet, this position cannot be reconciled with the text of the Charter. Pursuant to Article 51, only an armed attack – and nothing short of an armed attack – can precipitate a forcible reaction by way of self-defence.

While the Court in the *Nicaragua* case did not paint a clear picture of the similarities and dissimilarities between the counter-measures which it found analogous, one striking difference is emphasized in the Judgment. The Court held that when non-self-defence counter-measures are employed, there is no counterpart to collective self-defence, namely, the right of a third State to resort to force in response to the wrongful act.[89] As a result, the options of response to forcible measures short of an armed attack are substantially reduced.[90] Moreover, since the Court did not brand as an armed attack the supply of weapons and logistical support to rebels against a foreign State (see *infra*, v), a 'no-man's-land' unfolds between the type of military assistance that a third State can legitimately provide and the direct exercise of collective self-defence in response to an armed attack.[91]

---

[85] *Nicaragua* case, *supra* note 37, at 110.   [86] *Ibid.*

[87] See J. L. Hargrove, 'The *Nicaragua* Judgment and the Future of the Law of Force and Self-Defense', 81 *AJIL* 135, 138 (1987).

[88] *Case Concerning Oil Platforms*, *supra* note 40, at 1428, 1433.

[89] *Nicaragua* case, *supra* note 37, at 110, 127.

[90] See T. M. Franck, 'Some Observations on the ICJ's Procedural and Substantive Innovations', 81 *AJIL* 116, 120 (1987).

[91] See L. B. Sohn, 'The International Court of Justice and the Scope of the Right of Self-Defense and the Duty of Non-Intervention', *International Law at a Time of Perplexity: Essays in Honour of Shabtai Rosenne* 869, 878 (Y. Dinstein ed., 1989).

All this is quite baffling.[92] The confusion generated by the Court's dicta is compounded by the fact that it also distinguished between an armed attack and 'a mere frontier incident', inasmuch as an armed attack must have some 'scale and effects'.[93] The question of a frontier incident is particularly bothersome. It stands to reason that, if a rifle shot is fired by an Arcadian soldier across the border of Utopia and the bullet hits a tree or a cow, no armed attack has been perpetrated. But it would be fallacious to dismiss automatically from consideration as an armed attack every frontier incident. As aptly put by Sir Gerald Fitzmaurice, '[t]here are frontier incidents and frontier incidents. Some are trivial, some may be extremely grave'.[94] When elements of the armed forces of Arcadia ambush a border patrol (or some other isolated unit) of Utopia, the assault has to rank as an armed attack and some sort of self-defence must be warranted in response.[95] Many frontier incidents comprise fairly large military engagements, and an attempt to dissociate them from other forms of armed attack would be spurious.

The criteria of 'scale and effects', as will be seen (*infra*, C), are of immense practical import. They are particularly relevant in appraising whether a counter-action taken in self-defence, in response to an armed attack, is legitimate. But unless the scale and effects are trifling, below the *de minimis* threshold, they do not contribute to a determination whether an armed attack has unfolded. There is certainly no cause to remove small-scale armed attacks from the spectrum of armed attacks. In the words of W. H. Taft, '[t]he gravity of an attack may affect the proper scope of the defensive use of force ..., but it is not relevant to determining whether there is a right of self-defense in the first instance'.[96] Article 51 'in no way limits itself to especially large, direct or important armed attacks'.[97] The position was summed up by J. L. Kunz: 'If "armed attack" means illegal armed attack it means, on the other hand, any illegal armed attack, even a small border incident.'[98]

The fact that an armed attack – justifying self-defence as a response under Article 51 – need not take the shape of a massive military operation, was conceded by the Court in the *Nicaragua* case when it held that the sending of armed bands into the territory of another State may count as

[92] See the Dissenting Opinion of Judge Schwebel, *Nicaragua* case, *supra* note 37, at 349–50.
[93] *Ibid.*, 103.
[94] G. G. Fitzmaurice, 'The Definition of Aggression', 1 *ICLQ* 137, 139 (1952).
[95] See G. M. Badr, 'The Exculpatory Effect of Self-Defense in State Responsibility', 10 *GJICL* 1, 17 (1980).
[96] W. H. Taft IV, 'Self-Defense and the *Oil Platforms* Decision', 29 *YJIL* 295, 300 (2004).
[97] Hargrove, *supra* note 87, at 139.
[98] Kunz, *supra* note 10, at 878.

an armed attack[99] (see *infra*, v) If 'low intensity' fighting qualifies, the 'scale and effects' required as a condition for an armed attack are minimal. Interestingly enough, in the *Oil Platforms* case, the Court specifically stated that it 'does not exclude the possibility that the mining of a single military vessel might be sufficient to bring into play the "inherent right of self-defence"'.[100]

The choice of arms by the attacking State is immaterial. As emphasized by the International Court of Justice, in its 1996 Advisory Opinion on the *Legality of the Threat or Use of Nuclear Weapons*, Article 51 does not refer to specific weapons; it applies to any armed attack, regardless of the weapon employed.[101] In other words, an armed attack can be carried out with conventional or unconventional, primitive or sophisticated, ordnance. At the onset of the third millennium, what especially looms on the horizon is an electronic 'computer network attack'. What counts here is the consequence of such an assault.[102] If it were to cause fatalities (resulting, e.g., from the shutdown of computers controlling waterworks and dams, with a consequent flooding of inhabited areas), it would qualify as armed attack.[103]

iii.   *The locale of an armed attack* Ordinarily, an armed attack (justifying self-defence) is mounted across the frontier of the aggressor State into the territory of the victim country. However, the crossing of the frontier can precede the armed attack, which may commence from within the territory of the target State. As mentioned (*supra*, i), Atlantican troops stationed by permission on Patagonian soil may commit a constructive armed attack, if they refuse to withdraw upon expiry of the time allotted for their presence. In fact, the armed attack need not be constructive. An Atlantican military unit based in Patagonia, under the terms of a military alliance, may – in violation of these terms – open fire on Patagonian personnel or installations. An Arcadian warship admitted into a Utopian port, ostensibly for refuelling, may shell Utopian shore facilities. The use of force within a host country by foreign military units, in contravention of the conditions of the consent to their entry into the receiving State's territory, is recognized as an act of aggression under Article 3(e) of the General Assembly's Definition[104] (see *supra*, Chapter 5, B).

---

[99] *Nicaragua* case, *supra* note 37, at 103.

[100] *Case Concerning Oil Platforms*, *supra* note 40, at 1360.

[101] Advisory Opinion on *Nuclear Weapons*, *supra* note 1, at 244.

[102] See H. B. Robertson, 'Self-Defense against Computer Network Attack under International Law', 76 *ILS* 121, 140 (M. N. Schmitt and B. T. O'Donnell eds., 2001).

[103] See Y. Dinstein, 'Computer Network Attacks and Self-Defense', 76 *ILS*, *ibid.*, 99, 105.

[104] General Assembly Resolution 3314, *supra* note 52, at 143.

An armed attack by Arcadia against Utopia can also involve (either in an active or in a passive way) the territory of a third State. For instance, Utopian targets may be bombed by Arcadian planes operating from airfields located in Ruritania (a country allied with or occupied by Arcadia). Another possibility is that Arcadian troops assault Utopian personnel stationed by consent within the territory of Numidia. As well, the destruction of a Utopian Embassy in Carpathia – brought about by Arcadian agents – will be deemed an armed attack against Utopia (whose embassy was destroyed), no less than Carpathia (in whose territory the act was perpetrated). Thus, the destructive bombings by foreign perpetrators of the US Embassies in Kenya and Tanzania in 1998 were definitely armed attacks, laying the ground for the exercise of self-defence.[105]

At times, an armed attack occurs beyond the boundaries of all States. As noted (*supra*, i), if Arcadia mines a Utopian warship on the high seas, this may amount to an armed attack (depending on the degree of damage ensuing from the explosion), bringing into play the right of self-defence. The situation would be identical if missiles, fired by Numidian armed forces, destroy a satellite put in orbit in outer space by Apollonia.

The State subjected to an armed attack is entitled to resort to self-defence measures against the aggressor, regardless of the geographic point where the attack was delivered. An armed attack need not even be cross-border in nature: it does not have to be perpetrated beyond the frontiers of the aggressor State. If force is used by Patagonia against Atlantican installations (such as a military base or an embassy) legitimately situated within Patagonian territory, this may constitute an armed attack, and Atlantica would be entitled to exercise its right of self-defence against Patagonia.[106]

In the *Tehran* case of 1980, the International Court of Justice used the phrase 'armed attack' when discussing the takeover by Iranian militants of the United States Embassy in Tehran, and the seizure of the Embassy staff as hostages, in November 1979.[107] The reference to an 'armed attack' is particularly significant in light of the ill-fated American attempt, in April 1980, to bring about the rescue of the hostages by military means.[108] The legality of the rescue mission was not an issue before the

---

[105] See R. Wedgwood, 'Responding to Terrorism: The Strikes against Bin Laden', 24 *YJIL* 559, 564 (1999).
[106] See O. Schachter, 'International Law in the Hostage Crisis: Implications for Future Cases', *American Hostages in Iran* 325, 328 (W. Christopher *et al.* eds., 1985).
[107] *Case Concerning United States Diplomatic and Consular Staff in Tehran*, [1980] *ICJ Rep.* 3, 29, 42.
[108] See T. L. Stein, 'Contempt, Crisis, and the Court: The World Court and the Hostage Rescue Attempt', 76 *AJIL* 499, 500 n. 8 (1982).

Court.[109] Yet, the Judgment registered the American plea that the operation had been carried out in exercise of the right of self-defence, with a view to extricating the victims of an armed attack against the US Embassy.[110] In his Dissenting Opinion in the *Nicaragua* case, Judge Schwebel called that plea 'a sound legal evaluation of the rescue attempt'.[111]

When inter-State force is employed inside the national boundaries of the acting State, one must not gloss over the rights of the territorial sovereign (which other States must respect). Sovereign rights allow a State to guard its borders from any unauthorized entry. There have been a number of incidents in which naval forces of coastal countries (e.g., Sweden and Norway) dropped depth charges and detonated sea-bottom mines, in order to force to the surface foreign submarines intruding into internal or territorial waters.[112] Both Article 14(6) of the 1958 Geneva Convention on the Territorial Sea and the Contiguous Zone,[113] and Article 20 of the 1982 United Nations Convention on the Law of the Sea,[114] prescribe that submarines passing through the territorial sea 'are required to navigate on the surface and to show their flag'. It is sometimes argued that, nevertheless, submerged passage does not give the coastal State a licence to resort to force against the foreign submarine.[115] But this assertion is unsustainable. The practice of States amply demonstrates that the use of force by the coastal State is not ruled out, if a submarine makes an unauthorized and submerged entry into the territorial or internal waters.[116] The intrusion by the submerged submarine may be regarded as an incipient armed attack (see *supra*, i), and the coastal State is allowed, therefore, to employ forcible counter-measures by way of self-defence.[117]

---

[109] *Tehran* case, *supra* note 107, at 43.   [110] *Ibid.*, 18.

[111] *Nicaragua* case, *supra* note 37, at 292.

[112] For the facts, see F. D. Froman, 'Uncharted Waters: Non-Innocent Passage of Warships in the Territorial Sea', 21 *SDLR* 625, 680–8 (1983–4).

[113] Geneva Convention on the Territorial Sea and the Contiguous Zone, 1958, 516 *UNTS* 205, 214.

[114] United Nations Convention on the Law of the Sea, 1982, Official Text, 7.

[115] See R. Sadurska, 'Foreign Submarines in Swedish Waters: The Erosion of an International Norm', 10 *YJIL* 34, 57 (1984–5).

[116] See D. P. O'Connell, *The International Law of the Sea*, I, 297 (1982).

[117] It has been suggested that the problem can be solved by excluding from the 'proscribed categories of article 2(4)' of the Charter the enforcement by a State of its territorial rights against an illegal incursion. O. Schachter, 'The Right of States to Use Armed Force', 82 *Mich.LR* 1620, 1626 (1984). But in this writer's opinion, the span of the prohibition of the use of inter-State force, as articulated in Article 2(4), is subject to no exception other than self-defence and collective security (see *supra*, Chapter 4, B). When one State uses force unilaterally against another, even within its own territory, this must be based on self-defence against an armed attack.

The status of surface warships engaged in non-innocent passage of the territorial sea of the coastal State is more problematic.[118] Article 19(2) of the Law of the Sea Convention enumerates a number of activities that are inconsistent with innocent passage.[119] But some of these activities (such as serious pollution or taking on board an aircraft), while at odds with innocent passage, cannot even remotely be considered an armed attack. The proper response on the part of the coastal State is to require the warship 'to leave the territorial sea immediately'.[120] Only if the warship refuses to withdraw, can there be an issue of an incipient armed attack.

When war is raging between Arcadia and Utopia, Patagonia – as a neutral State – is not only entitled but is legally bound to prevent entry into its territory by belligerent land and air forces (see *supra*, Chapter 1, D, (b), i). Should Arcadian aircraft penetrate Patagonia's territory in breach of its neutrality, their intrusion into the neutral airspace may also be viewed as an incipient armed attack. Patagonian military units are accordingly allowed to open fire on the Arcadian aircraft, in the exercise of both the right of self-defence and the duties of neutrality.[121] If long-range Arcadian missiles transit through Patagonian airspace – *en route* to striking Utopian targets – Arcadia is in breach of the neutrality of Patagonia.[122] All the same, assuming that Patagonia is militarily incapable of shooting those missiles down, Patagonia cannot be blamed for being in violation of its duty as a neutral.[123] Moreover, since the missiles are merely overflying its territory, it is doubtful whether Patagonia may treat their illegal transit through its airspace as an armed attack and invoke the right of self-defence.

iv.   The target of an armed attack The foremost target of an armed attack (justifying counter-measures of self-defence) is the territory of a foreign State or any section thereof – land, water or air – including

---

[118] See D. G. Stephens, 'The Impact of the 1982 Law of the Sea Convention on the Conduct of Peacetime Naval/Military Operations', 29 *CWILJ* 283, 309 (1998–9).

[119] United Nations Convention on the Law of the Sea, *supra* note 114, at 6–7.

[120] Article 30 of the Convention, *ibid.*, 1276.

[121] M. Bothe is of the opinion that the Patagonian measures are legitimate independently of the issues of armed attack and self-defence. International Law Association, *Report of the Committee on Neutrality and Naval Warfare* 3 (Cairo, 1992; M. Bothe, Rapporteur). But the traditional laws of neutrality must be adapted to the law of the Charter, which permits a unilateral deviation from the general prohibition of inter-State use of force only in circumstances of self-defence against an armed attack.

[122] See N. Ronzitti, 'Missile Warfare and Nuclear Warheads – An Appraisal in the Light of the 1996 ICJ Advisory Opinion on the Legality of the Threat or Use of Nuclear Weapons', 27 *IYHR* 251, 256–7 (1997).

[123] See *ibid.*, 257.

persons or property (of whatever type) within the affected area. Another obvious target is a military unit belonging to the armed forces of the victim State, stationed or in transit outside the national territory. Taking forcible measures against any public (military or civilian) installation of the victim State, located outside the national territory, may also amount to an armed attack.

Does the use of force by Arcadia against a private vessel or aircraft, registered in Utopia but attacked beyond the national boundaries, qualify as an armed attack against Utopia? The consensus Definition of Aggression, in Article 3(d), brings within its scope an attack on 'marine and air fleets of another State'[124] (listing them separately from 'sea or air forces'; see *supra*, Chapter 5, B). The expression 'fleets' was chosen advisedly, so as to exclude from the purview of the Definition the use of force by Arcadia against a single or a few commercial Utopian vessels or aircraft, especially when they enter Arcadian jurisdiction.[125] A reasonable degree of force (in the form of search and seizure) may be legitimate against foreign merchant ships even on the high seas.[126] Hence, the United States erred in 1975, when it treated the temporary seizure of the merchant ship *Mayaguez* by Cambodian naval units as an armed attack (invoking self-defence to legitimize the use of force in response).[127]

Another question is whether recourse to force by Arcadia (within its own territory) against Utopian nationals, away from any Utopian installation or vessel, may also constitute an armed attack against Utopia (thus justifying counter-force as self-defence). The answer is certainly affirmative if the Utopian victims are diplomatic envoys or visiting dignitaries.[128] A more intricate problem is whether Utopia may treat as an armed attack the use of force (within the boundaries of Arcadia) against ordinary Utopian nationals holding no official position. Is an attack against such nationals tantamount to an armed attack against Utopia itself, so that Utopia is entitled to resort to counter-force in self-defence? D. W. Bowett upholds the thesis that the protection of nationals abroad can be looked upon as protection of the State.[129] While many scholars strongly

---

[124] General Assembly Resolution 3314, *supra* note 52, at 143.

[125] See B. Broms, 'The Definition of Aggression', 154 *RCADI* 299, 351 (1977).

[126] See W. J. Fenrick, 'Legal Limits on the Use of Force by Canadian Warships Engaged in Law Enforcement', 18 *CYIL* 113, 125–45 (1980).

[127] See J. J. Paust, 'The Seizure and Recovery of the *Mayaguez*', 85 *YLJ* 774, 791, 800 (1975–6).

[128] *Cf.* G. Arangio-Ruiz, 'The Normative Role of the General Assembly of the United Nations and the Declaration of Principles of Friendly Relations', 137 *RCADI* 419, 535 (1972).

[129] Bowett, *supra* note 49, at 91–4.

disagree,[130] others share that conception.[131] The present writer agrees in principle with Bowett, although much may depend on the circumstances of the attack. The allegation that an attack against nationals abroad can never be regarded as an attack against the State itself[132] swings away from reality: it carries the legal fiction of the State to extreme and illogical lengths.[133]

Some commentators believe that a novel rule concerning the protection of nationals abroad is currently being moulded in the crucible of customary international law.[134] The process is animated by new challenges to law and order within the international community, in particular the remarkable increase in episodes involving the taking of hostages and other incidents of transnational terrorism. If and when such a new rule becomes a part of customary international law, the protection of nationals abroad may join self-defence as another (and separate) exception to the general prohibition of the use of inter-State force. However, no such independent exception exists in the meantime.[135] At present, any forcible measures taken in a foreign territory in the interest of nationals must be based on self-defence in response to an armed attack. We shall return to this topic *infra* (Chapter 8, A, (a), iii).

v. Support of armed bands and terrorists In the *Nicaragua* case, the International Court of Justice held that 'it may be considered to be agreed that an armed attack must be understood as including not merely action by regular armed forces across an international border', but also the dispatch of armed bands or 'irregulars' into the territory of another State.[136] The Court quoted Article 3(g) of the General Assembly's Definition of Aggression[137] (see *supra*, Chapter 5, B), which it took 'to reflect customary international law'.[138]

---

[130] See J. E. S. Fawcett, 'Intervention in International Law. A Study of Some Recent Cases', 103 *RCADI* 343, 404 (1961); T. Schweisfurth, 'Operations to Rescue Nationals in Third States Involving the Use of Force in Relation to the Protection of Human Rights', 23 *GYIL* 159, 162–5 (1980).

[131] See G. Fitzmaurice, 'The General Principles of International Law Considered from the Standpoint of the Rule of Law', 92 *RCADI* 1, 172–3 (1957).

[132] See R. Zedalis, 'Protection of Nationals Abroad: Is Consent the Basis of Legal Obligation?', 25 *TILJ* 209, 236–7 (1990).

[133] '[S]ince population is one of the attributes of statehood, an attack upon a state's population would seem to be just as much an attack upon that state as would an attack upon its territory.' C. Greenwood, 'International Law and the United States' Air Operation against Libya', 89 *WVLR* 933, 941 (1986–7).

[134] See N. Ronzitti, *Rescuing Nationals Abroad through Military Coercion and Intervention on Grounds of Humanity* 65–8 (1985).

[135] See *ibid.*, 64–5.   [136] *Nicaragua* case, *supra* note 37, at 103.

[137] General Assembly Resolution 3314, *supra* note 52, at 143.

[138] *Nicaragua* case, *supra* note 37, at 103.

It may be added that, under the Declaration on Principles of International Law Concerning Friendly Relations and Co-operation among States in accordance with the Charter of the United Nations, adopted unanimously by the General Assembly in 1970, 'every State has the duty to refrain from organizing or encouraging the organization of irregular forces or armed bands ... for incursion into the territory of another State'.[139] The Draft Code of Offences against the Peace and Security of Mankind, formulated by the International Law Commission in 1954, listed among these offences the organization (or the encouragement of organization) by the authorities of a State of armed bands for incursions into the territory of another State, direct support of such incursions, and even the toleration of the use of the local territory as a base of operations by armed bands against another State.[140]

Since assaults by irregular troops, armed bands or terrorists are typically conducted by small groups, employing hit-and-run pin-prick tactics, the question whether they are of 'sufficient gravity' and reach the *de minimis* threshold of an armed attack – or of the consensus Definition of Aggression – is clearly apposite[141] (see *supra*, ii). This is not to say that every single incident, scrutinized independently, has to meet the standard of sufficient gravity. A persuasive argument can be made that, should a distinctive pattern of behaviour emerge, a series of pin-prick assaults might be weighed in its totality and count as an armed attack[142] (see *infra*, Chapter 8, A, (a), ii).

The Judgment in the *Nicaragua* case pronounced that 'while the concept of an armed attack includes the despatch by one State of armed bands into the territory of another State, the supply of arms and other support to such bands cannot be equated with armed attack'.[143] The Court did 'not believe' that 'assistance to rebels in the form of the provision of weapons or logistical or other support' rates as an armed attack.[144] These are sweeping statements that ought to be narrowed down.[145] In his Dissenting Opinion, Judge Jennings expressed the view that, whereas 'the mere provision of arms cannot be said to amount to an armed attack', it may qualify as such when coupled with 'logistical or

---

[139] General Assembly Resolution 2625 (XXV), 25 *RGA* 121, 123 (1970).
[140] Draft Code of Offences against the Peace and Security of Mankind, Report of the International Law Commission, 6th Session, [1954] II *ILC Ybk* 140, 149, 151 (Article 2(4)).
[141] See V. Cassin, W. Debevoise, H. Kailes and T. W. Thompson, 'The Definition of Aggression', 16 *HILJ* 589, 607–8 (1975).
[142] See Y. Z. Blum, 'State Response to Acts of Terrorism', 19 *GYIL* 223, 233 (1976).
[143] *Nicaragua* case, *supra* note 37, at 126–7.   [144] *Ibid.*, 104.
[145] See Randelzhofer, *supra* note 71, at 801.

other support'.[146] In another dissent, Judge Schwebel stressed the words 'substantial involvement therein' (appearing in Article 3(g) of the Definition of Aggression), which are incompatible with the language used by the majority.[147]

When terrorists are sponsored by Arcadia against Utopia, they may be deemed '*de facto* organs' of Arcadia.[148] '[T]he imputability to a State of a terrorist act is unquestionable if evidence is provided that the author of such act was a State organ acting in that capacity.'[149] Arms shipments alone may not be equivalent to an armed attack.[150] But an armed attack is not extenuated by the subterfuge of indirect aggression or by reliance on a surrogate.[151] There is no real difference between the activation of a country's regular armed forces and a military operation carried out at one remove, pulling the strings of a terrorist organization (not formally associated with the governmental apparatus). Not one iota is diminished from the full implications of State responsibility if a 'group of persons is in fact acting on the instructions of, or under the direction or control of, that State in carrying out the conduct'.[152]

An issue that arose in the *Nicaragua* Judgment was the 'degree of dependence on the one side and control on the other' that would equate hostile paramilitary groups with organs of the foreign State.[153] The Court held that what is required is 'effective control' of the operation by that State.[154] In 1999, the Appeals Chamber of the International Criminal Tribunal for the Former Yugoslavia (ICTY), in the *Tadic* case, sharply contested the *Nicaragua* test of 'effective control', maintaining that it is inconsonant with logic and with law.[155] The ICTY Appeals Chamber pronounced that acts performed by members of a paramilitary group organized by a foreign State may be considered 'acts of *de facto* State organs regardless of any specific instruction by the controlling State

---

[146] *Nicaragua* case, *supra* note 37, at 543.   [147] *Ibid.*, 349.

[148] R. Ago, 'Fourth Report on State Responsibility', [1972] II *ILC Ybk* 71, 120.

[149] L. Condorelli, 'The Imputability to States of Acts of International Terrorism', 19 *IYHR* 233, 234 (1989).

[150] See J. P. Rowles, '"Secret Wars", Self-Defense and the Charter – A Reply to Professor Moore', 80 *AJIL* 568, 579 (1986).

[151] See M. A. Harry, 'The Right of Self-Defense and the Use of Armed Force against States Aiding Insurgency', 11 *SIULJ* 1289, 1299 (1986–7).

[152] The quotation is from Article 8 of the Draft Articles on State Responsibility as formulated by the International Law Commission, Report of the 53rd Session 43, 45 (mimeographed, 2001).

[153] *Nicaragua* case, *supra* note 37, at 62.   [154] *Ibid.*, 65.

[155] *Prosecutor v. Tadic*, Judgment, ICTY Case No. IT-94–1-A, Appeals Chamber, 1999, 38 *ILM* 1518, 1540–5 (1999).

concerning the commission of each of those acts'.[156] The ICTY focused on the subordination of the group to overall control by the foreign State: that State does not have to issue specific instructions for the direction of every individual operation, nor does it have to select concrete targets.[157] Terrorists can thus act quite autonomously and still remain *de facto* organs of the controlling State. Notwithstanding the disagreement between the two international tribunals, it must be appreciated that both actually agree on the fundamental thesis that at some point a red line is crossed, and the acts of terrorists can be imputed to a foreign State.

(bb)   An armed attack by non-State actors

Whereas Article 2(4) of the Charter, in proscribing the use of force, refers solely to 'Members ... in their international relations' (see *supra*, Chapter 4, B, (a)) – *i.e.* State actors on both sides – Article 51 mentions a State (a Member of the United Nations) only as the potential target of an armed attack. The perpetrator of that armed attack is not identified necessarily as a State.[158] An armed attack can therefore be carried out by non-State actors.

It is true that in its 2004 Advisory Opinion on *Legal Consequences of the Construction of a Wall in the Occupied Palestinian Territory*, the International Court of Justice enunciated:

Article 51 of the Charter thus recognizes the existence of an inherent right of self-defence in the case of armed attack by one State against another State.[159]

However, as correctly observed by Judge Higgins in her Separate Opinion:

There is, with respect, nothing in the text of Article 51 that *thus* stipulates that self-defence is available only when an armed attack is made by a State.[160]

Similar criticism was expressed in the Separate Opinion of Judge Kooijmans[161] and in the Declaration of Judge Buergenthal.[162] Indeed, the Court itself noted without demur Security Council Resolutions 1368 and 1373 (see *infra*), drawing a distinction between the situation contemplated by them (cross-border terrorism) and occupied territories.[163]

Of course, when non-State actors attack a State from within – and no other State is involved – this is a case of either an internal armed conflict or domestic terrorism. In neither instance does Article 51 come into play

[156] *Ibid.*, 1545.   [157] *Ibid.*
[158] See S. D. Murphy, 'Terrorism and the Concept of "Armed Attack" in Article 51 of the U.N. Charter', 43 *HILJ* 41, 50 (2002).
[159] Advisory Opinion on *Legal Consequences of the Construction of a Wall in the Occupied Palestinian Territory* , 2004, 43 *ILM* 1009, 1050 (2004).
[160] *Ibid.*, 1063.   [161] *Ibid.*, 1072.   [162] *Ibid.*, 1079.   [163] *Ibid.*, 1050.

at all. An armed attack against a State, in the meaning of Article 51, posits some element external to the victim State. Non-State actors must strike at a State from the outside.

In theory, terrorists can attack a State within or from an area outside the jurisdiction of all States, to wit, the high seas or outer space. Such terrorist attacks may constitute piracy as defined in Article 15 of the 1958 Geneva Convention on the High Seas[164] or in Article 101 of the 1982 UN Convention on the Law of the Sea.[165] However, when an attack is launched against Utopia by non-State actors operating from outside its territory, the violent action may be expected to originate in another State (Arcadia). That does not denote that the Arcadian Government is necessarily implicated in the attack. Terrorists or members of armed bands who do not qualify as 'de facto organs' of Arcadia (see supra, (aa), i) may still use Arcadian territory either as a springboard for striking at Utopia or as a haven for regrouping thereafter (or both). In other words, the non-State actors may establish within Arcadian territory their base of operations. The usual pattern would consist of terrorists or armed bands located in Arcadia – without being inspired or prodded by the Arcadian Government (and while possibly taking evasive action against the Arcadian security forces) – emerging, when the opportunity presents itself, for hit-and-run attacks against Utopia and then returning to Arcadia for shelter. Arcadia may actually be a 'failed State', embroiled in a temporary situation of total collapse of the State apparatus.[166] Alternatively, Arcadia – constrained by political or military considerations – may passively tolerate the use of its soil by terrorists or armed bands operating against Utopia, without actively sponsoring their activities or even encouraging them.[167] In any event, if self-defence is to be exercised by Utopia against the terrorists or the armed bands, any forcible measures will have to take place 'in the territory of a state where the attackers are headquartered or have taken refuge',[168] i.e. Arcadia.

In the Corfu Channel case of 1949, the International Court of Justice pronounced that every State is under an obligation 'not to allow knowingly its territory to be used for acts contrary to the rights of other

---

[164] Geneva Convention on the High Seas, 1958, 450 UNTS 82, 90.

[165] United Nations Convention on the Law of the Sea, supra note 114, at 34.

[166] See C. Stahn, 'International Law at a Crossroads? The Impact of September 11', 62 ZAORV 183, 214–5, 222–3 (2002).

[167] On the difference between State terrorism, State-assisted or State-encouraged terrorism, and State-tolerated terrorism, see S. Sucharitkul, 'Terrorism as an International Crime: Questions of Responsibility and Complicity', 19 IYHR 247, 256–7 (1989).

[168] See J. Delbrück, 'The Fight against Global Terrorism: Self-Defense or Collective Security as International Police Action? Some Comments on the International Legal Implications of the "War against Terrorism"', 44 GYIL 9, 15 (2001).

States'.[169] Accordingly, a State must not knowingly permit its territory to be used as a sanctuary for terrorists or armed bands bent on attacking military targets or civilian objects in another country. It is irrefutable that the toleration by a State of activities by terrorists or armed bands, directed against another country, is unlawful.[170] Under the 1954 Draft Code of Offences against the Peace and Security of Mankind, as formulated by the International Law Commission, such toleration even constitutes a crime under international law[171] (see *supra*, (aa), v).

In its Judgment of 1980, in the *Tehran* case, the International Court of Justice held that, if the authorities of one State are required under international law to take appropriate acts in order to protect the interests of another State, and – while they have the means at their disposal to do so – completely fail to comply with their obligations, the inactive State bears international responsibility towards the other State.[172] Indeed, a State that does not fulfil its international obligation of 'vigilance', and fails 'in its specific duty not to tolerate the preparation in its territory of actions which are directed against a foreign Government or which might endanger the latter's security', assumes international responsibility for this international wrongful act of omission[173] (see *supra*, Chapter 4, F, (a)).

Irrespective of questions of State responsibility, the principal issue is whether acts of violence unleashed against Utopia from Arcadian territory by terrorists or armed bands – not sponsored by Arcadia – may amount to an armed attack within the meaning of Article 51 of the UN Charter (thereby triggering the right of self-defence). The simple proposition that forcible action taken against a State may constitute an armed attack, even if the perpetrators are non-State actors operating from a foreign State – albeit not organs of the latter State – was categorically upheld in previous editions of the present book.[174] In the past, many commentators admittedly argued that the expression 'armed attack' in Article 51 does not apply to every armed attack, 'regardless of the source', but only to an armed attack by another State.[175] However, all lingering doubts on this issue have been dispelled as a result of the

---

[169] *Corfu Channel* case (Merits), [1949] *ICJ Rep.* 4, 22.
[170] See I. Brownlie, 'International Law and the Activities of Armed Bands', 7 *ICLQ* 712, 734 (1958).
[171] Draft Code of Offences against the Peace and Security of Mankind, *supra* note 140, at 151 (Article 2(4)).
[172] *Tehran* case, *supra* note 107, at 32–3, 44.
[173] Ago, 'Fourth Report on State Responsibility', [1972] II *ILC Ybk* 71, 120.
[174] See pp. 213–15 of the 3rd ed. of this book (2001).
[175] See, e.g., O. Schachter, 'The Lawful Use of Force by a State against Terrorists in Another Country', 19 *IYHR* 209, 216 (1989).

response of the international community to the shocking events of 9 September 2001 (9/11).[176]

The attacks against the United States on 9/11 were mounted by the Al-Qaeda terrorist organization masterminded from within Taliban-led Afghanistan but not controlled by that State (indeed, there were indications that the Taliban regime was to some extent controlled by Al-Qaeda).[177] The terrorists hijacked passenger airliners within the US and used them as explosive devices, bringing about the destruction of the twin towers of the World Trade Center in New York and causing serious damage to the Pentagon, with thousands of human lives lost. The fact that these acts amounted to an armed attack – laying the ground for the exercise of self-defence pursuant to Article 51 – has been fully corroborated by a number of legal measures taken by international bodies:

i. Both in Resolution 1368 (2001)[178] – adopted a day after 9/11 – and in Resolution 1373 (2001),[179] the Security Council recognized and reaffirmed in this context 'the inherent right of individual or collective self-defence in accordance with the Charter'. Complaining that the Security Council refers to 'horrifying terrorist attacks' – without mentioning specifically the expression 'armed attack'[180] – stands the argument on its head. If the right of self-defence can be actuated, this ineluctably implies that an armed attack is concerned. The whole point about the contention that an armed attack has indeed taken place on 9/11 is that this would warrant the exercise of the right of self-defence, a right recognized and reaffirmed by the Security Council.

ii. The day after the attack, the North Atlantic Council also met and 'agreed that if it is determined that this attack was directed from abroad against the United States,[181] it shall be regarded as an action

---

[176] Even those who regard as 'problematic to say the least' the categorization of terrorist action as an armed attack within the meaning of Article 51, have to concede that the response of the international community to 9/11 has left its mark on the law. See E. P. J. Myjer and N. D. White, 'The Twin Towers Attack: An Unlimited Right to Self-Defence?', 7 *JCSL* 5, 7–9 (2002).

[177] The situation seemed to 'reverse the traditional formula of state-sponsored terrorism: Afghanistan was a terrorist-sponsored state'. M. J. Glennon, 'The Fog of Law: Self-Defense, Inherence, and Incoherence in Article 51 of the United Nations Charter', 25 *HJLPP* 539, 544 n. 17 (2001–2).

[178] Security Council Resolution 1368 (2001), [2001–2] *RDSC* 290, 291.

[179] Security Council Resolution 1373 (2001), [2001–2] *RDSC* 291, *id* .

[180] See M. A. Drumbl, 'Victimhood in our Neighborhood: Terrorist Crime, Taliban Guilt, and the Asymmetries of the International Legal Order', 81 *NCLR* 1, 29 (2002–3).

[181] Such a factual determination was made subsequently on the basis of additional information. See J. M. Beard, 'America's New War on Terror: The Case for Self-Defense under International Law', 25 *HJLPP* 559, 568 (2001–2).

covered by Article 5 of the Washington Treaty, which states that an armed attack against one or more of the Allies in Europe or North America 'shall be considered an attack against them all'.[182] It is noteworthy that this was the first time in the history of NATO that Article 5 of the 1949 (Washington) North Atlantic Treaty, was invoked. The Article, which uses the expression 'armed attack', does so explicitly in the context of Article 51 of the UN Charter and the right of self-defence.[183]

iii. In a September 2001 meeting of the Ministers of Foreign Affairs, acting as an Organ of Consultation, in application of the 1947 (Rio de Janeiro) Inter-American Treaty of Reciprocal Assistance, it was resolved that 'these terrorist attacks against the United States of America are attacks against all American States'.[184] This must be understood in light of Article 3 of the Rio Treaty, which refers specifically to an armed attack and to the right of self-defence pursuant to Article 51 (see *infra*, Chapter 9, B, (a)).[185]

The fact that terrorist attacks qualify as armed attacks means that they are subject to the full application of Article 51: no more and no less. Thus, the present writer cannot accept the argument made by R. Müllerson that – whereas self-defence against an armed attack by a State must (as a minimum) be interceptive rather than anticipatory – purely preventive measures are justified against terrorist attacks.[186]

C.   Conditions precedent to the exercise of self-defence

The International Court of Justice pointed out, in the *Nicaragua* case, that Article 51 'does not contain any specific rule whereby self-defence would warrant only measures which are proportional to the armed attack and necessary to respond to it, a rule well established in customary international law'.[187] In its 1996 Advisory Opinion on the *Legality of the Threat or Use of Nuclear Weapons*, the Court – citing these words – added that '[t]he submission of the exercise of the right of self-defence to the conditions of necessity and proportionality is a rule of customary

---

[182] North Atlantic Treaty Organization (NATO): Statement by the North Atlantic Council, 2001, 40 *ILM* 1267, *id.* (2001).

[183] North Atlantic Treaty, 1949, 34 *UNTS* 243, 246.

[184] Organization of American States (OAS): on Terrorist Threat to the Americas, 2001, 40 *ILM* 1273, *id.* (2001).

[185] Rio de Janeiro Inter-American Treaty of Reciprocal Assistance, 1947, 21 *UNTS* 77, 95.

[186] See R. Müllerson, '*Jus ad Bellum* and International Terrorism', 32 *IYHR* 1, 41–2 (2002).

[187] *Nicaragua* case, *supra* note 37, at 94.

international law', but '[t]his dual condition applies equally to Article 51 of the Charter, whatever the means of force employed'.[188] The two conditions of necessity and proportionality were reaffirmed by the Court in its Judgment of 2003 in the *Oil Platforms* case.[189]

In fact, the two conditions of necessity and proportionality are accompanied by a third condition of immediacy. As will be seen *infra* (Chapter 8, B, (c)), these three conditions are distilled from yardsticks set out by the American Secretary of State, D. Webster, more than 160 years ago.

The three conditions will be dissected *infra*, in the contexts of the different modes of self-defence, in Chapter 8. Still, in broad outline, the first condition of necessity entails the following requirements:

  (i) It is incumbent on the State invoking self-defence (Utopia) to establish in a definite manner that an armed attack was launched by a particular country (Arcadia) and no other (Ruritania). As shown in the *Oil Platforms* case, this is especially true if – during a war between Arcadia and Ruritania – damage is caused to a Utopian neutral vessel by an incoming missile or the explosion of a mine: conclusive evidence is required that the attack was carried out by Arcadia and not by Ruritania.[190]

  (ii) Utopia must verify that the use of force amounted to a genuine armed attack and not to a mere accident or mistake for which Arcadia may incur State responsibility without, however, bearing the blame for an armed attack. In the *Oil Platforms* case, the Court took the position that the attack must be 'aimed specifically' at the target country.[191] If this specificity implies that Arcadia does not incur full responsibility for an indiscriminate attack (e.g., through mine-laying carried out in international shipping lanes) – without due regard for the possibility that a Utopian objective can be the eventual victim – then the Court went too far.[192] But, in all likelihood, the Court's dictum ought to be construed narrowly against the factual background of the case (the Iran–Iraq War). Thus, when – in the course of war between Arcadia and Numidia – a neutral Utopian objective is struck by Arcadia, it is necessary to determine whether the attack was 'aimed specifically' at Utopia (as opposed to Numidia) and that the Utopian objective did not fall prey to a mistaken identity.[193]

  (iii) Utopia must ascertain that there exists a necessity to rely on force – in response to the armed attack – because no realistic alternative means

---

[188] Advisory Opinion on *Nuclear Weapons*, *supra* note 1, at 245.
[189] *Case Concerning Oil Platforms*, *supra* note 40, at 1361–2.
[190] *Ibid.*, 1356–7, 1360.   [191] *Ibid.*, 1358.   [192] See Taft, *supra* note 96, at 302–3.
[193] See C. Gray, *International Law and the Use of Force* 119 (2nd ed., 2004).

of redress is available.[194] In other words, 'force should not be considered necessary until peaceful measures have been found wanting or when they clearly would be futile'.[195] If efforts to resolve the problem amicably are made, they should be carried out in good faith and not only as a matter of 'ritual punctilio'.[196]

The second condition of proportionality is frequently depicted as 'of the essence of self-defence'.[197] However, as correctly remarked by Ago, the principle of proportionality must be applied with some degree of flexibility.[198] We shall discuss *infra* (Chapter 8, A) the different implications of proportionality, depending on whether the measures taken in self-defence constitute war or are 'short of war'. It is perhaps best to look at the demand for proportionality in the province of self-defence as a standard of reasonableness in the response to force by counter-force.[199]

Immediacy signifies that there must not be an undue time-lag between the armed attack and the exercise of self-defence. Again, this condition ought not to be construed too strictly.[200] Lapse of time is almost unavoidable when – in a desire to fulfil letter and spirit the condition of necessity – a tedious process of information gathering or diplomatic negotiations evolves. The first phase of the Gulf War is a prime example. The invasion of Kuwait by Iraq took place on 2 August 1990, yet the Security Council authorized the use of 'all necessary means' only as from 15 January 1991,[201] namely, after almost half a year (see *infra*, Chapter 8, A, (b), iii).

In the *Nicaragua* case, the Court rejected on other grounds a claim of (collective) self-defence by the United States. As a result, no decision in respect of necessity and proportionality (or immediacy) was required *stricto sensu*.[202] All the same, the Court commented that the condition of necessity (coupled with the condition of immediacy) was not fulfilled, inasmuch as the United States commenced its activities several months after the presumed armed attack had occurred and when the main danger could be eliminated in a different manner.[203] The condition of proportionality was not met either, according to the Judgment, in view of the relative scale of the initial measures and counter-measures.[204] But it must

---

[194] See Ago, *supra* note 17, at 69.   [195] See Schachter, *supra* note 117, at 1635.
[196] N. Rostow, 'Nicaragua and the Law of Self-Defense Revisited', 11 *YJIL* 437, 455 (1985–6).
[197] I. Brownlie, *International Law and the Use of Force by States* 279 n. 2 (1963).
[198] Ago, *supra* note 17, at 69.
[199] See K. W. Quigley, 'A Framework for Evaluating the Legality of the United States Intervention in Nicaragua', 17 *NYUJILP* 155, 180 (1984–5).
[200] See K. C. Kenny, 'Self-Defence', *United Nations: Law, Policies and Practice*, II, 1162, 1167 (R. Wolfrum ed., 1995).
[201] Security Council Resolution 678, 45 *RDSC* 27, 27–8 (1990).
[202] *Nicaragua* case, *supra* note 37, at 122.   [203] *Ibid.*   [204] *Ibid.*

be noted that Judge Schwebel strongly disagreed with these factual find-
ings in his Dissenting Opinion.[205]

D.   The role of the Security Council

(a)   The two phases rule

The excuse of self-defence has often been used by aggressors bent on
scoring propaganda points. Brutal armed attacks have taken place while
the attacking State sanctimoniously assured world public opinion that it
was only responding with counter-force to the (mythical) use of force by
the other side. If every State were the final arbiter of the legality of its own
acts, if every State could cloak an armed attack with the disguise of self-
defence, the international legal endeavour to hold force in check would
have been an exercise in futility.

From another perspective, the gist of self-defence is self-help (see
supra, A, (a)). The facts of life at present are such that a State confronted
with an armed attack cannot seriously expect an effective international
police force to come to its aid and repel the aggressor (see *infra*, Chapter
10, C). The State under attack has no choice but to defend itself as best it
can. It must also act without undue loss of time, and, most certainly, it
cannot afford the luxury of waiting for any juridical (let alone judicial)
scrutiny of the situation to run its course.

The upshot is that the process of self-defence must consist of two
separate stages.[206] Phase one is when the option of recourse to self-
defence is left to the unfettered discretion of the victim State (and any
third State ready to oppose the aggressor). The acting State determines
whether the occasion calls for the use of forcible measures in self-defence,
and, if so, what specific steps ought to be taken. But all this is preliminary.
In the second and final phase, a competent international forum has to be
empowered to review the whole flow of events and to gauge the legality of
the force employed. Above all, the competent forum must be authorized
to arrive at the conclusion that the banner of self-defence has been falsely
brandished by an aggressor.

The Judgment of the International Military Tribunal at *Nuremberg* fully
endorsed the two stages concept:

It was further argued that Germany alone could decide, in accordance with the
reservations made by many of the Signatory Powers at the time of the conclusion
of the Kellogg–Briand Pact, whether preventive action was a necessity, and that in

---

[205] *Ibid.*, 362–9.   [206] See Oppenheim, *supra* note 57, at 187–8.

making her decision her judgment was conclusive. But whether action taken under the claim of self-defense was in fact aggressive or defensive must ultimately be subject to investigation and adjudication if international law is ever to be enforced.[207]

The International Military Tribunal for the Far East at *Tokyo* rephrased the same idea in its own words:

The right of self-defence involves the right of the State threatened with impending attack to judge for itself in the first instance whether it is justified in resorting to force. Under the most liberal interpretation of the Kellogg–Briand Pact, the right of self-defence does not confer upon the State resorting to war the authority to make a final determination upon the justification for its action.[208]

The decisive issue, of course, is whether a competent international forum has actually been assigned the task of investigating the legality of any forcible measures taken by a State in reliance on self-defence. One of the great achievements of the UN Charter is that Article 51 enables the Security Council to undertake a review of self-defence claims made by Member States.

The Security Council is the sole international organ mentioned in Article 51. Nevertheless, as the 1986 Judgment in the *Nicaragua* case elucidated, the legitimacy of recourse to self-defence may also be explored – in appropriate circumstances – by the International Court of Justice. There is a general problem (to be discussed *infra*, Chapter 10, E, (b)) engendered by the potential concurrent jurisdictions of the Council and the Court. The Court in the *Nicaragua* case held (in 1984) that, because self-defence is a right, it has legal dimensions and judicial proceedings are not foreclosed in consequence of the authority of the Council.[209]

In his Dissenting Opinion of 1986, Judge Schwebel completely quashed the argument (advanced by some writers) that 'the use of force in self-defence is a political question which no court, including the International Court of Justice, should adjudge'.[210] He then grappled with a different (albeit related) view, pressed by the United States, that the capacity to determine the legality of the exercise of self-defence, especially in an on-going armed conflict, is exclusively entrusted by Article 51 to the Security Council and withheld from the Court.[211] After some deliberation, Judge Schwebel denied the validity of this contention, and yet, in his opinion – owing to the special circumstances of the

---

[207] *Nuremberg* trial, *supra* note 78, at 208.   [208] *Tokyo* trial, *supra* note 34, at 364.
[209] *Case Concerning Military and Paramilitary Activities in and against Nicaragua* (Jurisdiction), [1984] *ICJ Rep.* 392, 436.
[210] *Nicaragua* case, *supra* note 37, at 285–7.   [211] *Ibid.*, 287.

case – the issue of self-defence was not justiciable at the time the Judgment was rendered.[212] The majority of the Court refused to admit the claim of injusticiability in whole or in part.[213]

Another problem connected with judicial proceedings is whether a State may resort to the use of force in self-defence after the dispute has been submitted to adjudication by the International Court of Justice. This is what the United States did, in 1980, in the unsuccessful attempt to release American hostages from Iranian captivity (see *supra*, B, (b)). The Judgment in the *Tehran* case included an *obiter dictum* to the effect that such an operation may 'undermine respect for the judicial process in international relations'.[214] Sir Robert Jennings admonished that 'force, even lawful and justifiable force, should not be undertaken in respect of a matter which is *sub judice*; perhaps least of all by the party which itself initiated the Court proceedings'.[215] However, in some exceptional situations, a litigant State may have no practical choice but to rely on forcible counter-measures *pendente lite* (for instance, when hostilities are resumed by the other side).[216]

(b)   The options before the Security Council

Under Article 51, a State using force in self-defence, in response to an armed attack, acts at its own discretion but also at its own risk. Measures implementing the right of self-defence must immediately be reported to the Security Council. The report consists, as a minimum, of mere notification of the invocation of the right of self-defence in response to an armed attack. There is nothing in Article 51 to substantiate a claim, occasionally made, that the report must provide clear evidence regarding the occurrence of the armed attack.[217] A study of all the relevant facts may be undertaken by the Council.[218] But the Council, too, is not compelled to set in motion a thorough fact-finding process.[219] With or without a careful examination of the background, the Council is entitled

---

[212] *Ibid.*, 288–96.   [213] *Ibid.*, 26–8.   [214] *Tehran* case, *supra* note 107, at 43.

[215] R. Jennings, 'International Force and the International Court of Justice', *The Current Legal Regulation of the Use of Force* 323, 330 (A. Cassese ed., 1986).

[216] See Schachter, *supra* note 106, at 341–2.

[217] See Y. Arai-Takahashi, 'Shifting Boundaries of the Right of Self-Defense – Appraising the Impact of the September 11 Attacks on *Jus ad Bellum*', 36 *Int.Law.* 1081, 1095 (2002).

[218] See N. Q. Dinh, 'La Légitime Défense d'après la Charte des Nations Unies', 52 *RGDIP* 223, 239 (1948).

[219] On the difficulties immanent in this process, see R. B. Bilder, 'The Fact/Law Distinction in International Adjudication', *Fact-Finding before International Tribunals* 95–8 (R. B. Lillich ed., 1992).

to take any action it deems fit in order to maintain or restore international peace and security.

The modes of action open to the Security Council are diverse. *Inter alia*, the Council can (i) give its retrospective seal of approval to the exercise of self-defence; (ii) impose a general cease-fire (see *supra*, Chapter 2, C, (a), ii); (iii) demand withdrawal of forces to the original lines;[220] (iv) insist on the cessation of the unilateral action of the defending State, supplanting it with measures of collective security (see *infra*, Chapter 10); or (v) decide that the State engaged in so-called self-defence is in reality the aggressor. Whatever it opts to do, a mandatory decision taken by the Council in this matter is binding on UN Members (see *infra*, Chapter 10, B, (a)). Once a Member State is instructed in a conclusive manner to refrain from any further use of force, it must comply with the Council's directive.

Evidently, the Security Council is not a judicial body. It is, in the words of Judge Schwebel, 'a political organ which acts for political reasons'.[221] As a political body, the Council may be inclined to sacrifice the interests of an individual State for the sake of more general interests of international peace (as perceived by the Council).[222] The Council may even impose an arms embargo on a State exercising the right of self-defence.[223] The State concerned may resent such a decision and sincerely believe that the Council has been extremely unfair. But under the Charter, the State has no remedy. If it chooses to disobey the decision, the State may bear the brunt of enforcement measures activated by the Council (see *infra*, Chapter 10, A).

Unfortunately, in almost six decades of operation, the Security Council has displayed time and again a reluctance or inability to adopt a decision identifying the aggressor in a specific armed conflict. For most of the period, the inaction of the Council was deemed to be largely due to the profound rift between the blocs in the context of the 'Cold War'. But the termination of this rivalry has not markedly transformed the Council's record. Even when faced with an obvious case of an armed attack, political considerations may prevent the Council from taking a concerted stand. In the absence of an authoritative determination as to who actually

---

[220] Such a step may be taken either separately or jointly with the preceding measure. For a resolution demanding both a cease-fire and a withdrawal of forces to internationally recognized boundaries, see, e.g., Security Council Resolution 598, 42 *RDSC* 5, 6 (1987). For two separate (albeit consecutive) resolutions making similar calls, see, e.g., Security Council Resolutions 508 and 509, 42 *ibid.*, 5–6 (1982).

[221] *Nicaragua* case, *supra* note 37, at 290.   [222] See Bowett, *supra* note 49, at 197.

[223] See C. Gray, 'Bosnia and Herzegovina: Civil War or Inter-State Conflict? Characterization and Consequences', 67 *BYBIL* 155, 191–4 (1996).

attacked whom, both opposing parties can pretend that they are acting in legitimate self-defence, and the hostilities are likely to go on. To avert further carnage, the Council tends to bring about at least a cease-fire.

Article 51 sets forth that the right of self-defence may be exercised until the Security Council has taken the measures necessary to maintain international peace and security. Whenever the Council decrees in a binding fashion a withdrawal of forces or a cease-fire, the legal position is unequivocal: every Member State is obligated to act as the Council ordains and there is no further room to invoke self-defence. Should the Council be paralyzed and fail to take any measure necessary to maintain international peace and security, the legal position is equally obvious: a Member State exercising the right of self-defence may persist in the use of force. But what is the legal status if the Council follows the middle of the road and refrains from issuing detailed instructions to the parties, merely calling upon them, say, to conduct negotiations aimed at settling their dispute? Does such a resolution terminate the entitlement of a Member State to rely on self-help?

Notwithstanding contrary views,[224] it is clearly not enough (under Article 51) for the Security Council to adopt just any resolution, in order to divest Member States of the right to continue to resort to force in self-defence against an armed attack.[225] Even when the Council imposes economic sanctions in response to aggression, such measures by themselves cannot override the right of self-defence of the opposing side.[226] The only resolution that will engender that result is a legally binding decision, whereby the cessation of the (real or imagined) defensive action becomes imperative.[227] Short of an explicit decree by the Council to desist from the use of force, the State acting in self-defence retains its right to go on doing so until the Council has taken measures which have actually 'succeeded in restoring international peace and security'.[228] However, the defending State still acts at its own risk,

---

[224] See A. Chayes, 'The Use of Force in the Persian Gulf', *Law and Force in the New International Order* 3, 5–6 (L.F. Damrosch and D.J. Scheffer eds., 1991). *Cf.* K.S. Elliott, 'The New World Order and the Right of Self-Defense in the United Nations Charter', 15 *HICLR* 55, 68–9 (1991–2).

[225] See O. Schachter, 'United Nations Law in the Gulf Conflict', 85 *AJIL* 453, 458 (1991). *Cf.* T.K. Plofchan, 'Article 51: Limits on Self-Defense?', 13 *Mich.JIL* 336, 372–3 (1991–2).

[226] See E.V. Rostow, 'Until What? Enforcement Action or Collective Self-Defense?', 85 *AJIL* 506, 512–13 (1991).

[227] See Waldock, *supra* note 73, at 495–6.

[228] M. Halberstam, 'The Right to Self-Defense Once the Security Council Takes Action', 17 *Mich.JIL* 229, 248 (1996–7).

perhaps more so than before. Continued hostilities may instigate a decision by the Council against a self-proclaimed victim of an armed attack.[229]

(c)   Failure to report to the Security Council

Article 51 promulgates that measures taken in exercise of the right of self-
defence 'shall be immediately reported to the Security Council'. In some
instances, States invoking the right of self-defence make sure that such a
report to the Security Council is promptly dispatched. A letter-perfect
example is the American communication to the Security Council on
7 October 2001, reporting to the Council that the US (together with
some allies) had initiated action that day against Taliban-led Afghanistan
in response to the armed attack of 9/11 (unleashed by Al-Qaeda terrorists
but endorsed by the Taliban regime).[230] However, in practice, such a
communication represents the exception rather than the rule. When
States exercise the right of self-defence, they rarely respect the duty of
reporting to the Security Council.[231] There are numerous reasons for
such an omission. In particular, Governments do not always couch their
official statements in correct juridical terms. They are apt to conjure up
wrong pleas justifying their action, instead of relying on self-defence.[232]

The International Court of Justice, in the *Nicaragua* case, held that the
reporting obligation to the Security Council pursuant to Article 51 does
not constitute a part of customary international law (on which the
Judgment was based).[233] Yet, the Court was of the opinion that, even
'for the purpose of enquiry into the customary law position, the absence
of a report may be one of the factors indicating whether the State in
question was itself convinced that it was acting in self-defence'.[234] The
Court implied that – when the use of force is governed by the law of the
Charter – a State is precluded from invoking the right of self-defence if it
fails to comply with the requirement of reporting to the Council.[235] When
put in this light, the duty of reporting becomes a substantive condition
and a limitation on the exercise of self-defence.[236]

---

[229] See Bowett, *supra* note 49, at 196.
[230] Letter from the Permanent Representative of the United States of America to the
President of the Security Council, 7 October 2001, 40 *ILM* 1281 (2001).
[231] See S. D. Bailey and S. Daws, *The Procedure of the UN Security Council* 103 (3rd ed.,
1998).
[232] See J. Combacau, 'The Exception of Self-Defence in U.N. Practice', *The Current Legal
Regulation of the Use of Force, supra* note 215, at 9, 14.
[233] *Nicaragua* case, *supra* note 37, at 121.
[234] *Ibid.*, 105.   [235] *Ibid.*, 121–2.
[236] See P. S. Reichler and D. Wippman, 'United States Armed Intervention in Nicaragua:
A Rejoinder', 11 *YJIL* 462, 471 (1985–6).

Judge Schwebel disputed the majority's position, maintaining that measures of self-defence may be either overt or covert (just as an armed attack may be overt or covert); covert actions – *ex hypothesi* – cannot be reported to the Security Council and thereby publicly espoused.[237] In the present writer's view, the limitation of the reporting duty to overt operations is not congruent with the Charter. Article 51 imposes a blanket obligation of reporting to the Council whenever the right of self-defence is relied on, and the text does not even hint at the possibility of making an exception for covert operations. Indeed, a covert military operation (supposedly undertaken in self-defence) may subvert the authority of the Council by creating a smokescreen concealing the true state of affairs.

But Judge Schwebel did not stop here. Proceeding to probe the purport of the duty under discussion, he arrived at the conclusion that the report to the Security Council is a procedural matter, and that, therefore, non-feasance must not deprive a State of the substantive (and inherent) right of self-defence.[238] The nature of the reporting duty is the real issue. Should the report to the Council be regarded as a *conditio sine qua non*, going to the heart of the right of self-defence, or is it a technical requirement?[239]

Article 51 does not say that non-performance of the reporting obligation carries irrevocable adverse consequences for the invocation of the right of self-defence. The sequence of events envisaged by the framers of the Charter is such that initially a State takes measures in self-defence, and only thereafter does it have to transmit a report to the Security Council. The proposition that a failure to comport with the subsequent duty (to report) undermines the legality of the preceding measures (of self-defence) does not fit the scheme of Article 51.[240]

It is submitted that the dispatch of a report to the Security Council is only one of many factors bearing upon the legal validity of a State's claim to self-defence. The instantaneous transmittal of a report is no guarantee that the Council will accept that claim. Conversely, the failure to file a report at an early stage should not prove an irremediable defect. When

---

[237] *Nicaragua* case, *supra* note 37, at 374.   [238] *Ibid.*, 376–7.

[239] D. W. Greig has argued that 'it hardly seems possible to have a mandatory provision in the Charter, to which there is no counterpart in customary international law, relating to the exercise of a power available under both sources'. D. W. Greig, 'Self-Defence and the Security Council: What Does Article 51 Require?', 40 *ICLQ* 366, 380 (1991). But this position is unsound. As the Court explicitly pronounced in the context of self-defence: 'The areas governed by the two sources of law thus do not overlap exactly, and the rules do not have the same content' (*supra* note 37, at 94).

[240] See M. Knisbacher, 'The Entebbe Operation: A Legal Analysis of Israel's Rescue Action', 12 *JILE* 57, 79 (1977–8).

convinced that forcible measures were taken by a State in self-defence, the Council ought to issue a ruling to that effect, despite the absence of a report. It would be a gross misinterpretation of Article 51 for the Council to repudiate self-defence, thus condoning an armed attack, only because no report has been put on record. Certainly, if measures responsive to an armed attack are brought to the attention of the Council in an indirect manner (not earning the formal status of a report), the defending State must be absolved.[241] But even if the Council is not promptly informed of what is going on, due to lack of skill in reducing complex patterns of behaviour to Article 51 phraseology, that need not doom the entitlement to self-defence. A failure by a State resorting to force to formally invoke self-defence should not be fatal, provided that the substantive conditions for the exercise of this right are met.[242] It makes no sense to allow an aggressor State to get away with an armed attack only by dint of mislabelling by the victim State of an otherwise legitimate conduct.

---

[241] See J. N. Moore, 'The Secret War in Central America and the Future of World Order', 80 *AJIL* 43, 90 n. 189 (1986).

[242] See L. C. Green, 'Armed Conflict, War, and Self-Defence', 6 *Ar. V.* 387, 434 (1956–7).

Having dealt in Chapter 7 with diverse problems pertaining to the interpretation of the expression 'armed attack' (which constitutes the foundation
of the right of self-defence under Article 51 of the Charter of the United
Nations),[1] it is now necessary to sketch the optional modes of self-defence
available to a State facing an armed attack. At the outset of the discussion it
should be pointed out that, for an armed attack to justify counter-measures
of self-defence under Article 51, it need not be committed by another State.
Ordinarily, the perpetrator of the armed attack is indeed a foreign State as
such. Yet, in exceptional circumstances, an armed attack – although
mounted *from* the territory of a foreign State – is not launched *by* that
State. Whether an armed attack is initiated by or only from a foreign country,
the target State is allowed to resort to self-defence by responding to unlawful
force with lawful counter-force. Given, however, the different features of the
two types of armed attack, they will be addressed separately.

A.   Self-defence in response to an armed attack by a State

The expression 'self-defence', as used in Article 51 or in customary
international law, is by no means self-explanatory. It is a tag attached to
the legitimate use of counter-force. Like its corollary (armed attack), self-
defence assumes more than one concrete form. The cardinal division,
here as elsewhere when the use of force by States is at issue, is between
war and measures 'short of war'.

(a)   Measures 'short of war'

i.   *On-the-spot reaction* The first category of self-defence relates to
the case in which a small-scale armed attack elicits at once, and *in situ*, the

---

[1] Charter of the United Nations, 1945, 9 *Int. Leg.* 327, 346.

employment of counter-force by those under attack or present nearby. In the parlance of United States Rules of Engagement, this is known as '[u]nit self defense' – *i.e.* '[t]he act of defending elements or personnel of a defined unit' or those 'in the vicinity thereof' – in contradistinction to '[n]ational self defense'.[2] The two subsets of 'unit' and 'national' self-defence are quite useful in laying out internal Rules of Engagement, since they clearly pin the authority and the responsibility for specific action on different echelons. However, this bifurcated phraseology is apt to be misleading in the context of the international law of armed conflict. It must be grasped that, from the standpoint of international law, all self-defence is national self-defence. There is a quantitative but no qualitative difference between a single unit responding to an armed attack and the entire military structure doing so. Once counter-force of whatever scale is employed by military units of whatever size – in response to an armed attack by another State – this is a manifestation of national self-defence, and the legitimacy of the action is determined by Article 51 as well as by customary international law. Ultimately, self-defence is always exercised by the State. Just like the conduct of a senior general or admiral, the action of a low-ranking unit commander (a junior or a non-commissioned officer) is attributed to the State that put him in charge. Consequently, the present writer believes that the phrase 'on-the-spot reaction', which underscores the principal characteristic of such a manner of using counter-force, is more accurate than 'unit' self-defence.

Two examples will illustrate on-the-spot reaction in practice. First, suppose that a Utopian patrol, moving along the common international frontier, is subjected to intense fire by troops from Arcadian outposts. The Utopian patrol (possibly aided by other units nearby) returns fire, in order to extricate itself from the ambush, or even assaults the Arcadian position whence the attack has been delivered. The clash consists of an armed attack by Arcadia and self-defence by Utopia, despite dicta by the International Court of Justice in the *Nicaragua* case attempting to set an armed attack apart from 'a mere frontier incident'[3] (see *supra*, Chapter 7, B, (b), (aa), ii).

Secondly, suppose that a Numidian destroyer on the high seas drops depth charges upon a Ruritanian submarine, and the submarine responds by firing torpedoes against the destroyer. Authorities agree that vessels on the high seas may use counter-force to repel an attack by other vessels or

[2] United States Army, Judge Advocate General's Legal Center and School, *Operational Law Handbook* 75 (2004).
[3] *Case Concerning Military and Paramilitary Activities in and against Nicaragua* (Merits), [1986] *ICJ Rep.* 14, 103.

by aircraft.[4] The International Court of Justice, in the *Corfu Channel* case of 1949, seems to have taken it for granted that warships passing through international waterways are entitled to 'retaliate quickly if fired upon' by coastal batteries.[5] These are clearly measures of self-defence warranted by Article 51 and by customary international law.

For on-the-spot reaction to be legitimized as self-defence, it must be in harmony with the three conditions of necessity, proportionality and immediacy (see *supra*, Chapter 7, C). Immediacy is immanent in the nature of on-the-spot reaction: the employment of counter-force must be temporally interwoven with the armed attack triggering it. The requirement of necessity should therefore be assessed from the vantage point of the local command. That is to say, alternative courses of action, not entailing the use of counter-force, can only be weighed as a matter of tactics rather than grand strategy. If the sequence of events includes 'time out' for high-level consultations between the two Governments, in an effort to defuse the explosive situation, on-the-spot reaction is no longer a relevant mode of self-defence. As for proportionality, it means that the 'scale and effects'[6] of force and counter-force must be similar. Excessive counter-force is ruled out as a permissible on-the-spot reaction.

Genuine on-the-spot reaction closes the incident. This category of self-defence does not cover operations by other units in distant zones, or even future actions taken by the same unit which bore the brunt of the original armed attack. Admittedly, one exchange of fire can lead to another in a chain effect, so that – through gradual escalation – large military contingents will be engaged in combat. Yet, if the fighting fades away soon, the closed episode may still be reckoned as on-the-spot reaction. By contrast, should the original small incident evolve into a full-scale invasion or a prolonged campaign, the rubric of on-the-spot reaction is no longer appropriate as a legal classification of what has transpired.

ii.   *Defensive armed reprisals* Generally speaking, reprisals constitute 'counter-measures that would be illegal if not for the prior illegal act of the State against which they are directed'.[7] While most reprisals are non-forcible, this section of the study will focus on armed reprisals. Apart from unarmed reprisals, the term ought to remove from consideration

---

[4] See I. Brownlie, *International Law and the Use of Force by States* 305 (1963).

[5] *Corfu Channel* case (Merits), [1949] *ICJ Rep.* 4, 31.

[6] These are the words of the International Court of Justice used, however, in a different context. *Nicaragua* case, *supra* note 3, at 103. See *supra*, Chapter 7, B, (b), (aa), ii.

[7] O. Schachter, 'International Law in Theory and Practice', 178 *RCADI* 9, 168 (1982).

'belligerent reprisals', namely, reprisals resorted to by belligerents in the midst of hostilities, after an armed conflict has begun.[8]

Armed reprisals are measures of counter-force, 'short of war', undertaken by one State against another in response to an earlier violation of international law. Like all other instances of unilateral recourse to force by States, armed reprisals are prohibited unless they qualify as an exercise of self-defence under Article 51. Only defensive armed reprisals are allowed. They must come in response to an armed attack, as opposed to other violations of international law, in circumstances satisfying all the requirements of legitimate self-defence.

A juxtaposition of defensive armed reprisals and on-the-spot reaction discloses points of resemblance as well as divergence. In both instances, the use of counter-force is limited to measures 'short of war'. But when activating defensive armed reprisals, the responding State strikes at a time and a place different from those of the original armed attack. In the two hypothetical examples adduced above, the script must be altered as follows: (i) a few days after the Utopian patrol is fired upon by Arcadian troops, an Arcadian patrol is shelled by Utopian artillery, or Utopian commandos raid a military base in Arcadia from which the original attack was sprung; (ii) subsequent to the depth-charging of the Ruritanian submarine by a Numidian destroyer on the high seas, a Ruritanian aircraft strafes a Numidian missile boat a thousand miles away.

The choice of the time and place for putting into operation defensive armed reprisals, like that of the objective against which they are to be directed, is made by the victim State (Utopia or Ruritania). The decision obviously depends on considerations of where, when and how to deal a blow that would be most advantageous to that State. The actions taken 'need not mirror offensive measures of the aggressor'.[9] All the same, the rights of third States must be taken into account. This is particularly true if the defensive armed reprisals are likely to endanger international shipping at sea.[10]

When States carry out defensive armed reprisals, their operations must be guided by the basic norms of the *jus in bello*. This is true of all uses of force, even 'short of war' (see *supra*, Chapter 1, B, (a)), and defensive armed reprisals are no exception. The interplay in this field between the *jus in bello* (belligerent reprisals) and the *jus ad bellum* (defensive armed reprisals) is complicated, however, by a number of treaty stipulations.

---

[8] See F. Kalshoven, *Belligerent Reprisals* 33–6 (1971).

[9] *Nicaragua* case, *supra* note 3, at 379 (Dissenting Opinion of Judge Schwebel).

[10] See *ibid.*, 379–80. See also *ibid.*, 112 (Judgment of the Court); 536–7 (Dissenting Opinion of Judge Jennings).

The four 1949 Geneva Conventions for the Protection of War Victims forbid certain acts of reprisals against protected persons (such as prisoners of war) and objects.[11] A parallel clause appears in Article 4(4) of the 1954 Hague Convention for the Protection of Cultural Property in the Event of Armed Conflict.[12] Protocol I of 1977, Additional to the Geneva Conventions, goes much further in banning a whole range of acts of reprisals.[13] Thus, '[a]ttacks against the civilian population or civilians by way of reprisals are prohibited' under Article 51(6) of the Protocol.[14] Article 60(5) of the 1969 Vienna Convention on the Law of Treaties makes it clear that 'provisions prohibiting any form of reprisals' against protected persons, contained in treaties of a humanitarian character, are not subject to the application of the general rules enabling termination or suspension of a treaty as a consequence of its material breach by another party.[15]

In essence, the measures of reprisals interdicted in the instruments cited amount to belligerent reprisals. By their nature, the strictures of the Geneva Conventions (or the Hague Convention) are germane to defensive armed reprisals no more than they are to other situations in which inter-State force is employed. If prisoners of war are captured in the course of defensive armed reprisals, they must be protected (as in all other types of hostilities), and the protection encompasses an immunity from belligerent reprisals. But even if a prisoner of war is unlawfully exposed to belligerent reprisals during a military operation characterized as a defensive armed reprisal, the legitimacy of the whole operation (as an act of counter-force in response to an armed attack) is not compromised by that breach.

A different outcome is apparently produced by the broader prohibitions of reprisals incorporated in Protocol I. Although the injunctions of the Protocol were intended to cope with the problem of belligerent reprisals,[16] it may be inferred from their language that the discretion of

[11] Geneva Convention (I) for the Amelioration of the Condition of the Wounded and Sick in Armed Forces in the Field, 1949, 75 *UNTS* 31, 60 (Article 46); Geneva Convention (II) for the Amelioration of the Condition of Wounded, Sick and Shipwrecked Members of Armed Forces at Sea, 1949, *ibid.*, 85, 114 (Article 47); Geneva Convention (III) Relative to the Treatment of Prisoners of War, 1949, *ibid.*, 135, 146 (Article 13); Geneva Convention (IV) Relative to the Protection of Civilian Persons in Time of War, 1949, *ibid.*, 287, 310 (Article 33).

[12] Hague Convention for the Protection of Cultural Property in the Event of Armed Conflict, 1954, 249 *UNTS* 240, 244.

[13] Protocol Additional to the Geneva Conventions of 12 August 1949, and Relating to the Protection of Victims of International Armed Conflicts (Protocol I), 1977, [1977] *UNJY* 95, 103, 114–16 (Articles 20, 51(6), 52(1), 53(c), 54(4), 55(2) and 56(4)).

[14] *Ibid.*, 114.

[15] Vienna Convention on the Law of Treaties, 1969, [1969] *UNJY* 140, 156.

[16] See S. E. Nahlik, 'Belligerent Reprisals as Seen in the Light of the Diplomatic Conference on Humanitarian Law, Geneva, 1974–1977', 42(2) *LCP* 36–66 (1978).

a State contemplating defensive armed reprisals is also curtailed where the choice of objectives for counter-strikes is concerned. If the original armed attack by Atlantica was directed against the Patagonian civilian population, Patagonia might wish (as a *quid pro quo*) to requite the wrongful action with defensive armed reprisals aimed equally at civilians. Nonetheless, under Article 51(6) of the Protocol, should Atlantican civilians be the target of Patagonian armed reprisals, the whole retaliatory operation would be illegal.[17]

Assuming that this is the correct reading of Protocol I, a considerable change is introduced in the potential application of defensive armed reprisals. Yet, it must be appreciated that the Protocol's provisions on the subject of reprisals are controversial.[18] While the Protocol irrefutably constitutes 'an authoritative text for extensive areas of international humanitarian law',[19] due account must be taken of the fact that the United States (among others) has formally decided not to ratify Protocol I because it 'is fundamentally and irreconcilably flawed'.[20] Despite a contrary assertion by a Trial Chamber of the International Criminal Tribunal for the Former Yugoslavia, in the *Kuperskic* case of 2000,[21] the sweeping proscription of reprisals in the Protocol has not crystallized as customary international law.[22]

As in other circumstances in which self-defence is invoked, defensive armed reprisals must meet the conditions of necessity, proportionality and immediacy. Proportionality is the quintessential factor in appraising the legitimacy of the counter-measures executed by the responding State. This was highlighted in the 1928 Arbitral Award, rendered in a dispute between Portugal and Germany, in the *Naulilaa* case.[23] The proceedings related to an incident that had taken place in 1914, shortly after the outbreak of World War I (at a time when Portugal was still a neutral State), on the border between the German colony of South-West Africa (present-day Namibia) and the Portuguese colony of Angola. In that incident, three German nationals (one civilian official and two army

---

[17] See F. J. Hampson, 'Belligerent Reprisals and the 1977 Protocols to the Geneva Conventions of 1949', 37 *ICLQ* 818, 837 (1988).

[18] See Y. Dinstein, *The Conduct of Hostilities under the Law of International Armed Conflict* 226 (2004).

[19] H. P. Gasser, 'Book Review' [of the first edition of this book], 29 *IRRC* 256, *id.* (1989).

[20] Agora: The U.S. Decision Not to Ratify Protocol I to the Geneva Conventions on the Protection of War Victims, 81 *AJIL* 910, 911 (1987).

[21] International Criminal Tribunal for the Former Yugoslavia, Trial Chamber, *Prosecutor v. Kuperskic et al.* (2000), Case IT-95–16-T, paras. 527–33.

[22] See F. Kalshoven and L. Zegveld, *Constraints on the Waging of War: An Introduction to International Humanitarian Law* 146 (3rd ed., 2001).

[23] *Naulilaa* case (1928), 2 *RIAA* 1011, 1026.

officers) were shot dead. In retaliation, the German forces attacked and destroyed a number of Portuguese installations in Angola over a period of several weeks. The Arbitrators held that these measures were excessively disproportionate.[24]

It is unrealistic to expect defensive armed reprisals to conform strictly and literally to the tenet of 'an eye for an eye'. A precise equation of casualties and damage, caused by both sides (in the course of the armed attack and the defensive armed reprisals), is neither a necessary nor a possible condition. All the more so, since in every military entanglement there is an element of chance, and defensive armed reprisals can unpredictably give rise to more casualties and damage than anticipated.[25] However, the responding State must adapt the magnitude of its counter-measures to the 'scale and effects' of the armed attack. A calculus of force, introducing some symmetry or approximation between the dimensions of the lawful counter-force and the original (unlawful) use of force, is imperative.

As for necessity, considering that defensive armed reprisals (unlike on-the-spot reaction) anyhow post-date the initial armed attack, reliance by the victim State on counter-force is contingent on its first seeking in vain a peaceful solution to the dispute. This is another requisite condition pronounced by the Arbitrators in the *Naulilaa* case.[26] If the attacking State is ready to discharge its duty of making adequate reparation to the victim State – in conformity with the general rules of State responsibility (see *supra*, Chapter 4, F, (a)) – defensive armed reprisals would be illicit. But the need to consider alternatives to the exercise of counter-force does not mean that the injured State must embroil itself in prolonged and frustrating negotiations. If no redress is offered within reasonable time, a State confronted with an armed attack is entitled to put in effect measures of defensive armed reprisals.

The right of the victim State to avoid dilatory stratagems is tied in with the rule that defensive armed reprisals must also meet the requirement of immediacy. It is unlawful to engage in these measures of counter-force in response to an event that occurred in the remote past. An inordinate procrastination is liable to erode the linkage between force and counter-force, which is the matrix of the legitimacy of defensive armed reprisals.

The view expressed here, whereby armed reprisals can be a permissible form of self-defence (in response to an armed attack) under Article 51, is

---

[24] *Ibid.*, 1028.
[25] *Cf.* J. H. H. Weiler, 'Armed Intervention in a Dichotomized World: The Case of Grenada', *The Current Legal Regulation of the Use of Force* 241, 250 (A. Cassese ed., 1986).
[26] *Nicaragua* case, *supra* note 3, at 1026–7.

supported by some scholars.[27] It must be conceded, however, that most writers deny that self-defence pursuant to Article 51 may ever embrace armed reprisals.[28] The International Law Commission, too, in its work on the Draft Articles on State Responsibility, neatly separated the concepts of armed reprisals and self-defence.[29] The separation is reflected in the two different Articles dealing with self-defence (Article 21) and with counter-measures (Article 22) in the final text adopted in 2001.[30] The Commission explained that '[t]he term "countermeasures" covers that part of the subject of reprisals not associated with armed conflict'.[31]

Counter-measures are the subject of a whole chapter in the Draft Articles (Articles 49–54).[32] Article 50(1) stipulates:

Countermeasures shall not affect:
(a) The obligation to refrain from the threat or use of force as embodied in the Charter of the United Nations.[33]

This is an unassailable statement of international law. If forcible counter-measures are taken in response to an ordinary breach of international law, not constituting an armed attack, they are unlawful.[34] Yet, it must be recalled that the general prohibition of recourse to inter-State force is subject to the exception of self-defence when an armed attack occurs. If forcible counter-measures come within the bounds of legitimate self-defence, they are no longer prohibited by the Charter.[35]

Those denying the possibility of armed reprisals ever earning the seal of legitimacy of self-defence do so on the ground that armed reprisals take place 'after the event and when the harm has already been inflicted', so that their purpose is always punitive rather than defensive.[36] In the present writer's opinion, this is a narrow approach influenced, to some extent, by nomenclature. The legal analysis might benefit if the term 'armed reprisals' were simply abandoned. Thus, O. Schachter comes to

---

[27] See, e.g., K. Skubiszewski, 'Use of Force by States. Collective Security. Law of War and Neutrality', *Manual of Public International Law* 739, 754 (M. Sørensen ed., 1968): 'armed reprisals that are taken in self-defence against an armed attack are permitted'. *Cf.* E S. Colbert, *Retaliation in International Law* 202–3 (1948).

[28] See especially Brownlie, *supra* note 4, at 281 (and authorities cited there). *Cf.* I. Brownlie, *The Rule of Law in International Affairs: International Law at the Fiftieth Anniversary of the United Nations* 205–6 (1998).

[29] Draft Articles on State Responsibility, Report of the International Law Commission, 32nd Session, [1980] II (2) *ILC Ybk* 1, 26, 53–4.

[30] Draft Articles on State Responsibility, International Law Commission, 53rd Session 43, 48 (mimeographed, 2001).

[31] *Ibid.*, 325.   [32] *Ibid.*, 56–8.   [33] *Ibid.*, 57.

[34] See H. Mosler, *The International Society as a Legal Community* 280 (1980).

[35] *Cf.* G. Arangio-Ruiz, 'Third Report on State Responsibility', [1991] II (1) *ILC Ybk* 1, 30.

[36] See D. Bowett, 'Reprisals Involving Recourse to Armed Force', 66 *AJIL* 1, 3 (1972).

the conclusion that, whereas punitive armed reprisals are forbidden, 'defensive retaliation' is justified when its prime motive is protective.[37]

Armed reprisals do not qualify as legitimate self-defence if they are impelled by purely punitive, non-defensive, motives.[38] But the motives driving States to action are usually multifaceted, and a tinge of retribution can probably be traced in every instance of response to force. The question is whether armed reprisals in a concrete situation go beyond retribution. To be defensive, and therefore lawful, armed reprisals must be future-oriented, and not limited to a desire to punish past transgressions. At bottom, the issue is whether the unlawful use of force by the other side is likely to repeat itself. The goal of defensive armed reprisals is to 'induce a delinquent state to abide by the law in the future', and hence they have a deterrent function.[39] A signal that playing with fire constitutes a dangerous game is what most armed reprisals are all about. At times, armed reprisals have immediate defensive implications. To borrow an example from W. Wengler, if Arcadian troops invade the territory of Utopia, it would be 'no less self-defence' for the Utopian armed forces to occupy an area belonging to Arcadia (in order to divert the military attention of the aggressor) than to resist the invading troops.[40]

There is no reason why the built-in time-lag between the original armed attack and the response of the victim State, which is an inevitable feature in all armed reprisals, should divest the counter-measures of their self-defence nature.[41] The allegation that lapse of time by itself turns armed reprisals into punitive – as distinct from defensive – action[42] is unfounded. The passage of time between the incidence of unlawful force and the activation of lawful counter-force is not unique to defensive armed reprisals. It is an attribute that defensive armed reprisals have in common with a war of self-defence undertaken in response to an armed attack 'short of war'. Such a war, too, commences after some deliberation by policy-makers in the victim State (see *infra*, (b)). By the time that a decision is taken to employ counter-force, it is possible that the attacking military formations have

---

[37] O. Schachter, 'The Right of States to Use Armed Force', 82 *Mich.LR* 1620, 1638 (1984).

[38] It has been suggested that '[i]n considering whether an armed reprisal is consistent with article 51, the retributive or other motivation of the state is irrelevant'. L. C. Green, 'Book Review' [of the first edition of this volume], 27 *CJTL* 483, 503 (1988–9). However, unmodulated retribution cannot be squared with self-defence.

[39] R. W. Tucker, 'Reprisals and Self-Defense: The Customary Law', 66 *AJIL* 586, 591 (1972).

[40] W. Wengler, 'Public International Law. Paradoxes of a Legal Order', 158 *RCADI* 9, 22 (1977).

[41] See D. W. Bowett, 'Book Review' [of the first edition of this book], 59 *BYBIL* 263, 265 (1988).

[42] See L. A. Sicilianos, *Les Réactions Décentralisées à l'Illicite: Des Contre-Mesures à la Légitime Défense* 412 (1990).

already accomplished the mission assigned to them (say, the occupation of a contested mountain ridge) and they are at a standstill. Even in circumstances of on-the-spot reaction, the initial strike (for instance, an artillery barrage) may come to an end before the target units set in motion measures of counter-force. It is occasionally propounded that self-defence must always be undertaken while the armed attack is in progress, and that it cannot be exercised once the attacking State has consummated active military operations.[43] But this is an unacceptable thesis that would merely encourage an aggressor to adopt *Blitz* methods of combat.

In the final analysis, defensive armed reprisals are post-attack measures of self-defence 'short of war'. The availability of such a weapon in its arsenal provides the victim State with a singularly important option. If this option were to have been eliminated from the gamut of legitimate self-defence, the State upon which an armed attack is inflicted would have been able to respond only with either on-the-spot reaction or war. On-the-spot reaction is dissatisfactory because it is predicated on employing counter-force on the spur of the moment, meaning that hostilities (i) erupt without any (or, at least, any serious) involvement of the political branch of the Government; and (ii) take place at a time as well as a place chosen by the attacking State, usually at a disadvantage for the defending State. War, for its part, requires a momentous decision that may alter irreversibly the course of history. Defensive armed reprisals enable the victim State to fine-tune its response to an armed attack by relying on an intermediate means of self-defence, avoiding war but adding temporal and spatial nuances to on-the-spot reaction.

It would be incomprehensible for war to be acknowledged – as it is – as a legitimate form of self-defence in response to an isolated armed attack, if defensive armed reprisals were inadmissible. Taking into account that Article 51 allows maximal use of counter-force (war) in self-defence, there is every reason for a more calibrated form of counter-force (defensive armed reprisals) to be legitimate as well.

Evidently, international law is created in the practice of States and not in scholarly writings. Even if clarity existed on the doctrinal level that a State 'is not entitled to exercise a right of reprisal in modern international law', this would merely serve 'to discredit doctrinal approaches to legal analysis'.[44] Since the entry into force of the UN Charter, the record is replete with measures of defensive armed reprisals implemented by many

---

[43] See G. M. Badr, 'The Exculpatory Effect of Self-Defense in State Responsibility', 10 *GJICL* 1, 26 (1980).

[44] R. A. Falk, 'The Beirut Raid and the International Law of Retaliation', 63 *AJIL* 415, 430 (1969).

countries (including all the Permanent Members of the Security Council), although statesmen frequently shy away from the expression 'reprisals'. Thus, in 1986, American air strikes were launched against several targets in Libya, in exercise of the right of self-defence, in response to Libyan State-sponsored terrorist attacks (especially, a bomb explosion in Berlin killing two American servicemen and wounding many others).[45] In substance, these were acts of defensive armed reprisals.

It is true that, on more than one occasion, the Security Council has condemned armed reprisals 'as incompatible with the purposes and principles of the United Nations'.[46] However, a careful examination of its decisions and deliberations seems to indicate that the Council has been 'moving towards a partial acceptance of "reasonable" reprisals'.[47] This development 'finds some support in theory and in practice'.[48]

The 1970 General Assembly Declaration on Principles of International Law Concerning Friendly Relations and Co-operation among States in accordance with the Charter of the United Nations proclaims that 'States have a duty to refrain from acts of reprisal involving the use of force'.[49] In like manner, President Singh, in his Separate Opinion in the *Nicaragua* case of 1986, stated that recourse to armed reprisals is illegal.[50] But it is interesting to note that the Judgment of the Court, in evaluating certain American actions in Nicaragua (such as the laying of mines in or close to Nicaraguan ports) which were clearly in the nature of armed reprisals – while rejecting their justification as acts of collective self-defence[51] – refrained from ruling that all armed reprisals are automatically unlawful.

In its 1996 Advisory Opinion on the *Legality of the Threat or Use of Nuclear Weapons*, the International Court of Justice stated:

Certain States asserted that the use of nuclear weapons in the conduct of reprisals would be lawful. The Court does not have to examine, in this context, the question of armed reprisals in time of peace, which are considered to be unlawful. Nor does it have to pronounce on the question of belligerent reprisals save to observe that in any case any right of recourse to such reprisals would, like self-defence, be governed *inter alia* by the principle of proportionality.[52]

---

[45] See W. V. O'Brien, 'Reprisals, Deterrence and Self-Defense in Counterterror Operations', 30 *VJIL* 421, 463–7 (1989–90).

[46] Security Council Resolution 188, 19 *RDSC* 9, 10 (1964). *Cf.* Security Council Resolution 270, 24 *ibid.*, 4, *id.* (1969).

[47] See Bowett, *supra* note 36, at 21.

[48] D. W. Greig, *International Law* 889 (2nd ed., 1976).

[49] General Assembly Resolution 2625 (XXV), 25 *RGA* 121, 122 (1970).

[50] *Nicaragua* case, *supra* note 3, at 151.   [51] *Ibid.*, 48, 146–7.

[52] Advisory Opinion on the *Legality of the Threat or Use of Nuclear Weapons*, [1996] *ICJ Rep.* 226, 246.

The Court's dictum is completely malapropos. The only question that the Court should have addressed – assuming that recourse to nuclear weapons is unlawful in the circumstances – was their legitimacy as belligerent reprisals. However, that *jus in bello* question arises only when war is already in progress.[53] The notion of 'first use' of nuclear weapons as an armed reprisal 'in time of peace' is unsound for the simple reason that, once these weapons are discharged, the situation between the parties can no longer be categorized as peacetime. Granted, it is not always easy to determine whether resort to force in a particular situation amounts to war or is merely 'short of war' (see *supra*, Chapter 1, A, (b), iii). Still, one would be hard put to find a better example than the detonation of nuclear weapons for an act leading *ipso facto* to an outbreak of war. It would be incongruous for Arcadia to target Utopia with nuclear weapons and then to contend that peace continues to govern the relations between the two States, since the strike allegedly constituted only an armed reprisal. Nuclear weapons must be completely divorced from the issue of armed reprisals (defensive or otherwise).

No country in the world seems to have adhered more consistently to a policy of defensive armed reprisals than the State of Israel. For those who negate the entire concept of defensive armed reprisals under the Charter, all acts labelled as such are lumped together in one mass of illegality. More correctly, each measure of counter-force should be put to the test whether it amounts to legitimate self-defence (in response to an armed attack), satisfying the requirements of necessity, proportionality and immediacy. When this is done, some of the Israeli armed reprisals appear to pass muster, whereas others do not. The crux of the issue in almost every instance is proportionality. The general problem is compounded in Israel's case by its predilection for a response in one extensive military operation to a cluster of pin-prick assaults taking place over a long stretch of time.[54]

When defensive armed reprisals are tailored to the measurements of an 'accumulation of events', they are susceptible of charges of disproportionality.[55] But much depends on the factual background. If continuous

---

[53] In his Dissenting Opinion, Vice-President Schwebel put the issue in the proper context: 'Furthermore, had Iraq employed chemical or biological weapons – prohibited weapons of mass destruction – against coalition forces [during the Gulf War], that would have been a wrong in international law giving rise to the right of belligerent reprisal. Even if, *arguendo*, the use of nuclear weapons were to be treated as also prohibited, their proportionate use by way of belligerent reprisal in order to deter further use of chemical or biological weapons would have been lawful.' *Ibid.*, 328.

[54] See B. Levenfeld, 'Israel Counter-*Fedayeen* Tactics in Lebanon: Self-Defense and Reprisal under Modern International Law', 21 *CJTL* 1, 40 (1982–3).

[55] See Bowett, *supra* note 36, at 7.

pin-prick assaults form a distinctive pattern, a cogent argument can be made for appraising them in their totality as an armed attack[56] (see *supra*, Chapter 7, B, (b), (aa), v). It is well worth observing that R. Ago, while disavowing the legitimacy of all armed reprisals, enunciated the following rule (in the context of self-defence) in a report to the International Law Commission:

If . . . a State suffers a series of successive and different acts of armed attack from another State, the requirement of proportionality will certainly not mean that the victim State is not free to undertake a single armed action on a much larger scale in order to put an end to this escalating succession of attacks.[57]

A legitimate application of what might be regarded as a book-keeping ledger to an aggregation of pin-prick attacks would only emphasize the element of elasticity, which is anyhow characteristic of the concept of proportionality.

iii.   *The protection of nationals abroad* As indicated (*supra*, Chapter 7, B, (b), (aa), iv), the use of force by Arcadia within its own territory, against Utopian nationals, is considered by many to constitute an armed attack against Utopia. If that is the case, forcible counter-measures employed by Utopia may rate as self-defence, provided that the usual conditions of necessity, proportionality and immediacy are complied with.[58] Sir Humphrey Waldock reiterated these conditions in somewhat different wording, fitting better the specific context of the protection of nationals abroad: 'There must be (1) an imminent threat of injury to nationals, (2) a failure or inability on the part of the territorial sovereign to protect them and (3) measures of protection strictly confined to the object of protecting them against injury.'[59]

    Contemporary international practice abounds with incidents in which one country uses force within the territory of another, in order to protect or rescue nationals, while invoking self-defence.[60] Obviously, rescue missions – usually conducted against terrorists holding foreign nationals as hostages – cannot be counted as genuine precedents for the application

---

[56] See N. M. Feder, 'Reading the U.N. Charter Connotatively: Toward a New Definition of Armed Attack', 19 *NYUJILP* 395, 415–16 (1986–7).

[57] R. Ago, 'Addendum to Eighth Report on State Responsibility', [1980] II (1) *ILC Ybk* 13, 69–70.

[58] See C. Greenwood, 'International Law and the United States' Air Operation against Libya', 89 *WVLR* 933, 941 (1986–7).

[59] C. H. M. Waldock, 'The Regulation of the Use of Force by Individual States in International Law', 81 *RCADI* 451, 467 (1952).

[60] See *Lillich on the Forcible Protection of Nationals Abroad*, 77 *ILS* 41–108 (T. C. Wingfield and J. E. Meyen eds., 2002).

of the inter-State law of self-defence if they are carried out with the consent of the Government of the local State[61] (on external use of force with local consent, see *supra*, Chapter 4, G, (a)). However, from time to time, either there is a complete breakdown of law and order in the local State or its Government aids and abets those who put the foreign nationals in jeopardy. In such circumstances, military operations have been put in motion unilaterally by the State of nationality, with a view to securing the lives of its citizens. As an illustration, one may cite the joint Belgian–American action to rescue nationals of the two countries in the Congo in 1964.[62] A more questionable case was the landing of American troops in the Dominican Republic in 1965.[63] A particularly controversial instance was the military action taken by the United States in Grenada, in 1983, the central justification of which was the protection of approximately a thousand endangered US citizens (mainly medical students) in a chaotic situation in the island.[64] It is not easy to reconcile the operation with the three conditions enumerated by Sir Humphrey.[65] The most telling point against the American expedition is that Grenada remained occupied for months, long after the evacuation of the US nationals had been wound up.[66] The principle of proportionality requires that any incursion of this nature be terminated as soon as possible, with a minimal encroachment on the sovereignty of the local State.[67] For the same reason, an attempt to predicate the legality of the United States invasion and occupation of Panama in 1989 on the need to safeguard the lives of American citizens in that country appears to be contrived.[68]

---

[61] See I. Brownlie, 'The Principle of Non-Use of Force in Contemporary International Law', *The Non-Use of Force in International Law* 17, 23 (W. E. Butler ed., 1989).

[62] See A. Gerard, 'L'Opération Stanleyville-Paulis devant le Parlement Belge et les Nations Unies', [1967] *RBDI* 242, 254–6.

[63] See V. P. Nanda, 'The United States' Action in the 1965 Dominican Crisis: Impact on World Order – Part I', 43 *DLJ* 439, 444–72 (1966).

[64] See W. C. Gilmore, *The Grenada Intervention* 31, 56 (1984).   [65] See *ibid.*, 61–4.

[66] See V. P. Nanda, 'The United States Armed Intervention in Grenada – Impact on World Order', 14 *CWILJ* 395, 410–11 (1984). An intriguing question has been raised 'why, in a case such as Grenada, a post hoc request by the local constitutional authorities for the U.S. forces to remain until order was restored could not be valid'. J. N. McNeill, 'Book Review' [of the first edition of this book], 84 *AJIL* 305, 306 (1990). But a *post hoc* request to stay in the local territory cannot escape suspicions concerning the genuine motives and objectives of the intervening State.

[67] See A. Abramovsky and P. L. Greene, 'Unilateral Intervention on Behalf of Hijacked American Nationals Held Abroad', [1979] *ULR* 231, 246.

[68] See V. P. Nanda, 'The Validity of United States Intervention in Panama under International Law', 84 *AJIL* 494, 496–7 (1990). *Cf.* R. Wedgwood, 'The Use of Armed Force in International Affairs: Self-Defense and the Panama Invasion', 29 *CJTL* 609, 621–2 (1991).

The 'clearest example' of a State fulfilling the three conditions, as listed by Sir Humphrey, was the Israeli rescue mission in Entebbe airport in 1976.[69] The action brought about the release of Israeli (and other Jewish) passengers of an Air France plane, hijacked by terrorists and held as hostages with the connivance of the Ugandan Government of the day headed by Idi Amin.[70] Even if the use of force on behalf of nationals abroad cannot be given open-ended approval as an exercise of self-defence, there are several exceptional features serving to legitimize the Entebbe raid:

(a) Although the terrorists did not use Uganda as their regular base of operations, the Ugandan Government was directly implicated in keeping the hostages under detention. It is necessary to distinguish between cases of civil disturbances (or riots) in Arcadia, in which Utopian nationals are attacked without any complicity on the part of the Arcadian Government, and actions against Utopian nationals committed with the blessing of the Arcadian Government. A rescue mission of the Entebbe type – aimed at releasing hostages held by terrorists in another country – is justifiable as self-defence when the powers-that-be collaborate with the terrorists, whereas in the absence of official wrongdoing, the prior consent of the local Government would usually be required before any forcible action is mobilized from the outside.[71]

(b) '[T]he hostages were seized and held as part of a political action against the state of their nationality. The attack on the individuals was clearly meant as an attack on their government.'[72] This is an immensely important factor at a time when international terrorists display a growing tendency to strike at innocent bystanders in Arcadia only because of their link of nationality to Utopia. If the victims are pre-selected as targets owing to their Utopian nationality, the equation between the use of force against them and an armed attack against Utopia (an equation which is the key to the exercise of the right of self-defence by Utopia) becomes unmistakable.

(c) The Israeli nationals did not go to Uganda volitionally: they were brought there against their will, in violation of international law.[73]

---

[69] Schachter, *supra* note 37, at 1630.

[70] For the facts, see L. C. Green, 'Rescue at Entebbe – Legal Aspects', 6 *IYHR* 312, 313–15 (1976).

[71] See F. C. Pedersen, 'Controlling International Terrorism: An Analysis of Unilateral Force and Proposals for Multilateral Cooperation', 8 *UTLR* 209, 222 (1976–7).

[72] O. Schachter, 'In Defense of International Rules on the Use of Force', 53 *UCLR* 113, 139 n. 107 (1986).

[73] See M. Akehurst, 'The Use of Force to Protect Nationals Abroad', 5 *Int.Rel.* 3, 21 (1977).

The exceptional circumstances of their entry into the territory of the local State affect the exceptional remedy (of recourse to force) made accessible to the State of nationality.

(d) The Entebbe raid was the epitome of a 'surgical' military sortie. It compares well with the massive intervention in some other instances, e.g., Grenada, because it was 'an in-out operation'.[74] Nobody could claim that Israel took the action 'as a pretext' to remain in Uganda.[75]

For all these reasons, Israel was entitled under Article 51 to use counter-force in self-defence, securing the release of its captive nationals in Uganda. Since the Entebbe raid was not in breach of the Charter, its legality is not affected by Article 14 of the 1979 International Convention against the Taking of Hostages,[76] which reads:

Nothing in this Convention shall be construed as justifying the violation of the territorial integrity or political independence of a State in contravention of the Charter of the United Nations.[77]

The fact that some non-Israeli hostages were also saved cannot diminish from the legality of the operation.[78] But it must be noted that the deliverance of the non-Israeli hostages was merely a by-product of the successful rescue of Israeli nationals. As an exercise of the right of self-defence, the protection of nationals abroad must not be confused with 'humanitarian intervention' (see *supra*, Chapter 3, B, (c)).[79] The rationale of self-defence, exercised in response to an armed attack against individuals abroad, is founded on the nexus of nationality; it is inapplicable when the human rights of non-nationals are deprived.[80]

---

[74] L. C. Green, 'The Rule of Law and the Use of Force – The Falklands and Grenada', 24 *Ar.V.* 173, 189 (1986).

[75] O. Schachter, 'International Law in the Hostage Crisis: Implications for Future Cases', *American Hostages in Iran* 325, 331 (W. Christopher *et al.* eds., 1985).

[76] See J. L. Lambert, *Terrorism and Hostages in International Law – A Commentary on the Hostages Convention 1979* 322–3 (1990).

[77] International Convention against the Taking of Hostages, 1979, [1979] *UNJY* 124, 127.

[78] See D. W. Bowett, 'The Use of Force for the Protection of Nationals Abroad', *The Current Legal Regulation of the Use of Force*, *supra* note 25, at 39, 44.

[79] The present writer cannot accept the proposition (advocated, e.g., by L. Henkin, 'The Invasion of Panama under International Law: A Gross Violation', 29 *CJTL* 293, 296–7 (1991)) that a so-called Entebbe principle – as a legitimate form of humanitarian intervention – constitutes an exception to the general prohibition of the use of inter-State force pursuant to Article 2(4) of the Charter, irrespective of the provision of Article 51.

[80] See A. Jeffery, 'The American Hostages in Tehran: The I.C.J. and the Legality of Rescue Missions', 30 *ICLQ* 717, 725 (1981).

(b)   War

War as an act of self-defence denotes comprehensive use of counter-force in response to an armed attack. It is sometimes hard to perceive that war can be a legitimate measure. But there is no doubt that, in some situations, '[t]he right of self-defense is ... a right to resort to war'.[81] In other words, '[a] forcible act of self-defense may amount to or may result in war'.[82] To lower the psychological barrier, H. Kelsen contrasted war (a delict) with counter-war (a sanction), saying: '[w]ar and counterwar are in the same reciprocal relation as murder and capital punishment'.[83] While the distinction is useful in many circumstances, it is not infallible. Utopia (the defending State) does not always respond with counter-war to war. Actually, Utopia may be the one initiating war, in response to an Arcadian armed attack 'short of war'. In such a case, what we are facing is not war (started by Arcadia) and counter-war (waged by Utopia), but an isolated armed attack (commenced by Arcadia) and war (conducted in response by Utopia).

It must be understood that, once a war is properly stamped with the legal seal of self-defence, this legal characterization is indelible regardless of the vicissitudes of the hostilities. If Utopia is fighting a war of self-defence against Arcadia, it does not matter whether Utopia is conducting its military operations in an offensive or in a defensive mode. The entire Utopian war is painted in the colour of self-defence, and, in a corresponding manner, Arcadia cannot shed the odium of being the aggressor. This contrapuntal relationship does not change even after a cease-fire (which, in suspending hostilities, does not terminate the on-going war; see *supra*, Chapter 2, C,(b)). Utopia continues to be the party waging a war of self-defence, and Arcadia remains the aggressor in that war, irrespective of the question of who resumes the hostilities after the cease-fire. A good example is the Gulf War (see *infra*, Chapter 10, C, (b)). The critical moment from the self-defence angle was August 1990, when Iraq invaded Kuwait. At that point, the status of the belligerents was fixed for the duration of the Gulf War: Iraq was the aggressor, whereas the Coalition that came to the aid of Kuwait was fighting in collective self-defence. This status was not altered by the lengthy cease-fire period (after the suspension of hostilities in 1991), and it continued to characterize the relations between

---

[81] J. L. Kunz, 'Individual and Collective Self-Defense in Article 51 of the Charter of the United Nations', 41 *AJIL* 872, 877 (1947). *Cf.* R. R. Baxter, 'The Legal Consequences of the Unlawful Use of Force under the Charter', [1968] *PASIL* 68, 74.

[82] P. C. Jessup, *A Modern Law of Nations* 163 (1948).

[83] H. Kelsen, *Principles of International Law* 28 (1st ed., 1952).

the parties in the final phase of the Gulf War in 2003. Hence, it is wrong to condition the military action of the Coalition in 2003 – as an act of self-defence – on a new armed attack by Iraq.[84]

A Utopian war of self-defence against Arcadia may come in response to an armed attack originally carried out by non-State actors but subsequently endorsed by Arcadia. This is where a 'war against terrorism' turns from a mere metaphor to a real (inter-State) war. The prime example is the war conducted by the United States (supported by allies) against the Taliban-led sovereign State of Afghanistan in the wake of the atrocities of 11 September 2001 (9/11). The war, which commenced on 7 October 2001, was waged against Afghanistan because the latter had given shelter to the Al-Qaeda terrorists – headed by Bin Laden – and refused to surrender them to justice (in defiance of binding Security Council resolutions predating September 9/11).[85] Although the terrorist acts of 9/11 were carried out by Al-Qaeda, once the Taliban regime persisted in its folly of protecting the terrorists, it assumed a (belated) responsibility for the armed attack and thereby exposed itself to exercise of self-defence: individual (by the United States) or collective (by allies, such as the United Kingdom).

The case of Taliban-led Afghanistan bears some resemblance to what happened in Iran at the time of the take-over of the US Embassy and the seizure of the Embassy staff as hostages in 1979. As the International Court of Justice held, in the 1980 *Tehran* case,[86] militants acting on their own initiative took over the Embassy initially, but later the Iranian Government gave its endorsement to the act by completely failing to take the means at its disposal to comply with its obligations under international law. At that point, the militants became the *de facto* organs of Iran. By the same token, Taliban-led Afghanistan assumed responsibility for the terrorist acts. The original outrage of 9/11 could not be imputed to Afghanistan *ex post facto*.[87] But, even though the Taliban were not accomplices to the 9/11 events before and during the act, they became accomplices after the act. By brazenly refusing to take any measures against Al-Qaeda and Bin Laden – and continuing to offer them shelter

---

[84] Such a condition is put in place, e.g., by F. Nguyen-Rouault, 'L'Intervention Armée en Irak et son Occupation au regard du Droit International', 107 *RGDIP* 835, 850 (2003).

[85] See especially Security Council Resolution 1267, 54 *RDSC* 148, 148–9 (1999).

[86] *Case Concerning United States Diplomatic and Consular Staff in Tehran*, [1980] *ICJ Rep.* 3, 31–44.

[87] Some commentators who are critical of the war against Afghanistan wrongly assume that such an *ex post facto* imputation is the issue. See, e.g., O. Corten and F. Dubuisson, 'Operation "Liberté Immuable": Une Extension Abusive du Concept de Légitime Défense', 106 *RGDIP* 51, 68 (2002).

within its territory – Afghanistan endorsed the armed attack against the US.[88] In consequence, from that moment on, the US could invoke the right of individual self-defence against Afghanistan and take direct action against it (as happened on 7 October). Any other State in the world could assist the US, invoking the right of collective self-defence (see *infra*, Chapter 9, A). The military operations in Afghanistan were a classical State versus State exercise of self-defence.

The salient questions arising in the context of a war of self-defence relate to the operation of the three conditions of necessity, proportionality and immediacy.

i.   *Necessity* When a war of self-defence is triggered by an all-out invasion, the issue of necessity usually becomes moot. The target State is by no means expected 'to allow an invasion to proceed without resistance on the ground that peaceful settlement should be sought first'.[89] Necessity comes to the fore when war is begun following an isolated armed attack. Before the defending State opens the floodgates to full-scale hostilities, it is obligated to verify that a reasonable settlement of the conflict in an amicable way is not attainable.

ii.   *Proportionality* The condition of proportionality has a special meaning in the context of a war of self-defence. When on-the-spot reaction or defensive armed reprisals are involved, proportionality points at a symmetry or an approximation in 'scale and effects' between the unlawful force and the lawful counter-force (see *supra*, (a)). To gauge proportionality in these settings, a comparison must be made between the quantum of force and counter-force used, as well as the casualties and damage sustained.[90] Such a comparison can only be drawn *a posteriori*, weighing in the balance the acts of force and counter-force in their totality (from the first to the last moment of fighting).

Proportionality in this sense, albeit appropriate for the purposes of on-the-spot reaction and defensive armed reprisals, is unsuited for an investigation of the legitimacy of a war of self-defence. There is no support in the practice of States for the notion that proportionality remains relevant – and has to be constantly assessed – throughout the hostilities in the course of war.[91] Once war is raging, the exercise of

---

[88] See M. Byers, 'Terrorism, the Use of Force and International Law after 11 September', 51 *ICLQ* 401, 408–9 (2002).

[89] Schachter, *supra* note 37, at 1635.   [90] See *ibid.*, 1637.

[91] This notion is advocated by J. G. Gardam, 'Proportionality and Force in International Law', 87 *AJIL* 391, 404 (1993).

self-defence may bring about 'the destruction of the enemy's army', regardless of the condition of proportionality.[92] The absence of congruence between the original injury and the ensuing conflagration is conspicuous when war is waged in response to an isolated armed attack. By its nature, war (as a comprehensive use of force) is virtually bound to be disproportionate to any measure 'short of war'. The scale of counterforce used by the victim State in a war of self-defence will be far in excess of the magnitude of the original force employed in an armed attack 'short of war', and the devastation caused by the war will surpass the destructive effects of the initial use of unlawful force. Proportionality, as an approximation of the overall force employed (or damage caused) by the two opposing sides, cannot be the yardstick for determining the legality of a war of self-defence caused by an isolated armed attack.

At the same time, it would be irrational to permit an all-out war whenever a State absorbs an isolated armed attack, however marginal. A war of self-defence is the most extreme and lethal course of action open to a State, and it must not be allowed to happen on a flimsy excuse. Some sort of proportionality has to be a major consideration in pondering the legitimacy of a defensive war. Still, the criteria for application of the prerequisite of proportionality ought to be different from what they are in settings 'short of war'. When war looms on the horizon, the comparative evaluation of force and counter-force has to take place not at the termination of the exercise of self-defence but at its inception. The decision has to be predicated on the gravity of the isolated armed attack and the degree to which the victim State is jeopardized.

War as a measure of self-defence is legitimate, in response to an armed attack 'short of war', only if vindicated by the critical character of the attack. There is no similarity between a minor skirmish and an artillery barrage in which hundreds of cannons are thundering. It is possible to say that, in certain situations, quantity turns into quality. Only when it is established (upon sifting the factual evidence) that the original armed attack was critical enough, is the victim State free to launch war in self-defence.

A better understanding of the applicability of the principle of proportionality to a war of self-defence may be facilitated by a legal analysis of the 'first use' of nuclear weapons. In its 1996 Advisory Opinion on the

[92] D. Alland, 'International Responsibility and Sanctions: Self-Defence and Countermeasures in the ILC Codification of Rules Governing International Responsibility', *United Nations Codification of State Responsibility* 143, 183 (M. Spinedi and B. Simma eds., 1987).

Legality of the Threat or Use of Nuclear Weapons, the International Court of Justice pronounced (by eleven votes to three):

> There is in neither customary nor conventional international law any comprehensive and universal prohibition of the threat or use of nuclear weapons as such.[93]

All the same, the Court dealt with the question whether recourse to nuclear weapons is illegal in light of general international humanitarian law, especially the two cardinal principles of (a) the distinction between combatants (or military targets) and non-combatants (or civilian objects), and (b) the prohibition to cause unnecessary suffering to combatants.[94] In view of the 'unique characteristics' of nuclear weapons, the Court felt that their use is 'scarcely reconcilable with respect for such requirements'; nevertheless, the Court refused to conclude with certainty that such use 'would necessarily be at variance with the principles and rules of law applicable in armed conflict in any circumstances'.[95] The majority (seven to seven, with the President's casting vote) did not reject the possibility of resort to nuclear weapons 'in an extreme circumstance of self-defence, in which the very survival of a State would be at stake'[96] (see *supra*, Chapter 6, C, (a)). It follows that the defending State – whose survival is at stake – may marshal nuclear weapons against the aggressor, although the latter has resorted only to conventional weapons. In other words, when its very existence is in jeopardy, the defending State can employ weapons of mass destruction, irrespective of their disproportionality to the arsenal of ordnance serving the aggressor. The Court specifically held:

> The proportionality principle may thus not in itself exclude the use of nuclear weapons in self-defence in all circumstances.[97]

Of course, the choice of targets for nuclear (as well as other) weapons must be made consonant with the rules of international humanitarian law.[98]

An aggressor State may lose its appetite for continuing with the hostilities, but the victim State need not be accommodating. It is occasionally maintained that, 'where the aggressor State indicates a willingness to end hostilities ... or where the manifestations of aggression disappear, there is, in principle, a duty to end defensive measures'.[99] That is not so. After

---

[93] Advisory Opinion on *Nuclear Weapons*, *supra* note 52, at 266. See also, *ibid.*, 256.
[94] *Ibid.*, 257.   [95] *Ibid.*, 262–3.   [96] *Ibid.*, 266.   [97] *Ibid.*, 245.
[98] The best example is 'a strike upon troops and armor in an isolated desert region with a low-yield air-burst in conditions of no wind'. M. N. Schmitt, 'The International Court of Justice and the Use of Nuclear Weapons', 362 *NWCR* 91, 108 (1998).
[99] K. H. Kaikobad, 'Self-Defence, Enforcement Action and the Gulf Wars, 1980–88 and 1990–91', 63 *BYBIL* 299, 337 (1992).

the outbreak of a war of self-defence, 'no moral or legal duty exists for a belligerent to stop the war when his opponent is ready to concede the object for which war was made'.[100] In the Iran–Iraq War, once the Iraqi invasion (launched in 1980) failed to crush Iran and degenerated into military stalemate, Iraq was more than willing to call off the fighting while Iran insisted on proceeding with the war to the point of decisively defeating the enemy.[101] Iran was fully empowered to take that stand, as long as it did not defy a legally binding Security Council resolution decreeing cease-fire (see *infra*, Chapter 10, B, (a)). After several resolutions of a recommendatory nature, the Council issued a mandatory demand for cease-fire in 1987.[102] This was Resolution 598,[103] actually complied with by Iran only in 1988.[104]

Unless the Security Council adopts a binding cease-fire resolution, a war of self-defence – once legitimately started – can be fought to the finish. As Ago commented, in a report to the International Law Commission:

It would be mistaken . . . to think that there must be proportionality between the conduct constituting the armed attack and the opposing conduct. The action needed to halt and repulse the attack may well have to assume dimensions disproportionate to those of the attack suffered. What matters in this respect is the result to be achieved by the 'defensive' action, and not the forms, substance and strength of the action itself.[105]

Thus, despite the condition of proportionality, a war of self-defence may be carried out until it brings about the complete collapse of the enemy belligerent, and (as in the case of World War II) it can be fought in an offensive mode to the last bunker of the enemy dictator.

Military operations by a State fighting a war of self-defence can legitimately take place anywhere within the region of war (see *supra*, Chapter 1, C), and there is no need to adjust to artificial geographic limitations conveniencing the aggressor. Once a war of self-defence is justified by the merits of the case, only the Security Council can contain the hostilities. An allegation often made is that recourse to counter-force in self-defence has to be confined to the space where the armed attack was launched

---

[100] L. Oppenheim, *International Law*, II, 225 (H. Lauterpacht ed., 7th ed., 1952).
[101] See S. H. Amin, 'The Iran-Iraq Conflict: Legal Implications', 31 *ICLQ* 167, 186 (1982).
[102] See M. J. Ferretti, 'The Iran-Iraq War: United Nations Resolution of Armed Conflict', 35 *Vill. LR* 197, 204–28 (1990).
[103] Security Council Resolution 598, 42 *RDSC* 5, 6 (1987).
[104] See Kaikobad, *supra* note 99, at 341.   [105] Ago, *supra* note 57, at 69.

and should not be extended to remote areas.[106] The *reductio ad absurdum* of this position is epitomized in the following question posed in connection with the terrorist events of 9/11: 'Does an attack against a small part of the United States, albeit one with devastating consequences for the people in the area hit, justify an armed response against a whole country, with the aim not only to root out the terrorists but to destroy and remove the effective, though unrecognized, government?'[107] The mere phrasing of the question is inconsistent with either law or history. Is it necessary to recall that the Japanese attack against Pearl Harbor in December 1941 – affecting an even smaller part of the United States – engendered the Pacific War with the United States, in which the whole Empire of Japan was embroiled and in the end dismembered, entire Japanese cities pulverized, and the Japanese system of government (with the exception of the Emperor) eradicated? Patently, when an armed attack brings about a war of self-defence, the attacker must realize that the stakes are mortal.

Indeed, the general experience of World War II shows that the liberation of the immediate victim of an armed attack is not necessarily enough, and a war of self-defence may aim much higher. Although Great Britain declared war on Nazi Germany in response to a German armed attack against Poland on 1 September 1939, the liberation of Poland was not viewed by Great Britain as sufficient in itself to end the war in Europe. Jointly with its Allies, Great Britain insisted – and rightly so – on the unconditional surrender of the enemy. As noted (*supra*, Chapter 6, B), insistence on the unconditional surrender of the Axis countries was declared the policy of the United Nations (the official name of the Allies) in World War II.[108] The text of the UN Charter (including Article 51) – signed in San Francisco, in June 1945, shortly after the victory in Europe but before the end of the hostilities with Japan and while that country was still an active enemy – was surely not intended to alter that. Article 107 of the Charter emphatically states:

Nothing in the present Charter shall invalidate or preclude action, in relation to any state which during the Second World War has been an enemy of any signatory to the present Charter, taken or authorized as a result of that war by the Governments having responsibility for such action.[109]

[106] See C. Greenwood, 'Self-Defence and the Conduct of International Armed Conflict', *International Law at a Time of Perplexity: Essays in Honour of Shabtai Rosenne* 273, 277 (Y. Dinstein ed., 1989).

[107] E. P. J. Myjer and N. D. White, 'The Twin Towers Attack: An Unlimited Right to Self-Defence', 7 *JCSL* 5, 8 (2002).

[108] Moscow Declaration on General Security, 1943, 9 *Int.Leg.* 327, 343–4.

[109] Charter of the United Nations, *supra* note 1, at 362–3.

In general, post-Charter State practice shows that 'self-defence, individual and collective, may carry the combat to the source of the aggression'.[110] War of self-defence, if warranted as a response to an armed attack, need not be terminated at the point when the aggressor is driven back: rather, it may be carried on by the defending State until final victory.[111] Particularly when engaged in a successful response to a large-scale invasion, the defending State – far from being bound to stop at the frontier – may pursue the retreating enemy forces, hammering at them up to the time of their total defeat.[112]

In the Gulf War (see *infra*, Chapter 10, C, (b)), the Coalition that stood up against Iraq in a war of collective self-defence fought the enemy until its total collapse in 2003. Granting that the Gulf War was triggered by Iraq's armed attack against Kuwait in 1990, the liberation of Kuwait was never looked at as the maximum goal by the Coalition. The cease-fire that Iraq was compelled to agree to in 1991, pursuant to Security Council Resolution 687, imposed on Iraq far-reaching obligations (especially in the field of disarmament) that went far beyond acceptance of the territorial integrity of Kuwait.[113] Later, 'no-fly' zones – severely limiting Iraqi sovereignty – were introduced by the Coalition. Ultimately, in 2003, in view of Iraqi 'material breach' of the cease-fire terms, hostilities were resumed: Iraq was occupied and the Saddam Hussein regime was overthrown. The Coalition in Iraq, just like the Grand Alliance in World War II, was fully entitled to carry out the war to its final conclusion. Indeed, the Saddam Hussein regime demonstrated the need not to look upon the liberation of the immediate victim of the armed attack (Kuwait) as the sole issue. Iraqi continued defiance of the world community served to underscore the danger that – unless the aggressor is utterly defeated – it is liable to revert to its policy of aggression as soon as circumstances permit.

iii.   Immediacy War may not be undertaken in self-defence long after an isolated armed attack. Yet, there are two notable provisos. First, a war of self-defence does not have to commence within a few minutes, or even a few days, from the original armed attack. A State under attack cannot be expected to shift gear from peace to war instantaneously. A description of a human being under attack as having 'no moment for deliberation' would

---

[110] *Nicaragua* case, *supra* note 3, at 371 (Dissenting Opinion of Judge Schwebel).

[111] See Kunz, *supra* note 81, at 876.

[112] See J. Zourek, 'La Notion de Légitime Défense en Droit International', 56 *AIDI* 1, 49–50 (Wiesbaden, 1975).

[113] Security Council Resolution 687, 46 *RDSC* 11 (1991).

be accurate. But when such an expression is applied to a State confronted with an armed attack (see *infra*, B, (b)), it is a hyperbolic statement. Front-line officers in the victim country must report to, and receive instructions from, headquarters. The high command is not inclined to embark upon full-scale hostilities, in response to an isolated armed attack, without some deliberation. When there is no military junta in power, the civilian Government will have to give a green light to the armed forces. In all, moving forward to a war of self-defence is a time-consuming process, especially in a democracy where the wheels of government grind slowly. P. C. Jessup remarked that '[t]elegraphic or radio communication between the officer and his superiors can be taken as a counterpart of the impulses in the nervous system of the individual whose brain instructs his arm to strike'.[114] This is true only in a metaphorical sense. Despite the means of modern communication available in the electronic age, States respond to pressure more tardily than individuals.

Secondly, even when the interval between an armed attack and a recourse to war of self-defence is longer than usual, the war may still be legitimate if the delay is warranted by circumstances. Suppose that Numidian troops forcibly occupy a part of the territory of Ruritania. Instead of promptly employing counter-force, Ruritania elects to give amicable negotiations a try (thus meeting the aforementioned condition of necessity). If the negotiations fail, and Ruritania then resorts to war, the action ought to be regarded as self-defence notwithstanding the lapse of time.[115] The first phase of the Gulf War shows that the use of counter-force in self-defence can begin almost half a year after the armed attack. The condition of immediacy was not transgressed, inasmuch as persistent attempts to resolve the conflict amicably were foiled by Iraqi obduracy. Claims that the option of self-defence existed in early August 1990 but expired a few months later are simply fallacious.[116]

A justifiable delay in the response of Ruritania may also occur when a region forcibly occupied by Numidia is distant from the centre of Government, and lengthy preparations are required before the military machinery can function smoothly. The Falkland Islands War of 1982 concretizes this state of affairs.[117]

---

[114] Jessup, *supra* note 82, at 164.

[115] J. Barboza, 'Necessity (Revisited) in International Law', *Essays in International Law in Honour of Judge M. Lachs* 27, 41 (J. Makarczyk ed., 1984).

[116] See T. Yoxall, 'Iraq and Article 51: A Correct Use of Limited Authority', 25 *Int.Law.* 967, 985 (1991).

[117] See A. Cassese, 'Article 51', *La Charte des Nations Unies* 769, 773 (J.-P. Cot and A. Pellet eds., 1985).

B.   Self-defence in response to an armed attack from a State

(a)   Extra-territorial law enforcement

Attention has already been drawn to the issue of terrorists or armed bands operating against Utopia from the territory of Arcadia without being deemed even 'de facto organs' of the latter State (see supra, Chapter 7, B, (b), (bb)). Clearly, Utopia is entitled to employ force within its own territory, so as to extirpate all hostile paramilitary groups (wherever they come from). The question is whether, when the terrorists or armed bands operate from within Arcadian territory but there is no complicity between them and the Arcadian Government, Utopia may take forcible counter-measures inside Arcadia.

The conduct of Arcadia may be unlawful under international law, without constituting an armed attack on its part against Utopia.[118] For that matter, not always is Arcadia in any breach of international law. When armed bands or terrorists turn a portion of Arcadian territory into a staging area for raids against Utopia, the Arcadian Government may not be aware of what is happening (especially when the armed bands or terrorists organize in remote and sparsely populated areas). As long as Arcadia does not 'knowingly' allow its territory to be used contrary to the rights of Utopia, Arcadia incurs no international responsibility towards Utopia under the Corfu Channel ruling[119] (cited supra, Chapter 7, B, (b), (aa), ii).

Even when the Government of Arcadia is fully aware of the presence within its territory of armed bands or terrorists hostile to Utopia, it may be incapable of putting an end to their activities. A Government does not always succeed in suppressing armed bands or terrorists, even when their activities are directed against itself. A fortiori, the Government of Arcadia may be unable to stop the use of its territory as a springboard for attacks by armed bands or terrorists against Utopia. However, it is incumbent on Arcadia, under international law, to exercise due diligence – that is, to take all reasonable measures called for by the situation – so as to prevent the armed bands or terrorists from mounting attacks against Utopia, or to apprehend and punish them after an attack has been perpetrated.[120]

---

[118] See P. L. Zanardi, 'Indirect Military Aggression', The Current Legal Regulation of the Use of Force, supra note 25, at 113.

[119] Corfu Channel case (Merits), [1949] ICJ Rep. 4, 22.

[120] See R. B. Lillich and J. M. Paxman, 'State Responsibility for Injuries to Aliens Occasioned by Terrorist Activities', 26 Amer. ULR 217, 268–9, 275 (1976–7).

If the Government of Arcadia does not condone the operations of armed bands or terrorists emanating from within its territory against Utopia, but it is too weak (militarily, politically or otherwise) to prevent these operations, Arcadian responsibility *vis-à-vis* Utopia (if engaged at all) may be nominal. Nevertheless, it does not follow that Utopia must patiently endure painful blows, only because no sovereign State is to blame for the turn of events. All the more so, if Arcadia is in breach of international law towards Utopia (a breach not qualifying as an inter-State armed attack). The armed bands or terrorists in Arcadia are not cloaked with a mantle of protection from Utopia. 'If a host country permits the use of its territory as a staging area for terrorist attacks when it could shut those operations down, and refuses requests to take action, the host government cannot expect to insulate its territory against measures of self-defense.'[121] Should Arcadia not grant its consent to a Utopian offer to send military forces into Arcadian territory, in order to eliminate the terrorist threat (see *supra*, Chapter 4, G, (a)), Arcadia must be prepared to bear certain unpleasant consequences. Just as Utopia is entitled to exercise self-defence against an armed attack by Arcadia, it is equally empowered to defend itself against armed bands or terrorists operating from within the Arcadian territory.[122]

This is an extraordinary case demanding, and getting, an extraordinary solution in international law. Article 51 permits Utopia to resort to self-defence in response to an armed attack. Utopia may, therefore, dispatch military units into Arcadian territory, in order to destroy the bases of the hostile armed bands or terrorists (provided that the destruction of the bases is the 'sole object' of the expedition).[123] Although acting beyond the limits of Arcadian consent, Utopia – in taking these measures – does what Arcadia itself should have done, 'had it possessed the means and disposition to perform its duty'.[124] The situation amounts to an international armed conflict since Utopia resorts to forcible measures on Arcadian soil in the absence of Arcadian consent, and thus two States are involved in the use of force without being on the same side. But there is no war between Utopia and Arcadia: the international armed conflict is 'short of war'.

---

[121] R. Wedgwood, 'Responding to Terrorism: The Strikes against Bin Laden', 24 *YJIL* 559, 565 (1999).

[122] See C. G. Fenwick, *International Law* 274 (4th ed., 1965).

[123] J. E. S. Fawcett, 'Intervention in International Law. A Study of Some Recent Cases', 103 *RCADI* 343, 363 (1961).

[124] C. C. Hyde, *International Law Chiefly as Interpreted and Applied by the United States*, I, 240 (2nd ed., 1945).

Like on-the-spot reaction, this category of self-defence has no generally accepted appellation. Now and then, there are references to 'hot pursuit', but the phrase – borrowed from the law of the sea – is rooted in 'a wholly untenable analogy'.[125] The right of maritime hot pursuit forms an exception to the freedom of the high seas.[126] It is governed by Article 23 of the 1958 Geneva Convention on the High Seas,[127] and Article 111 of the 1982 United Nations Convention on the Law of the Sea.[128] In conformity with both provisions, the right of hot pursuit relates to a foreign ship that has violated the laws and regulations of the coastal State. Hot pursuit has to be uninterrupted, and it must be commenced when the offending ship (or one of its boats) is within the internal waters, the territorial sea or the contiguous zone of the coastal State (under the 1958 Convention), as well as the archipelagic waters (under the 1982 Convention, which also extends the right of hot pursuit *mutatis mutandis* to violations occurring in the exclusive economic zone or the continental shelf). Most significantly, the right of hot pursuit ceases as soon as the vessel being chased enters the territorial sea of its own country or of a third State. On land, the operation undertaken against hostile armed bands or terrorists need not begin while they are still within the territory of the acting State; it does not have to be uninterrupted; and, far from coming to a halt at the border of a foreign State, it consists of an incursion into the territory of that State.

More often, the exercise of self-defence in the factual setting under discussion used to be called 'necessity'.[129] This labelling may prove confusing, since necessity – as shown by the International Law Commission – has many diverse connotations in international law.[130] Within the very framework of self-defence, necessity has already been encountered (together with proportionality and immediacy) as a condition for the admissibility of counter-force when an armed attack occurs. More significantly, and regrettably, the International Law Commission – on the initiative of its Special Rapporteur on State Responsibility (Ago)[131] – while accepting the existence of a state of affairs characterized as 'state of necessity', chose to disconnect it in its work from the concept of self-defence.[132] Thus, 'self-defence' and 'necessity' are the subjects of two

---

[125] M. R. Garcia-Mora, *International Responsibility for Hostile Acts of Private Persons against Foreign States* 123 (1962).
[126] See N. M. Poulantzas, *The Right of Hot Pursuit in International Law* 39 (1969).
[127] Geneva Convention on the High Seas, 1958, 450 *UNTS* 82, 94–5.
[128] United Nations Convention on the Law of the Sea, 1982, Official Text, 36–7.
[129] See L. Oppenheim, *International Law*, I, 298–9 (H. Lauterpacht ed., 8th ed., 1955).
[130] See Draft Articles on State Responsibility, *supra* note 29, at 34–52.
[131] Ago, *supra* note 57, at 39–40, 61–2.
[132] Draft Articles on State Responsibility, *supra* note 29, at 34, 57.

separate provisions (Articles 21 and 25) in the Commission's Draft Articles on State Responsibility of 2001.[133] As a result of the notional disjunction between necessity and self-defence, the Commission did not really find an adequate solution to the problem of a State exposed to an armed attack from (rather than by) another State.[134]

The distinction by the International Law Commission between self-defence and necessity, which is supported by some scholars,[135] is artificial and erroneous. The Commission goes so far as to classify the *Caroline* incident (to be examined *infra*, (b)) outside the scope of self-defence.[136] Although the Commission is right in noting that at the time of the incident the law concerning the use of force was completely different from what it is today,[137] the incontrovertible fact is that (as will be seen) the parties expressly employed the language of self-defence and that language has left its footprints on the future law on the subject. There is no way to cut retrospectively that historical umbilical cord.

In this study, it is proposed to use the idiom 'extra-territorial law enforcement' to describe the phenomenon of recourse to cross-border counter-force against terrorists and armed bands. The present writer believes that this idiom properly telescopes the notion of measures enforcing international law, taken by one State within the territory of another without the latter's consent. Extra-territorial law enforcement is a form of self-defence, and it can be undertaken by Utopia against terrorists and armed bands inside Arcadian territory only in response to an armed attack unleashed by them from that territory. Utopia is entitled to enforce international law extra-territorially if and when Arcadia is unable or unwilling to prevent repetition of that armed attack.

(b)   The practice of States

Extra-territorial law enforcement as a mode of self-defence has been manifested, throughout the 1990s, in repeated crossings by Turkish troops into Northern Iraq, in an attempt to deny Kurdish armed bands a sanctuary in an enclave carved out of Iraq in the aftermath of the hostilities in the Gulf War. However, the best contemporary illustration of extra-territorial law enforcement was provided by the Israeli incursion

---

[133] Draft Articles on State Responsibility, *supra* note 30, at 48–9.

[134] *Cf.* P. Malanczuk, 'Countermeasures and Self-Defence as Circumstances Precluding Wrongfulness in the International Law Commission's Draft Articles on State Responsibility', 43 *ZAORV* 705, 779–85 (1983).

[135] See O. Schachter, 'The Lawful Use of Force by a State against Terrorists in Another Country', 19 *IYHR* 209, 228–9 (1989).

[136] See Draft Articles on State Responsibility, *supra* note 30, at 196–7.   [137] *Ibid.*, 196.

into Lebanon, in 1982, designed to destroy a vast complex of Palestinian bases from which multiple armed attacks across the international frontier had originated.[138] The Government of Lebanon was incapable of putting an end to the formidable Palestinian military presence within its territory, and Israel felt compelled to cope with the problem by sending a sizeable expeditionary force into Southern Lebanon. Israeli and Lebanese forces did not exchange fire at any point in 1982, and the Israeli operation did not amount to a war with Lebanon. Yet, Israeli and Syrian armed forces in Lebanon did clash vigorously. These hostilities formed another round in an on-going war between Israel and Syria that has been in progress (interspersed by lengthy cease-fires) since 1967 (see *supra*, Chapter 2, C, (b)).

A case of striking similarity was the American military expedition of 1916 into Mexico, provoked by attacks across the Rio Grande by Mexican armed bands headed by Francisco Villa, at a time when the central Government in Mexico City had little control over the outlying areas.[139] President Wilson justified the dispatch of a substantial force, pursuing the bandits deep into Mexican territory, as necessary to protect the American border from hostile attacks, since the Mexican authorities were powerless and there was no other remedy.[140]

There are other historical precedents for extra-territorial law enforcement in self-defence.[141] The most famous among them is the *Caroline* incident.[142] In 1837, during the Mackenzie Rebellion against the British rule in Upper Canada, the insurgents took over an island on the Canadian side of the Niagara River. The American population along the border largely sympathized with the cause of the rebellion, and the steamboat *Caroline* was used for transporting men and materials from the US bank of the Niagara River to the rebel-held island. When British protests failed to stop the line of supplies, a British unit crossed the border in the dark of night, boarded the vessel, set it on fire, and sent it drifting to eventual destruction upon the awesome Falls. In the course of the incident, several American citizens were killed or injured. The United States lodged a protest with the British Government for violating American sovereignty, but the British invoked self-defence. In his correspondence about the

---

[138] For the facts, see B. A. Feinstein, 'The Legality of the Use of Armed Force by Israel in Lebanon – June 1982', 20 *Is.LR* 362, 365–70 (1985).
[139] For the facts, see G. A. Finch, 'Mexico and the United States', 11 *AJIL* 399–406 (1917).
[140] Quoted by Hyde, *supra* note 124, at 244 n. 21.
[141] See, e.g., *ibid.*, 240 n. 7 (the case of the US incursion into West Florida in 1818).
[142] For the facts, see R. Y. Jennings, 'The *Caroline* and McLeod Cases', 32 *AJIL* 82, 82–9 (1938).

incident with British envoys (in 1841–2), Secretary of State D. Webster took the position that – for the claim of self-defence to be admitted – Britain is required to 'show a necessity of self-defence, instant, overwhelming, leaving no choice of means, and no moment for deliberation'.[143] The action taken must also involve 'nothing unreasonable or excessive; since the act, justified by the necessity of self-defence, must be limited by that necessity, and kept clearly within it'.[144] The British reply finally conciliated the United States, and the case was closed.[145]

(c)   Webster's formula

The language used in Webster's correspondence, in the *Caroline* incident, made history. It came to be looked upon as transcending the specific legal contours of extra-territorial law enforcement, and has markedly influenced the general *materia* of self-defence. This has happened despite the lack of evidence that Webster had in mind any means of self-defence other than extra-territorial law enforcement, and notwithstanding the time-frame of the episode, which preceded the prohibition of the use of inter-State force.[146] R. Y. Jennings called the *Caroline* incident the '*locus classicus*' of the law of self-defence.[147] More than a century after the episode, the International Military Tribunal at *Nuremberg* quoted Webster's formulation as a standard for evaluating (and rejecting) the German allegation that the invasion of Norway in 1940 – which had amounted to war and not to extra-territorial law enforcement – constituted a legitimate exercise of self-defence.[148] It is sometimes put forward that the rule emerging from the *Caroline* incident is no longer valid under the UN Charter.[149] But there is no corroboration of this view in the text of the Charter.

Although Webster's prose was inclined to overstatement, the three conditions of necessity, proportionality and immediacy can easily be detected in it. These conditions are now regarded as pertinent to all categories of self-defence (see *supra*, Chapter 7, C). We have seen in what different ways they are to be applied to on-the-spot reaction, defensive armed reprisals and war (see *supra*, A).

---

[143] 29 *BFSP* 1129, 1138 (Webster to Fox) (1840–1).   [144] *Ibid.*
[145] 30 *BFSP* 195, 196–8 (Lord Ashburton to Webster); 201, *id.* (Webster to Lord Ashburton) (1841–2).
[146] See T. Kearley, 'Raising the Caroline', 17 *WILJ* 325, 330 (1999).
[147] Jennings, *supra* note 142, at 92.
[148] International Military Tribunal (*Nuremberg* trial), Judgment (1946), 1 *IMT* 171, 207.
[149] See Garcia-Mora, *supra* note 125, at 119.

When Utopia resorts to extra-territorial law enforcement within the territory of Arcadia, the necessity to infringe upon Arcadian sovereignty has to be manifest. The forcible measures employed by Utopia must be reactive to an attack already committed by hostile armed bands or terrorists, and not only anticipatory of what is no more than a future threat (see *supra*, Chapter 7, B, (a)). Additionally, a repetition of the attack has to be expected, so that the extra-territorial law enforcement can qualify as defensive and not purely punitive. The absence of alternative means for putting an end to the operations of the armed bands or terrorists has to be demonstrated beyond reasonable doubt.

The condition of immediacy requires that the incursion by Utopia into Arcadian territory will take place soon after the assault by the terrorists or armed bands, so that the cause (armed attack) and effect (self-defence) are plain for all to see. Besides, as accentuated by Webster, there has to be a perception of urgency impelling extra-territorial law enforcement before the armed bands or terrorists strike again. On the other hand, as rightly pointed out by R. Müllerson, since 'the source of [terrorist] attacks may not be immediately obvious', the process of gathering intelligence data and pinning the blame on a particular non-State group (operating from within the territory of Arcadia) may ineluctably stretch the interval between the armed attack and the forcible response.[150]

As for proportionality, when Utopia sends an expeditionary force into Arcadia, the operation is to be directed exclusively against the armed bands or terrorists, and it must not be confused with defensive armed reprisals.[151] Surely, no forcible action may be taken against the Arcadian civilian population.[152] Furthermore, even the Arcadian armed forces and installations ought not to be harmed. If the Utopian expeditionary force – on its way to or from the target (viz. the bases of the armed bands or terrorists) – encounters Arcadian military units, it is disallowed to open fire on them. Correspondingly, international law imposes on Arcadia a duty of 'acquiescence', or non-interference, with the Utopian operation;[153] for there is no self-defence against self-defence (see *supra*, Chapter 7, A (b)).

---

[150] R. Müllerson, '*Jus ad Bellum*: Plus Ça Change (le Monde) Plus C'est la Même Chose (le Droit)?', 7 *JCSL* 149, 179 (2002).

[151] At least one writer uses the term 'enforcement' in adverting to what is actually a defensive armed reprisal (directed at a Government). See A. D'Amato, *International Law: Process and Prospect* 29 (1987).

[152] See J. L. Taulbee, 'Retaliation and Irregular Warfare in Contemporary International Law', 7 *Int.Law*. 195, 203 (1973).

[153] D. W. Bowett, *Self-Defence in International Law* 60 (1958).

If the Arcadian Government is too weak to suppress the activities of armed bands or terrorists from within its territory against Utopia, Arcadia must not display unwonted prowess against the Utopian expeditionary force (which is only doing what Arcadia ought to have done in the first place). Should Arcadian troops open fire on the Utopian units, they are likely to become accomplices after the act to the armed attack committed by the armed bands or terrorists against Utopia. Arcadia will thereby transform the international armed conflict from a 'short of war' situation into war (in which Utopia is acting in self-defence).

9   Collective self-defence

A.   The meaning of collective self-defence

The phrase 'individual or collective self-defence', as used in Article 51 of the Charter of the United Nations[1] (see *supra*, Chapter 7, A, (a)), is not easily comprehensible. A close examination of the text, in light of the practice of States, shows that more than a simple dichotomy is involved. It seems necessary to distinguish between no less than four categories of self-defence: (i) individual self-defence individually exercised; (ii) individual self-defence collectively exercised; (iii) collective self-defence individually exercised; and (iv) collective self-defence collectively exercised.

The first category represents the most straightforward implementation of the right of self-defence, and it has been dealt with in Chapter 8: Arcadia perpetrates an armed attack against Utopia, and in response Utopia invokes self-defence. This is a one-on-one encounter, and the right of individual self-defence is applied individually.

The second category relates to the situation where an armed attack is launched by the same aggressor (Arcadia), either simultaneously or consecutively, against several States (Utopia, Ruritania, etc.). Both Utopia and Ruritania are entitled to resort to measures of individual self-defence against Arcadia. These measures may still be taken individually, each victim State declining any suggestion of cooperation with the other. Utopia and Ruritania, while resisting armed attacks by the same aggressor (Arcadia), are not obliged to consolidate a united front. When recent relations between Utopia and Ruritania have been characterized by a deeply felt animosity, let alone a long-standing antagonism with historical roots, either country is apt to be opposed to the idea of recasting the political landscape, and it may elect to act on its own.

However, particularly when a large-scale invasion is in progress, States trying to resist aggression tend to overlook past grievances and forge a coalition, proceeding on the basis of the principle that 'the enemy of my

---

[1] Charter of the United Nations, 1945, 9 *Int.Leg.* 327, 346.

enemy is my friend'. The essence of a coalition is that its members marshal their combined resources and act jointly in effecting their aggregate rights of self-defence. It is sometimes argued that such a situation was envisaged by the authors of the Charter when they referred to 'collective' self-defence.[2] In actuality, rather than collective self-defence, what we have here is 'nothing more than a plurality of acts of "individual" self-defence committed collectively'.[3]

A coalition in self-defence, dictated by expediency, emerged in the course of World War II, following the Nazi invasion of the Soviet Union in June 1941. By July of that year, an Agreement was made by Great Britain and the USSR (Powers that had not been on the best of terms prior to this date) Providing for Joint Action between the Two Countries in the War against Germany.[4] In May 1942, the same two States concluded a follow-up Treaty for an Alliance in the War against Hitlerite Germany and Her Associates in Europe, and Providing also for Collaboration and Mutual Assistance Thereafter.[5]

The 1942 Anglo-Soviet Alliance illuminates two interesting points. First, the Contracting Parties sought to extend the operation of the instrument into the post-War period. Future events did not bear out the optimism engendered by the constellation of World War II. In general, a military alliance, if welded in the course of war by otherwise polarized countries, is not likely to outlast the advent of peace. For that reason, many wartime alliances are confined to the immediate needs of combating a common foe. Secondly, the Soviet–British treaty proved that an alliance concluded in the midst of hostilities need not embrace all the belligerents positioned on the same side, nor does it have to be directed against all the enemies of the allies. Thus, (i) the United States (and other countries waging war at the time against Nazi Germany) did not accede to the treaty; (ii) the stated goal of the treaty was to fight together against Germany and its associates in Europe, thereby excluding Japan with which Britain – but not the USSR – was then at war.

Collective self-defence has a different meaning. The scenario is that Arcadia initiates an armed attack against Utopia (and only against Utopia), but Atlantica – although beyond the range of the attack – decides

---

[2] See D. W Bowett, *Self-Defence in International Law* 216 (1958).

[3] R. Ago, 'Addendum to Eighth Report on State Responsibility', [1980] II (1) *ILC Ybk* 13, 68.

[4] Great Britain–USSR, Moscow Agreement Providing for Joint Action between the Two Countries in the War against Germany, 1941, 204 *LNTS* 277.

[5] Great Britain–USSR, London Treaty for an Alliance in the War against Hitlerite Germany and Her Associates in Europe, and Providing also for Collaboration and Mutual Assistance Thereafter, 1942, 204 *LNTS* 353.

to come to the assistance of Utopia. There is no doubt that, in principle, Article 51 permits any UN Member to help another if the latter has fallen prey to an armed attack.[6] That is to say, Greece may respond to an armed attack against Peru.[7] When Greece avails itself of the option, this is a case of collective self-defence, exercised individually, as per the third category listed above.

The fourth category is that of collective self-defence carried out collectively. It becomes apposite when two or more States (Atlantica, Patagonia and so forth) act together in supporting the victim country (Utopia).

The question is whether, from an analytical standpoint, the aid furnished to Utopia by Atlantica (acting alone or in conjunction with other countries) may properly be considered *self*-defence. Occasionally, the concept is repudiated.[8] But there is no good reason to deny the existence of a 'collective' self of groupings of States.[9] If Utopian 'safety and independence are deemed vital to the safety and independence' of Atlantica, any assistance offered by Atlantica to Utopia in repelling an armed attack by Arcadia can be viewed as a measure of Atlantican self-defence.[10] The security of various States is frequently interwoven, so that when Atlantica helps Utopia, it is truly defending itself.[11]

The actual stake that Atlantica may have in the security of Utopia is a matter of perception. Insofar as legal theory is concerned, it may be advisable to refer again (see *supra*, Chapter 4, F, (b)) to the statement of the International Court of Justice – in the *Barcelona Traction* case of 1970 – that the outlawing of aggression has created obligations applicable *erga omnes*, since all States have valid interests in the protection of the rights involved.[12] Of course, in pragmatic terms, 'it is highly unlikely' that Atlantica will immerse itself in an armed conflict with Arcadia, unless there is a clear and present danger to Atlantican security.[13] Nevertheless,

---

[6] See H. Kelsen, 'Collective Security and Collective Self-Defense under the Charter of the United Nations', 42 *AJIL* 783, 792 (1948).

[7] The question whether Greece can exercise collective self-defence in response to an armed attack against Peru is raised by M. Akehurst, *Modern Introduction to International Law* 317 (P. Malanczuk ed., 7th ed., 1997).

[8] See D. W. Bowett, 'The Interrelation of Theories of Intervention and Self-Defense', *Law and Civil War in the Modern World* 38, 46–7 (J. N. Moore ed., 1974).

[9] M. S. McDougal and F. P. Feliciano, *Law and Minimum World Public Order* 248–50 (1961).

[10] L. Oppenheim, *International Law*, II, 155 (H. Lauterpacht ed., 7th ed., 1952).

[11] See the Dissenting Opinion of Judge Jennings in *Case Concerning Military and Paramilitary Activities in and against Nicaragua* (Merits), [1986] *ICJ Rep.* 14, 545.

[12] *Case Concerning the Barcelona Traction, Light and Power Company, Limited*, [1970] *ICJ Rep.* 3, 32.

[13] O. Schachter, 'The Right of States to Use Armed Force', 82 *Mich. LR* 1620, 1639 (1984).

there are many utilitarian considerations that may galvanize Atlantica into action against Arcadia when Utopia is attacked.

To begin with, if Atlantica is a super-Power, it is apt to think of the whole world as its bailiwick. In that case, an armed attack initiated anywhere, no matter where and against whom it is unleashed, may be interpreted by Atlantica as a direct challenge to its vital interests.

Additionally, from the vantage point of minor Powers (particularly, although by no means exclusively, within a prescribed geographic region), their overall security is detrimentally affected when one of them is invaded by a potent aggressor. The repeated lesson of history (epitomized by World War II) has been that, once an aggressor starts out on the path of territorial expansion, attaining a rapid and facile success, it develops an appetite for further conquests. When multiple States – none of which is strong enough to withstand alone the steamroller of an armed attack – face the danger of overwhelming force, the only chance of averting 'piecemeal annihilation' lies in closing ranks together while there is still time.[14] Believing as they do that, in the long run, all of them are anyhow destined to become victims of aggression, each may opt to join the fray as soon as one of the others is subjected to an armed attack. In truth, it is the selfish interest of the State expecting to be next in line for an armed attack that compels it not to be indifferent to what is happening across its borders.

It may be said that an armed attack is like an infectious disease in the body politic of the family of nations. Every State has a demonstrable self-interest in the maintenance of international peace, for once the disease starts to spread there is no telling if and where it will stop. This is the fundamental concept underlying the Charter of the United Nations. As long as the system of collective security within the UN Organization is ineffective (see *infra*, Chapter 10, C), collective self-defence constitutes the sole insurance policy against an armed attack.

Collective self-defence may be exercised either spontaneously (as an unplanned response to an armed attack after it has become a reality) or premeditatedly (on the footing of a prior agreement contemplating a potential armed attack). There are those who deny one possibility or the other. It has been contended that support of a State in the grip of an armed attack is contingent on the existence of a collective self-defence treaty.[15] Conversely, it has been maintained that Article 51 precludes Member States (acting outside the pale of the United Nations) from

---

[14] Oppenheim, *supra* note 10, at 156.   [15] See A. Martin, *Collective Security* 170 (1952).

elaborating strategic plans, or coordinating their military forces under a combined high command, before an armed attack takes place.[16] In reality, there is no sustenance in the text for either interpretation. The latter position has been rightly termed 'astonishing',[17] and so is the former. States are entitled to exercise the right of collective self-defence either on the spur of the moment or after thorough preparation for a rainy day. The military action taken by the American-led Coalition against Iraq in support of Kuwait, with the blessing of the Security Council (see *infra*, E), shows that 'any state may come to the aid of a state that has been illegally attacked'.[18]

In the *Nicaragua* case of 1986, the International Court of Justice held that the right of collective self-defence is well established not only in Article 51 of the UN Charter but also in customary international law.[19] Judge Oda, in his Dissenting Opinion, criticized the majority for not sufficiently probing the concept that the right of collective (as opposed to individual) self-defence is 'inherent' in pre-Charter customary law.[20] There is indeed some authority for the proposition that, in opening the door to collective self-defence by any State, Article 51 expanded the right of self-defence as previously understood.[21] However, whether or not the right of collective self-defence can be traced back to pre-Charter customary norms, there is hardly any doubt that it constitutes an integral part of customary international law as it stands today. Consequently, States that are non-Members of the United Nations have an equal right to exercise, and to benefit from, collective self-defence.[22]

B.   Collective self-defence treaties

Article 52(1) of the United Nations Charter sets forth:

Nothing in the present Charter precludes the existence of regional arrangements or agencies for dealing with such matters relating to the maintenance of international peace and security as are appropriate for regional action, provided that such

---

[16] See F. B. Schick, 'The North Atlantic Treaty and the Problem of Peace', 62 *Jur.R.* 26, 49 (1950).

[17] A. L. Goodhart, 'The North Atlantic Treaty of 1949', 79 *RCADI* 183, 229 (1951).

[18] See O. Schachter, 'United Nations Law in the Gulf Conflict', 85 *AJIL* 452, 457 (1991).

[19] *Nicaragua* case, *supra* note 11, at 102–4.

[20] *Ibid.*, 256–8 (Dissenting Opinion of Judge Oda).

[21] See Oppenheim, *supra* note 10, at 155. But *cf. supra*, Chapter 4, A, regarding the Preamble of the Kellogg–Briand Pact (General Treaty for Renunciation of War as an Instrument of National Policy, 1928, 94 *LNTS* 57, 59–61).

[22] See S. A. Alexandrov, *Self-Defense against the Use of Force in International Law* 103 (1996).

arrangements or agencies and their activities are consistent with the Purposes and Principles of the United Nations.[23]

A region in the sense of Article 52(1) should not be construed narrowly, along lines of 'geographical propinquity', and it may comprise any limited community of States 'joined together by ties of interests'.[24] Every group of like-minded States, having a common interest in activities relating to the maintenance of international peace and security, is entitled to make such arrangements.[25] Since the size of the group is not delineated in Article 52, a regional arrangement may apparently be limited to two States.[26]

As for the nature of regional arrangements under Article 52(1), while they may have manifold purposes, surely one of the most important is to pave the road for collective self-defence. It has been suggested that a joint defence of a region against an external danger of an armed attack, originating from another region, exceeds the limits of a regional arrangement within the meaning of Article 52(1).[27] But this restrictive interpretation of Article 52(1) is specious.

In anticipation of a future armed attack, States can conclude several forms of treaties. The three principal categories are: (i) mutual assistance; (ii) military alliance; or (iii) guarantee. Only a State placed under a permanent neutrality regime (see *supra*, Chapter 1, C, (a)) is barred from engaging in a mutual assistance treaty or a military alliance – and, whereas it may benefit from a guarantee, it must never become a guarantor – for permanent neutrality is incompatible with any obligations liable to implicate the State concerned in war.[28]

(a)   Mutual assistance treaties

A mutual assistance treaty is an instrument whereby the Contracting Parties proclaim that an armed attack against one of them will be regarded as an armed attack against all, pledging to help out each other in such circumstances. A treaty of mutual assistance may be either

---

[23] Charter of the United Nations, *supra* note 1, at 346–7.

[24] A. V. W. Thomas and A. J. Thomas, *Non-Intervention: The Law and Its Import in the Americas* 178 (1956).

[25] H. Kelsen, *The Law of the United Nations: A Critical Analysis of Its Fundamental Problems* 920 (1951).

[26] See M. Akehurst, 'Enforcement Action by Regional Agencies, with Special Reference to the Organization of American States', 42 *BYBIL* 175, 177 (1967).

[27] See J. Stone, *Legal Controls of International Conflict: A Treatise on the Dynamics of Disputes – and War – Law* 249 (1954).

[28] See A. Verdross, 'Austria's Permanent Neutrality and the United Nations Organization', 50 *AJIL* 61, 64 (1956).

bilateral or multilateral in scope. An agreement made by the United States and South Korea in 1953 may serve as a telling example for a bilateral treaty of this nature.[29]

The downside of a mutual assistance treaty is that, as a rule, a State is ready to employ force in aid of another country only if such conduct is consonant with its vital interests as perceived at the time of action, rather than in the past (when the treaty was signed). Hence, when an armed attack occurs, Atlantica may rush to Utopia's rescue despite the absence of a mutual assistance treaty between them, yet fail to succour Numidia notwithstanding the existence of such a treaty.

If Atlantica is disinclined to abide by its obligations under a mutual assistance treaty, it will not have to contrive to find an ingenious escape clause in the text. Even if the treaty is formulated in an unequivocal manner, and does not have legal loopholes enabling a reluctant party to refuse to take action altogether, a sufficient margin of discretion is always left to Contracting Parties. It is simply impossible to resolve beforehand, except in crude outlines, pragmatic issues that in the reality of an armed attack assume crucial significance, like the precise scale of the military support to be afforded, its pace and the concrete shape that it will take.[30] There are no objective comparative benchmarks by which these matters can be assessed. Decisions have to be taken against the background of the armed attack, once it unfolds in fact, and there is no way to settle differences of opinion in advance through airtight juridical clauses.

It may be deduced that a mutual assistance treaty *per se* cannot provide assurance that meaningful aid will actually be obtained when called for. The main benefit derived from such a treaty lies in the political sphere, for publication of the text serves notice on friends and foes alike as to the cords of affiliation uniting the Contracting Parties. This may deter potential enemies and encourage States that are favourably disposed. Nonetheless, a mutuality of political interests must not be confused with a binding commitment for reciprocal military support.

Admittedly, Contracting Parties do not always seek ways to evade carrying out the stipulations of a treaty of mutual assistance. The most momentous illustration of compliance with such a treaty is that of the

---

[29] United States–Republic of Korea, Washington Treaty, 1953, 48 *AJIL*, Supp., 147 (1954).

[30] Military supplies can be transported at once by airlift, but they can also be shipped slowly and arrive after the fighting is over. Should an expeditionary force be dispatched, its size might range from a token detachment to several army corps. The type of military units sent over (air squadrons, armoured units, paratroopers, regular infantry, etc.), their combat readiness and mastery of state-of-the-art equipment would all make a tremendous difference.

1939 British–Polish Agreement of Mutual Assistance,[31] the implementation of which turned the Nazi invasion of Poland into World War II. But we must be mindful of the relevant dates: the formal agreement was signed on 25 August, the Nazi invasion of Poland began on 1 September, and the British Declaration of War was issued on 3 September. Thus, it all happened within the span of ten days. The longer the lapse of time following the conclusion of a mutual assistance treaty, the fewer the chances for its being respected in practice.

A treaty of mutual assistance may be multilateral (often regional in the geographic sense) instead of bilateral. Here the obligation to help a Contracting Party, upon the outbreak of an armed attack, is imposed not on a single State but on a cluster of States. In principle, collective self-defence ought to be exercised collectively by the entire group. If any member of the group is averse to the idea of participating in an armed conflict when the need arises, it may still shirk its duty in practice. However, the assumption is that, among a whole host of parties, there will be at least one ready to honour its commitment.

The question is whether a single Contracting Party in a multilateral mutual assistance treaty is permitted to act on its own, offering assistance to the victim State, without waiting for an authoritative decision on behalf of the group. The treaty may require a group decision, and the process of arriving at it can be frustrated by opposition on the part of one or more countries, or at least delayed by protracted debates. All the same, a multilateral mutual assistance treaty, in creating a collective *duty* of collective self-defence, does not diminish from the individual *right* of collective self-defence under the Charter.[32] This right may be exercised by any State, including any Contracting Party to the mutual assistance treaty that is unwilling to wait inertly while the victim of an armed attack is gradually strangulated.

The paradigmatic multilateral treaty of mutual aid is the 1947 Rio de Janeiro Inter-American Treaty of Reciprocal Assistance.[33] The basic principle is spelt out in Article 3(1):

The High Contracting Parties agree that an armed attack by any State against an American State shall be considered as an attack against all the American States and, consequently, each one of the said Contracting Parties undertakes to assist in

---

[31] Great Britain–Poland, London Agreement of Mutual Assistance, 1939, 199 *LNTS* 57.
[32] See J. N. Moore, 'The Secret War in Central America and the Future of World Order', 80 *AJIL* 43, 104–5 (1986).
[33] Rio de Janeiro Inter-American Treaty of Reciprocal Assistance, 1947, 21 *UNTS* 77, 93. (A Protocol of Amendment to the Rio Treaty was done at San José in 1975 (14 *ILM* 1122 (1975)), but has not entered into force.)

meeting the attack in the exercise of the inherent right of individual or collective self-defense recognized by Article 51 of the Charter of the United Nations.[34]

When an armed attack occurs, Article 3(2) permits response on two levels: (i) at the request of the attacked State, each Contracting Party may take immediate measures individually; (ii) a central Organ of Consultation of the American States may put in motion measures of a collective character.[35] The distinction between collective self-defence exercised individually (as a first stage) and collective self-defence exercised collectively (as a second stage) is plainly discernible.[36] On both levels of response, actual recourse to collective self-defence depends on the free will of each Contracting Party. Under Article 17, resolutions of the Organ of Consultation are to be adopted by a two-thirds majority.[37] But the minority cannot be dragged into hostilities against its wishes. Article 20 clarifies that no Contracting Party is 'required to use armed force without its consent'.[38] The obligation of mutual assistance is in effect. Yet, assistance in the only form that really counts is not automatic.

(b)   Military alliances

An acute practical problem in the field of mutual assistance is that, in the absence of prior coordination, it is immensely difficult for separate armed forces of sovereign States (with divergent command structures, equipment, training and usually languages) to act in unison against an aggressor, even if the political decision to resort to collective self-defence has been taken. This is why a peacetime military alliance becomes a natural extension of a mutual assistance arrangement. Such an alliance is motivated by the concept that 'if you want peace, prepare for war (*si vis pacem, para bellum*)'. A treaty of alliance goes beyond an abstract commitment for mutual assistance in the event of an armed attack. Induced by the apprehension of a future armed attack, the parties undertake to start preparing their common defence right away.

The hallmarks of a military alliance are the integration of the military high command, the amalgamation of staff planning, the unification of ordnance, the establishment of bases on foreign soil, the organization of joint manoeuvres and the exchange of intelligence data. The political decision whether or not to use force (and especially to go to war), in support of a State subjected to an armed attack, is retained by each of the

---

[34] *Ibid.*, 95.   [35] *Ibid.*, 95–7.

[36] See J. L. Kunz, 'The Inter-American Treaty of Reciprocal Assistance', 42 *AJIL* 111, 120 (1948).

[37] Rio de Janeiro Inter-American Treaty, *supra* note 33, at 101.   [38] *Ibid.*, 103.

allied Governments.[39] But an integrated high command reduces considerably the freedom of action of the individual States, and the sense of solidarity is reinforced by the presence of military units belonging to other members of the alliance within the territory of a country directly threatened by an armed attack.[40] The forces of the allied nations may be so inextricably intertwined that it becomes impossible to disentangle them once hostilities begin. When armed units of Atlantica are stationed on Utopian soil, they can become hostages to fate. Should the Atlantican troops sustain severe casualties as a result of an Arcadian armed attack against Utopia, the theoretical discretionary power of Atlantica to avoid discharging its duty towards Utopia would be eliminated in practice. In this fashion, an armed attack against one allied State may sweep the entire group into the flow of hostilities, preempting any genuine opportunity for the exercise of individual choice in the matter.

It is not always easy to tell on the face of the text of a given document whether it is only a treaty of mutual assistance or the constituent instrument of a military alliance. Nor is the nature of the undertaking invariably determined by the language of the seminal treaty. The initial instrument may be limited to enunciating the guiding principle of mutual assistance and setting up central organs, while the details of military cooperation can be worked out in supplementary agreements or empirically. This is the case of the 1949 North Atlantic Treaty.[41] Article 5 of the Treaty, which lays down the principle of mutual assistance in response to an armed attack,[42] is couched in terms similar to those used in Article 3(1) of the Rio Inter-American Treaty. There is no 'automatism' in this provision: decision-making as to actual recourse to counter-force in specific instances is left to each Contracting Party.[43] Additionally, Article 3 of the North Atlantic Treaty further sets forth that the parties 'will maintain and develop their individual and collective capacity to resist armed attack'.[44] Article 9 provides for the creation of some central organs.[45] These innocuous clauses have brought into being the North Atlantic Treaty Organization (NATO), which has evolved over the years (particularly in the aftermath of the Korean War) into a sophisticated military

---

[39] See W. E. Beckett, *The North Atlantic Treaty, the Brussels Treaty and the Charter of the United Nations* 28 (1950).

[40] See M. Virally, 'Panorama du Droit International Contemporain', 183 *RCADI* 9, 298 (1983).

[41] North Atlantic Treaty, 1949, 34 *UNTS* 243.   [42] *Ibid.*, 246.

[43] N. Schrijver, 'Responding to International Terrorism: Moving the Frontiers of International Law for "Enduring Freedom"?', 48 *NILR* 271, 282 (2001).

[44] North Atlantic Treaty, *supra* note 41, at 246.   [45] *Ibid.*, 248.

alliance with a vast structure.[46] After the end of the 'Cold War', far from being regarded as an anachronism, NATO has enlarged its membership (most recently, in 2004). NATO has also undertaken new missions exceeding the bounds of collective self-defence (see *infra*, Chapter 10, D, (c)).

Since most States succumb to a touch of paranoia, perennially suspecting the intentions of other countries, a single State may concurrently assume assorted reciprocal commitments to support potential victims of aggression. The drawback is that the agendas and concerns of diverse associations of States do not always mesh. When small States – in an elusive quest for added security – reinsure themselves in a number of ways, a chain effect may be generated. A case in point is the trilateral Treaty of Alliance, Political Co-operation and Mutual Assistance, concluded in Bled in 1954 (at the peak of the 'Cold War') between Greece, Turkey and Yugoslavia.[47] The first two parties were members of NATO, whereas the third was not. Pressures on Yugoslavia could have produced a suction process, drawing in non-Contracting Parties belonging to NATO (through the pipeline of Greece and Turkey). This is also true of a super-Power straddling several political groupings. Thus, the United States is a party to a wide range of military alliances and mutual assistance treaties. It may well be asked whether the involvement of the United States in collective self-defence in Europe (under the North Atlantic Treaty) may not trigger the obligations incurred by other American countries in accordance with the Rio Treaty.[48]

On the other hand, the fact that two countries are associated in the same multilateral military alliance, provides no assurance of good bilateral relations between them. Thus, because of the Cyprus issue (see *infra*, (c)), Greece and Turkey periodically behave as if they were foes, rather than allies.

Often, military alliances and mutual assistance treaties are aligned in fact, albeit not necessarily on paper, against each other. Accordingly, opposite NATO, there stood for many years (during the 'Cold War') the Warsaw Pact alliance.[49] Although the machinery constructed in the Warsaw Pact was the political and military antithesis of NATO, there was no legal contradiction immanent in their coexistence. The rationale was that, under either treaty of alliance, Contracting Parties undertook to

---

[46] See D. W. Bowett, *The Law of International Institutions* 180–5 (4th ed., 1982).

[47] Greece–Turkey–Yugoslavia, Bled Treaty of Alliance, Political Co-operation and Mutual Assistance, 1954, 211 *UNTS* 237.

[48] *Cf.* C. G. Fenwick, 'The Atlantic Pact', 43 *AJIL* 312, 314–16 (1949).

[49] Warsaw Treaty of Friendship, Co-operation and Mutual Assistance, 1955, 219 *UNTS* 3, 24.

render military assistance to one another only in response to an armed attack, had it occurred (presumably on the initiative of members of the opposite group).[50] Both treaties expressly subordinated themselves to the Charter of the United Nations.[51]

The duty of collective self-defence, under a military alliance or a mutual assistance treaty, may be restricted to the occurrence of a specifically defined armed attack (instead of being linked to any armed attack against a Contracting Party, wherever and whenever it takes place). The condition activating the duty of a Contracting Party to lend support to the victim of aggression is called *casus foederis*.[52] The obligation of affording military aid may be reduced to the eventuality of an armed attack mounted by a certain State (and no other) or in a given region (and no other). For example, in 1925 two treaties were concluded in Locarno between France (on one side), Poland and Czechoslovakia (respectively, on the other), whereby the parties undertook to assist each other in case of an attack by Germany (and none but Germany).[53] In conformity with the aforementioned Article 5 of the North Atlantic Treaty, an armed attack against one of the Contracting Parties is deemed an armed attack against all only if it takes place in Europe or North America, in contradistinction to other regions of the world.

A military alliance may rely primarily on a super-power (like the United States in NATO) whose might constitutes the backbone of the association. An alliance may also be based on the combined strengths of many a small State. Either way, a military alliance hinges on the principle of reciprocity. A super-power (like the United States) not only spreads a nuclear umbrella over its allies, but also benefits from their contribution to the alliance, actively (through contingents of armed forces, equipment and supplies) as well as passively (permission to station troops on their soil).

(c)   Treaties of guarantee

A completely different legal technique for ensuring military assistance to a State dreading an armed attack is the issuance of a guarantee. The term

[50] North Atlantic Treaty, *supra* note 41, at 246 (Article 5); Warsaw Treaty, *supra* note 49, at 28 (Article 4).
[51] North Atlantic Treaty, *supra* note 41, at 246, 248 (Articles 5, 7); Warsaw Treaty, *supra* note 49, at 28 (Article 4).
[52] See Oppenheim's *International Law*, I, 1322 (R. Jennings and A. Watts eds., 9th ed., 1992).
[53] France–Poland, Locarno Treaty of Mutual Guarantee, 1925, 54 *LNTS* 353, 355 (Article 1); France–Czechoslovakia, Locarno Treaty of Mutual Guarantee, 1925, *Ibid.*, 359, 361 (Article 1).

'guarantee' demands an explanation. When Carpathia undertakes to carry out its part of an agreement with Apollonia, it may be said that Carpathia guarantees performance. As well, a certain territory or other property belonging to a State may be considered a guarantee. Thus, Article 428 of the 1919 Versailles Treaty of Peace prescribed that the German territory situated west of the Rhine (the Rhineland) would be occupied by Allied and Associated troops, for a period of fifteen years, as a guarantee for the execution of the Treaty by Germany.[54] However, a 'guarantee' in the sense commanding our attention in the context of collective self-defence is of a different nature.

A guarantee for our purposes is 'essentially a trilateral transaction'.[55] Just as Atlantica may guarantee to Utopia that Arcadia will honour a financial debt (so that Atlantica will secure payment if Arcadia defaults),[56] Atlantica may promise Utopia to respond in a certain way to prescribed conduct by Arcadia (which is not necessarily a party to the transaction). In a genuine guarantee, Atlantica does not merely 'endorse' – or undertake to 'respect' – arrangements of a political-military character made by Utopia and Arcadia.[57]

The thrust of the guarantee is that, should Utopia become a victim of an Arcadian armed attack, Atlantica undertakes to come to its aid. A guarantee may be given *erga omnes* (encompassing any country in the world) or it may be linked to a well-defined danger faced by Utopia from a specific source (Arcadia). The guarantee is generally granted by a major Power (militarily capable of offering credible aid) – or by a group of States – to a small country (which is in need of it) as part of a territorial arrangement, a political settlement, a regime of permanent neutrality, and the like.

Although a guarantee may be issued as a binding unilateral declaration by the guarantor, or a mandatory decision of the Security Council, it is chiefly incorporated in a treaty between the guarantor and the State benefiting from the guarantee. A treaty of guarantee is similar in form to a mutual assistance treaty, but the two instruments are dissimilar in substance. In a mutual assistance treaty, all the Contracting Parties are obligated to come to each other's help in the event of an armed attack.

---

[54] Versailles Treaty of Peace with Germany, 1919, *Peace Treaties*, II, 1265, 1524.
[55] Lord McNair, *The Law of Treaties* 240 (1961).
[56] See J. H. W. Verzijl, *International Law in Historical Perspective*, VI, 457 (1973).
[57] Hence, the 1995 General Framework Agreement for Peace in Bosnia and Herzegovina, negotiated in Dayton, Ohio, and signed in Paris (35 *ILM* 75, 90 (1996)), does not truly qualify as a treaty of guarantee on the part of the former Yugoslavia and Croatia. *Per contra*, see P. Gaeta, 'The Dayton Agreements and International Law', 7 *EJIL* 147, 153 (1996).

What stands in stark contrast in a treaty of guarantee is that it is unidirectional in nature. Should an armed attack occur, only the guarantor would be required to extend aid to the guaranteed State, and there is no reciprocity. A disparity in the relative positions and undertakings of the Contracting Parties is an intrinsic trait of a treaty of guarantee.

When added to a treaty, the epithet 'guarantee' is liable to be used loosely. Thus, in 1988, the United States and the USSR signed a Declaration on International Guarantees, in which they undertook to refrain from any form of interference or intervention in the internal affairs of Afghanistan and Pakistan, as well as to respect commitments contained in a bilateral agreement between the two latter countries.[58] In the bilateral agreement, Afghanistan and Pakistan renounced the threat or use of force against each other in any form (such as fomenting rebellion or secessionist activities).[59] While on the face of it, the United States and the USSR were pledged to respect conduct by other States, in reality they primarily engaged themselves: the Soviet Union to withdraw its armed forces from Afghanistan, and the United States to cease covert assistance to Afghan resistance fighters.[60] The so-called guarantee was merely a semantic device to produce 'interlocked' treaties, which constituted component parts of a single settlement.[61] This was practically acknowledged in an Agreement on the Interrelationships for the Settlement of the Situation Relating to Afghanistan, concluded simultaneously by all four parties (and referring to a phased withdrawal of the Soviet troops).[62]

At times, a complex treaty is formulated embodying mixed components of guarantee and mutual assistance. A case in point is the 1925 Locarno Treaty of Mutual Guarantee between Germany, Belgium, France, Great Britain and Italy.[63] In Article 1, the Contracting Parties 'collectively and severally' guaranteed the German–French and the German–Belgian frontiers.[64] From the angle of France and Belgium (each being both a guarantor, as far as the other's frontiers with Germany were concerned, and a guaranteed State), this was in effect a mutual assistance treaty. Insofar as Britain and Italy were concerned, it was an authentic treaty of guarantee. The phrase 'mutual guarantee', appearing in the titles of the various Locarno Treaties (see also the

[58] USA–USSR, Declaration on International Guarantees, 1988, 27 *ILM* 584, *id.* (1988).
[59] Afghanistan–Pakistan, Agreement on the Principles of Mutual Relations, in Particular on Non-Interference and Non-Intervention, 1988, 27 *ILM* 581, 582 (1988).
[60] See C. Chinkin, *Third Parties in International Law* 47 (1993).   [61] *Ibid.*
[62] Agreement on the Interrelationships for the Settlement of the Situation Relating to Afghanistan, 1988, 27 *ILM* 587, 590 (1988).
[63] Locarno Treaty of Mutual Guarantee, 1925, 54 *LNTS* 289.   [64] *Ibid.*, 293.

other accords mentioned *supra*, (b)), actually merges two separate concepts of mutual assistance and guarantee.

Whenever a guarantee is collective, it is debatable whether the obligation arises for each guarantor independently or is only enforceable in respect of all the guarantors together.[65] If the duty devolving on the guarantors is activated jointly or not at all, a single party refusing to budge can effectively frustrate the guarantee. A multilateral treaty of guarantee may expressly permit action to be taken either jointly or severally (as was done in Article 1 of the Locarno Treaty), and anyhow the right of collective self-defence remains unimpaired. Nevertheless, individual action will be a right rather than a duty: no guarantor in a collective guarantee is legally compelled to act alone.[66]

When a multilateral treaty of guarantee reserves the right of each guarantor to take the necessary measures on its own, this may ultimately prove counter-productive from the perspective of the guaranteed State. A poignant illustration is the 1960 Nicosia Treaty of Guarantee.[67] Here – in Article II – Greece, Turkey and the United Kingdom guaranteed the independence, territorial integrity and security of Cyprus, as well as the state of affairs established by its Constitution.[68] In Article IV, each of the guarantors reserved the right to take action where necessary to reestablish the state of affairs created by the Treaty.[69] Turkey relied on Article IV when it carried out, in 1974, an armed intervention on behalf of the Turkish minority in the island (leading to the nascence of the so-called Turkish Republic of Northern Cyprus).[70] The circumstances of the case were admittedly exceptional, bearing in mind not only the broad language of Article IV but also another agreement signed in 1960: the tripartite Nicosia Treaty of Alliance authorizing Greece and Turkey to keep military contingents in Cyprus.[71]

In any event, to the extent that Article IV purports to enable a guarantor to use force other than in the legitimate exercise of collective self-defence, it is incompatible with the Charter.[72] Pursuant to the Charter, a 'humanitarian intervention' on behalf of a persecuted minority

---

[65] See McNair, *supra* note 55, at 240–1.
[66] See J. F. Williams, 'Sanctions under the Covenant', 17 *BYBIL* 130, 135 (1936).
[67] Nicosia Treaty of Guarantee, 1960, 382 *UNTS* 3.   [68] *Ibid.*, 4.   [69] *Ibid.*, 6.
[70] See Z. M. Necatigil, *The Cyprus Question and the Turkish Position in International Law* 129–32 (2nd ed., 1993). On the juridical evolution of the Turkish enclave, see *ibid.*, 67–8.
[71] Greece–Turkey–Cyprus, Nicosia Treaty of Alliance, 1960, 397 *UNTS* 287, 289, 291 (Articles III–IV and Additional Protocol I).
[72] See R. St. J. Macdonald, 'International Law and the Conflict in Cyprus', 19 *CYIL* 3, 12–17, 25–6 (1981).

can only take place at the behest of the Security Council (see *supra*, Chapter 3, B, (c)).

As a legal institution, a guarantee suffers from all the shortcomings of a mutual assistance treaty (not linked to a military alliance), for there is no certainty that actual military aid will materialize when the moment of truth arrives. In light of the guarantee's asymmetrical nature, and the fact that it lays a burden on the guarantor without spawning any direct benefit for it (unless the treaty is exploited as a lever of intervention *à la* Cyprus), the chances of implementation of a guarantee in reality are perceptibly lower than those of a mutual assistance treaty.

C.   The legal limitations of collective self-defence

(a)   The primacy of the Charter of the United Nations

In the past, States used to conclude treaties of mutual assistance and military alliances of an offensive–defensive nature.[73] Arcadia and Patagonia would undertake to render aid to one another, whenever war was waged against Utopia, regardless of the identity of the side that started the war. At the present time, an agreement projecting complicity in aggression will be in violation of the United Nations Charter. Article 103 of the Charter promulgates that, in the event of a conflict between obligations assumed by UN Members under the Charter and other international agreements, their Charter obligations shall prevail.[74] The juridical consequences of Article 103 are controversial.[75] Some commentators believe that any treaty conflicting with the Charter (even if concluded with a non-Member State) is abrogated.[76] Others take the position that such a treaty is legally valid, but a Member is required to breach it and, if necessary, compensation will be paid to the non-Member Contracting Party.[77] Whatever the correct interpretation of Article 103 may be, there can be no doubt about the nullity of treaties in the specific case when they countenance aggression. This is a direct outcome of the peremptory nature of the prohibition of the use of inter-State force as *jus cogens* (see *supra*, Chapter 4, E, (a)).

---

[73] See Verzijl, *supra* note 56, at 444–5.
[74] Charter of the United Nations, *supra* note 1, at 361.
[75] See R. St. J. Macdonald, 'Reflections on the Charter of the United Nations', *Des Menschen Recht zwischen Freiheit und Verantwortung: Festschrift für Karl Josef Partsch* 29, 37–42 (J. Jekewitz *et al.* eds., 1989).
[76] See H. Lauterpacht, '[First] Report on Law of Treaties', [1953] II *ILC Ybk* 90, 157.
[77] See G. G. Fitzmaurice, 'Third Report on Law of Treaties', [1958] II *ILC Ybk* 20, 43.

The general practice with respect to mutual assistance treaties or military alliances is to subordinate them expressly to the provisions of the UN Charter. The North Atlantic Treaty and the now defunct Warsaw Pact both exemplify this trend (see *supra*, B, (b)). Under Article 30(2) of the 1969 Vienna Convention on the Law of Treaties, '[w]hen a treaty specifies that it is subject to, or that it is not to be considered as incompatible with, an earlier or later treaty, the provisions of that other treaty prevail'.[78] Therefore, the Charter must govern the exercise of collective self-defence by Contracting Parties to the North Atlantic Treaty or formerly the Warsaw Pact.

(b)   The requirement of an armed attack

As the International Court of Justice in the *Nicaragua* case emphasized, States do not have a right to employ force in collective self-defence, under either the Charter or customary international law, except in response to acts constituting an armed attack.[79] If Atlantica resorts to force against Arcadia, invoking collective self-defence, it must show that an armed attack has been initiated by Arcadia against Utopia.[80]

The insistence on an armed attack as a condition of collective self-defence sounds like a truism. But even a truism may be lost sight of in intricate situations. For instance, if Utopia conducts a legitimate operation of extra-territorial law enforcement against terrorists or armed bands ensconced within the territory of Arcadia, this is an act of self-defence in which Arcadia has to acquiesce (see *supra*, Chapter 8, B, (c)). Since Utopia does not commit an armed attack against Arcadia, Pacifica cannot employ counter-force against Utopia in reliance on collective self-defence. To be regarded as a defending State, Pacifica must first demonstrate that Utopia is an attacking State. This ties in with the principle that there is no self-defence against self-defence (see *supra*, Chapter 7, A, (b)).

In the *Nicaragua* case, the Court also ruled that a State may not exercise the right of collective self-defence merely 'on the basis of its own assessment of the situation'.[81] The direct victim of an armed attack must first 'form and declare the view' that it has been subjected to such an attack.[82] Moreover, a request for help has to be made by the victim State: in the absence of such a request, collective self-defence by a third State is excluded.[83] In 2003, in the *Case Concerning Oil Platforms*, the Court

---

[78] Vienna Convention on the Law of Treaties, 1969, [1969] *UNJY* 140, 148.
[79] *Nicaragua* case, *supra* note 11, at 110.   [80] *Ibid.*   [81] *Ibid.*, 104.   [82] *Ibid.*
[83] *Ibid.*, 105.

reiterated this requirement of a request made to the third State by the direct victim of an armed attack.[84]

In his Dissenting Opinion in the *Nicaragua* case, Judge Jennings doubted whether the prerequisite of 'some sort of formal declaration and request' by the victim State (a declaration that it is under an armed attack and a request for assistance) is realistic in all instances.[85] Indisputably, military aid (especially the dispatch of troops to the combat zone) may not be forced by Ruritania on Utopia against the latter's will. As Judge Jennings remarked, '[o]bviously the notion of collective self-defence is open to abuse and it is necessary to ensure that it is not employable as a mere cover for aggression disguised as protection'.[86] However, the majority appears to have missed the kernel of collective self-defence. The Judgment referred to 'the use of collective self-defence by the third State for the benefit of the attacked State'.[87] In fact, collective self-defence is above all the defence of self (see *supra*, A), and, when Ruritania responds to an armed attack by Arcadia against Utopia, it is not a 'third State' in the strict sense. Judge Jennings rightly commented that the Court's way of looking at collective self-defence 'seems to be based almost upon an idea of vicarious defence by champions', whereas, legally speaking, Ruritania (at least in some measure) should be defending itself.[88]

The issue has important practical dimensions. In certain situations, such as the notorious *Anschluss* of Austria by the German *Reich* in March 1938, the direct victim of an armed attack (Utopia) does not resist the aggressor. In general, as already observed (*supra*, Chapter 7, A, (b)), self-defence is a right and not a duty. Utopia is not obligated, therefore, to attempt to repel an invasion or any other form of an armed attack by Arcadia (unless a pledge to exercise individual self-defence is incorporated in a treaty in force, such as a permanent neutrality arrangement). Ruritania cannot coerce Utopia to accept help against its will (again, unless both parties are bound by a specific treaty regulating collective self-defence, e.g., a military alliance).[89] Yet, there is a palpable distinction between a case in which Ruritania proceeds to send its troops into the territory of Utopia (in order to fight there against the invading armed

---

[84] *Case Concerning Oil Platforms*, 2003, 42 *ILM* 1334, 1355 (2003).
[85] *Nicaragua* case, *supra* note 11, at 544–5.   [86] *Ibid.*, 544.   [87] *Ibid.*, 104.
[88] *Ibid.*, 545.
[89] The requirement of a request by the victim of an armed attack, as a condition for outside assistance, is apparently not reconcilable with many existing treaties. See F. L. Morrison, 'Legal Issues in the *Nicaragua* Opinion', 81 *AJIL* 160, 163 (1987). *Cf.* D. K. Linnan, 'Self-Defense, Necessity and U. N. Collective Security: United States and Other Views', 1 *DJCIL* 57, 103 (1991).

forces of Arcadia) and a setting in which Ruritania announces that, exercising its right of collective self-defence in response to an Arcadian armed attack (of which Utopia is the direct victim), it will use forcible measures against Arcadia outside Utopian territory.

In the absence of a special treaty conferring on Ruritania the right to dispatch an expeditionary force to Utopia, the unsolicited arrival of Ruritanian troops on Utopian soil – notwithstanding the avowed desire of Utopia to be left alone – amounts to an invasion (no different from the previous invasion by Arcadia), namely, an armed attack. Before its troops enter Utopian territory, Ruritania must await a call for help from the country that it purportedly seeks to assist (Utopia).

The legal position is completely different when the Ruritanian response to the Arcadian armed attack takes place outside the territorial boundaries of Utopia. In this factual situation, why should there be any need of a declaration or a request emanating from Utopia? Ruritania's right of collective self-defence is independent of Utopia's right of individual self-defence. Ruritania's right corresponds to the duty binding all nations (and applicable *erga omnes*) to refrain from an armed attack. When Arcadia commences an armed attack (the direct victim of which is Utopia), and Ruritania perceives that its own security is endangered, Ruritania is entitled under Article 51 of the Charter to resort to counter-force. There is no allusion in the Article to prior approval by Utopia as a condition to the exercise of the right of collective self-defence by Ruritania.

If Utopia categorically denies that it has been the target of an armed attack by Arcadia, any collective self-defence measures directed by Ruritania against Arcadia – even beyond the frontiers of Utopia – would be suspect. But this is merely one factor among many, to be weighed by the Security Council when it reviews the entire series of events at a later stage (see *supra*, Chapter 7, D, (a)). During the first phase, Ruritania should be allowed to gauge the Arcadian action by itself, irrespective of any protestations by Utopia.

(c)   Other conditions for the exercise of collective self-defence

The three conditions precedent to the exercise of the right of self-defence (see *supra*, Chapter 7, C) – necessity, proportionality and immediacy – are applicable to collective, no less than to individual, self-defence. This was underscored by the Court in the *Nicaragua* case.[90]

---

[90] *Nicaragua* case, *supra* note 11, at 122–3.

As indicated (*supra*, Chapter 7, D, (c)), Article 51 imposes on a State exercising the right of self-defence a duty of immediately reporting to the Security Council. In establishing the reporting duty, the Article does not differentiate between individual and collective self-defence. It emerges from the Judgment in the *Nicaragua* case (where the obligation was looked upon as a material rather than a technical condition) that each State resorting to measures of self-defence has to submit such a report.[91] If so, it is not enough for Utopia (the direct victim) to communicate a message to the Security Council about the Arcadian armed attack and the forcible counter-measures taken in individual self-defence. When Ruritania invokes the right of collective self-defence, it must file a separate report. Such a report by Ruritania is particularly called for if (as just explained) it acts alone against Arcadia, whereas Utopia declines to exercise its right of individual self-defence.

In addition, Article 54 of the Charter stipulates that when activities for the maintenance of international peace and security are undertaken (or even contemplated) by regional agencies under regional arrangements, the Security Council must be kept fully informed.[92]

D. The modality of collective self-defence

The modality of individual self-defence (see *supra*, Chapter 8) is not available in its full range to a State invoking collective self-defence. Thus, the protection of nationals abroad (when it qualifies as legitimate self-defence) is a proper remedy only for the State directly affected. This mode of response to an armed attack is based, by definition, on a nexus of nationality. Hence, it may not be subrogated by another country in the name of collective self-defence. Otherwise, the limited right for the protection of nationals abroad (as a measure of self-defence) will spin off a general freedom of 'humanitarian intervention' (see *supra*, Chapter 3, B, (c)).

On-the-spot reaction, too, is not usually germane to the right of collective self-defence. This is due to the limited scope of the clash of arms and the fact that the incident is closed rapidly. It is conceivable that Patagonian troops, stationed on Utopian soil as a result of a military alliance, will be attacked by Arcadian armed forces and return fire (thereby closing the incident). Here is a characteristic instance of on-the-spot reaction, but it has nothing to do with collective self-defence. The exchange of fire represents a run-of-the-mill case of individual self-defence, exercised by

---

[91] *Ibid.*, 105, 121–2.   [92] Charter of the United Nations, *supra* note 1, at 348.

Patagonia against an Arcadian armed attack. The only extraordinary aspect of the clash is that both the Arcadian armed attack and the Patagonian response occur within the territory of a third State (Utopia) (see *supra*, Chapter 7, B, (b), (aa), iii). On-the-spot reaction as a manifestation of collective self-defence takes place only if the Arcadian attack is directed at a Utopian patrol, yet a Numidian military unit deployed nearby (either within Utopia or in Numidia itself, assuming that these are allied and neighbouring countries) rushes immediately to the assistance of the Utopian patrol, and the incident is presently closed.

There are no clear-cut precedents for extra-territorial law enforcement measures, taken by Apollonia within Arcadian territory against terrorists or armed bands striking at Utopian targets from bases in Arcadia (without the backing of the Arcadian Government). On the one hand, since the dispatch of armed forces into a foreign territory (with a view to performing the neglected functions of the local sovereign) is an exceptional course of action, it may be argued that extra-territorial law enforcement should be left to the bilateral relations between Utopia and Arcadia. On the other hand, given the growing realization that terrorism is a global bane threatening to spread far and wide, Apollonia may claim that such assaults against Utopia constitute an armed attack against itself.

The position is perhaps less ambiguous when defensive armed reprisals are at issue. It has been argued that these may be carried out by allied nations within the framework of collective self-defence.[93] To a degree, the practice of States corroborates the argument. The United States employed armed reprisals against Nicaragua in 1984, invoking the right of collective self-defence.[94] The International Court of Justice rejected the American claim to collective self-defence, determining that the measures taken had not come in response to an armed attack.[95] At the same time, the Court passed no judgment on the specific issue of the legality of armed reprisals, either in individual or in collective self-defence (*supra*, Chapter 8, A, (a), ii).

The archetypical case of the implementation of the right of collective self-defence is war. Multipartite recourse to war, in response to an armed attack, is the primary goal of collective self-defence treaties (see *supra*, B). But irrespective of treaty obligations, when Carpathia exercises in practice the theoretical right of collective sell-defence against Arcadia – in response to an Arcadian armed attack against Utopia – it will normally do so by embarking upon war (although it may avoid using this term). In all

---

[93] See J.-C. Venezia, 'La Notion de Représailles en Droit International Public', 64 *RGDIP* 465, 490 (1960).

[94] *Nicaragua* case, *supra* note 11, at 22.   [95] *Ibid.*, 103–6.

likelihood, the Carpathian action will be in the form of a counter-war (as opposed to war in response to an isolated armed attack 'short of war'). To reiterate (see *supra*, A), there is little prospect of Carpathia plunging into war against Arcadia when Utopia is attacked, unless what is at stake is perceived as critical to Carpathia's own security. Ordinarily, nothing short of a full-scale invasion of Utopia will induce Carpathia to get involved in a war of self-defence with Arcadia, considering that Carpathia itself is not the direct victim of the Arcadian attack.

E.   The Gulf War and collective self-defence

The invasion of Kuwait by Iraq on 2 August 1990 triggered within a few hours Security Council Resolution 660, which determined the existence of 'a breach of international peace and security', and demanded immediate and unconditional withdrawal of the Iraqi forces.[96] Afterwards, the Council imposed on Iraq economic sanctions (Resolution 661)[97] and even a blockade (Resolution 665)[98] (*infra*, Chapter 10, C, (b)). When Iraq did not relent, the Council reached a crossroads. A vital decision had to be made whether to proceed to military enforcement measures by the United Nations – in the exercise of collective security (*infra*, Chapter 10, A) – or to recommend, and rely on, collective self-defence. Surmounting some apparent hesitation, the Council opted for the latter path.

In Resolution 678 of 29 November 1990, the Security Council authorized the 'Member States co-operating with the Government [in exile] of Kuwait' – should Iraq not fully comply with previous Council resolutions by 15 January 1991 – 'to use all necessary means to uphold and implement resolution 660 (1990) and all subsequent relevant resolutions and to restore international peace and security in the area'.[99] Although Resolution 678 did not speak in a lapidary manner about the employment of force by the countries cooperating with Kuwait, nobody could fail to grasp the purport of the authorization 'to use all necessary means' in order to secure full compliance with the Council's decisions. Resolution 678 'has to be read against the background of the earlier resolutions on Kuwait', taking into account that Iraq had impudently (and imprudently) disregarded other means falling short of comprehensive force.[100]

---

[96] Security Council Resolution 660, 45 *RDSC* 19, *id.* (1990).
[97] Security Council Resolution 661, 45 *RDSC* 19, 19–20 (1990).
[98] Security Council Resolution 665, 45 *RDSC* 21, 21–2 (1990).
[99] Security Council Resolution 678, 45 *RDSC* 27, 27–8 (1990).
[100] C. Greenwood, 'New World Order or Old? The Invasion of Kuwait and the Rule of Law', 55 *Mod.LR* 153, 166 (1992).

Pursuant to Resolution 678, and upon the expiry of the ultimatum, the armed forces of a large American-led Coalition struck at Iraq on the night of 16/17 January 1991. At the outset, the military operations were confined to air warfare (missiles, bombings and strafings). On 24 February, a massive land offensive was launched: Kuwait was liberated (and about 15 percent of Iraq's territory was occupied) within 100 hours. At this point, on 28 February, President G. Bush announced the suspension of hostilities. Preliminary conditions of a cease-fire were proclaimed by the Council on 2 March, in Resolution 686.[101] Definitive cease-fire terms were dictated to Iraq only on 3 April, in Resolution 687.[102] All these conditions and terms were reluctantly accepted by Iraq.

The role that the Security Council played in the first phase of the Gulf War deserves an intense scrutiny. Did the armed forces of the Coalition constitute a United Nations force predicated on genuine collective security (see *infra*, Chapter 10, A)? The answer is emphatically negative. At no time did the Council establish a United Nations force for combat purposes against Iraq.[103] All that happened was that the Council determined conclusively (in Resolution 660) that there had been an Iraqi invasion – *i.e.* an armed attack – against Kuwait, and then (primarily in Resolution 678) authorized recourse to force against Iraq by the Coalition cooperating with Kuwait. The use of force by the Coalition against Iraq was legitimized by the Council within the purview of collective self-defence (Article 51), as opposed to collective security.[104]

Resolution 678 has animated diverse comments in the legal literature. One can put aside extravagant (and incongruous) allegations that the resolution 'was contrary to the United Nations Charter'.[105] Closer attention must be paid to the assertion that '[t]he use of force to liberate Kuwait ... involved not self-defense but, rather, the interpretation and application of a Security Council resolution'.[106] Yet, an interpretation of a Council's resolution and collective self-defence, far from being mutually

---

[101] Security Council Resolution 686, 46 *RDSC* 8–9 (1991).

[102] Security Council Resolution 687, 46 *RDSC* 11–15 (1991).

[103] See K. Boustany, 'La Guerre du Golfe et le Système d'Intervention Armée de l'ONU', 28 *CYIL* 379, 391–2 (1990). It may be added that, following the cease-fire, the United Nations Iraq-Kuwait Observation Mission (UNIKOM) – a non-combat force – was established to monitor a demilitarized zone. See Security Council Resolution 687, *supra* note 102, at 12; and Security Council Resolution 689, 46 *RDSC* 15–16 (1991).

[104] See Schachter, *supra* note 18, at 459–60.

[105] Y. Le Bouthillier and M. Morin, 'Réflexions sur la Validité des Opérations Entreprises contre l'Iraq en regard de la Charte des Nations Unies et du Droit Canadien', 29 *CYIL* 142, 220 (1991).

[106] B. M. Carnahan, 'Protecting Nuclear Facilities from Military Attack: Prospects after the Gulf War', 86 *AJIL* 524, 527 (1992).

exclusive, are interlinked in this instance. In the words of N. Rostow, '[A]rticle 51 rights can be exercised in the context of Security Council approval.'[107]

A specific affirmation of 'the inherent right of individual or collective self-defence, in response to the armed attack by Iraq against Kuwait, in accordance with Article 51 of the Charter', was incorporated already in Resolution 661.[108] At the time, this reference to Article 51 puzzled some commentators.[109] Later events proved that it was not accidental.[110] Resolution 678 denotes that, while the Security Council abstained from deploying a veritable United Nations force as an instrument of collective security, it gave its blessing in advance to the voluntary exercise of collective self-defence by the members of the Coalition (following an interval of several weeks designed for the exhaustion of the political process). The core of the resolution was the prospective approval of future action.[111] In an ordinary constellation of events, States first employ force in individual or collective self-defence and only then report to the Council about the measures that they have taken, so that the Council investigates the nature of the hostilities retrospectively. As noted (*supra*, Chapter 7, D, (c)), this is the chronological sequence envisaged by the framers of the Charter. In the particular case of Iraq, the Coalition sought and obtained from the Council a green light for the exercise of collective self-defence against the perpetrator of an armed attack (Iraq) well before the projected military clash. Thereafter, the Coalition did not have to worry about the reaction of the Council, inasmuch as that reaction had predated the actual combat.

The principal beneficiaries of the collective self-defence orientation of the operations against Iraq were the Americans who led the Coalition. They, rather than the UN, were in command. Consequently, theirs – and almost theirs alone – was the decision when and in what form to strike subsequent to 15 January 1991, at what juncture (if at all) to mount a ground offensive, and under what circumstances to halt the advance. It is useful to recall that, as a Permanent Member of the Security Council, the

---

[107] N. Rostow, 'The International Use of Force after the Cold War', 32 *HILJ* 411, 420 (1991).

[108] Security Council Resolution 661, *supra* note 97, at 19.

[109] See, e.g., L. C. Green, 'Iraq, the U.N. and the Law', 29 *ALR* 560, 565–6 (1991).

[110] Even the phrase 'Member States co-operating with the Government of Kuwait' suggests that these are 'nations engaged in collective [self-]defense with Kuwait'. J. N. Moore, *Crisis in the Gulf: Enforcing the Rule of Law* 151 (1992).

[111] See A. Pyrich, 'United Nations: Authorizations of Use of Force', 32 *HILJ* 265, 268 (1991).

United States could also veto any posterior resolution that might have obstructed the military moves of the Coalition.

Considering that the military operations of the Coalition in 1991 were a manifestation of collective self-defence – rather than collective security – there was technically no need for the specific mandate of Resolution 678 to legally validate the launching of the strikes against Iraq.[112] Article 51 *per se* ought to have sufficed in authorizing the Coalition to resort to force in response to the Iraqi armed attack, and arguably Resolution 678 only tied the hands of the countries cooperating with Kuwait in that they had to hold their fire until 15 January.[113] Of course, in political and psychological terms, Resolution 678 had an incalculable effect: internationally (cementing the solidarity of the Coalition and swelling its ranks) as well as domestically (mobilizing public opinion to political support of the action against Iraq).

There is a resemblance between the Gulf War and the Korean War, although they are four decades apart temporally and light years apart psychologically. In both instances, the Security Council determined the existence of a breach of the peace, yet refrained from taking legally binding decisions activating genuine collective security (see *infra*, Chapter 10, C, (a)–(b)). In both cases, an international coalition led by the United States came to the aid of the victim of an armed attack, heeding the Council's recommendation or authorization.[114] Still, there are some unmistakable dissimilarities.[115] First, whereas in Korea the fighting was continuous, in the Gulf – since Kuwait had been completely overrun by the Iraqi forces – there was an interlude between the original armed attack and the military response. Secondly, in contrast to the near unanimity that characterized relations between the Permanent Members during the Gulf War,[116] the resolutions in the Korean War (which occurred in the heyday of the 'Cold War') were made possible only by a fortuitous albeit fleeting Soviet boycott of the Council's sessions. Thirdly, and conversely, in Korea the contingents confronting the aggressor were allowed to fly the United Nations flag (see *supra*, Chapter 6, B), whereas

---

[112] See Greenwood, *supra* note 100, at 163. *Cf.* D. R. Penna, 'The Right to Self-Defense in the Post-Cold War Era: The Role of the United Nations', 20 *DJILP* 41, 49–50 (1991–2).

[113] See C. Dominicé, 'La Sécurité Collective et la Crise du Golfe', 2 *EJIL* 85, 104 (1991).

[114] The difference between authorization and recommendation (stressed by J. Frowein and N. Krisch, 'Article 42', *The Charter of the United Nations: A Commentary*, I, 749, 756–8 (B. Simma ed., 2nd ed., 2002)) is more verbal than real. See *infra*, Chapter 10, D, (c).

[115] See S. M. De Luca, 'The Gulf Crisis and Collective Security under the United Nations Charter', 3 *PYIL* 267, 295–6 (1991).

[116] China alone abstained in the vote on Resolution 678 (1990). It voted in favour of all the preceding resolutions against Iraq.

the Coalition that came to the rescue of Kuwait had no similar status. But here as there the command was American and the financing of the operation formed no part of the United Nations budget. Legally speaking, in both wars the American-led expeditionary force fought in exercise of collective self-defence (approved by the Council) as distinct from collective security.

The reopening of full-scale hostilities against Iraq in 2003, in the final phase of the Gulf War (see *infra*, Chapter 10, C, (b), iii), represented a renewal of the exercise of the right of collective self-defence after twelve years of cease-fire. A cease-fire, which merely suspends hostilities without terminating the war, does not extinguish the right of collective self-defence that remains legally intact for the duration of the war.[117] Moreover, the criteria for the legitimate exercise of this right remain anchored to the circumstances of the outbreak of the war (in this case, in 1990). The disintegration of a cease-fire by dint of its violation by one belligerent party – and the forcible response of the adversary – is not to be confused with the initiation of a new war (see *supra*, Chapter 8, A, (b)).

---

[117] See A. E. Wall, 'The Legal Case for Invading Iraq and Toppling Hussein', 32 *IYHR* 165, 188 (2002).

10   Collective security

A.   The meaning of collective security

(a)   Definition

Collective security postulates the institutionalization of the lawful use of force in the international community.[1] What is required is a multilateral treaty, whereby Contracting Parties create an international agency vested with the power to employ force against aggressors (and perhaps other law-breakers). Such an instrument is basically 'introverted' in character (designed against a potential future aggressor from among the Contracting Parties), unlike a collective self-defence treaty (see *supra*, Chapter 9, B) which is 'extroverted' (envisaging aggression from outside the system).[2] Collective security shares with collective self-defence the fundamental premise that recourse to force against aggression can (and perhaps must) be made by those who are not the immediate and direct victims. But self-defence, either individual or collective, is exercised at the discretion of a single State or a group of States. Collective security operates on the strength of an authoritative decision made by an organ of the international community.

(b)   The Covenant of the League of Nations

The system of collective security has its roots in the League of Nations. Article 10 of the League's Covenant empowered the Council to advise Member States on the means to be taken in case of aggression or threat of aggression.[3] Article 11 declared that any war or threat of war, whether or not immediately affecting any Member, was a matter of concern to the

---

[1] See G. Schwarzenberger and E. D. Brown, A *Manual of International Law* 153 (6th ed., 1976).
[2] H. Rumpf, 'The Concepts of Peace and War in International Law', 27 *GYIL* 429, 440 (1984).
[3] Covenant of the League of Nations, 1919, 1 *Int.Leg.* 1, 7.

whole League, which had to take action as required to safeguard peace among nations.[4] Article 16 stipulated that, if any Member resorted to war in violation of its obligations under Articles 12, 13 or 15 of the Covenant (see *supra*, Chapter 3, E, (c)), it was *ipso facto* deemed to have committed an act of war against all other Members.[5] All trade or financial relations with the transgressor, including commerce between nationals, had to be severed. The Article went on to instruct the Council to recommend to the Governments concerned what effective military, naval or air contribution they should make to the armed forces which were to be used for the protection of the Covenant's obligations. Expulsion of a Member from the League for violation of any of the Covenant's obligations was also authorized. Article 17 applied the provisions of Article 16 in the event that a non-Member State embarked upon war against a Member.[6]

Article 16 of the Covenant drew a line of distinction between economic sanctions and military action. Member States were duty-bound to apply commercial and financial measures against an aggressor, but – insofar as military action was concerned – the League's Council was only entitled to make (non-binding) recommendations.[7] Economic sanctions (partial, temporary and ineffective in nature) were indeed imposed on Italy, instigated by the latter's aggression against Ethiopia in 1935/6.[8] Yet, even mandatory economic sanctions are not likely to stop war by themselves. As long as an international organization cannot obligate Member States to impose military sanctions against an armed attack, one cannot speak of a veritable collective security system.

(c)   The Charter of the United Nations

The main objective of the framers of the Charter of the United Nations was to introduce into international relations a genuine mechanism of collective security. The UN organ entrusted with the task of activating and supervising the mechanism is the Security Council. In Article 24(1), Member States 'confer on the Security Council primary responsibility for the maintenance of international peace and security, and agree that in carrying out its duties under this responsibility the Security Council acts on their behalf'.[9]

---

[4] *Ibid.*   [5] *Ibid.*, 11.   [6] *Ibid.*, 12.

[7] See J. F. Williams, *Some Aspects of the Covenant of the League of Nations* 156–7 (1934).

[8] See J. H. Spencer, 'The Italian-Ethiopian Dispute and the League of Nations', 31 *AJIL* 614, 624–41 (1937).

[9] Charter of the United Nations, 1945, 9 *Int.Leg.* 327, 339.

The Charter's collective security system is constructed in Chapter VII (Articles 39 to 51).[10] Article 39, in opening Chapter VII, reads:

The Security Council shall determine the existence of any threat to the peace, breach of the peace, or act of aggression and shall make recommendations, or decide what measures shall be taken in accordance with Articles 41 and 42, to maintain or restore international peace and security.[11]

The last words in Article 39 put in a nutshell the Security Council's mandate: it is to maintain or restore international peace and security.[12] The notion of maintaining international peace and security has a pre-emptive thrust. The purpose is to ensure, before it is too late, that no breach of the peace will in fact occur. Measures taken by the Council to forestall a breach of international peace and security have deterrence and prevention as their goals. Once a breach of international peace and security occurs (notwithstanding any prophylactic measures that may have been taken), the situation changes dramatically. At this point, the Council's mission is to restore the peace. It has to take steps calculated to reestablish international law and order.

The Charter endows the Security Council with a whole array of powers, enabling it to maintain or restore international peace and security. The fulcrum of Article 39 is the determination by the Council of the existence of a threat to the peace, a breach of the peace or an act of aggression. Once that determination is made, 'the door is automatically opened to enforcement measures of a non-military or military kind'.[13] The determination is binding on Member States, even if the Council subsequently proceeds to adopt a mere recommendation for action (as distinct from a binding decision).

Naturally, recommendations – even when issued by the Security Council – are not binding,[14] and they can only urge Member States to action. Recommendations can address the country held responsible for a threat to the peace, a breach of the peace or an act of aggression. They can also be directed at other States, calling upon them to take certain action with a view to maintaining or restoring international peace and security.

---

[10] *Ibid.*, 343–6. Of course, the last clause in Chapter VII (Article 51) deals with self-defence, rather than collective security.

[11] *Ibid.*, 343.

[12] On the meaning of the term 'security', as used in Article 39 in combination with 'international peace', see H. Vetschera, 'International Law and International Security: The Case of Force Control', 24 *GYIL* 144, 145–6 (1981).

[13] I. Osterdahl, *Threat to the Peace: The Interpretation by the Security Council of Article 39 of the UN Charter* 28 (1998).

[14] See G. Schwarzenberger, *International Constitutional Law* (*International Law as Applied by International Courts and Tribunals*, III) 204–5 (1976).

Either way, Member States can make up their own minds whether to follow or to ignore non-compulsory calls for action issued by the Council. But it must be borne in mind that (i) if a recommendation is disregarded, the Council may be impelled to adopt a binding decision; (ii) if Member States choose to heed a Council's recommendation authorizing them to take measures predicated on a binding determination concerning the existence of a threat to the peace etc., these measures must be regarded as lawful notwithstanding their permissive character (see *infra*, B, (a)). Interestingly, the Council has more leeway under Article 39 when it resorts to recommendations. As the punctuation of the text clearly indicates, the reference to Articles 41 and 42 appears in conjunction with decisions rather than recommendations. The upshot is that, when the Council is making mere recommendations under Article 39, it is not restricted to the compass of Articles 41 and 42: '[t]he Council may adopt every measure it deems appropriate for the restoration of international peace and security'.[15]

Article 41 prescribes:

The Security Council may decide what measures not involving the use of armed force are to be employed to give effect to its decisions, and it may call upon the Members of the United Nations to apply such measures. These may include complete or partial interruption of economic relations and of rail, sea, air, postal, telegraphic, radio, and other means of communication, and the severance of diplomatic relations.[16]

The list of measures enumerated in Article 41 is not exhaustive, but none of the steps taken under this provision of the Charter involves the use of force.[17]

Article 50 expounds that, if a State (whether or not a UN Member) is confronted with special economic problems arising from the carrying out by the Security Council of preventive or enforcement action against another State, it may consult the Council as regards the solution of these problems.[18] The text is devised to cope with the plight of a country that – owing to geographic proximity to, or special trade with, the State against which steps are taken – suffers unduly from the imposition of the economic sanctions, and requires special assistance.[19] A telling example is that of the Kingdom of Jordan in the first phase of the Gulf War. This

[15] A. Orakhelashvili, 'The Legal Basis of the United Nations Peace-Keeping Operations', 43 *VJIL* 485, 492–3 (2002–3).
[16] Charter of the United Nations, *supra* note 9, at 343.
[17] See B. Broms, *The United Nations* 313 (1990).
[18] Charter of the United Nations, *supra* note 9, at 346.
[19] See L. M. Goodrich, E. Hambro and A. P. Simons, *Charter of the United Nations* 341 (3rd ed., 1969).

country was exceptionally affected by the economic sanctions imposed on Iraq, and it invoked Article 50 in September 1990.[20] In response to Jordanian and other requests for special assistance,[21] the Security Council adopted Resolution 669, which established a procedure examining requests under Article 50 with a view to appropriate action.[22] In the event, Jordan chose the course of continuing to trade with Iraq in violation of Resolution 661[23] (*infra*, C, (b), i). The Council dealt with Article 50 situations both before the Gulf War (in response to an application by Mozambique after sanctions had been imposed on Southern Rhodesia (Resolution 386 (1976))[24] and subsequently (in the context of the air embargo imposed on Libya in Resolution 748 (1992),[25] as well as on other occasions[26]).

Conceptually, Article 41 may be viewed as an outgrowth of the Covenant of the League of Nations. However, the framers of the Charter were not content with non-forcible sanctions. A far-reaching leap forward was made in Article 42:

Should the Security Council consider that measures provided for in Article 41 would be inadequate or have proved to be inadequate, it may take such action by air, sea, or land forces as may be necessary to maintain or restore international peace or security. Such action may include demonstrations, blockade, and other operations by air, sea, or land forces of Members of the United Nations.[27]

In brief, under Article 42, the Council may exert force, either on a limited or on a comprehensive scale.

Article 40 warrants recourse by the Security Council to provisional measures, without prejudice to the positions of the parties, before final decisions or recommendations are adopted.[28] The original object of this clause was to ensure that a threat to the peace does not become an actual breach.[29] In the practice of the Council, it is principally utilized – after

[20] See V. P. Nanda, 'The Iraqi Invasion of Kuwait: The U.N. Response', 15 *SIULJ* 431, 443 (1990–1).
[21] Ultimately, no less than twenty-one States from all over the world (including Jordan) applied for assistance under Article 50. See P. Conlon, 'Lessons from Iraq: The Functions of the Iraq Sanctions Committee as a Source of Sanctions Implementation Authority and Practice', 35 *VJIL* 633, 654 n. 94 (1994–5).
[22] Security Council Resolution 669, 45 *RDSC* 24, *id.* (1990).
[23] US Department of Defense Report to Congress on the Conduct of the Persian Gulf War, 1992, 31 *ILM* 612, 638–9 (1992).
[24] Security Council Resolution 386, 31 *RDSC* 7, *id.* (1976).
[25] Security Council Resolution 748, 47 *RDSC* 52, *id.* (1992).
[26] See R. Kolb, *Ius Contra Bellum: Le Droit International Relatif au Maintien de la Paix* 153 (2003).
[27] Charter of the United Nations, *supra* note 9, at 343–4.
[28] *Ibid.*, 343.   [29] See Goodrich, Hambro and Simons, *supra* note 19, at 303–4.

hostilities have broken out – to bring about a cease-fire (*see supra*, Chapter 2, C, (a), iii)), to mandate a withdrawal of troops from a disputed area, etc.[30]

(d)   The discretion of the Security Council

The scope of the discretion granted to the Security Council, in discharging its duties within the ambit of the Charter of the United Nations, is very wide. A comparison between Article 39 and Article 51 of the Charter[31] highlights the Council's freedom of action. As per Article 51 (quoted *supra*, Chapter 7, A, (a)), individual or collective self-defence is allowed only in response to an armed attack. Conversely, in keeping with Article 39, collective security can be brought into action whenever the Security Council determines that there exists a threat to the peace, a breach of the peace or an act of aggression. An unambiguous bifurcation ensues in respect of lawful use of inter-State force consonant with the Charter. On the one hand, every State or group of States is entitled to resort to force in international relations, although only in the exceptional circumstances of self-defence in response to an armed attack and subject to ultimate review by the Council (see *supra*, Chapters 7–9). On the other hand, the Council is empowered to employ force in the name of collective security, and the degree of latitude bestowed upon it by the Charter is well-nigh unlimited. The Council may wield force to counter any type of aggression, not necessarily amounting to an armed attack,[32] and it may even respond to a mere threat to the peace.

Since the Charter seems to give the Security Council a *carte blanche* in exercising its authority in pursuit of collective security, the Council is not just free to decide whether and how to use force, but it is also at liberty to determine when to do so and against whom. Patently, the Council may initiate a preventive war in anticipation of a future breach of the peace (figuring only as a threat to the peace at the time of action), a privilege that the Charter withholds from any individual State or group of States acting alone (see *supra*, Chapter 7, B, (a)). The Council's entitlement to act preventively is derived not only from Chapter VII of the Charter but also

---

[30] See J. A. Frowein and N. Krisch, 'Article 40', *The Charter of the United Nations: A Commentary*, I, 729, 733 (B. Simma ed., 2nd ed., 2002).

[31] Charter of the United Nations, *supra* note 9, at 346.

[32] It has been argued, in the context of the consensus Definition of Aggression, that 'it would presumably be absurd to suggest that any act that (according to the definition) the Security Council might properly find to qualify as an "aggression" might not give rise at least to the right of self-defense'. J. L. Hargrove, 'The *Nicaragua* Judgment and the Future of the Law of Force and Self-Defense', 81 *AJIL* 135, 139 n. 15 (1987). But there is no absurdity in an act of aggression failing to qualify as an armed attack.

from Article 1(1) – quoted *supra*, Chapter 4, B, (a) – which, in listing the Purposes of the United Nations, refers explicitly to the taking of 'effective collective measures for the prevention and removal of threats to the peace'.[33]

Nowhere is the Security Council under less strictures than in its determination that a threat to the peace exists. A 'threat to the peace' (adverted to in Article 39) is not to be confused with a 'threat ... of force', mentioned in Article 2(4)[34] (see *supra*, Chapter 4, B, (a)).[35] Evidently, a threat of force by one State against another may be considered by the Council a threat to the peace. But the expression 'threat to the peace' is elastic enough to stretch away from a contemplated use of force and beyond inter-State relations.[36] A determination of a threat to the peace is not contingent on any (past, present or future) use of force. Nor is it linked even to any breach of international law.[37] 'It is completely within the discretion of the Security Council to decide what constitutes a "threat to the peace".'[38] The Council is free to deal with 'remote threats':[39] it can go as far 'upstream' as it desires in identifying a threat to the peace. Indeed, a threat to the peace is not necessarily a state of facts: it can be merely a state of mind; and the mind that counts is that of the Council. It may opt to stigmatize as a threat to the peace a situation that does not appear to anyone else as disturbing the equilibrium of international security. In other words, 'a threat to the peace in the sense of Article 39 seems to be whatever the Security Council says is a threat to the peace'.[40]

It is true that some scholars adhere in theory to the view that the discretion of the Council to determine the existence of a threat to the peace is not unlimited.[41] But what, then, is the legal source of the limitation? In the *Tadic* case of 1995, the Appeals Chamber of the International Criminal Tribunal for the Former Yugoslavia (ICTY) opined that 'the determination that there exists such a threat is not a totally unfettered discretion, as it has to remain, at the very least, within the limits of the Purposes and Principles of the Charter'.[42] This dictum is not particularly helpful. One can, of course, disagree on the facts with the Council's determination of the existence of a threat to the peace. Yet, it is well-nigh

---

[33] Charter of the United Nations, *supra* note 9, at 331.   [34] *Ibid.*, 332.

[35] See H. Kelsen, *The Law of the United Nations: A Critical Analysis of Its Fundamental Problems* 727 (1951).

[36] See B. Conforti, *The Law and Practice of the United Nations* 173 (2nd ed., 2000).

[37] See Kolb, *supra* note 26, at 68.   [38] See Kelsen, *supra* note 35, at 727.

[39] A. Garwood-Gowers, 'Pre-Emptive Self-Defence: A Necessary Development or the Road to International Anarchy', 23 *AYBIL* 51, 63 (2002).

[40] M. Akehurst, *Modern Introduction to International Law* (P. Malanczuk ed., 7th ed., 1997).

[41] See E. de Wet, *The Chapter VII Powers of the United Nations Security Council* 134–44 (2004).

[42] *Prosecutor v. Tadic*, Judgment, ICTY Case No. IT-94-1-AR72 (Jurisdiction), Appeals Chamber, 1995, 35 *ILM* 35, 43 (1996).

impossible to conjure up circumstances in which that determination *per se* may conceivably be regarded as invalid on the ground of a head-on collision with the Purposes and Principles of the Charter. Even those wishing to limit the Council's wide discretion usually concede that the Purposes and Principles of the Charter can play a restrictive role only as regards concrete measures taken by the Council subsequent to such a determination.[43]

It is important to remember that the Security Council is a political and not a judicial organ (see *supra*, 7, D, (b)). It is composed of Member States, and its decisions are (and have every right to be) linked to political motivations that are not necessarily congruent with legal considerations. As a non-judicial body, the Council is not required to set out reasons for its decisions.[44] Yet, a determination by the Council that a threat to the peace exists is conclusive. All Member States must accept the Council's verdict, despite any misgivings that they may entertain concerning the merits of the case.

On 12 September 2001, in Resolution 1368, the Security Council unequivocally condemned the horrifying terrorist attacks of the previous day (9/11), regarding 'such acts, like any act of international terrorism, as a threat to international peace and security'.[45] Before the end of the month, the Council reaffirmed that statement in Resolution 1373, acting under Chapter VII.[46] Resolution 1377, adopted by a special meeting of the Council on a Ministerial level in November, declared that 'acts of international terrorism constitute one of the most serious threats to international peace and security in the twenty-first century'.[47] The general proposition introduced in Resolution 1368 has subsequently been reiterated in the context of specific terrorist attacks: in Bali (Resolution 1438 (2002));[48] Moscow (Resolution 1440 (2002));[49] Kenya (Resolution 1450 (2002));[50] and Bogotá (Resolution 1465 (2003)).[51]

Resolutions 1368 and 1373 also recognized the right of self-defence which presupposes an armed attack[52] (see *supra*, Chapter 7, B, (b), (bb)). Obviously, a threat to the peace is a much broader concept than an armed

---

[43] See de Wet, *supra* note 41, at 191–215.
[44] See J. E. S. Fawcett, 'Security Council Resolutions on Rhodesia', 41 *BYBIL* 103, 116–17 (1965–6).
[45] Security Council Resolution 1368 (2001), [2001–2] *RDSC* 290, 291.
[46] Security Council Resolution 1373 (2001), [2001–2] *RDSC* 291, 291–2.
[47] Security Council Resolution 1377 (2001), [2001–2] *RDSC* 294, *id.*
[48] Security Council Resolution 1438 (2002), [2002–3] *RDSC* 69, *id.*
[49] Security Council Resolution 1440 (2002), [2002–3] *RDSC* 70, *id.*
[50] Security Council Resolution 1450 (2002), [2002–3] *RDSC* 70, 71.
[51] Security Council Resolution 1465 (2003), [2002–3] *RDSC* 75, *id.*
[52] Security Council Resolutions 1368 and 1373, *supra* notes 45–6, at 291.

attack, inasmuch as the former is not conditioned on any use of force. Still, it must be stressed that 'the categories of threat to the peace and armed attack are not mutually exclusive'.[53] When the same situation can be characterized both as an armed attack and a threat to the peace, the difference between the two categories relates to the consequences ensuing therefrom. Whereas any State or group of States can forcibly respond to an armed attack by invoking the right of individual or collective self-defence, only the Security Council can put in motion measures of collective security that (in the Council's judgement) are called for in the face of a threat to the peace.

The two different lines of action may be followed simultaneously. Thus, irrespective of measures of self-defence exercised by the US (and its allies) in response to the armed attack of 9/11 (see *supra*, Chapter 7, B, (b), (bb)), the Security Council – in Resolution 1373 – decided in a binding fashion on a series of steps that States must take to prevent the financing of terrorist acts, suppress recruitment to terrorist groups, eliminate supply of weapons to terrorists, etc.[54] The Council was fully aware of the fact that all the latter measures, 'useful as they might be', would not suffice 'to deal decisively with the threat to international peace and security posed by Al Qaeda and its Taliban defenders'.[55] Only the use of counter-force, in the exercise of individual and collective self-defence, could root out Al-Qaeda from Afghanistan. Of course, the Security Council is free to deem the collective security measures that it has decided to take as adequate under the circumstances. In that case, it can always insist (in a binding decision) on the suspension of hostilities carried out by States in self-defence. But, as long as no clear-cut cease-fire resolution is adopted by the Security Council, the two sets of counter-measures (self-defence and collective security) may proceed independently of each other.

Resolutions 1368 and 1373 refer to any act of international terrorism as a threat to international peace and security. It should be added, therefore, that the Security Council is free to determine that even an act of domestic terrorism constitutes a threat to international peace. On several occasions, an internal situation (within the boundaries of a single State) was deemed by the Council a threat to international peace and security.[56] The Security Council can deem a non-international armed conflict a threat to

---

[53] C. Greenwood, 'International Law and the "War against Terrorism"', 78 *Int.Aff.* 301, 307 (2002).

[54] Security Council Resolution 1373, *supra* note 46, at 292–3.

[55] T. M. Franck, 'Terrorism and the Right of Self-Defense', 95 *AJIL* 839, 841 (2001).

[56] See F. L. Kirgis, Jr., 'The Security Council's First Fifty Years', 89 *AJIL* 506, 513–14 (1995).

the peace, and it 'is free to take measures against any entity which it considers to be an obstructive factor in the restoration of peace'.[57] Thus, in Resolution 1127 (1997), the Council – having determined that the situation in Angola constituted 'a threat to international peace and security in the region', and acting under Chapter VII – imposed sanctions on UNITA (Union for the Total Independence of Angola), a non-State entity.[58]

In Resolution 1540 (2004), the Security Council affirmed that proliferation of nuclear, chemical and biological weapons – as well as their means of delivery – constitutes 'a threat to international peace and security'.[59]

A threat to the peace may be determined by the Security Council even in the face of mere violations of human rights not entailing the use of force.[60] It is a debatable – but moot – point whether the Council is necessarily animated by concern about trans-boundary spill-over effects on neighbouring countries, for instance through the flow of refugees.[61] The undeniable fact is that the Council is sometimes willing to determine the existence of a threat to the peace, and take action accordingly, in the face of events that are occurring internally.

The paradigmatic case is the overthrow by a military junta of the legitimate Government of Haiti in 1993. In Resolution 841 (1993), the Security Council determined that, in these 'unique and exceptional circumstances', the continuation of the situation 'threatens international peace and security in the region'.[62] In Resolution 940 (1994), the Council authorized Member States to form a multinational force under unified command and control, using 'all necessary means' to bring about the removal of the military junta and the restoration of the legitimate Government in Haiti.[63] A multinational force, led by the United States, soon accomplished this task without bloodshed.[64] But the resolution was 'unprecedented in authorizing force to remove one regime and install

---

[57] P. H. Kooijmans, 'The Security Council and Non-State Entities as Parties to Conflicts', *International Law: Theory and Practice (Essays in Honour of Eric Suy)* 333, 339 (K. Wellens ed., 1998).

[58] Security Council Resolution 1127, 52 *RDSC* 50, 50–1 (1997).

[59] Security Council Resolution 1540, 43 *ILM* 1237, *id.* (2004).

[60] T. D. Gill, 'Legal and Some Political Limitations on the Power of the UN Security Council to Exercise Its Enforcement Powers under Chapter VII of the Charter', 26 *NYIL* 33, 42–3 (1995).

[61] See M. Toufayan, 'Deployment of Troops to Prevent Impending Genocide: A Contemporary Assessment of the UN Security Council's Powers', 40 *CYIL* 195, 229–41 (2002).

[62] Security Council Resolution 841, 48 *RDSC* 119, *id.* (1993).

[63] Security Council Resolution 940, 49 *RDSC* 51, *id.* (1994).

[64] See 48 *Yearbook of the United Nations* 427 (1994).

another (however democratically elected) within a Member State'.[65] It is noteworthy that Article 2(7) of the Charter, in precluding intervention by the United Nations 'in matters which are essentially within the domestic jurisdiction of any state', expressly adds a reservation that 'this principle shall not prejudice the application of enforcement measures under Chapter VII'.[66] The broad powers conferred on the Council in the province of collective security override, where necessary, the sovereignty of any UN Member State.

Once the Security Council determines that a threat to the peace exists, that determination remains valid irrespective of the passage of time or even radical changes in the factual situation: the threat to the peace continues to exist until the Council expressly decides otherwise.[67]

Attempts are occasionally made to demarcate an unblurred line between the categories of a breach of the peace and aggression.[68] But the Charter (or, for that matter, the practice of the Security Council) does not provide any clear guidance in distinguishing between the two expressions. In pragmatic terms, as long as the authority of the Council to act in a given context is unassailable under the Charter, it is of little weight whether one stamp or the other is affixed to the measures taken.

Just as the Security Council may take action against a threat to the peace that is imperceptible to the public eye, it may also decline to acknowledge the existence of a manifest threat to the peace. Indeed, by the time that the Council formally discerns a threat to the peace, the state of affairs may have deteriorated past the mark of mere threats. This is what happened in May 2000, when – following a resumption of hostilities that had been raging between Eritrea and Ethiopia – the Council formally determined that the situation constituted 'a threat to regional peace and security'.[69] By the same token, in mid-July 1948, two months after an inter-State war had been in progress in the area, the Council determined that the situation in Palestine constituted 'a threat to the peace within the

---

[65] D. Malone, *Decision-Making in the UN Security Council: The Case of Haiti, 1990–1997* 110 (1998).
[66] Charter of the United Nations, *supra* note 9, at 332.
[67] See K.Wellens, 'The UN Security Council and New Threats to the Peace: Back to the Future', 8 *JCSL* 15, 27 (2003).
[68] See G. Cohen Jonathan, 'Article 39', *La Charte des Nations Unies* 645, 657–9 (J.-P.Cot and A. Pellet eds., 1985).
[69] Security Council Resolution 1298, 55 *RDSC* 146, 147 (2000). This resolution cited Chapter VII of the Charter. Already in February 1999, the Council – without citing Chapter VII – 'stressed' (but did not formally determine) that the situation constituted 'a threat to peace and security'. Security Council Resolution 1227, 54 *RDSC* 65, 66 (1999).

meaning of Article 39'.[70] Factually, the resolution seemed unsynchronized with what was happening in the conflict region.[71] Legally, the Council was fully competent to make the specific determination as and when it deemed appropriate.

B.   The decision-making process

(a)   The duties incumbent on UN Member States

As noted (*supra*, A, (c)), it is the function of the Security Council, in conformity with Article 39 of the Charter, to decide or recommend what measures are to be taken in order to maintain or restore international peace and security. Decisions, unlike recommendations, are binding on all Member States. Under Article 25 of the Charter:

The Members of the United Nations agree to accept and carry out the decisions of the Security Council in accordance with the present Charter.[72]

It is not altogether free of doubt which decisions are covered by Article 25. But indisputably, decisions adopted by the Council under the aegis of Chapter VII, aimed at maintaining or restoring the peace, are legally binding.

In its 1971 Advisory Opinion on *Namibia*, the International Court of Justice held that Article 25 does not apply solely to Security Council decisions under Chapter VII.[73] However, there was no question about the mandatory nature of the Council's decisions under Chapter VII. The Court pronounced that the binding effect of such decisions is vouchsafed not only by the general stipulation of Article 25, but also by the specific terms of Articles 48 and 49.[74]

Article 48 sets forth:

1. The action required to carry out the decisions of the Security Council for the maintenance of international peace and security shall be taken by all the Members of the United Nations or by some of them, as the Security Council may determine.

---

[70] Security Council Resolution 54, 3 *RDSC* 22, *id.* (1948).
[71] For the 'discrepancy between the nature of events in Palestine and the response of the Security Council', see I. S. Pogany, *The Security Council and the Arab-Israeli Conflict* 27–44 (1984).
[72] Charter of the United Nations, *supra* note 9, at 339.
[73] Advisory Opinion on *Legal Consequences for States of the Continued Presence of South Africa in Namibia (South West Africa) notwithstanding Security Council Resolution 276 (1970)*, [1971] *ICJ Rep.* 16, 52–3.
[74] *Ibid.*, 53.

2. Such decisions shall be carried out by the Members of the United Nations directly and through their action in the appropriate international agencies of which they are members.[75]

Article 49 enjoins all Member States to afford mutual assistance in carrying out the measures decided upon by the Council.[76]

The importance of Article 48 lies first in its specific context: decisions adopted by the Security Council under Chapter VII for the maintenance of international peace and security. Secondly, Article 48 clarifies that the Council may lay the burden of implementing its decisions on a few of the Member States (presumably, those better equipped to do so), or it may apportion different assignments to all Members. Thirdly, Article 48 allows the Council's decisions to be carried out through regional organizations. However, it must be emphasized that Article 48 deals only with decisions of the Council which ordain States to take action: it does not apply to 'permissive action' not prescribed in a mandatory fashion by the Council.[77]

Permissive action, animated by a mere recommendation adopted by the Security Council, is anchored in Article 39 and not in Article 48. No Member State is required to take part in any enforcement operation in the absence of a binding decision to that effect by the Council. Nevertheless, should Member States (acting jointly or severally) voluntarily carry out enforcement action in response to a non-obligatory call issued by the Council, these measures would be fully legitimized by the Council's binding determination that there exists a threat to the peace, a breach of the peace or an act of aggression (see *supra*, A, (c)).

(b)   The responsibility of the Security Council

Chapter VII obligations devolve not only on Member States, but also on the Security Council itself. After all, the Council is charged by the Charter with the primary responsibility for the maintenance of international peace and security (see *supra*, A, (c)). Article 39 employs the mandatory expression 'shall' to describe the Council's task in the field of collective security: the Council 'shall' determine the existence of a threat to the peace, a breach of the peace or an act of aggression, and 'shall' either make recommendations or decide what is to be done in order to maintain or restore international peace and security.

---

[75] Charter of the United Nations, *supra* note 9, at 345–6.   [76] *Ibid.*, 346.

[77] See O. Schachter, 'Legal Aspects of the Gulf War of 1991 and Its Aftermath', *Law, Policy, and International Justice (Essays in Honour of Maxwell Cohen)* 5, 20 (W. Kaplan and D. McRae eds., 1993).

Any action taken by the Security Council is contingent on the adoption of an enabling resolution. Under Article 27, as amended, resolutions of the Council can only be carried by an affirmative vote of at least nine of its fifteen Members.[78] Moreover, a resolution must obtain the concurring votes of the five Permanent Members of the Council. This is the celebrated veto power: even should fourteen of the fifteen Members of the Council support a draft resolution, a lone dissenter – if it is one of the Permanent Members (China, France, Russia,[79] the United Kingdom and the United States) – would prevent adoption of the proposed text by casting a negative vote.

Article 27 has been construed in the Security Council's proceedings in such a way that only a negative vote by a Permanent Member signifies that it does not concur with a resolution, thus constituting a veto (which defeats the motion), whereas an abstention (or non-participation in a vote) does not count.[80] When the generally accepted interpretation of Article 27 was challenged, in the *Namibia* proceedings, the International Court of Justice endorsed the consistent and uniform practice of the Council.[81] Abstention (or non-participation in a vote) by one or more Permanent Members is a common phenomenon, registered in approximately a quarter of the resolutions adopted by the Council.[82]

Article 27 lays down that, in certain matters, a party to a dispute must abstain from voting in the Security Council. But the obligation does not apply to decisions under Chapter VII. Hence, a Permanent Member may cast the veto, in a vote on the application of Chapter VII measures, notwithstanding the fact that it is a party to the dispute. That is to say, a Permanent Member may always bar the adoption of any resolution putting into effect the scheme of Chapter VII, if the action decided upon (or recommended) is pointed at itself (or at a State with which it is closely

---

[78] Charter of the United Nations, *supra* note 9, at 340. The numbers involved were amended as of 1965. Protocol of Entry into Force of the Amendments to Articles 23, 27 and 61 of the Charter of the United Nations, [1965] *UNJY* 159, 160.

[79] The five Permanent Members are listed in Article 23(1) of the Charter (Charter of the United Nations, *supra* note 9, at 338), which refers to the Union of Soviet Socialist Republics. Following the collapse of the USSR, its permanent membership in the Security Council – and its membership in other organs of the United Nations – is continued by the Russian Federation. On the manner in which this change was brought about, see B. Fassbender, *UN Security Council Reform and the Right of Veto: A Constitutional Perspective* 183–9 (1998).

[80] See C. A. Stavropoulos, 'The Practice of Voluntary Abstentions by Permanent Members of the Security Council under Article 27, Paragraph 3, of the Charter of the United Nations', 61 *AJIL* 737, 742–4 (1967).

[81] Advisory Opinion on *Namibia*, *supra* note 73, at 22.

[82] For a list of 319 such instances – out of 1,322 resolutions – see T. M. Franck, *Recourse to Force: State Action against Threats and Armed Attacks* 8 n.16 (2002).

associated). In realistic terms, there is more than an element of truth in the cynical observation that the collective security system of the Charter is only geared to handle 'minor disturbers of the peace'.[83] Armed conflicts (whether international or internal) – in which Permanent Members are directly or indirectly involved – are, to most intents and purposes, practically excluded from the reach of the Charter's system of collective security.

C.   An overview of the Security Council's record

(a)   The 'Cold War' era

The record of the Security Council over a period of forty-five years, from the inception of the United Nations to the outbreak of the Gulf War, was disappointing in the extreme. That record is replete with cases in which, notwithstanding the outbreak of hostilities, the Council was deadlocked – due to the political cleavages splitting the five Permanent Members – and unable to take a common stand. The Council was primarily hampered by the use and abuse of the veto power, for which there were abundant illustrations.[84]

During the entire time span of the 'Cold War', the Security Council expressly determined that a breach of the peace existed on just three occasions: in the Korean War (Resolution 82 (1950)),[85] the Falkland Islands War (Resolution 502 (1982)),[86] and the Iran–Iraq War (Resolution 598 (1987)).[87] Relatively speaking, the Council took the strongest action in the Korean War (in the temporary absence of the Soviet delegation owing to a badly timed boycott). Even there, as observed (*supra*, Chapter 6, B), the Council merely recommended to Member States to render assistance to the Republic of Korea in order to repel the North Korean armed attack,[88] and permitted the use of the

---

[83] I. L. Claude, 'The United Nations and the Use of Force', 532 *Int.Con.* 323, 330 (1961).
[84] By 2004, the veto was cast in the Security Council on more than 250 occasions (in some instances, more than one Permanent Member wielded its power to prevent the adoption of a resolution). The veto was used much more frequently prior to the Gulf War. See S. D. Bailey and S. Daws, *The Procedure of the UN Security Council* 230–7 (3rd ed., 1998). The figures do not tell the whole story for two countervailing reasons: (a) in many instances, the veto has had nothing to do with collective security; however, (b) in a host of cases affecting peace and security, the mere threat of a veto has had a chilling effect, so that the Council did not proceed to a formal vote.
[85] Security Council Resolution 82, 5 *RDSC* 4, *id.* (1950).
[86] Security Council Resolution 502, 37 *RDSC* 15, *id.* (1982).
[87] Security Council Resolution 598, 42 *RDSC* 5, 6 (1987).
[88] Security Council Resolution 83, 5 *RDSC* 5, *id.* (1950).

UN flag by the Coalition that volunteered to do so under American command.[89] In the Falkland Islands War, the Council did not specify who had committed the armed attack: the resolution only determined that 'there exists a breach of the peace in the region of the Falkland Islands (Islas Malvinas)', and confined itself to anodyne demands for immediate cessation of hostilities and withdrawal of Argentine forces from the Islands.[90] In the political atmosphere prevalent at the time, enforcement measures involving military action could not be seriously contemplated by the Council.[91] In the Iran–Iraq War, after seven years of hostilities, the Council determined that 'there exists a breach of the peace as regards the conflict between Iran and Iraq' and (acting under Articles 39 and 40) demanded an immediate cease-fire.[92]

Additionally, in 1984, the Security Council also condemned armed attacks by South Africa against Angola, reaffirmed Angola's right to defend itself under Article 51 and requested Member States to extend assistance to the victim country.[93] Had that resolution become the catalyst for another international coalition, the ensuing use of force would have amounted once again to collective self-defence exercised with the *imprimatur* of the Council. In actuality, the resolution remained virtually unheeded.

In three situations, the Security Council formally determined the existence of a threat to the peace: during Israel's War of Independence, citing both Articles 39 and 40 (Resolution 54 (1948));[94] as regards the situation in Southern Rhodesia (Resolution 232 (1966));[95] and with respect to the acquisition of arms by South Africa (Resolution 418 (1977)).[96]

On several additional occasions, the Security Council employed the phrase 'threat to the peace' in an informal manner. For example, in Resolution 353 (1974) relating to Cyprus, the Council stated that it was '[g]ravely concerned about the situation which has led to a serious threat to international peace'.[97] Similar language had been used in Resolution 161 (1961) in reference to the situation in Congo.[98] Trying another tack, the Council – in Resolution 405 (1977) – strongly

---

[89] Security Council Resolution 84, 5 *RDSC* 5, 6 (1950).
[90] Security Council Resolution 502, *supra* note 86, at 15.
[91] See A. C. Arend, 'The Falklands War and the Failure of the International Legal Order', *The Falklands War* 52, 54–5 (A. R. Coll and A. C. Arend eds., 1985).
[92] Security Council Resolution 598, *supra* note 87, at 6.
[93] Security Council Resolution 546, 39 *RDSC* 1, 1–2 (1984).
[94] Security Council Resolution 54, *supra* note 70, at 22.
[95] Security Council Resolution 232, 21 *RDSC* 7, *id.* (1966).
[96] Security Council Resolution 418, 32 *RDSC* 5, *id.* (1977).
[97] Security Council Resolution 353, 29 *RDSC* 7, *id.* (1974).
[98] Security Council Resolution 161, 16 *RDSC* 2, 2–3 (1961).

condemned 'as an act of armed aggression' mercenary attacks from out-side Benin against the airport and city of Cotonou.[99] However, absent a formal determination under Chapter VII of the existence of a threat to the peace or an act of aggression, any allusion by the Council to such an event can be dismissed as a non-binding locution.

In two cases, the Security Council also imposed mandatory sanctions: a trade embargo on Southern Rhodesia, referring to Articles 39 and 41 (Resolution 232 (1966));[100] and an arms embargo on South Africa, acting under Chapter VII in general (Resolution 418 (1977)).[101]

(b)   The Gulf War

The Gulf War started in 1990 and is still not over in 2004. It is a mistake to regard the major hostilities against Iraq that occurred in 2003 as an armed conflict independent of the invasion of Kuwait in 1990. Yet, the different phases of the single Gulf War deserve a discrete analysis.

i.   The invasion and liberation of Kuwait (1990–1) The invasion of Kuwait by Iraq in August 1990 was a turning point in the history of the Security Council, since it signified the end of the 'Cold War' (even prior to the collapse of the Soviet Union). A unanimity among the five Permanent Members in 1990/1 (or, at certain points, at least a readiness to allow the majority to proceed with appropriate measures) enabled the adoption of a whole string of resolutions under Chapter VII for effective action against Iraq. Several of these resolutions call for an examination in detail, as they vividly show how the Council gradually flexed its muscles while recoiling from the application of Article 42.

First came Resolution 660 of 2 August 1990 (the very day of the invasion of Kuwait), in which the Security Council determined the exis-tence of 'a breach of international peace and security', and – acting specifically under Articles 39 and 40 of the Charter – condemned the invasion, demanding immediate and unconditional withdrawal of the Iraqi forces.[102] A few days later, the Council adopted Resolution 661, which – citing Chapter VII – imposed on Iraq mandatory economic sanctions: the Council decided in particular that all States must prevent any imports or exports from or to Iraq or occupied Kuwait (except for

[99] Security Council Resolution 405, 32 *RDSC* 18, *id.* (1977).
[100] Security Council Resolution 232, *supra* note 95, at 7–8.
[101] Security Council Resolution 418, *supra* note 96, at 5.
[102] Security Council Resolution 660, 45 *RDSC* 19, *id.* (1990).

medications and, in humanitarian circumstances, foodstuffs), as well as any other type of trade, supply or transfer of funds.[103]

In Resolution 665, the Security Council recorded that Resolution 661 had imposed 'economic sanctions under Chapter VII of the Charter of the United Nations'.[104] It called upon the 'Member States co-operating with the Government [in exile] of Kuwait' (which were deploying maritime forces in the area) to use such measures 'as may be necessary under the authority of the Security Council to halt for inspection purposes all inward and outward maritime shipping', in order 'to ensure strict implementation' of Resolution 661.[105] In practical terms, Iraq was subjected in consequence to a blockade, although Resolution 665 avoided that expression.[106]

While the mandatory economic sanctions imposed on Iraq in Resolution 661 were plainly predicated on Article 41, the blockade went beyond the scope of that clause. As noted (*supra*, A, (c)), the expression 'blockade' appears in the Charter in Article 42 (military sanctions) rather than in Article 41 (economic sanctions). Did the Security Council introduce and apply 'Article 41 and a half'?[107] The maritime operations intercepting imports and exports to and from Iraq were conducted by the United States, the United Kingdom and other naval Powers cooperating with Kuwait on the basis of the right of collective self-defence pursuant to Article 51.[108] Resolution 661, which Resolution 665 was designed to implement, makes an all-inclusive reference to Chapter VII. It ought to be recalled that Article 51 (just like Articles 41 and 42) figures in that chapter.

The Security Council acted again under Chapter VII in Resolution 670, deciding that – irrespective of any rights or obligations conferred or imposed by any international agreement,[109] contract or licence – all States must deny permission to any aircraft to take off from or overfly their territories when destined to land in Iraq or occupied Kuwait (unless authorized by a Sanctions Committee).[110] The Council further called

---

[103] Security Council Resolution 661, 45 *RDSC* 19, 19–20 (1990).
[104] Security Council Resolution 665, 45 *RDSC* 21, *id.* (1990).   [105] *Ibid.*, 21–2.
[106] On the similarities and dissimilarities to blockade, see H. B. Robertson, 'Specific Means and Methods of Application of Force', 1 *DJCIL* 1, 11 (1991).
[107] The phrase was coined, in the general context of the Council's activities in the Gulf War, by P. Weckel, 'Le Chapitre VII de la Charte et son Application par le Conseil de Sécurité', 37 *AFDI* 165, 202 (1991).
[108] See C. Greenwood, 'New World Order or Old? The Invasion of Kuwait and the Rule of Law', 55 *Mod.LR* 153, 161 (1992).
[109] The Council expressly recalled in this context the provision of Article 103 of the Charter (*Cf. supra*, Chapter 9, C, (a)). Security Council Resolution 670, 45 *RDSC* 24, 25 (1990).
[110] *Ibid.*

upon all States to detain any ships of Iraqi registry which entered their ports in violation of Resolution 661, and threatened to consider measures in case of evasion of either resolution.[111]

Chapter VII was invoked by the Security Council in Resolution 678, authorizing the 'Member States co-operating with the Government of Kuwait' – after a prescribed space of time – 'to use all necessary means to uphold and implement resolution 660 (1990) and all subsequent relevant resolutions and to restore international peace and security in the area'.[112] As indicated (*supra*, Chapter 9, E), this landmark resolution constituted a specific mandate for the exercise of collective self-defence under Article 51 by a coalition of the willing.[113] Claims that the resolution was based on Article 42[114] are totally unwarranted.[115]

Both before and after the Iraqi military defeat at the hands of the Coalition, the Security Council also alluded to Chapter VII in multiple additional texts, the most important of which is Resolution 687,[116] dictating the definitive terms of a cease-fire that Iraq reluctantly accepted. As pointed out (*supra*, Chapter 2, C, (a), iii), this text – albeit unprecedented in many respects[117] – was merely a scheme for a cease-fire. It has to be appreciated that, although the conditions of the cease-fire were delineated by Resolution 687, the ensuing cease-fire constituted an agreement between the Coalition – rather than the United Nations (which remained above the fray) – and Iraq.

ii.   *The cease-fire period (1991–2003)* The cease-fire in Iraq went on for a dozen years, but it failed to spawn peace. Instead of moving towards a peaceful settlement, the Coalition and Iraq were constantly at logger-heads, inasmuch as Iraq – from the very onset of the cease-fire – was unwilling to comply with its agreed terms, especially as regards disarmament. Quite frequently between 1991 and 2003 (in particular, in 1998/9), Coalition warplanes raided Iraqi targets striving unsuccessfully to compel Iraq to abide by the cease-fire conditions and especially to cooperate with UN disarmament inspectors.[118] The sundry air strikes by the Coalition

---

[111] *Ibid.*   [112] Security Council Resolution 678, 45 *RDSC* 27, 27–8 (1990).
[113] See O. Schachter, 'United Nations Law in the Gulf Conflict', 85 *AJIL* 452, 459–60 (1991).
[114] See C. Warbrick, 'The invasion of Kuwait by Iraq – Part II', 40 *ICLQ* 965, 966 (1991).
[115] See P.-M. Dupuy, 'Après la Guerre du Golfe', 95 *RGDIP* 621, 624–5 (1991).
[116] Security Council Resolution 687, 46 *RDSC* 11, 12 (1991).
[117] On the meaning and significance of the resolution, see S. Sur, 'La Résolution 687 (3 Avril 1991) du Conseil de Sécurité dans l'Affaire du Golfe: Problèmes de Rétablissement et de Garantie de la Paix', 37 *AFDI* 25–97 (1991).
[118] For an overview of the sporadic hostilities between the Coalition and Iraq, from 1992 to 2002, see A. E. Wall, 'The Legal Case for Invading Iraq and Toppling Hussein', 32 *IYHR* 165, 183–7 (2002).

must be construed as a resumption of combat operations in the face of
Iraqi violations of the cease-fire terms.[119]

Already under Resolution 688, adopted within in a few days of the
onset of the cease-fire, the Security Council (without naming Chapter
VII) held that the Iraqi repression of the civilian population (preeminently, the Kurds) 'threaten international peace and security in the
region', and insisted that Iraq 'allow immediate access by international
humanitarian organizations to all those in need of assistance in all parts of
Iraq and to make available all necessary facilities for their operation'.[120]
As a result, with the military help of armed forces of the United States and
other Coalition countries, 'access' to humanitarian aid was achieved
through the creation of an air exclusion ('no-fly') zone securing a
Kurdish enclave in the north of Iraq. In 1992, another 'no-fly' zone was
established over the Shiite areas in the south of the country. In the next
decade, many air strikes were launched by Coalition warplanes against
Iraq in response to Iraqi defiance of the 'no-fly' zones.[121]

iii.   The occupation of Iraq (2003) The state of war between Iraq and
the Coalition continued notwithstanding the suspension of general hostilities in 1991. When the friction between Iraq and the Coalition culminated in the resumption of general hostilities in 2003, events were
examined by numerous commentators against the backdrop of a doctrine
of 'preemption' set out by President G. W. Bush[122] (see *supra*, Chapter 7,
B, (a)). But references to preemption by the Bush Administration were
only part of the US argument for resort to force, and they can possibly be
looked at as not much more than 'rhetorical flourish'.[123] As conceded by
the Legal Adviser of the Department of State:

> Was Operation Iraqi Freedom an example of preemptive use of force? Viewed as
> the final episode in a conflict initiated more than a dozen years earlier by Iraq's
> invasion of Kuwait, it may not seem so.[124]

There is absolutely nothing preemptive about the resumption of hostilities when a cease-fire disintegrates. The leading partner of the US in the
Coalition against Iraq – the United Kingdom – formally took the position

---

[119] See R. Wedgwood, 'The Enforcement of Security Council Resolution 687: The Threat
of Force against Iraq's Weapons of Mass Destruction', 92 *AJIL* 724, 726(1998).
[120] Security Council Resolution 688, 46 *RDSC* 31, 32 (1991).
[121] See Wall, *supra* note 118, at 184–7.
[122] See C. Henderson, 'The Bush Doctrine: From Theory to Practice', 9 *JCSL* 3, 8–13
(2004).
[123] D. Kritsiotis, 'Arguments of Mass Confusion', 15 *EJIL* 233, 249 (2004).
[124] W. H. Taft IV and T. F. Buchwald, 'Preemption, Iraq, and International Law', 97 *AJIL*
557, 563 (2003).

that the legal basis of the 2003 hostilities was a revival of the Coalition's right to use force against Iraq consequent upon the Iraqi 'material breach' of the cease-fire.[125]

The Coalition of 2003 (still led by the US) was of a different composition compared to the original anti-Iraq array of 1990/1, but this is largely immaterial. Wartime coalitions are not engraved in stone: the Grand Alliance that defeated Germany and Japan in World War II underwent even greater permutations within a shorter period of time.

Of the manifold obligations imposed on Iraq in the cease-fire of 1991, the one that it found most onerous was the requirement to disarm itself of weapons of mass destruction (WMD). Huge quantities of chemical weapons agents, and a variety of biological weapons production equipment and materials, were subsequently destroyed under the supervision of UN inspectors.[126] But reports about continuous violations by Iraq of its disarmament obligation persisted. The fact that no WMD were found in Iraq in 2003 is irrelevant: on the eve of the resumption of hostilities, everybody – including the UN inspectors – believed that Iraq had not fully observed its disarmament undertakings.[127] Iraqi refusal to cooperate unreservedly with UN inspectors led to a series of Security Council resolutions; these climaxed with Resolution 1441 (2002), determining (under Chapter VII) that Iraq was in 'material breach' of its disarmament obligations (see *supra*, Chapter 2, C, (c)).[128]

Many commentators maintain that – subsequent to Resolution 1441 – the Coalition could not take military action against Iraq in 2003 without obtaining a specific go-ahead signal from the Security Council to resort to force.[129] The fact that the Coalition failed to persuade the Security Council to adopt a further resolution expressly authorizing – in the vein of Resolution 678 – 'all necessary means' (*i.e.* the use of force) against Iraq was regrettable from a political standpoint. But, legally speaking, such an additional resolution was not required. Even those contending that Resolution 1441 'does not contain any "automaticity" as concerns the potential use of force' have to concede that the text lends itself to a different interpretation.[130] It assuredly does not prescribe – or even

[125] Foreign and Commonwealth Office Paper, 'Iraq: The Legal Basis for the Use of Force', 52 *ICLQ* 812–14 (2003).

[126] See S. D. Murphy, 'Missile Attacks against Iraq', 93 *AJIL* 471, 472 (1999).

[127] See J. Yoo, 'International Law and the War in Iraq', 97 *AJIL* 563, 566 (2003).

[128] Security Council Resolution 1441 (2002), [2002–3] *RDSC* 114, 116.

[129] See, e.g., R. Wolfrum, 'The Attack of September 11, 2001, the Wars against the Taliban and Iraq: Is There a Need to Reconsider International Law on the Recourse to Force and the Rules in Armed Conflict?', 7 *MPYUNL* 1, 15–18 (2003).

[130] R. Hofman, 'International Law and the Use of Military Force against Iraq', 45 *GYIL* 9, 25–8 (2002).

necessarily imply – that, prior to recourse to force, the Coalition must return to the Security Council for a second (confirmatory) resolution.[131]

The clear inference from the determination by the Security Council as regards the Iraqi 'material breach' was that the other side to the cease-fire agreement was released from its obligation to continue to respect the cease-fire (see *supra*, Chapter 2, C, (c)).[132] A salient point, often missed by commentators on this topic,[133] is that the other side to cease-fire in the on-going state of war with Iraq was not the United Nations as such but a coalition of the willing. Resumption of the hostilities, therefore, did not require an explicit seal of approval from the Security Council.

In reality, even the determination of the existence of an Iraqi 'material breach' need not have been made by the Security Council.[134] By right, this determination could have been made by the Coalition itself. Differently put, there was no legal (as distinct from a political) need for the Coalition to have turned to the Security Council in the first place (just as in 1990/1 the Coalition did not have to go the Security Council for Resolution 678 or, for that matter, Resolution 687). Yet, since the Coalition chose to bring the matter before the Security Council in 2002 – and since the Council did set up an enhanced inspection regime, giving Iraq a 'final opportunity' to comply with the disarmament obligation[135] – the Coalition was constrained to give that inspection regime a chance of success. Like Resolution 678, which equally offered Iraq a 'final opportunity'[136] and tied the hands of the Coalition by introducing a temporal interval when it had to hold its fire (see *supra*, Chapter 9, E), Resolution 1441 did not leave the Coalition the option of recommencing hostilities immediately. Despite the determination of the existence of a 'material breach' of the cease-fire terms, the Coalition had to await new UN inspectors' reports. However, when a number of reports were in, it plainly emerged that there were still unresolved issues and that Iraq had failed to meet all the demands (made by the UN inspectors) with a view to putting an end to its 'material breach'.[137] Whereupon the freedom of action of the Coalition was regained.

---

[131] See Taft and Buchwald, *supra* note 124, at 560–2.
[132] See M. Byers, 'Preemptive Self-Defense: Hegemony, Equality and Strategies of Legal Change', 11 *JPP* 171, 183 (2003).
[133] See, e.g., P. Weckel, 'L'Usage Déraisonnable de la Force', 107 *RGDIP* 378, 386 (2003).
[134] See Taft and Buchwald, *supra* note 124, at 560.
[135] Security Council Resolution 1441, *supra* note 128, at 116.
[136] Security Council Resolution 678, *supra* note 112, at 27.
[137] See C. Greenwood, 'International Law and the Pre-emptive Use of Force: Afghanistan, Al-Qaida, and Iraq', 4 *SDILJ* 7, 31–2 (2003).

It is wrong to argue (as was done by the UK) that the legality of the Coalition's right to use force against Iraq in 2003 hinged on a revival of Security Council Resolution 678.[138] Resolution 678 gave the blessing of the Security Council to the military action taken in 1991, and evidently it had nothing to do with operations conducted a dozen years later under totally different circumstances. However, there was no need for a revival of Resolution 678 in 2003, just as there was no strict need for its original adoption in 1990. Both in 1991 and in 2003, the Coalition acted on the basis of the right of collective self-defence with which it was directly vested by Article 51 of the Charter and by customary international law. The exercise of that right could not be terminated by a cease-fire.

Following a final ultimatum, the Coalition resumed general hostilities against Iraq on 20 March 2003. Baghdad fell on 9 April, and in a few days major combat operations were over. All the same, irregular fighting has persisted long after the occupation of Iraq (with an upsurge in the violence in 2004). Already in May 2003, the Security Council determined in Resolution 1483 that the situation in Iraq, although improved, continued to constitute 'a threat to international peace and security'.[139] In October 2003, in Resolution 1511, the Council expressly authorized 'a multinational force under unified command' (structured around the Coalition military units) 'to take all necessary measures to contribute to the maintenance of security and stability in Iraq'.[140] In June 2004, in accordance with Security Council Resolution 1546, the formal occupation of Iraq by the Coalition ended, and an Interim Government reasserted full responsibility and authority; but the multinational (Coalition) force remained in the country – at the request of the Interim Government – and its authority 'to take all necessary measures' was reaffirmed by the Council.[141] Late in 2004, the US forces engaged in a major battle that destroyed an insurgents' base of operations in the city of Fallujah.

(c)   The post-'Cold War' era (other than the Gulf War)

In the years since the outbreak of the Gulf War, the Security Council has become inured to citing Chapter VII, and has frequently adverted to it in diverse contexts.[142] The Council has not determined since August 1990

---

[138] Foreign and Commonwealth Office Paper, *supra* note 125, at 812–14.
[139] Security Council Resolution 1483 (2003), [2002–3] *RDSC* 139, 140.
[140] Security Council Resolution 1511 (2003), 43 *ILM* 254, *id.*, 256 (2004).
[141] Security Council Resolution 1546, 43 *ILM* 1459, 1460–2.
[142] Between 1990 and 1996, the Council adopted no less than 107 resolutions under Chapter VII. Bailey and Daws, *supra* note 84, at 273. Since then, the number has grown at a brisk pace.

the existence of a breach of the peace. However, in no less than twenty-five specific cases (unrelated to Iraq; not counting reiterations; and in addition to a general reference to terrorist attacks as well as the proliferation of nuclear, chemical and biological weapons), it has formally determined the existence of a threat to the peace (either globally or at least in a particular region). This was done in Resolution 733 (1992) relating to Somalia;[143] Resolution 748 (1992) concerning Libyan failure to renounce terrorism (as demonstrated by its refusal to surrender to justice suspects in the Lockerbie bombing (see *infra*, E, (b), ii);[144] Resolution 757 (1992) pertaining to the situation in Yugoslavia, especially in Bosnia-Herzegovina;[145] Resolution 788 (1992) in respect of Liberia;[146] Resolution 807 (1993) motivated by repeated violations of the cease-fire in Croatia;[147] Resolution 841 (1993) as regards Haiti;[148] Resolution 918 (1994) on Rwanda;[149] Resolution 1054 (1996) prompted by Sudan's non-compliance with demands for extradition of suspected terrorists;[150] Resolution 1078 (1996) generated by the situation in Eastern Zaire (Great Lakes Region);[151] Resolution 1101 (1997) about Albania;[152] Resolution 1125 (1997) *re* the Central African Republic;[153] Resolution 1127 (1997) dealing with Angola;[154] Resolution 1132 (1997) applying to Sierra Leone;[155] Resolution 1199 (1998) as to Kosovo;[156] Resolution 1264 (1999) in the matter of East Timor;[157] Resolution 1267 (1999) engendered by the Taliban authorities providing a safe haven in Afghanistan to the terrorist Osama bin Laden;[158] Resolution 1291 (2000) germane to Congo;[159] Resolution 1298 (2000) triggered by the war between Eritrea and Ethiopia;[160] Resolution 1343 (2001) generated by Liberian support for rebels in Sierra Leone;[161] Resolution 1363 (2001) brought about by

---

[143] Security Council Resolution 733, 47 *RDSC* 55, *id.* (1992).
[144] Security Council Resolution 748, *supra* note 25, at 52.
[145] Security Council Resolution 757, 47 *RDSC* 13, 14 (1992).
[146] Security Council Resolution 788, 47 *RDSC* 99, *id.* (1992).
[147] Security Council Resolution 807, 48 *RDSC* 23, *id.* (1993).
[148] Security Council Resolution 841, *supra* note 62, at 119.
[149] Security Council Resolution 918, 49 *RDSC* 6, 7 (1994).
[150] Security Council Resolution 1054, 51 *RDSC* 75, *id.* (1996).
[151] Security Council Resolution 1078, 51 *RDSC* 115, 116 (1996).
[152] Security Council Resolution 1101, 52 *RDSC* 58, *id.* (1997).
[153] Security Council Resolution 1125, 52 *RDSC* 92, 93 (1997).
[154] Security Council Resolution 1127, *supra* note 58, at 50.
[155] Security Council Resolution 1132, 52 *RDSC* 83, 84 (1997).
[156] Security Council Resolution 1199, 53 *RDSC* 13, 14 (1998).
[157] Security Council Resolution 1264, 54 *RDSC* 128, 129 (1999).
[158] Security Council Resolution 1267, 54 *RDSC* 148, *id.* (1999).
[159] Security Council Resolution 1291, 55 *RDSC* 51, 53 (2000).
[160] Security Council Resolution 1298, *supra* note 69, at 147.
[161] Security Council Resolution 1343 (2001), [2001–2] *RDSC* 204, 205.

post-Taliban Afghanistan;[162] Resolution 1464 (2003) affecting the Ivory Coast;[163] Resolution 1484 (2003) contending with the Ituri Region (Bunia) in the Congo;[164] Resolution 1529 (2004) linked once more to Haiti;[165] Resolution 1545 (2004) instigated by Burundi;[166] and Resolution 1556 (2004) stimulated by the crisis in the Darfur region in Sudan.[167]

On at least eighteen occasions (not counting Iraq), the Security Council decided to resort to sanctions: Resolution 713 (1991) imposed an arms embargo on Yugoslavia;[168] Resolution 733 (1992) imposed an arms embargo on Somalia;[169] Resolution 748 (1992) imposed various sanctions on Libya, especially air and arms embargo;[170] Resolution 757 (1992) imposed economic sanctions on Serbia and Montenegro;[171] Resolution 781 (1992) the Council banned military flights in the airspace of Bosnia-Herzegovina;[172] Resolution 788 (1992) imposed an arms embargo on Liberia;[173] Resolution 841 (1993) imposed a trade embargo on Haiti;[174] Resolution 918 (1994) imposed an arms embargo on Rwanda;[175] Resolution 942 (1994) imposed economic sanctions on the Bosnian Serbs;[176] Resolution 1070 (1996) imposed an air embargo on Sudan;[177] Resolution 1127 (1997) imposed sanctions on UNITA, a non-State entity in Angola;[178] Resolution 1132 (1997) imposed an arms embargo on Sierra Leone;[179] Resolution 1160 (1998) imposed a new arms embargo on Yugoslavia in connection with the Kosovo crisis;[180] Resolution 1267 (1999) imposed an air embargo on Afghanistan and froze funds controlled by the Taliban;[181] Resolution 1298 (2000) imposed an arms embargo on Eritrea and Ethiopia;[182] Resolution 1343

---

[162] Security Council Resolution 1363 (2001), [2001–2] *RDSC* 268, *id.*
[163] Security Council Resolution 1464 (2003), [2002–3] *RDSC* 176, 177.
[164] Security Council Resolution 1484 (2003), [2002–3] *RDSC* 24, 25.
[165] Security Council Resolution 1529, 43 *ILM* 963, *id.* (2004).
[166] Security Council Resolution 1545, 43 *ILM* 1453, 1455 (2004).
[167] Security Council Resolution 1556, 43 *ILM* 1244, 1245 (2004).
[168] Security Council Resolution 713, 46 *RDSC* 42, 43 (1991).
[169] Security Council Resolution 733, *supra* note 143, at 55.
[170] Security Council Resolution 748, *supra* note 25, at 52.
[171] Security Council Resolution 757, *supra* note 145, at 14.
[172] Security Council Resolution 781, 47 *RDSC* 27, *id.* (1992).
[173] Security Council Resolution 788, *supra* note 146, at 100.
[174] Security Council Resolution 841, *supra* note 62, at 119.
[175] Security Council Resolution 918, *supra* note 149, at 7.
[176] Security Council Resolution 942, 49 *RDSC* 30, 31 (1994).
[177] Security Council Resolution 1070, 51 *RDSC* 75, *id.* (1996).
[178] Security Council Resolution 1127, *supra* note 58, at 51.
[179] Security Council Resolution 1132, *supra* note 155, at 84.
[180] Security Council Resolution 1160, 53 *RDSC* 10, 11 (1998).
[181] Security Council Resolution 1267, *supra* note 158, at 149.
[182] Security Council Resolution 1298, *supra* note 69, at 147.

(2001) imposed sanctions on Liberia, primarily on the import of diamonds from that country;[183] Resolution 1556 (2004) – which also expressed the intention of considering measures under Article 41 against the Government of Sudan – imposed an arms embargo on non-governmental entities and individuals operating in Darfur;[184] and Resolution 1572 (2004) imposed an arms embargo on the Ivory Coast.[185]

In nine cases (again, not counting Iraq), the Security Council authorized Member States to use 'all necessary means' (or 'measures'), with a view to attaining a specific enforcement goal (see *infra*, D, (c)). Thus, Resolution 787 (1992) allowed States, acting either individually or regionally, to use 'such measures commensurate with the specific circumstances as may be necessary' – a euphemism for the use of force – to inspect cargoes and to ensure strict implementation of Resolutions 713 and 757 relating to Yugoslavia;[186] Resolution 794 (1992) authorized Member States the use of 'all necessary means' to establish 'a secure environment for humanitarian relief operations in Somalia';[187] Resolution 816 (1993) authorized the use of 'all necessary means' in the airspace of Bosnia-Herzegovina;[188] Resolution 929 (1994) authorized the use of 'all necessary means' to protect civilians at risk in Rwanda;[189] Resolution 940 (1994) authorized the use of 'all necessary means' to bring about the removal of the military leadership and the restoration of the legitimate Government in Haiti (*supra*, A, (d));[190] and Resolution 1264 (1999) – stirred by a request from Indonesia – authorized 'the establishment of a multinational force under a unified command structure', with the task of restoring peace and security in East Timor, coupled with a specific authorization to 'the States participating in the multinational force to take all necessary measures to fulfil this mandate'.[191] Similarly, Resolution 1386 (2001) authorized the establishment of an International Assistance Force to assist in the maintenance of security in Kabul and its surrounding areas in Afghanistan – after the fall of the Taliban regime – and the Member States participating in the Force were explicitly authorized 'to take all necessary measures to fulfil its mandate'.[192] Exactly the same formula was used in Resolution 1484 (2003), as regards the Interim Emergency Multinational Force deployed in Bunia,

[183] Security Council Resolution 1343, *supra* note 161, at 206.
[184] Security Council Resolution 1556, *supra* note 167, at 1246.
[185] Security Council Resolution 1572, doc. S/RES/1572 at 2 (2004).
[186] Security Council Resolution 787, 47 *RDSC* 29, 30–1 (1992).
[187] Security Council Resolution 794, 47 *RDSC* 63, 64 (1992).
[188] Security Council Resolution 816, 48 *RDSC* 4, *id.* (1993).
[189] Security Council Resolution 929, 49 *RDSC* 10, *id.* (1994).
[190] Security Council Resolution 940, *supra* note 63, at 51.
[191] Security Council Resolution 1264, *supra* note 157, at 129.
[192] Security Council Resolution 1386 (2001), [2001–2] *RDSC* 272, 273.

Congo (not to be confused with the UN Mission in Congo (MONUC)).[193] In Resolution 1464 (2003), relating to the Ivory Coast, ECOWAS and French forces were authorized 'to take the necessary steps' and to use 'the means available to them' for protection of civilians and for force protection.[194]

It is manifest from the spate of resolutions that the Security Council currently interprets its mandate under Chapter VII in the most liberal manner. That being said, it is remarkable that – despite the litany of references to Chapter VII – the Council has never attempted to activate the key clause in the collective security system: Article 42 of the Charter. In 1992, the then Secretary-General, B. Boutros-Ghali, was invited by the Council (following a special and unprecedented meeting at the level of Heads of States and Governments) to submit recommendations for strengthening the effectiveness of the collective security system of the Charter.[195] Boutros-Ghali addressed the issue in a report entitled 'An Agenda for Peace'.[196] He noted that the Council had not made use of Article 42, and suggested that such a move 'is essential to the credibility of the United Nations as a guarantor of international security'.[197] Since a pre-condition is the conclusion of the special agreements required by Article 43 (see *infra*, D, (a)), the Secretary-General thought that negotiations should be initiated.[198] However, the Council was disinclined to pursue this path.[199]

D.   The mechanism of employing collective force

(a)   *Article 42 and the absence of special agreements*

The Charter does not envisage the establishment of a permanent international force with troops recruited directly by the UN Organization itself.[200] Instead, Article 42 refers to the carrying out of military

---

[193] Security Council Resolution 1484, *supra* note 164, at 25.

[194] Security Council Resolution 1464 *supra* note 163, at 177–8.

[195] 'The Responsibility of the Security Council in the Maintenance of International Peace and Security', 47 *RDSC* 65, 66 (1992).

[196] Report of the Secretary-General, 'An Agenda for Peace', 31 *ILM* 956 (1992).

[197] *Ibid.*, 966.   [198] *Ibid.*

[199] For the Council's response to the Report of the Secretary-General, see 'An Agenda for Peace: Preventive Diplomacy, Peacemaking and Peace-Keeping', 47 *RDSC* 101–4 (1992).

[200] It is consequently doubtful whether the Council is authorized by the Charter to require States (without their consent) to allow the enlistment of individual volunteers against an aggressor. Such a view is expressed by L. C. Green, *The Contemporary Law of Armed Conflict* 272 (2nd ed., 2000).

operations (as decided by the Security Council) through the forces of Member States. How will these forces be accessible to the Council? Under Article 43, UN Members are obligated to make available to the Council the necessary armed forces, but the duty is subject to the condition that this will be done 'in accordance with a special agreement or agreements' (governing the numbers and types of forces, their degree of readiness and general location).[201] The rationale underlying the scheme of the special agreements is plain. The Council cannot accomplish the mission assigned to it by the Charter unless it acts swiftly once a crisis breaks out. Since no permanent international force exists, advance preparations have to be made for the rapid deployment of forces belonging to Member States. In particular, Member States must identify combat-ready units that can be drawn upon by the Council at a moment's notice.

It stands to reason that the Security Council is not required to conclude special agreements with all UN Members, not even all Permanent Members of the Council.[202] But the question is whether a Member State is bound to place armed forces for enforcement action at the disposal of the Council when no special agreement has been signed. There are two conflicting interpretations of the Charter on this issue. One approach is that the Council may insist on Member States deploying military units at its behest, despite the non-conclusion of special agreements (or in excess of the forces pledged in the agreements).[203] The other, and more common, opinion is that the duty of Member States under the Charter – to do their share in a collective security operation mounted by the Council – is purely abstract, and, unless it is concretized in special agreements, the Members may evade their undertaking.[204]

Article 43 prescribes that the special agreements 'shall be negotiated as soon as possible on the initiative of the Security Council'. Nevertheless, six decades later, no special agreements have been reached. Article 106 enunciates that, pending the coming into force of the special agreements referred to in Article 43, the five Permanent Members shall consult with a view to taking 'such joint action on behalf of the Organization as may be necessary for the purpose of maintaining international peace and security'.[205] Since no special agreement pursuant to Article 43 has ever

---

[201] Charter of the United Nations, *supra* note 9, at 344.
[202] See L. M. Goodrich and A. P. Simons, *The United Nations and the Maintenance of International Peace and Security* 395–6 (1955).
[203] See Kelsen, *supra* note 35, at 756.
[204] See C. Chaumont, 'Nations Unies et Neutralité', 89 *RCADI* 1, 39–40 (1956).
[205] Charter of the United Nations, *supra* note 9, at 362.

been concluded, the transition period envisaged in Article 106 'has not yet ended'.[206] However, '[s]o far, Art. 106 has not attained any practical significance'.[207]

Article 44 stipulates that, before being called upon to provide armed forces, a UN Member State not represented in the Security Council will be invited to participate in any decisions concerning the employment of these forces.[208] The case is exceptional, for a regular UN Member is hereby entitled not just to have its voice heard in the deliberations of the Council, but actually to take part in the Council's decision-making process by voting on any proposal (albeit only in regard to the use made of the Member's own armed forces).[209] All the same, the Member has only one vote, and it may be overruled by the majority in the Council.

To enable carrying out a combined UN enforcement action in urgent cases, Member States are instructed by Article 45 to keep air force contingents immediately available.[210] This clause, too, is conditional on the existence of the special agreements projected in Article 43.

Articles 46 and 47 establish a Military Staff Committee, consisting of the Chiefs of Staff of the five Permanent Members of the Security Council or their representatives, its mission being to advise and assist the Council on all military matters.[211] The Committee was stalemated in the early days of the UN, and, while continuing to meet periodically, proposals to activate it have so far met with little enthusiasm.[212] Interestingly enough, in Resolution 665 (1990), the Security Council requested the States 'co-operating with the Government of Kuwait' – while carrying out a blockade of Iraq – to coordinate their actions using the mechanism of the Military Staff Committee.[213] However, the American-led Coalition preferred to leave the Committee dormant.[214]

By dint of the failure to conclude special agreements, as perceived in Article 43, no advance preparations have been made for prompt action in the event of a breach of the peace, and no standing military units are ready to do as the Security Council bids. Yet, in the words of the International

---

[206] R. Geiger, 'Article 106', *The Charter of the United Nations: A Commentary,* II, *supra* note 30, at 1327, 1328.

[207] *Ibid.,* 1329.   [208] Charter of the United Nations, *supra* note 9, at 344.

[209] See Goodrich, Hambro and Simons, *supra* note 19, at 327.

[210] Charter of the United Nations, *supra* note 9, at 344–5.

[211] *Ibid.,* 345.   [212] Bailey and Daws, *supra* note 84, at 280.

[213] Security Council Resolution 665, *supra* note 104, at 22.

[214] See G. K. Walker, 'The Crisis over Kuwait, August 1990 – February 1991', 1 *DJCIL* 25, 49 (1991).

Court of Justice in its Advisory Opinion on *Certain Expenses of the United Nations*:

It cannot be said that the Charter has left the Security Council impotent in the face of an emergency situation when agreements under Article 43 have not been concluded.[215]

Over the years, two mechanisms have evolved: (i) peacekeeping, and (ii) non-Article 42 enforcement actions.

(b)   Peacekeeping forces

Since the 1950s, dozens of United Nations forces have been set up (principally by the Security Council but exceptionally by the General Assembly) for 'peacekeeping' purposes.[216] The common denominator of all UN peacekeeping forces is that they have come into being *ad hoc*, as and when required in specific emergencies, and their dependence on voluntary cooperation by Member States (willing to contribute the military contingents of which the forces are composed) has been absolute.[217] The original idea of peacekeeping was primarily that of creating a *cordon sanitaire*, setting opponents apart and preventing bloodshed.[218] But, especially after the end of the 'Cold War', peacekeeping operations have gradually become more multi-dimensional.[219] An extreme example is that of UNAMSIL (United Nations Mission in Sierra Leone) whose mandate was revised in 2000 to provide security at key locations and installations, as well as to facilitate the free flow of people, goods and humanitarian assistance, and to assist local law enforcement authorities (affording protection to civilians under imminent threat of violence).[220]

A peacekeeping operation is supposed to be completely different from an enforcement action. The two special attributes of a peacekeeping force are that (i) it is established and maintained with the consent of all the States concerned; and (ii) it is not authorized to take military action

[215] Advisory Opinion on *Certain Expenses of the United Nations (Article 17, Paragraph 2, of the Charter)*, [1962] *ICJ Rep.* 151, 167.
[216] For an updated survey of all UN peacekeeping operations until mid-2001, see M. Bothe, 'Peace-Keeping', *The Charter of the United Nations: A Commentary*, I, *supra* note 30, at 648–700.
[217] See R. Sommereyns, 'United Nations Forces', 4 *EPIL* 1106, 1109.
[218] See E. Jiménez de Aréchaga, 'International Law in the Past Third of a Century', 159 *RCADI* 1, 130 (1978).
[219] See W. J. Durch, 'Keeping the Peace: Politics and Lessons of the 1990s', *UN Peacekeeping, American Politics, and the Uncivil Wars of the 1990s* 1, 3–4 (W. J. Durch ed., 1996).
[220] Security Council Resolution 1289, 55 *RDSC* 96, 97–8 (2000).

against any State.[221] These special features are generally conceded in theory, yet they are not free of complications in practice.

The concept of consent has stirred up a number of thorny problems in its application,[222] although it is still accepted in principle as a condition precedent for the stationing of a peacekeeping force.[223] It has to be recognized that consent may be induced by the Security Council in circumstances where the host State has little or no real choice. Thus, the United Nations Iraq-Kuwait Observation Mission (UNIKOM) was set up with Iraq's reluctant consent after that country's military defeat in the first phase of the Gulf War.[224] While, as a rule, a withdrawal of prior consent by a host-State would terminate a peacekeeping operation,[225] Resolution 689 (1991) proclaimed categorically that the deployment of UNIKOM 'can only be terminated by a decision of the Council'.[226] The special regime must be understood against the background of a cease-fire imposed on Iraq.

In essence, peacekeeping forces are not designed for combat. Nevertheless, it has always been understood that they are entitled to defend themselves. This specific right of self-defence, applicable to peacekeeping forces, should not be confused with the much broader right of self-defence vested in States (see *supra*, Chapters 7–9). A peace-keeping force's exercise of self-defence is more akin to a military unit's self-defence,[227] in the context of on-the-spot reaction (see *supra*, 8, A, (a), i). It is noteworthy that the Security Council occasionally refers to 'armed attacks' against United Nations personnel.[228]

The Security Council has granted some peacekeeping forces permis-sion to use force in circumstances going beyond self-defence. Already in Bosnia-Herzegovina, UNPROFOR (United Nations Protection Force) was explicitly authorized in Resolution 836 (1993), 'acting in self-defence, to take the necessary means, including the use of force, in reply to bombardments against the safe areas' (free from hostile acts) established by the Council, as well as to protect freedom of movement

---

[221] See Advisory Opinion on *Certain Expenses of the United Nations*, *supra* note 215, at 170, 177.

[222] See J. I. Garvey, 'United Nations Peacekeeping and Host State Consent', 64 *AJIL* 241–69 (1970).

[223] See C. Gray, *International Law and the Use of Force* 232 (2nd, 2004).

[224] Security Council Resolution 687, *supra* note 116, at 12.

[225] See D. Wippman, 'Military Intervention, Regional Organizations, and Host-State Consent', 7 *DJCIL* 209, 234 (1996–7).

[226] Security Council Resolution 689, 46 *RDSC* 15, *id.* (1991).

[227] See N. D. White, *Keeping the Peace: The United Nations and the Maintenance of International Peace and Security* 240 (2nd ed., 1997).

[228] See, e.g., Security Council Resolution 837, 48 *RDSC* 83, *id.* (1993).

and humanitarian convoys.[229] In Resolution 1101 (1997), the multinational protection force in Albania was authorized 'to ensure the security and freedom of movement' of its personnel.[230] Most significantly, ONUB (United Nations Operation in Burundi) was authorized by the Council, in Resolution 1545 (2004), 'to use all necessary means' to carry out its extensive mandate.[231] Clearly, this is a new robust concept of 'peacekeeping with teeth', which is viewed by some as 'a mutation between traditional peace-keeping and peace-enforcement operations'.[232]

Whatever the scope of their mission may be, '[a]ll UN peace-keeping forces have so far been made up of national contingents, supplied by member states'.[233] The component units are neither fully integrated nor released from national discipline. In the words of Lord Pearce in the *Nissan* case (which arose before the House of Lords, in 1969, and related to the United Nations force in Cyprus):

the commander of the United Nations force is head in the chain of command and is answerable to the United Nations. The functions of the force as a whole are international. But its individual component forces have their own national duty and discipline and remain in their own national service.[234]

When an international force is put together consensually for strictly peacekeeping – as opposed to enforcement – purposes, it need not be set up specifically by the Security Council (or, for that matter, by any other organ of the United Nations). Under a Protocol annexed to the Egyptian–Israeli Treaty of Peace of 1979, the parties requested the United Nations to provide forces and observers for supervising the implementation of the terms agreed upon between them.[235] When it turned out that the Security Council was unable to accede to that request, Egypt and Israel (with the active assistance of the United States) concluded in 1981 another Protocol Establishing the Sinai Multinational Force and Observers.[236] This force operates successfully in lieu of the UN force originally visualized, without being linked to the UN Organization.[237]

[229] Security Council Resolution 836, 48 *RDSC* 13, 14 (1993).
[230] Security Council Resolution 1101, *supra* note 152, at 58.
[231] Security Council Resolution 1545, *supra* note 166, at 1455.
[232] See D. Kritsiotis, 'Security Council Resolution 1101 (1997) and the Multinational Protection Force of Operation Alba in Albania', 12 *LJIL* 511, 538 (1999).
[233] R. C. R. Siekmann, *National Contingents in United Nations Peace-Keeping Operations* 9 (1991).
[234] *Attorney-General v. Nissan* (1969), [1970] *AC* 179, 223.
[235] Egypt–Israel, Treaty of Peace, 1979, 18 *ILM* 362, 367, 372 (1979) (Article VI).
[236] Egypt–Israel, Protocol Establishing the Sinai Multinational Force and Observers, 1981, 20 *ILM* 1190 (1981).
[237] See M. Tabory, *The Multinational Force and Observers in the Sinai: Organization, Structure and Function passim* (1986).

(c)   Enforcement action beyond the purview of Article 42

In the 1990s, the Security Council found a pragmatic way to circumvent Article 42 in flagrant cases of a threat to the peace. In the absence of special agreements required by Article 43 (*supra*, (a)), the Council still refrains from imposing on Member States the obligation to take military measures. Instead, the Council now resorts to the strategy of authorizing Member States – acting either individually or within the framework of regional organizations – to use force in sharply defined situations on a voluntary basis. Some scholars adhere to the view that, whereas a mere 'recommendation' would not suffice to activate Article 42, an 'authorization' of military action by Member States comes within the ambit of the Article.[238] This view is untenable. In the final analysis, there is no genuine differentiation between an authorization of military action and its recommendation. Authorization is no less permissive than recommendation.[239] Both authorization and recommendation share a non-mandatory nature and, therefore, neither action comes under the rubric of Article 42. Enforcement measures in keeping with Article 42 must be based on mandatory decisions by the Security Council, and nothing short of such decisions will do. Permissive enforcement action, predicated either on a recommendation or on an authorization issued by the Council, acquires its intrinsic legal validity not from Article 42 but from Article 39 (see *supra*, A, (c) – B, (a)).

The most intriguing aspect of the policy of authorization of the use of force by the Security Council – *i.e.* voluntary enforcement action – is the element of 'sub-contracting' the use of force to regional organizations.[240] This *modus operandi* is specifically envisaged in Chapter VIII of the Charter (Articles 52–4).[241] Article 52(1) (referred to *supra*, Chapter 9, B) expressly permits the existence of 'regional arrangements or agencies' for dealing with matters that relate to the maintenance of international peace and security (and are appropriate for regional action), provided that such arrangements or agencies (and their activities) are consistent with the Purposes and Principles of the United Nations.[242] Article 53(1) promulgates:

---

[238] See J. A. Frowein and N. Krisch, 'Article 42', *The Charter of the United Nations: A Commentary*, I, *supra* note 30, at 749, 756–8.

[239] See E. V. Rostow, 'Until What? Enforcement Action or Collective Self-Defense?', 85 *AJIL* 506, 509 (1991).

[240] N. D. White, 'The UN Charter and Peacekeeping Forces: Constitutional Issues', *The UN, Peace and Force* 43, 58 (M. Pugh ed., 1997).

[241] Charter of the United Nations, *supra* note 9, at 346–8.   [242] *Ibid.*, 346–7.

The Security Council shall, where appropriate, utilize such regional arrangements or agencies for enforcement action under its authority. But no enforcement action shall be taken under regional arrangements or by regional agencies without the authorization of the Security Council.[243]

Already in Resolution 199 (1964), the Security Council expressed its conviction that the Organization of African Unity should be able – in the context of Article 52 of the Charter – to help find a peaceful solution to the problem of the Congo.[244] Similarly, in Resolution 217 (1965) concerning Southern Rhodesia, the Council called upon the Organization of African Unity to assist in the implementation of the resolution, in conformity with Chapter VIII of the Charter.[245]

A contextual interpretation of its language might lead to the conclusion that Article 53(1) can only be invoked when the State 'in which action is intended to take place' is a member of the regional organization invited by the Security Council to intervene.[246] But (as demonstrated by the Southern Rhodesia case), that is not the way in which the Council has construed the Charter in practice. The Council may utilize a regional organization for enforcement action beyond the bounds of the region, simply because the organization in question is willing and able to serve as an instrument for performing the task assigned to it.

The functioning of a regional organization does not modify the fundamental rules governing the use of force. The position of a regional group of States is not appreciably different from that of an individual State.[247] Chapter VIII of the Charter interlocks with Chapter VII to retain the monopoly of the Council in the field of collective security. The wording of Article 53(1) is unequivocal: the legality of regional enforcement action is entirely contingent on Security Council authorization.[248] An authorization resolution 'produces a permissive effect by making lawful a conduct otherwise prohibited by article 2(4) of the charter'.[249] Unless it gets a clear-cut go-ahead signal from the Council to perform enforcement functions, a regional organization (like any single State) can resort to lawful force only within the ambit of collective self-defence (see *supra*, Chapter 9).

[243] *Ibid.*, 347.   [244] Security Council Resolution 199, 19 *RDSC* 18, 19 (1964).
[245] Security Council Resolution 217, 20 *RDSC* 8, 9 (1965).
[246] G. Gaja, 'Use of Force Made or Authorized by the United Nations', *The United Nations at Age Fifty: A Legal Perspective* 39, 44 (C. Tomuschat ed., 1995).
[247] See D. Sarooshi, *The United Nations and the Development of Collective Security: The Delegation by the UN Security Council of Its Chapter VII Powers* 248–9 (1999).
[248] See C. Walter, 'Security Council Control over Regional Action', 1 *MPYUNL* 129, 154 (1997).
[249] T. Gazzini, 'NATO's Role in the Collective Security System', 8 *JCSL* 231, 255 (2003).

Addressing the same subject from a complementary angle, one can say that when an armed attack occurs, any State or cluster of States derives directly from the Charter a right to use force in collective self-defence. There is no need in such an instance to procure any prior authorization of the Council (although any exercise of self-defence is ultimately subject to review by the Council; see *supra*, Chapter 7, D, (a)). The Council may choose to give its blessing to the initiation of collective self-defence measures against an armed attack (as it did in the first phase of the Gulf War), but a mere blessing for action taken by right must not be confused with a Council authorization of action not otherwise permissible by the Charter.[250] As long as no armed attack is mounted, a regional organization (like any individual State) is disentitled under the Charter to have any recourse to force. Only the authorization by the Council can vest a regional organization with the right to use force in circumstances short of an armed attack.

A conspicuous authorization by the Security Council of the use of force by a regional organization occurred in Bosnia-Herzegovina. In Resolution 816 (1993), the Council – invoking Chapter VII – decided that Member States, 'acting nationally or through regional organizations or arrangements' could, 'under the authority of the Security Council', take 'all necessary measures' in the airspace of Bosnia-Herzegovina.[251] Resolution 816 was designed to ensure compliance with a ban on flying in the airspace of Bosnia-Herzegovina.[252] In Resolution 836 (1993), the same call was made with a view to supporting UNPROFOR in the performance of its mandate (including the protection of safe areas).[253] Accordingly, in 1994/5, NATO aircraft repeatedly conducted air strikes in the area, in close coordination with the UN.[254]

If the premise is accepted that a regional organization may exceed the reach of its membership when acting under Article 53(1), Resolutions 816 and 836 lend full legitimacy to the NATO military operation in Bosnia-Herzegovina. NATO is a regional organization in the meaning of Article 53(1).[255] The fact that it was originally envisioned merely as a collective self-defence organization (see *supra*, Chapter 9, B, (b)) does not diminish from NATO's objective character as a regional arrangement. Any attempt to erect a barrier between collective self-defence

---

[250] For an example of such confusion, see L.-A. Sicilianos, 'L'Autorisation par le Conseil de Sécurité de Recourir à la Force: Une Tentative d'Evaluation', 106 *RGDIP* 5, 23–4 (2002).
[251] Security Council Resolution 816, *supra* note 188, at 4.   [252] *Ibid.*
[253] Security Council Resolution 836, *supra* note 229, at 14.
[254] See S. M. Hill and S. P. Malik, *Peacekeeping and the United Nations* 181–4 (1996).
[255] See Kelsen, *supra* note 35, at 920.

organizations and regional arrangements for enforcement purposes is artificial.[256] For sure, there is a difference between the exercise of collective self-defence and an enforcement undertaking stemming from Article 53(1). But that difference relates to the organization's interface with the Security Council. When exercising collective self-defence, NATO does not require the advance authorization of the Security Council. Contrarily, when functioning as a regional organization in keeping with Article 53(1), NATO must seek first the authorization of the Security Council. Once that authorization was obtained with respect to Bosnia-Herzegovina, NATO's air-raids constituted a lawful enforcement action compatible with the UN Charter.

The role played by NATO in Bosnia-Herzegovina gained a new dimension when it was agreed in Article I(1)(a) of Annex IA (Military Aspects of the Peace Settlement) of the 1995 General Framework Agreement for Peace in Bosnia and Herzegovina (negotiated in Dayton, Ohio, and signed in Paris):

The United Nations Security Council is invited to adopt a resolution by which it will authorize Member States or regional organizations and arrangements to establish a multinational military Implementation Force (hereinafter 'IFOR'). The Parties understand and agree that this Implementation Force may be composed of ground, air and maritime units from NATO and non-NATO nations, deployed to Bosnia and Herzegovina to help ensure compliance with the provisions of this Agreement.[257]

The transfer of authority from the United Nations Protection Force (UNPROFOR) to IFOR was accomplished by the Security Council in Resolution 1035 (1995).[258] Under Resolution 1088 (1996), IFOR was succeeded by SFOR (Stabilization Force),[259] run by NATO. In 2004, NATO transferred its responsibilities to the European Union. In Resolution 1575 (2004), the Council recognized EUFOR as the legal successor to SFOR.[260]

Unlike its operation in Bosnia, NATO did not act within the confines of the Charter in 1999, when it deemed fit to compel Yugoslavia – without prior authorization by the Council – to accept a settlement of the issue of Kosovo. NATO relied on the fact that the Security Council (acting

---

[256] *Cf.* E. P. J. Myjer, 'Some Reflections on Collective Security and the Use of Force: A Critical Review of Dinstein's *War, Aggression and Self-Defence*', 44 *NILR* 89, 96–100 (1997).
[257] General Framework Agreement for Peace in Bosnia and Herzegovina, 1995, 35 *ILM* 75, 92 (1996).
[258] Security Council Resolution 1035, 50 *RDSC* 23, *id.* (1995).
[259] Security Council Resolution 1088, 51 *RDSC* 42, 44–5 (1996).
[260] Security Council Resolution 1575, doc. S/RES/1575 at 4 (2004).

under Chapter VII) had twice determined that the situation in Kosovo constituted 'a threat to peace and security in the region': in Resolutions 1199 (1998)[261] and 1203 (1998).[262] However, as long as there is no specific authorization by the Council to take enforcement action, no State or group of States is entitled to resort to forcible measures in response to a mere threat to the peace.[263] Had the Council decided that there was a breach of the peace (assuming that it amounts to an armed attack), the legal state of affairs would have been entirely different, inasmuch as NATO could then have exercised the right of collective self-defence. But there was no question of armed attack and self-defence in Kosovo (which is an integral part of Yugoslavia and not a sovereign State).[264] Any decision or recommendation as to whether, when and how to respond to a threat to the peace is a matter within the exclusive prerogative of the Security Council.

It is true that the Security Council did not condemn NATO's air campaign in Kosovo.[265] But inaction by the Council does not amount to authorization of enforcement measures, even by a regional organization.[266] As for Resolution 1244 (1999),[267] adopted by the Security Council following an agreement between the parties which ended the NATO attacks, it was not phrased in language implying retroactive ratification of the use of force by NATO.[268] In any event, barring exceptional circumstances, the Council's authorization of regional enforcement action must be sought before – and not subsequent to – the operation.[269] The supremacy of the Council in the province of international peace and security can be utterly eroded if the expression 'authorization' in Article 53(1) is construed in a manner encompassing tacit acquiescence with a *fait accompli*.[270] One reason is that a Permanent

---

[261] Security Council Resolution 1199, *supra* note 156, at 14.

[262] Security Council Resolution 1203, 53 *RDSC* 15, 16 (1998).

[263] See N. Krisch, 'Unilateral Enforcement of the Collective Will: Kosovo, Iraq, and the Security Council', 3 *MPYUNL* 59, 86–9 (1999).

[264] See M. Byers and S. Chesterman, 'Changing the Rules about Rules? Unilateral Humanitarian Intervention and the Future of International Law', *Humanitarian Intervention: Ethical, Legal, and Political Dilemmas* 177, 182 (J. L. Holzgrefe and R. O. Keohane eds., 2003).

[265] See R. Wedgwood, 'NATO's Campaign in Yugoslavia', 93 *AJIL* 828, 830–1 (1999).

[266] See O. Schachter, 'The Right of States to Use Armed Force', 82 *Mich. LR* 1620, 1640–1 (1984).

[267] Security Council Resolution 1244, 54 *RDSC* 32 (1999).

[268] See U. Villani, 'The Security Council's Authorization of Enforcement Action by Regional Organizations', 8 *MPYUNL* 535, 547–8 (2002).

[269] See G. Ress and J. Bröhmer, 'Article 53', *The Charter of the United Nations: A Commentary*, I, *supra* note 30, at 854, 864–5.

[270] See N. D. White, *The Law of International Organisations* 215 (1996).

Member is apt to 'shift the burden of the veto' by acting unilaterally and then frustrating the adoption of any resolution terminating the action.[271]

The NATO operation may also be viewed as 'an important and undeniable invocation of the so-called right of humanitarian intervention in state practice'[272] (see *supra*, Chapter 3, B, (c)). Yet, 'humanitarian intervention is not an exception to the Charter prohibitions on the use of force'.[273] If the situation in Kosovo in 1999 was so agonizing that it warranted humanitarian intervention from the outside, this should have been decided upon by the Security Council and not unilaterally by NATO. Obviously, in Kosovo – as in Bosnia-Herzegovina – there was room for 'synergy' between the Security Council and NATO, but only on condition that the Council authorized NATO action against Yugoslavia.[274] The fact that NATO acted independently of the Council is a source of considerable disquiet, since a precedent has been created wreaking havoc on the Charter's system of collective security.

E.   Is there an alternative to the Security Council?

(a)   The General Assembly

The impasse reached by the Security Council during the 'Cold War' – due to the frequent exercise of the veto power – became apparent shortly after the entry into force of the Charter. In 1950, the General Assembly adopted a famous resolution – entitled 'Uniting for Peace' – which was supposed to surmount the obstacles standing in the way of concerted international action in the face of aggression:

Resolves that if the Security Council, because of lack of unanimity of the permanent members, fails to exercise its primary responsibility for the maintenance of international peace and security in any case where there appears to be a threat to the peace, breach of the peace, or act of aggression, the General Assembly shall consider the matter immediately with a view to making appropriate recommendations to Members for collective measures, including in the case of a breach of the peace or act of aggression the use of armed force when necessary, to maintain or restore international peace and security. If not in session at the time, the General

---

[271] L. Henkin, 'Kosovo and the Law of "Humanitarian Intervention"', 93 *AJIL* 824, 827 (1999).

[272] D. Kritsiotis, 'The Kosovo Crisis and NATO's Application of Armed Force against the Federal Republic of Yugoslavia', 49 *ICLQ* 330, 357–8 (2000).

[273] J. I. Charney, 'Anticipatory Humanitarian Intervention in Kosovo', 93 *AJIL* 834, 836 (1999).

[274] See B. Simma, 'NATO, the UN and the Use of Force: Legal Aspects', 10 *EJIL* 1, 12 (1999).

Assembly may meet in emergency special session within twenty-four hours of the request therefor.[275]

When adopted, the 'Uniting for Peace' Resolution was greeted as 'epoch-making'.[276] With the passage of time, much of the original appeal of the Resolution has vanished.[277] The radical increase in the composition of the General Assembly has turned it into an unwieldy body, ill-suited for the task at hand. Apart from its size, the overall record of the General Assembly has given rise to a lot of criticism and a sense of disenchantment.[278]

There is no need to dwell upon the fact that the 'Uniting for Peace' Resolution did not, and could not, amend the Charter. Nowhere in the text did the General Assembly purport to arrogate powers exceeding those allotted to it in the Charter.[279] Nor does the Resolution say that the General Assembly will supplant the Security Council.

The central question concerning 'Uniting for Peace' is often presented as one of defining a failure on the part of the Security Council to exercise its responsibility or, at least, ascertaining which UN organ is to decide that such a failure has occurred.[280] But in reality this is a side issue. The main problem is that, in all matters pertaining to international peace and security, the General Assembly is authorized (under Chapter IV)[281] to adopt only non-binding recommendations. Each Member State 'remains legally free to act or not to act on such recommendation'.[282] In its 1962 Advisory Opinion on *Certain Expenses of the United Nations*, the International Court of Justice held that – although, generally speaking, the responsibility of the Security Council respecting the maintenance of international peace and security is 'primary' rather than exclusive – only the Council possesses the power to impose explicit obligations of compliance under Chapter VII.[283]

During the 'Cold War' era, the General Assembly tried to 'usurp the primary responsibility of the Security Council on quite a number of occasions', although in recent years it appears to have largely reconciled

---

[275] General Assembly Resolution No. 377 (V), 5 *RGA* 10, *id.* (1950).
[276] L. H. Woolsey, 'The "Uniting for Peace" Resolution of the United Nations', 45 *AJIL* 129, 130 (1951).
[277] See P. R. Baehr and L. Gordenker, *The United Nations in the 1990s* 75–6 (2nd ed., 1994).
[278] See T. M. Franck, *Nation against Nation* 117 (1985).
[279] See J. Andrassy, 'Uniting for Peace', 50 *AJIL* 563, 572 (1956).
[280] See H. Reicher, 'The Uniting for Peace Resolution on the Thirtieth Anniversary of Its Passage', 20 *CJTL* 1, 10 (1981).
[281] Charter of the United Nations, *supra* note 9, at 334–8.
[282] J. Stone, *Legal Controls of International Conflict: A Treatise on the Dynamics of Disputes – and War – Law* 274–5 (1954).
[283] Advisory Opinion on *Certain Expenses of the United Nations*, *supra* note 215, at 163.

itself to taking 'a secondary or silent role'.[284] In any event, when the General Assembly adopts a recommendation for action by States in the realm of international peace and security, such a resolution – while not bereft of political significance – does not alter the legal rights and duties of those States. In particular, the General Assembly is incapable of placing any forcible measures employed on a new juridical footing.[285] In that, a General Assembly resolution falls conspicuously short of a Security Council decision, which (pursuant to Chapter VII) can legitimize an otherwise unlawful use of force.

A General Assembly recommendation to employ force should be interpreted as an exhortation addressed to Member States, to take joint action in the exercise of their inherent right of collective self-defence[286] (see *supra*, Chapter 9). Unlike a similar recommendation by the Security Council (see *supra*, A, (c)), the General Assembly is unable even to attach to the action the cachet of *bona fide* self-defence. That is not to assert (as some scholars stringently do)[287] that the General Assembly lacks competence to recommend that Member States resort to self-defence. As long as the Security Council retains its ultimate power to come to grips with the situation, it is the prerogative of the General Assembly to encourage Member States to exercise a right which is bestowed upon them under the Charter (as well as by customary international law).

Collective security differs from collective self-defence in that the right to decide whether to fight an aggressor is accorded not to every single State, but to a central organ of the international community. It is settled in the Charter that the organ in question is the Security Council. When the Council fails to carry out its mandate, no other UN organ can serve as its surrogate. Collective self-defence may be organized on the initiative of the General Assembly. But if it is, freedom of inaction redounds on every Member State.

When the Security Council refrains from setting in motion collective security measures, any force used by States must be restricted to self-defence (individual or collective), namely, a response to an armed attack. The 'Uniting for Peace' Resolution was carefully phrased in specifying that the General Assembly may recommend recourse to armed force only when an actual breach of the peace or aggression occurs, and not in circumstances of a threat to the peace. Perhaps the Resolution ought to

---

[284] White, *supra* note 227, at 143.
[285] See C. Leben, 'Les Contre-Mesures Inter-Etatiques et les Réactions a l'Illicite dans la Société Internationale', 28 *AFDI* 9, 33 (1982).
[286] See A. V. W. Thomas and A. J. Thomas, *Non-Intervention: The Law and Its Import in the Americas* 175–6 (1956).
[287] See H. Kelsen, *Recent Trends in the Law of the United Nations* 979 (1951).

have been drafted even more meticulously, for, under the Charter, a breach of the peace or aggression as such is not an adequate justification for the use of counter-force (unauthorized by the Security Council), unless it constitutes an armed attack.

(b)   The International Court of Justice

There are two separate, albeit related, issues concerning the interaction of the Security Council and the International Court of Justice. The first is the concurrent or consecutive competence of the Council and the Court. The second is whether the Court can invalidate Council resolutions, adopted under Chapter VII.

i.   Concurrent or consecutive competence of the Council and the Court In the *Nicaragua* case, the United States challenged the jurisdiction of the International Court of Justice (as a judicial organ) to deal with complaints concerning the unlawful use of force (including acts of aggression or other breaches of the peace), on the ground that this is a task assigned by the Charter to the political organs of the United Nations, chiefly the Security Council.[288] The Court, in 1984, rejected the argument, inasmuch as the responsibility ascribed to the Security Council in this domain is only 'primary' and not exclusive.[289] The Judgment distinguished between the purely judicial role of the Court and the political duties entrusted to the Council.[290] In the Court's words, '[b]oth organs can therefore perform their separate but complementary functions with respect to the same events'.[291] Judge Schwebel upheld the same line of approach in his Dissenting Opinion of 1986:

while the Security Council is invested by the Charter with the authority to determine the existence of an act of aggression, it does not act as a court in making such a determination. It may arrive at a determination of aggression – or, as more often is the case, fail to arrive at a determination of aggression – for political rather than legal reasons. However compelling the facts which could give rise to a determination of aggression, the Security Council acts within its rights when it decides that to make such a determination will set back the cause of peace rather than advance it. In short, the Security Council is a political organ which acts for political reasons. It may take legal considerations into account but, unlike a court, it is not bound to apply them.[292]

---

[288] *Case Concerning Military and Paramilitary Activities in and against Nicaragua* (Jurisdiction), [1984] *ICJ Rep.* 392, 431–3.
[289] *Ibid.*, 434.   [290] *Ibid.*, 435.   [291] *Ibid.*
[292] *Case Concerning Military and Paramilitary Activities in and against Nicaragua* (Merits), [1986] *ICJ Rep.* 14, 290.

This is a correct analysis of the powers of the Security Council. Under the Charter, the Council is put in charge of the all-important mission of maintaining or restoring international peace and security. The Council must concentrate on that task, functioning as a political rather than a judicial organ. As stressed by Sir Gerald Fitzmaurice, the Council is not supposed to settle a dispute as such, or to prevent or punish any violation of international law, although indirectly it may achieve these results as well.[293] The Council is not the most suitable body to pass judgment as to which side in an armed conflict is 'guilty of violating its legal obligations'; such a determination may indeed impede it from taking the measures conducive to the safeguarding of international peace and security.[294] By contrast, the Court, not being hampered by political constraints or by motivations of expediency, is fully qualified to bring legal yardsticks to bear upon the armed conflict in a dispassionate fashion.[295]

Since the Security Council and the International Court of Justice are both authorized to pronounce on the same events – one body applying political, and the other legal, criteria – the question that comes to mind is how to obviate the theoretical contingency of two contradictory, equally binding, decisions being reached by the two organs simultaneously. Most assuredly, such a head-on collision is not likely to happen in reality.[296] The Court is not often seized with disputes affecting the maintenance or restoration of international peace and security. For jurisdictional and other reasons, it is reasonable to assume that the judicial regulation of such matters will 'remain peripheral' in the future.[297] In any event, once the Council issues a verdict about the occurrence of an act of aggression, it is hard to believe that the Court would be inclined to contradict it. Nevertheless, as a matter of speculative inquiry, the scenario of a potential discord between the Council and the Court cannot be lightly dismissed. What happens if the Council determines that an act of aggression has been committed by Arcadia against Utopia, whereas the Court rules that

[293] G. G. Fitzmaurice, 'The Foundations of the Authority of International Law and the Problem of Enforcement', 19 *Mod. LR* 1, 5 (1956).

[294] O. Schachter, 'The Quasi-Judicial Role of the Security Council and the General Assembly', 58 *AJIL* 960, *id.* (1964).

[295] See B. S. Chimni, 'The International Court and the Maintenance of Peace and Security: The Nicaragua Decision and the United States Response', 35 *ICLQ* 960, 967–9 (1986).

[296] The present author was taken to task for this statement, reflecting 'an optimism readily dispelled by the events leading to the Lockerbie cases in 1992'. S. A. M. Pasha, 'Book Review' [of the second edition of this book], 37 *IJIL* 790, 794 (1997). But as will be shown *infra*, ii, in the event, the author's guarded optimism was only confirmed by the International Court of Justice.

[297] O. Schachter, 'Self-Defense and the Rule of Law', 83 *AJIL* 259, 276–7 (1989).

Arcadia is not to blame and that it is actually the victim of aggression initiated by Utopia? In the *Nicaragua* case, the Court observed that, in the context of those proceedings, it was not 'asked to say that the Security Council was wrong'.[298] But what would the Court do in the future, if it is requested to say precisely that?

One way to resolve the difficulty is to apportion different time-frames for the performance of the dissimilar functions of the Security Council and the Court. Thus, in an on-going armed conflict (as argued by the United States),[299] it would be preferable for the Council alone to exercise its mission of restoring international peace and security. The Council may ordain a cease-fire, insist on withdrawal of forces and even initiate an enforcement action, without tackling the legality of the underlying issues. The measures taken by the Council need not diminish from the power of the Court to investigate the legality of the use of force – as well as other legal rights and wrongs – after the hostilities are over. In the aftermath of the fighting, the Court will be at liberty to take a fresh look at the situation from the perspective of juridical standards. It may then come to conclusions that are at variance with those previously reached by the Council. For instance, the Court may rule that a disputed territorial zone, from which Arcadia was ordered by the Council to withdraw, actually belongs to it. In that case, Arcadian troops would be allowed to reoccupy the area.

Analytically, given different time-frames and divergent criteria for decision-making, there need be no real clash between a decree by the Security Council and a different ruling by the Court. The Council's responsibility in an on-going conflict is to restore international peace and security. The Court's role is to settle disputes in accordance with international law. The restoration of peace is more urgent than the settlement of the dispute, and it should be given temporal priority. But the measures taken by the Council are not necessarily the last word on the subject. The final judgment is left to the Court (provided, of course, that it has jurisdiction).

There is a remote possibility that the parties to an international armed conflict, acting together, may elect to submit their dispute to the Court even in the midst of hostilities. Should that happen, there is no reason for the Court to decline jurisdiction.[300] Under these circumstances, the Security Council ought to allow the Court to exercise its judicial powers without undue interference, although a cease-fire

---

[298] *Nicaragua case, supra* note 288, at 436.   [299] *Ibid.*
[300] See R. B. Bilder, 'Judicial Procedures Relating to the Use of Force', 31 *VJIL* 249, 265 (1990–1).

order will not be out of place. However, if the parties to the conflict are not at one in their desire to bring their dispute before the Court, and as long as hostilities are not terminated, it is submitted that the Court ought to exercise judicial restraint. The reason is not that the 'factual matrix is fluid and constantly changing',[301] but that the Court should do whatever it can to avoid an actual or potential dissension with the Council. While the armed conflict continues, and in the absence of agreement between the parties as to the Court's jurisdiction, the Court ought to defer to the Council, letting it discharge its duties pursuant to the Charter. If an application instituting contentious proceedings is filed with the Court *pendente bello*, unless all the parties explicitly urge the Court to entertain the dispute without delay, it is on the whole better to regard the case as unripe – as yet – for judicial determination.

ii.   *Can the Court invalidate binding decisions adopted by the Council?* Does the International Court of Justice have the power of judicial review over binding resolutions, adopted by the Security Council under Chapter VII? The question came to the fore in the wake of the *Lockerbie* case.[302] Here a bomb was placed aboard a Pan American aircraft, which exploded in mid-air over Lockerbie (Scotland) with vast loss of life. Two Libyan officials were suspected of responsibility for the terrorist act, and Libya was requested to surrender them to trial either to the United States (the State of nationality of the airline) or the United Kingdom (the State in whose airspace the explosion occurred). Libya refused to do so. The Council adopted three resolutions on the subject. In the first (Resolution 731 of January 1992), it merely urged Libya to cooperate fully in establishing responsibility for the terrorist act by responding to the requests for the surrender of the suspects.[303] In the second (Resolution 748 of March 1992), the Council – acting under Chapter VII – decided that Libya must comply with those requests, determined that failure by Libya to demonstrate by concrete action its renunciation of terrorism constitutes 'a threat to international peace and security', and imposed on Libya sundry sanctions (mainly, arms and air embargo).[304] In the third (Resolution 883 of November 1993), the Council – again acting under Chapter VII and reiterating the existence of a threat to the peace – extended the range of the sanctions (primarily, by the freezing of Libyan assets abroad).[305]

---

[301] K. Highet, 'Evidence, the Court, and the Nicaragua Case', 81 *AJIL* 1, 43 (1987).
[302] For the facts, see F. Beveridge, 'The Lockerbie Affair', 41 *ICLQ* 907–20 (1992).
[303] Security Council Resolution 731, 47 *RDSC* 51, 52 (1992).
[304] Security Council Resolution 748, *supra* note 25, at 52–3.
[305] Security Council Resolution 883, 48 *RDSC* 113, 114 (1993).

In March 1992, after Resolution 731 but prior to Resolution 748 (and, of course, Resolution 883), Libya instituted legal proceedings against the United Kingdom and the United States before the International Court of Justice. The Libyan claim was that the 1971 Montreal Convention for the Suppression of Unlawful Acts against the Safety of Civil Aviation[306] should be applicable to the case. The UK and the US maintained that the case was inadmissible, being governed by Security Council resolutions which supersede any obligations under the Montreal Convention in light of Articles 25 (*supra*, B, (a)) and 103 of the Charter.[307] Article 103 sets forth that obligations under the Charter prevail over any obligations assumed by Member States under other international agreements[308] (see *supra*, Chapter 9, C, (a)).

In an early phase of the proceedings, in 1992, the Court practically confirmed the binding effect of Resolution 748 (given the provisions of Articles 25 and 103) *vis-à-vis* any rights claimed by Libya under the Montreal Convention.[309] However, in 1998, the Court upheld a Libyan submission that admissibility must be determined by the critical date of the filing of the Libyan Application:

Security Council resolutions 748 (1992) and 883 (1993) cannot be taken into consideration in this regard, since they were adopted at a later date. As to Security Council resolution 731 (1992), adopted before the filing of the Application, it could not form a legal impediment to the admissibility of the latter because it was a mere recommendation without binding effect.[310]

Clearly, had the Libyan Application been filed subsequent to Resolution 748, this binding text would have formed a legal impediment to its admissibility.

As it is, the Court's ruling was issued at a Preliminary Objections stage. How the Court would have pronounced itself on the merits is a matter of conjecture. In the event, the two Libyan suspects were surrendered to the Netherlands, which undertook to host a Scottish Court for the purpose of their trial.[311] The Security Council, in Resolution 1192 (1998), agreed to

---

[306] Montreal Convention for the Suppression of Unlawful Acts against the Safety of Civil Aviation, 1971, [1971] *UNJY* 143.

[307] *Case Concerning Questions of Interpretation and Application of the 1971 Montreal Convention Arising from the Aerial Incident at Lockerbie* (Preliminary Objections) (*Libya v. the UK*), [1998] *ICJ Rep.* 9, 24; (*Libya v. US*), *ibid.*, 115, 129–30.

[308] Charter of the United Nations, *supra* note 9, at 361.

[309] *Case Concerning Questions of Interpretation and Application of the 1971 Montreal Convention Arising from the Aerial Incident at Lockerbie* (Request for the Indication of Provisional Measures) (*Libya v. the UK*), [1992] *ICJ Rep.* 3, 15; (*Libya v. US*), *ibid.*, 114, 127.

[310] *Lockerbie case*, *supra* note 307, at 26, 130–1.

[311] The Netherlands–United Kingdom, Agreement Concerning a Scottish Trial in the Netherlands, 1998, 38 *ILM* 926, 927 (1999) (Articles 2–3(1)).

suspend the sanctions against Libya once the accused arrived in the Netherlands.[312] Ultimately, one of the two accused was convicted in 2001 of murder.[313] The conviction was upheld on appeal in 2002.[314] In 2003, Libya consented to pay appropriate compensation to the families of the victims (a payment of $2.7 billion was made), and its cases in the International Court of Justice against the UK and the US were withdrawn.[315] For its part, the Security Council terminated the sanctions in Resolution 1506 (2003).[316]

The Court in the *Lockerbie* case shied away from a direct confrontation with the Security Council, although it is evident that the Court did not exclude the feasibility of simultaneous proceedings before the Council and itself.[317] But the case triggered the question whether the Court has the power to override binding decisions of the Council (such as Resolution 748). In his Dissenting Opinion, in 1998, President Schwebel denied that the Court is generally 'empowered to exercise judicial review of the decisions of the Security Council', and enunciated that the Court 'is particularly without power to overrule or undercut decisions of the Security Council made by it in pursuance of its authority under Articles 39, 41 and 42 of the Charter'.[318]

The present writer believes that President Schwebel went too far. A more modulated assessment of the inter-relationship between the Court and the Council was made by Judge Weeramantry, in his Dissenting Opinion of 1992:

Thus, any matter which is the subject of a valid Security Council decision under Chapter VII does not appear, prima facie, to be one with which the Court can properly deal.[319]

The word that should be underlined in this proposition is the adjective 'valid'. The Council is vested by Chapter VII with extensive powers coupled with the widest possible discretion, and as a rule the Court

---

[312] Security Council Resolution 1192, 53 *RDSC* 74, *id.* (1998).
[313] Scottish High Court of Justiciary at Camp Zeist (the Netherlands): *Her Majesty's Advocate v. Al Megrahi* et al. (2001), 40 *ILM* 582, 612–13 (2001).
[314] Verdict in Libya Terrorist Case: Pan Am 103, [2002] *Digest of United States Practice in International Law* 111, *id.*
[315] See S. D. Murphy, 'Libyan Payment to Families of Pan Am Flight 103 Victims', 97 *AJIL* 987, 990–1 (2003). The Court placed on record the discontinuance of the proceedings in *Case Concerning Questions of Interpretation and Application of the 1971 Montreal Convention arising from the Aerial Incident at Lockerbie* (Order) (*Libya v. UK*), [2003] *ICJ Rep.* 149, 150; (*Libya v. US*), *ibid.*, 152, 153.
[316] Security Council Resolution 1506, 43 *ILM* 251, *id.* (2004).
[317] See B. Martenczuk, 'The Security Council, the International Court and Judicial Review: What Lessons from Lockerbie?', 10 *EJIL* 517, 532 (1999).
[318] *Lockerbie case, supra* note 307, at 73, 164–5.
[319] *Lockerbie case, supra* note 309, at 66, 176.

cannot gainsay the Council. To take but one prime example, a determination by the Council that a particular situation constitutes a threat to the peace is non-reviewable on the facts by the Court[320] (see *supra*, A, (d)). Nevertheless, the Council's decisions – to be binding – must be legally valid.

As implied in Judge Weeramantry's words, there must be a *prima facie* presumption that the Security Council's resolutions are valid. But it must not be forgotten that the Council's powers and competence flow from the Charter. Consequently, if any resolution adopted by the Council is *ultra vires* the Charter itself (owing to exceptional circumstances rebutting the presumption), the Court may have no choice but to declare it invalid.[321] Even the pivotal text establishing the Council's power to adopt binding decisions – Article 25 – proclaims that these decisions are to be accepted and carried out by Member States 'in accordance with the present Charter' (*supra*, B, (a)).[322] For instance, should a professed decision of the Council run afoul of the procedural requirements laid down in the Charter, the result may be held by the Court to be null and void.

Whereas it is true that a binding decision of the Security Council may supersede an ordinary norm of international law (by virtue of the combined thrust of Articles 25 and 103 of the Charter), the position is different as regards peremptory norms of general international law (*jus cogens*) (see *supra*, Chapter 4, E, (a)). It is noteworthy that the reach of Article 103 is confined to a conflict between Charter obligations and 'obligations under any other international agreement'.[323] Article 103 is, therefore, not germane to a conflict with *jus cogens* anchored in customary international law.[324] It may follow that '[a]ny Security Council decision in conflict with a norm of *jus cogens* must necessarily be without effect'.[325] To cite an illustration offered by Judge *ad hoc* E. Lauterpacht in his Separate Opinion in the *Application of the Genocide Convention* case of

---

[320] See J. G. Merrills, *International Dispute Settlement* 251 (3rd ed., 1998).

[321] D. Bowett, 'The Impact of Security Council Decisions on Dispute Settlement Procedures', 5 *EJIL* 89, 95–6 (1994). The possibility of a UN organ acting *ultra vires* was touched upon tangentially in the International Court's Advisory Opinion on *Certain Expenses of the United Nations, supra* note 215, at 167.

[322] See V. Gowlland-Debbas, 'Security Council Enforcement Action and Issues of State Responsibility', 43 *ICLQ* 55, 90 (1994).

[323] See R. F. Kennedy, '*Libya v. United States*: The International Court of Justice and the Power of Judicial Review', 33 *VJIL* 899, 908 (1992–3).

[324] See M. N. Shaw, 'The Security Council and the International Court of Justice: Judicial Drift and Judicial Function', *The International Court of Justice: Its Future Role after Fifty Years* 219, 229 (A. S. Muller *et al.* eds., 1997).

[325] D. Akande, 'The International Court of Justice and the Security Council: Is There Room for Judicial Control of Decisions of the Political Organs of the United Nations?', 46 *ICLQ* 309, 322 (1997).

1993,[326] should the Council require States to participate in the perpetration of genocide, the obligation may be set aside by the Court. However, due account must be given to the fact that the prohibition of aggression is the paradigmatic illustration of a peremptory norm. When the Council ordains collective security measures to counter aggression (with a view to safeguarding this peremptory norm), and the action entails a violation of another peremptory norm, the legal situation may boil down to a clash between two norms of *jus cogens* and it may be debatable which one should prevail.[327]

All these scenarios are more easily imaginable in theory than in practice. Still, the present writer agrees with those who take the position that *en principe* the Court is competent to declare invalid a purportedly binding decision, adopted by the Security Council, on the ground of being either *ultra vires* the Charter or incompatible with peremptory norms of international law (*jus cogens*).[328]

---

[326] *Case Concerning Application of the Convention on the Prevention and Punishment of the Crime of Genocide* (Further Requests for the Indication of Provisional Measures), 1993, [1993] *ICJ Rep.* 325, 440.

[327] See K. Svanberg-Torpman, 'The Security Council as a Law Enforcer and Legislator', *Peace and Security: Current Challenges in International Law* 85, 94–5 (D. Amnéus and K. Svanberg-Torpman eds., 2004).

[328] See K. Doehring, 'Unlawful Resolutions of the Security Council and Their Legal Consequences', 1 *MPYUNL* 91, 108 (1997).

Conclusion

Aggressive war is currently forbidden by the Charter of the United Nations, as well as by customary international law, and it even constitutes a crime against peace. The legal proscription of war forms the bedrock of the contemporary international legal system. Admittedly, to date, the prohibition has not had a profound impact on the actual conduct of States. As of now, its imprint has been more noticeable in the vocabulary of States. An international climate has been generated in which the term 'war' has an unsavoury connotation. Hence, while States continue to wage war,[1] they prefer taking the moral high ground and describe their activities in palatable euphemisms. One may say, in a combination of cynicism and realism, that so far the legal abolition of war has stamped out not wars but declarations of war. This lip-service to the cause of peace may be hypocritical. However, as pithily put by La Rochefoucauld, *'l'hypocrisie est un hommage que le vice rend à la vertu'*.[2] The recognition of virtue is an indispensable first step without which no vice is likely to be eliminated.

Nevertheless, a taboo on the use of the word 'war' in legal analysis makes no sense at all.[3] The fact that war is banished linguistically will not make it vanish empirically. Whether we employ this or that phrase does not alter the incontrovertible truth that comprehensive armed conflicts still permeate international relations. If the phenomenon of war is to be eradicated, it must be faced and not ignored. Otherwise, all that we are left with is hypocrisy.

For aggressive war (as well as unlawful uses of force 'short of war') to disappear, the international community must establish effective measures of collective security. The 'harnessing' of force to international

---

[1] For a comprehensive list of armed conflicts (both inter-State and intra-State) occurring between 1945 and 1995, see K. J. Holsti, *The State, War, and the State of War* 210–14 (1996). The list requires continuous updates.

[2] La Rochefoucauld, *Oeuvres Complètes* 432 (*Maxime* 218) (Gallimard ed., 1964).

[3] See R. R. Baxter, 'The Law of War', 62 *ILS* 209, *id.* (R. R. Lillich and J. N. Moore eds., 1980).

procedures of law and order is the real challenge of our day.[4] Unfortunately, the lacklustre performance of the UN Security Council (which has been entrusted with this task by the Charter) has instigated widespread disappointment and dissatisfaction. The binding enforcement mechanism of the United Nations – embedded in Article 42 of the Charter[5] – has not been activated despite the end of the 'Cold War' (and notwithstanding concrete proposals submitted by the Secretary-General in 1992, in response to the Council's invitation).[6] A Security Council policy of permissive enforcement action based on 'sub-contracting' to a regional organization – NATO – in Bosnia-Herzegovina has led to the disquieting precedent of NATO imposing law and order in Kosovo, in 1999, without the authorization of the Council.

As long as the Charter's scheme of collective security fails to function adequately, States are left to their own devices when confronted with an unlawful use of force. Again and again, they invoke the right of (individual or collective) self-defence in response to an 'armed attack', in conformity with Article 51 of the Charter.[7] Thus, instead of being a provisional interlude pending the exercise of collective security, self-defence (individual as well as collective) has virtually taken the place of collective security.[8] During the 'Cold War', the very 'centre of gravity in the United Nations has swung from Article 39 to Article 51'.[9] Notwithstanding the palpable changes in the world political landscape since the termination of the 'Cold War', the right of self-defence – individual and collective – remains the principal shield against armed attacks.

Drawing an unambiguous distinction between collective self-defence and collective security is particularly important when the Security Council gives its direct or indirect blessing to the former without committing the international community to the latter. Only genuine collective security – namely, the activation by the Council of binding enforcement mechanism pursuant to Article 42 – can turn the use of counter-force into an approximation of an international police action. The exercise of collective self-defence, even by a large coalition of the willing, is apt to trigger political doubts and plant the seeds of legal confusion. The Gulf

---

[4] R. Y. Jennings, 'General Course on Principles of International Law', 121 *RCADI* 323, 584 (1967).
[5] Charter of the United Nations, 1945, 9 *Int.Leg.* 327, 343–4.
[6] Secretary-General, 'An Agenda for Peace', 31 *ILM* 956, 966 (1992).
[7] Charter of the United Nations, *supra* note 5, at 346.
[8] See H. Kelsen, 'Collective Security and Collective Self-Defense under the Charter of the United Nations', 42 *AJIL* 783, 785 (1948).
[9] N. Feinberg, *Studies in International Law* 70 (1979).

War in all its phases, from the invasion of Kuwait to the occupation of Iraq, is a paradigmatic illustration of such doubts and confusion.

The new challenges posed by international terrorism have only added to the complexity of the situation. Paradoxically, the idiom 'war' is freely used – as a figure of speech – in the context of the struggle against terrorism. But the crux of the issue is that the concept of an 'armed attack' is now clearly understood as embracing acts of terrorism (when launched from abroad). Self-defence against terrorists can develop into a full-scale war, as happened in Afghanistan following the devastating events of 11 September 2001. However, anti-terrorist strikes can involve forcible measures 'short of war', and these may be carried out even interceptively. The spectrum of options available in exercise of the right of self-defence appears to be wider and more intricate than ever.

Index of persons

Index of subjects